Signals Passed at Danger

Signals Passed at Danger
Railway Power and Politics in Britain

Richard Faulkner and Christoper Austin

crecy.co.uk

First published 2023

© Richard Faulkner and Christoper Austin 2023

ISBN 9781800352568

All rights reserved. Apart from any fair dealing for the purpose of private study, research, criticism or review, as permitted under the Copyright, Design and Patents Act 1988, no part of this publication may be reproduced, stored in a retrieval system, or transmitted in any form or by any means, electronic, electrical, chemical, mechanical, optical, photocopying, recording or otherwise, without prior written permission. All enquiries should be directed to the publisher.

Printed in Malta by Melita

Crécy Publishing Ltd
1a Ringway Trading Estate, Shadowmoss Rd,
Manchester M22 5LH
www.crecy.co.uk

Front cover:
Lack of a clear policy framework and with a blind eye to signals from the industry meant frustration and disappointment for rail customers, managers and staff as well as for Government. At a time of great uncertainty in July 1961, but under clear signals, the 'Elizabethan' races south through Durham behind one of the iconic 'A4' class locomotives, Kingfisher.
Alexander McBlain/Online Transport Archive

Rear cover main:
Open Access operations. The complexity of regulation was predicated by the assumption of on-track competition between operators. In fact it has had minimal effect and is inconsistent with making best use of the infrastructure. Here a Grand Central Class 180 is seen at East Boldon.
citytransportinfo (CC0 1.0 Universal Public Domain Dedication)

Rear cover inset from top:
Railways in the shadow politics: with the Houses of Parliament in the background, a Class 450 unit accelerates through Vauxhall on the start of its journey to Portsmouth Harbour in 2022. *Christopher Austin*

Before the days of North Sea gas. A train of coke hoppers is hauled past the former Finchley Road (Midland) station by a WD 2-8-0 heading north. The sidings are now occupied by Homebase and Sainsbury superstores and car parks.
Harry Luff/Online Transport Archive

Picture credits
Every effort has been made to identify and correctly attribute photographic credits. Should any error have occurred this is entirely unintentional.

Contents

1 **The Railway and the Nation** 7
   The Railway Dichotomy
   Strategic Objectives

2 **Origins of State Involvement:**
   Regulation from 1839 to State Control in 1920 11
   In the Beginning …
   Parliamentary Powers
   Dialogue of the Deaf: the Great Engineers Challenged in Parliament
   The Dalhousie Board and the Railway Mania, 1845
   Regulation of Railways
   Westminster Offices and Early Lobbying
   Lloyd George and the Railways
   Government and Industrial Relations: the Railway Strike of 1911
   The 1919 Railway Strike

3 **Railwaymen in Parliament** 35
   Railway Staff in Public Service
   In the Railway Interest: Railway Directors as Politicians
   ASRS/NUR Representation, 1900–45
   The Railway Clerks' Association's MPs
   ASLEF MPs
   Union Representation, 1946–92
   Expanding the Rail Unions' Group
   NUR/NUS Merger
   Ending of Union Sponsorship
   Special Advisers

4 **Wartime Control and the Big Four, 1921–47** 54
   Wartime Control
   Post-War Uncertainty and the Grouping
   Ministry of Transport
   British Transport Police
   Herbert Morrison and the Creation of London Transport
   Working with the Main-Line Companies
   The Square Deal Campaign
   Big Four Achievements
   Government Control in War

5 **British Railways, 1948–94** 72
   Nationalisation
   The LNER's Track Authority Proposal
   The Minor Railways
   British Transport Commission
   The Beeching Whirlwind
   BR Chairmen
   Integration and Co-ordination
   BR's Parliamentary Relationships
   Channel Tunnel Rail Link

6 **Fifty Years of British Railways** 96
   Aunt Sally: Which Was the Target?
   Changing Perceptions: BR's Advertising
   The 'Agonising Beauty Parade'
   New Lines and Stations
   What did BR Ever do for us?

7 **The Great Privatisation Debate, 1992–97** 106
   First Steps
   Privatising the Railway: Theoretical Structures
   The 1992 Election
   The Railways Act, 1993
   The Politics of Privatisation
   The Prospects for the Privatised Railway
   The Rush to Sell Railtrack
   The Cost of Privatisation
   Could Labour have Stopped it?
   Some Conclusions
   What BR Could have Done

8 **Labour in Control, 1997–2010** 125
   Passenger Growth and Service Expansion
   Customer Service
   Strategy: the 1998 White Paper
   Safety Management
   The Strategic Rail Authority
   The Collapse of Railtrack
   The Regulator Sets out the Cost
   Open Access Operators

9 **The Freight Story** 138
   Freight Growth and Decline
   Coal
   Other Goods Traffic
   Government Role
   International
   Potential for Freight Growth
   Rates of Return
   Privatisation

10 **Back in Public Control, 2005** 147
   Abolition of the SRA
   Costs and Complexity
   Electrification
   High Speed Two: Andrew Adonis's Vision
   Devolution or Balkanisation
   The Williams Review

11 **Analysis and Conclusions** 166
   Ministers' Perspectives
   Regulation, Control and Ownership
   Renationalisation
   Reorganisations
   Oversight and Scrutiny
   Expectations
   Funding

12 **Postscript** 176

Stop the Presses 179

Appendices

1 Statutory Returns Required from the Railway 180
   Companies, 1901
2 Transport Ministers and Secretaries of State 181
   1919–2022
3 Principal Acts of Parliament Affecting the Nature 182
   and Structure of Railways in the United Kingdom,
   1838–2022
4 Parliamentary Inquiries and Reports on Railway, ... 184
   1995–2022
5 Government Reviews of Rail Policy, Including 186
   White Papers, 1839–2022
6 Letter from Sir George Young to Conservative 187
   Backbenchers on Privatisation
7 Minor Railways Excluded from the Railways Act, ... 188
   1947
8 List of Passenger Service Agreements 189
   in Place in October 2022

Bibliography 190

Acknowledgements 190

Index 191

1

The Railway and the Nation

'No other improvement can equal in utility the railroad.'
Abraham Lincoln, March 1832, a politician who understood the value of railways

The Railway Dichotomy

This book looks at the relationship between politicians and the railways, their people and particularly their managers and owners. It considers why it has always been fraught and frustrating for both sides, and the effect political influence has had on the development of the railway and its effectiveness in serving the people of Great Britain.

Regulation starts early and morphs into control following two world wars and after the collapse of Railtrack, which really marked the beginning of the end of the privatisation experiment. Change has generally been piecemeal and often in response to a specific event, such as the Armagh accident of 1879 or the Hatfield derailment of 2001. There is no discernible thread of a railway strategy throughout two centuries, and the railways themselves have tended to react to changing policies and have rarely combined effectively to set their own agenda. One consequence of this is that, when major changes have been made, they have not been successful because the strategy was not clear and because too many radical changes were being attempted at the same time.

One of the more surprising conclusions from the research is that, prior to the recent Williams/Shapps review,[1] no government has ever set out clearly what it expects from the railway in Britain. Another is that there has never been any attempt by governments to measure the wider value of the railway, but only ever to look at the narrow issue of profitability or costs.

In the nineteenth century, it was not seen as the government's role to do this, and so their involvement was mainly on regulation and restrictions on railway managers and directors. This covered safety, fares and the terms on which goods traffic was carried, and is covered in Chapter 2. The one thing the government did want in the nineteenth century was more railways, and this was eventually encouraged by simplifying the approvals process through the Light Railways Act, 1896, as also described in Chapter 2. 'None of the Governments between then (1870) and the outbreak of war in 1914 had any clear railway policy', wrote Alderman in his detailed analysis *The Railway Interest*, published in 1973.

At the start of the First World War, government took control of the railways, which were an essential part of the supply chain for the army, navy and the newly formed Royal Flying Corps, the story told at the start of Chapter 4. The actual operation of the railway was sensibly left in the hands of the Railway Executive Committee, made up of senior managers of the railway companies themselves. However, the financial mismanagement of the government during the war years left the railways crippled and, given the choice between paying for the damage caused and fudging the finances through reorganising, the government of David

---

[1] Great British Railways: William–Shapps plan for rail. The government's plan to transform the railways in Great Britain. Department for Transport, May 2021. Keith Williams (b 1956) is a British businessman who has served as chairman of British Airways and Royal Mail. He was the independent chair of the government's Rail Review. Grant Shapps (b 1968) has been Conservative MP for Welwyn Hatfield since 2015. He was Secretary of State for Transport between 2019 and 2022, and had previously served as minister of state for housing and local government, and as chairman of the Conservative Party.

The Southwold Railway served the Suffolk town for just 50 years from 1879 to 1929, when bus competition forced its premature closure. A beneficiary of the Tramways Act, 1870 and subsequently a Light Railway Order, construction and operating costs were kept down, enabling Southwold to be linked to the national rail network.
Barry Cross Collection/Online Transport Archive

Lloyd George[2] chose the latter course of action, even though Lloyd George himself played a crucial role during his time as Prime Minister, which we chronicle in Chapter 2.

Between the wars, the Big Four were largely left to get on with things, even though the transport market was changing dramatically with the growth of road transport. Many returning servicemen bought army lorries and started their own goods services by road, competing directly with the railway. These were mainly owner–drivers, nimble and with low overheads, completely unregulated, and paying nothing for their infrastructure until 1930. With the common carrier obligations and the requirement to publish rates for goods traffic imposed on the railways, these new highway buccaneers could pick and choose the traffic they carried, just undercutting railway rates to secure the traffic while maximising their profit. This problem was known about from the formation of the Ministry of Transport in 1919, yet it took over forty years, until 1962, before the railways were relieved of these obligations, by which time huge swathes of traffic had been lost and the nature of logistics was changing fast to a form that excluded rail from all but the heaviest flows.

Other ex-servicemen converted their lorries to buses and without any form of regulation, or even a driving test, were able to carry passengers to and from the centre of villages and towns at low fares. The effect of this is seen in the early withdrawal of vulnerable passenger services like the Wantage Tramway (1925), the Derwent Valley Light Railway (1926) and the 3ft-gauge Southwold Railway (1929), which we describe in *Holding the Line*[3].

During the Second World War, the railways were again under direct government control, and again served Britain well but were, in the process, run down with deferred maintenance and renewals. New works focused on military objectives, such as the expansion of the Didcot, Newbury and Southampton line in preparation for D-Day, rather than those planned for an expanding peacetime network. Catching up the backlog had to wait until the modernisation plan ten years after the end of the war, and the overriding priority of the Attlee government was both nationalisation and transport integration, which is described in Chapter 5.

Between 1955 and 1985, the overwhelming issue for government was the cost of the railway. This was essentially treated in isolation – it was the cost that was the issue, not the value for money, or the outputs bought by the subsidies being paid to run services.

On fares, the railways had been able to apply to the Transport Tribunal to raise fares to meet rising costs, but in March 1952 the minister, John Maclay, gave a statutory direction to the British Transport Commission (see Chapter 5) to freeze fares pending a review of sub-standard fares, which the BTC wanted to 'level up'. Following this precedent, government did not hesitate to intervene and the government policy during the 1960s and '70s was unclear. BR tried each year to secure a fares increase that would keep down the call on public funds, but government frequently limited the increase allowed because it breached the general policy on prices and incomes. This was not compensated by increased public support for the railway to make up the shortfall, but by requiring the BR Board to close the gap through 'efficiencies'.

From 1978 onwards, the policy was clear and required BR to meet a larger share of its costs through fares and freight income with a lower proportion coming from the taxpayer. Broadly speaking, the proportion was around 70 per cent of costs being met by fares and 30 per cent through support levels. As freight and InterCity were profitable, that meant that the subsidy for fares in London

---

[2] David Lloyd George, 1st Earl Lloyd-George of Dwyfor (1863–1945), charismatic statesman widely credited for winning the First World War and for the creation of the welfare state but with a controversial legacy. Born in Lancashire, he was a Welsh-speaking Liberal MP representing Caernarvon Boroughs from 1890 to 1945, Father of the House of Commons, 1929–45. He was successively President of the Board of Trade, 1905–08; Chancellor of the Exchequer, 1908–15; Minister of Munitions, 1915–16; Secretary of State for War, July–December 1916; Prime Minister (as head of a coalition government), 1916–22; Leader of the Liberal Party, 1926–31. Awarded earldom, 1 January 1945, but never took his seat in the House of Lords and died on 26 March 1945. See Chapter 2.

[3] *Holding the Line*, Richard Faulkner and Christopher Austin, Ian Allan Publishing (OPC), 2012.

The Wantage Tramway serving the Berkshire town, birthplace of King Alfred the Great, was originally linked to the GWR main line at Wantage Road by a 2½ mile roadside tramway. It was the first tramway to use steam traction rather than horses from 1876 onwards. Losing its passenger service in 1925, the track was damaged by US army trucks based at Grove Camp during the Second World War, and the tramway finally closed to all traffic in 1945. Locomotive No 5 *Shannon* is now preserved at the Didcot Railway Centre. *Barry Cross Collection/Online Transport Archive*

and the South-East and on regional services, including those in Scotland and Wales, attracted a higher proportion of support than these overall figures would suggest. This has remained substantially the same approach through privatisation, although only around half of the fares basket is regulated, the rest being a plethora of cheaper advance fares, some which derive from regulated fares but are not directly regulated themselves. Again, the level of fares derives from fairly arbitrary decisions made over thirty years ago, and little attempt has been made to use fares to drive policy. One result is that fares are perceived to be high, because the higher open fare is the one always quoted, whereas the majority of passengers travel on discounted fares, either using season tickets, advance tickets or railcards. So, the fares levels are actually set in broad terms by government, currently with annual increases of RPI plus one, but it is the train operating companies that are demonised by the media and passenger groups for putting fares up each year.

After 1985, and particularly after the Conservative manifesto for the 1992 election, the only policy government had for the railways was privatisation, which was assumed by the Conservative administration to be a panacea for the 'problems' of the industry. This is examined fully in Chapter 7, while the problems and benefits are explored in Chapter 8. One problem here is that the government tried to do too many untested things simultaneously (franchising, privatisation of Railtrack, open access operation and outsourcing of maintenance and renewal work), so when they were hurriedly implemented, many problems combined to require radical changes to the original concept and to take most of the industry back under public ownership or control within a decade. Despite the dramatic changes that were made in the early 1990s, they were again made in a policy vacuum, not linked to other aspects of government, or even of transport policy.

Just prior to 2020, the picture was more complex. The requirement for passenger operators was set out in some detail in the franchise agreement. Network Rail's plans were specified in the periodic settlements agreed with ORR. No objectives were set for freight, although access to the network for freight operators is regulated.

The expectations of government and public are huge, though. Safety is taken as a given and underpins everything, with a zero tolerance policy of accidents, similar to the airline industry, but a far cry from road where the safety criteria are completely different with a tolerance of 1,558 fatalities a year and 128,209 injuries in 2021, most of which would be preventable with stricter controls.

Accessibility has improved dramatically over the last forty years and has opened up new opportunities for people who a generation ago would have been virtually housebound. This is now a basic requirement for the railway but comes at a high price in terms of meeting the highly prescriptive requirements for stations and trains. There are objectives in relation to diversity, and in terms of conditions of service for staff.

Strategic Objectives

Beyond these specific tactical objectives that have grown piecemeal, there is no overarching strategy for the railway, nor any link with associated transport strategies relating to the competitive modes of air and road, and perhaps more specifically, electronic communications.

What is the purpose of the railway? Is it there to support economic development, to provide the basic public transport network for Britain, to encourage modal shift from more polluting modes like car and air, or reduce social isolation by providing connectivity? The answer is probably 'all of the above' and these benefits are enjoyed by government, but were not previously overtly acknowledged or specified. More importantly, these unspoken requirements change frequently, sometimes dependent on changing public opinion, sometimes in the light of a *Daily Mail* headline. For the railway managers and staff, it was confusing, and inhibited them from contributing as effectively as they otherwise might.

Railways have a great role to play in environmental terms, and rail is the only network in the country that is relatively easy to decarbonise. Electrification allows power to be provided from a wide range of sustainable sources, yet the electrification programme has repeatedly stalled and government attention switched to experiments on the much more difficult technology of hydrogen trains, or those operated by batteries. The setbacks to the electrification programme are described in Chapter 10.

Apart from a lack of clear rail objectives from successive governments, policies for the railway have been developed in isolation from other aspects of government policy. Government departments tend to work in silos and this is particularly true in transport where road, rail, ports and civil aviation have always been managed separately, from the very beginning in 1919 (see Chapter 4). Apart from transport (DfT), railways support business and the economy (BEIS), take people to work and school (DWP and DfE), are essential for tourism and major sporting activities (DCMS) and can contribute hugely to meeting Britain's environmental targets (DEFRA). They also employ around 130,000 people, many of them highly skilled, and support training and apprenticeships, diversity and bring work to areas that would otherwise be able to offer little in the way of skilled employment (DWP's area). Examples are the maintenance of the sleeping car fleets at Penzance and Inverness, or Network Rail's Whitemoor rail recycling centre at March in Cambridgeshire. Rail can also be the basis of a healthy lifestyle (DHSC), and those using it tend to walk more, with benefits to their cardiovascular system, than those who are car dependent.

Yet nothing brought these disparate issues together and there was little recognition of the range of benefits that rail brings, quite apart from transporting people and freight. Such considerations did start to be recognised through the Community Rail Network but have never been recognised or used by governments to inform their decisions across these disparate areas of policy. Nor did many of these benefits feature in government set objectives. The huge number of external benefits that railways bring in environmental, social and economic terms are there to be had, but need to be explicitly recognised and paid for.

A significant problem for government has been the importance and high public profile of the railway. It affects everyone's life, and has turned out to be too important politically to leave entirely to the private sector, as John Major's government would have wished. It has also turned out to be too big for government to manage. This was manifestly so in the period of the British Transport Commission, which attempted in vain to manage all forms of inland transport. It has even proved to be the case in the case of the slimmed down railway that has been under direct government control since 2005. The most recent white paper quite properly replaces that with management by Great British Railways, which could provide a proper separation between the Secretary of State's strategic responsibilities and those of the companies providing the actual services to customers (both freight and passenger). For the first time, it also recognises the wide range of external benefits that the railway provides and confirms the need for their continuation.

The great changes in the railway have always been triggered by concerns over its costs, even though governments have never set out strategic objectives or tried to measure whether the actual cost is still good value, in the light of the outputs delivered. This failure to set or measure strategic objectives has resulted in friction between ministers, their officials and railway managers, especially when they have led to major reorganisation of the industry, and it is no surprise that no satisfactory long-term organisational solution has been found.

The cost of the railway in wartime and the demands made on it were the basis of the creation of the Big Four main-line railways in 1923, and was also a factor in the formation of British Railways in 1948. The financial inadequacy of the British Transport Commission led to its demise in 1962 and the creation of the British Railways Board. Further financial pressures resulted in many reorganisations during BR's half century of existence. Privatisation was, like nationalisation before it, based on political dogma rather than the needs of customers or the industry that served them. The demise of the SRA was largely down to the financial crisis that affected the industry after Hatfield, and the collapse of Railtrack and the current cost of the railway have also led to the proposals set out in the recent white paper.

During the Covid pandemic, advice from government (generated by the Department of Health rather than Transport) specifically advised people not to use public transport to avoid the risk of infection, even though research by the Rail Safety and Standards Board[4] showed that rail remained the safer and greener mode of travel compared with road. There was no evidence that train travel resulted in an increase in infections by the virus. This hugely damaged confidence in public transport and helped to delay recovery from the very low levels of travel experienced during the lockdown periods. This too has raised questions again about the cost of the railway that will influence both political perceptions of the railway and planning for its future.

Future reorganisations can confidently be expected in the years to come, but would be far more effective if government first defined the sort of railway it needed in the age of the climate crisis and how funding is to be divided between users of the system and the other beneficiaries of it. We outline our thoughts on this at the end of Chapter 11.

---

[4] Rail Standards and Safety Board website report on infection risks updated on 27 September 2021.

2
Origins of State Involvement: Regulation from 1839 to State Control in 1920

*'The idiot who, in railway carriages, scribbles on window panes,
We only suffer to ride on a buffer of parliamentary trains.'*
W S Gilbert, *The Mikado*, 1884

In the Beginning ...

What led to the involvement of politicians with railways in the first place? Why did the state become involved in the activities of private companies and how did railways become so politicised?

The roots of this go well back to the eighteenth century and even earlier, and originated in the railways' need for rights over land. By their nature in linking A and B, the construction of railways involved crossing privately owned land, for which wayleaves were needed to enable the line to be built.

As railways were developed for public use rather than as private colliery lines, even the *laissez-faire* governments of early nineteenth-century Britain were involved in legislating to protect the public, particularly in relation to safety and fares. The need for Parliamentary powers for construction and operation led inevitably to government regulation but it is perhaps surprising that this started so early and spread quickly to every aspect of railway operation.

Nevertheless, our Victorian ancestors would have been astonished at the degree of government control exercised over today's railway. In order to see how we got here, though, we need to go back to the very beginning of the seventeenth century, to the year when Shakespeare's *Othello* was first performed and King James I was on the throne.

Parliamentary Powers

The earliest railways did not involve politicians at all when the owner built the line on his own land. The earliest written record of a railway in Britain is the Wollaton Wagonway of 1604, built to carry coal for 2 miles from Strelley to Wollaton in Nottinghamshire as a joint venture between the landowner, Sir Percival Willoughby of Wollaton Hall, and Huntingdon Beaumont, an entrepreneur who built the line and managed the mine. No powers were sought from Parliament for this pioneering line.

The following year, a shorter ½-mile line at Broseley in Shropshire was opened to carry coal from a mine to the River Severn, but in this case, the builders, Richard Wilcox and William Wells, had to take their line over the land of a rival coalmaster, James Clifford, the local lord of the manor. The promoters therefore sought a licence from the Privy Council, although this did not prevent Clifford's men damaging the line, once built.

The first railway to be built under authority of an Act of Parliament was the Middleton Railway in Leeds, in 1758, as a private venture to carry coal. The principal reason to seek Parliamentary powers was to ensure the ability to build the line over land belonging to other owners, by wayleave, as described in the preamble:

> An ACT for Establishing Agreement made between Charles Brandling, Esquire, and other Persons, Proprietors of Lands, for laying down a Waggon-Way in order for the better supplying the Town and Neighbourhood of Leeds in the County of York, with Coals.

The Middleton Railway in Leeds was the first to be built under the authority of an act of Parliament in 1758. This picture shows the *Salamanca*, the first commercially successful steam locomotive, with its cog wheel and toothed track designed by Blenkinsop to aid adhesion. Now a successful heritage railway it tells the story of Leeds locomotive manufacturers like the Hunslet Engine Company and Manning Wardle, that exported industrial locomotives all over the world.
Public domain via Commons Wikimedia

The first public railway to be opened under an Act of Parliament was the Surrey Iron Railway of 1801, between Wandsworth and Croydon, and the powers sought here were much wider, including the incorporation of the company, authorising the construction of the line and the charging of tolls, as the line was open to the public to use (the first example anywhere of 'open access').

From this point onwards, the building of permanent lines (as opposed to temporary tracks to serve quarries or mines) was generally done under authority of an Act of Parliament. This had the advantage for promoters of:

- Granting compulsory purchase powers for land
- Providing for the crossing of public roads and watercourses
- Authorising the construction and operation of the railway, and protecting the promoter against actions for nuisance
- Permitting the levying of tolls and charges

These advantages were counterbalanced by the need to address the objections of those whose rights were affected, and the process did not always guarantee success. The first Liverpool & Manchester Railway Bill of 1825 was rejected by Parliament and the route was revised and resubmitted the following year. Three further Bills were necessary to provide for route variations and raising a loan before the line was opened in 1830.

The process could be expensive too, exemplified by the Great Northern Railway Bill in the 1845–46 session, which cost its promoters the huge sum of £433,000 (£48.3 million in today's money) after a long tussle in Parliament with the promoters of rival schemes.

Dialogue of the Deaf: the Great Engineers Challenged in Parliament

The early railways faced opposition from their competitors, the canals and the turnpike trusts, as well as from landowners affected and a group of unbelievers who foresaw disaster from the new mode of transport. Some were straightforward. The Provost of Eton College wanted the Great Western Railway kept as far away from the school as possible, as its presence would be a temptation to the boys to visit the fleshpots of London. Others were more complex, as theoretical scientists like Dr Dionysius Lardner[5] produced spurious claims about the danger and problems that the railways would cause. Others asserted that people could not live at the speeds proposed, or that the smoke from the engines would cause cattle to run dry and all sorts of other nonsense.

George Stephenson, 'father of the railways.' Pioneer in all aspects of the early railway. Engineer for the Stockton & Darlington and Liverpool & Manchester Railways as well as many others. *Public domain via Commons Wikimedia*

---

[5] Professor Dionysius Lardner FRS FRSE (1793–1859) was an Irish scientific writer who popularised science and technology, and edited the 133-volume *Cabinet Cyclopædia*.

These opponents employed articulate barristers to make their case before the Parliamentary committees and the treatment by these people of the great pioneering engineers was shameful. These early encounters served to establish a mistrust between practical railwaymen and politicians that has lasted to the present day.

In March 1825, George Stephenson[6] was cross-examined by the leading opposition counsel Mr (later Lord) Alderson,[7] who was instructed by the directors of the Bridgewater, and Leeds and Liverpool canals. He pressed him on the levels of the Liverpool and Manchester where it crossed the Irwell. This was a weak point for Stephenson, and Alderson knew the levels to be inaccurate. After a gruelling session, the suave Alderson sealed his advantage by humiliating the Northumbrian engineer in an unforgiveable way:

'It was the most ridiculous thing I ever heard stated by any man.' Said Alderson in summing up, 'I am astonished that any man standing in that box would make such a statement without shrinking to nothing … Did any ignorance ever arrive at such a pitch as this? Was there ever any ignorance exhibited like this? Is Mr Stephenson to be the person upon whose faith this committee is to pass this Bill involving property to the extent of £400/500,000 when he is so ignorant of his profession as to propose to build a bridge not sufficient to carry off the flood water of the river or to permit any of the vessels to pass which of necessity must pass under it, and leave his own railroad liable to be several feet under water.'[8]

After more of this rhetoric, the Bill was thrown out by the committee and it was the following year when a new one was passed successfully, when the young engineer

---

[6] George Stephenson (1781–1848), civil engineer and mechanical engineer. With his son Robert he built the first steam railway locomotive – *Locomotion No. 1* – to carry passengers on the Stockton and Darlington railway in 1825 and the first intercity line – the Liverpool and Manchester – which opened in 1830. Their locomotive *Rocket* won the Rainhill trials in 1829 staged by the directors of the railway company. They went on to design and build numerous other railways and ensured railways' place in the story of the Industrial Revolution.

[7] Sir Edward Hall Alderson (1787–1857), barrister and recorder who became a judge on the northern circuit.

[8] Proceedings quoted in *George and Robert Stephenson* by L T C Rolt, Amberley Publishing, 2009.

Above: Charles Vignoles was an early railway surveyor and engineer who played a key role in securing Parliamentary Powers for the Liverpool and Manchester Railway. *Public Domain/Grace's Guides*

Right: Robert Stephenson, son of George Stephenson, the 'father of the railways' worked with him on Locomotion no 1 as well as on the Liverpool & Manchester Railway. He was appointed Chief Engineer of the London & Birmingham Railway at the age of 29. He was MP for Whitby from 1849 until his untimely death in 1859, but declined a knighthood. At that stage, he had been involved in the engineering of one third of the country's railway system. *Engraving by D. J. Pound/Wellcome Trust*

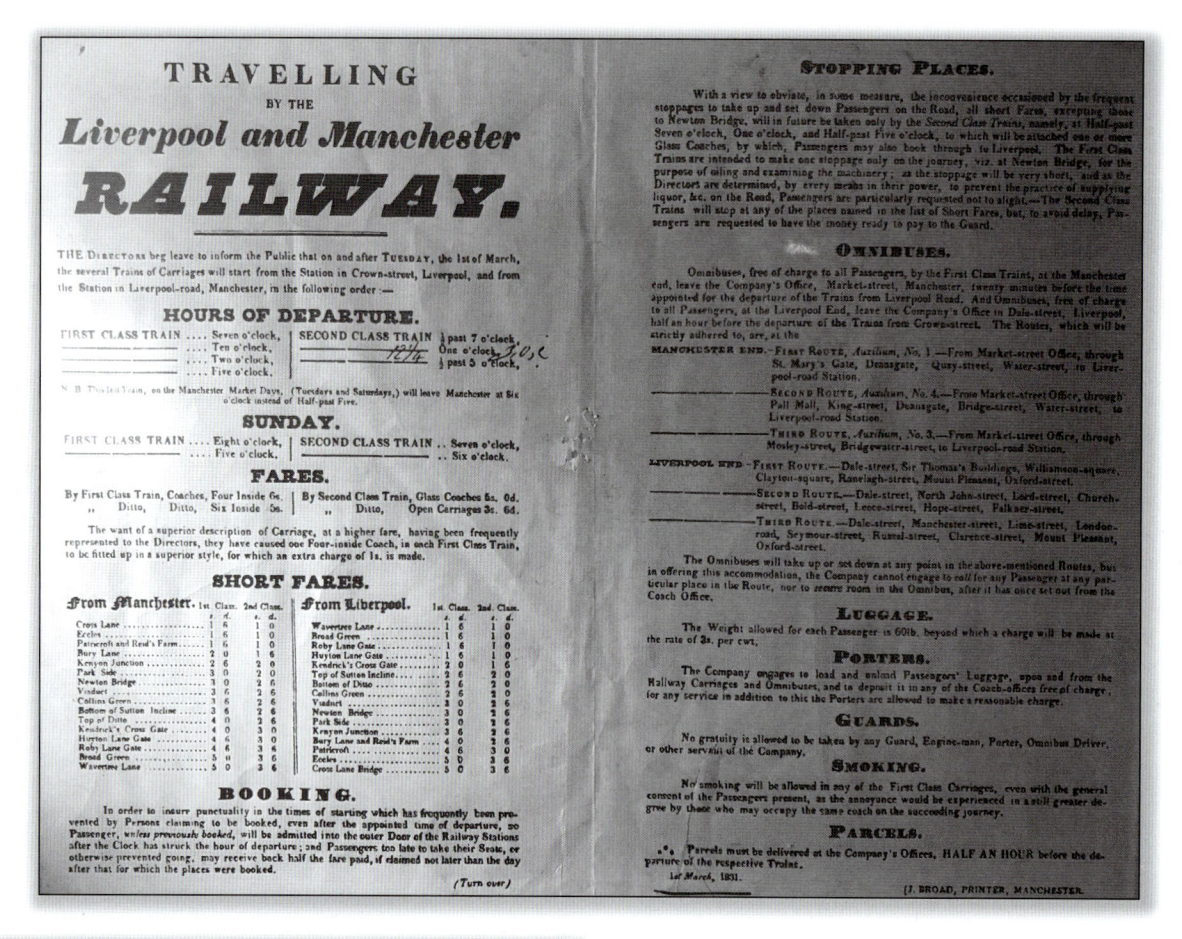

Top: Liverpool & Manchester Railway handbill, 1831. Punctuality was an issue from the dawn or railways, and the notice makes clear passengers will not be admitted to trains after the booked time of departure, even if they have a booking. Integration with omnibuses at both end of the line is impressive, as is the early ban on smoking in first class. *Public domain via Commons Wikimedia*

Above left: Chat Moss. 4¾ miles of peat bog between Patricroft and Newton le Willows was seen by many as impassable by many in the years before 1830. Using layers of brushwood and heather, and covering these with moss and turf from the surrounding bog, the formation was complete in early 1830 and stood five feet above the bog, with a total depth of embankment of 25 feet. *Public domain via Commons Wikimedia*

Above right: Euston. Famous for the Doric Arch that was demolished in 1962, the station built for the London & Birmingham Railway was also the first example of a wrought iron truss roof, designed by Charles Fox. This design was used for the train shed built for the opening of the line in 1837. *Public domain via Commons Wikimedia*

Charles Vignoles[9] sorted out the levels and gave evidence to the committee. Stephenson's courage and underlying ability overcame this and he is rightly now recognised as one of England's greatest engineers and the father of railways. But the experience had given George, in his own words, 'great grief' and he was bitterly resentful of the treatment he had received in London. He put his son, Robert, through private schools and ensured that he spoke 'received pronunciation' English, while he himself never lost his broad Northumbrian accent. His subsequent achievements showed his sceptical opponents to be wrong, but the seeds of distrust had been sown between engineers and legislators.

The subsequent opening of the Liverpool & Manchester Railway in 1830 also saw the death of the former President of the Board of Trade, William Huskisson,[10] who was run over by the *Rocket* at Parkside. The presence of mind of George Stephenson after this first railway accident led to the injured man's removal on a special train hauled by *Rocket* to Eccles, where he was conveyed to the vicarage and died later in the evening. With such a light load, the train ran the 15 miles at an average speed of 36mph. It was, however, an inauspicious beginning, not least because Huskisson's previous role at the Board of Trade meant that he was then effectively the minister for railways. The holder of the office of President of the Board of Trade remained in that role until 1919, when the first Minister of Transport (Sir Eric Geddes[11]) was appointed.

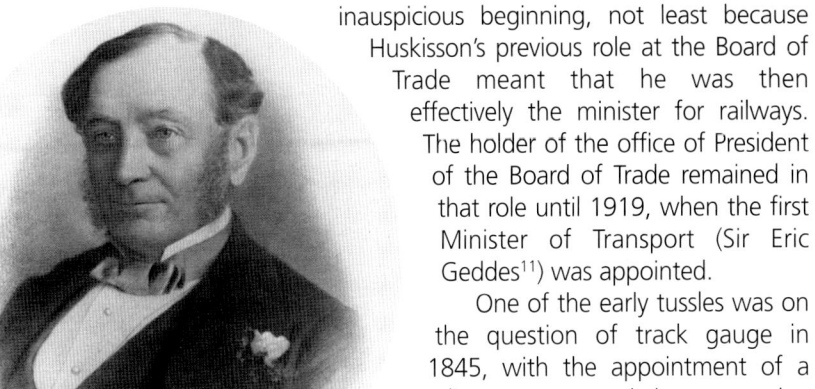

One of the early tussles was on the question of track gauge in 1845, with the appointment of a Parliamentary commission to examine the merits of the broad and standard gauges and to make recommendations in respect of future railways. As we shall see later, in relation to many other inquiries, the commissioners appointed lacked the railway knowledge for the task, although to be fair, the dispute itself was an internal railway one rather than one between the industry and government. Daniel Gooch[12] was then 29, but already a successful engineer and Isambard Kingdom Brunel's[13] right-hand man. In his memoirs, he recalled the names of the three commissioners[14], saying 'Sir F. Smith[15] had been for a time Inspector of Railways, but knew nothing about them. They were certainly a most incompetent tribunal, yet when it is considered that the fight was to be between one railway Co

Sir Daniel Gooch was recruited by Brunel as his first Superintendent of locomotive engines of the GWR in 1837 and he went on to become Chairman of the GWR in 1865, the year he was elected MP for Cricklade, a constituency which he represented for 20 years. *Published in* History of the Great Western Railway *by E. T. MacDermot; Peter Waller Collection*

---

[9] Charles Vignoles (1793–1875), railway surveyor and engineer who worked on numerous projects in the period leading up to the 1850s. The 'Vignoles rail' was named after him: he first suggested its use on the London and Croydon railway in 1836. The rail had a flat-bottom design that became widely used in the twentieth century.

[10] William Huskisson (1770–1830), Conservative MP for numerous constituencies in the early nineteenth century, finally including Liverpool. He served as a minister in several departments, including President of the Board of Trade, 1823–27; Secretary of State for War and the Colonies and Leader of the House of Commons, 1827–28. First fatal casualty in a railway accident.

[11] Sir Eric Campbell Geddes GCB GBE PC (1875–1937), Britain's first Minister of Transport, serving from 1919 to 1922. Joined the North Eastern Railway in a clerical role in 1904 and rose to become deputy general manager in 1911. Appointed by Lloyd George as deputy director general of munitions supply in 1915, later promoted to director general of military railways and inspector-general of transportation with the rank of major general. To counter the German U-boat offensive he was moved to the Admiralty as civilian lord in charge of shipbuilding. In 1917 he became First Lord of the Admiralty, a political post that required him to be in the House of Commons: he was elected as MP for Cambridge in 1917 and served until he retired in 1922. He was minister without portfolio 1919, and then minister of transport 1919–22, by which time he had decided that politics was not for him. Brother of Sir Auckland Geddes (*qv*).

[12] Sir Daniel Gooch, 1st Baronet (1816–89) was an English railway locomotive and transatlantic cable engineer and Conservative MP for Cricklade from 1865 to 1885. He was the first Superintendent of Locomotive Engines on the Great Western Railway from 1837 to 1864 and its chairman from 1865 to 1889.

[13] Isambard Kingdom Brunel (1806–59), British civil engineer who is widely regarded as one of the most influential figures of the nineteenth-century Industrial Revolution. Known principally for the construction of much of the Great Western Railway to a gauge of 7ft ¼in (as opposed to Stephenson's gauge of 4ft 8½in), he also designed dockyards, steam ships, under-river tunnels, viaducts and bridges. In 2002 Brunel was placed second in a BBC poll to decide the '100 greatest Britons'.

[14] The Gauge Commissioners were Professor George Biddell Airy, the Astronomer Royal; Professor Peter Barlow, Professor of Mathematics at the Royal Military Academy, Woolwich; and Lieutenant Colonel Sir Frederick Smith.

[15] Sir Frederick Smith (1790–1874) was inspector-general of railways at the Board of Trade, 1840–41. Army officer, military engineer, fellow of the Royal Society, an associate of the Institution of Civil Engineers, and a member of several learned societies. Conservative MP for Chatham, 1852–53 and 1857–65.

Left: William Ewart Gladstone was involved in the regulation of railways from the earliest days and even proposed a reversion clause in the 1844 Act to take railways into state control after 25 years of operation. His influence continued through the nineteenth century as he served as an MP from 1832 until his death in 1898. He was Prime Minister four times.
Public domain via Commons Wikimedia

Below: GWR cut off lines. By 1912, GWR had built new lines to shorten distances between London and Birmingham, Cardiff and the West of England, as well as the cross-country route from Cardiff to Birmingham. The Westbury and Frome cut-off lines were still to come in 1933.
Published in History of the Great Western Railway *by E. T. MacDermot; Peter Waller Collection*

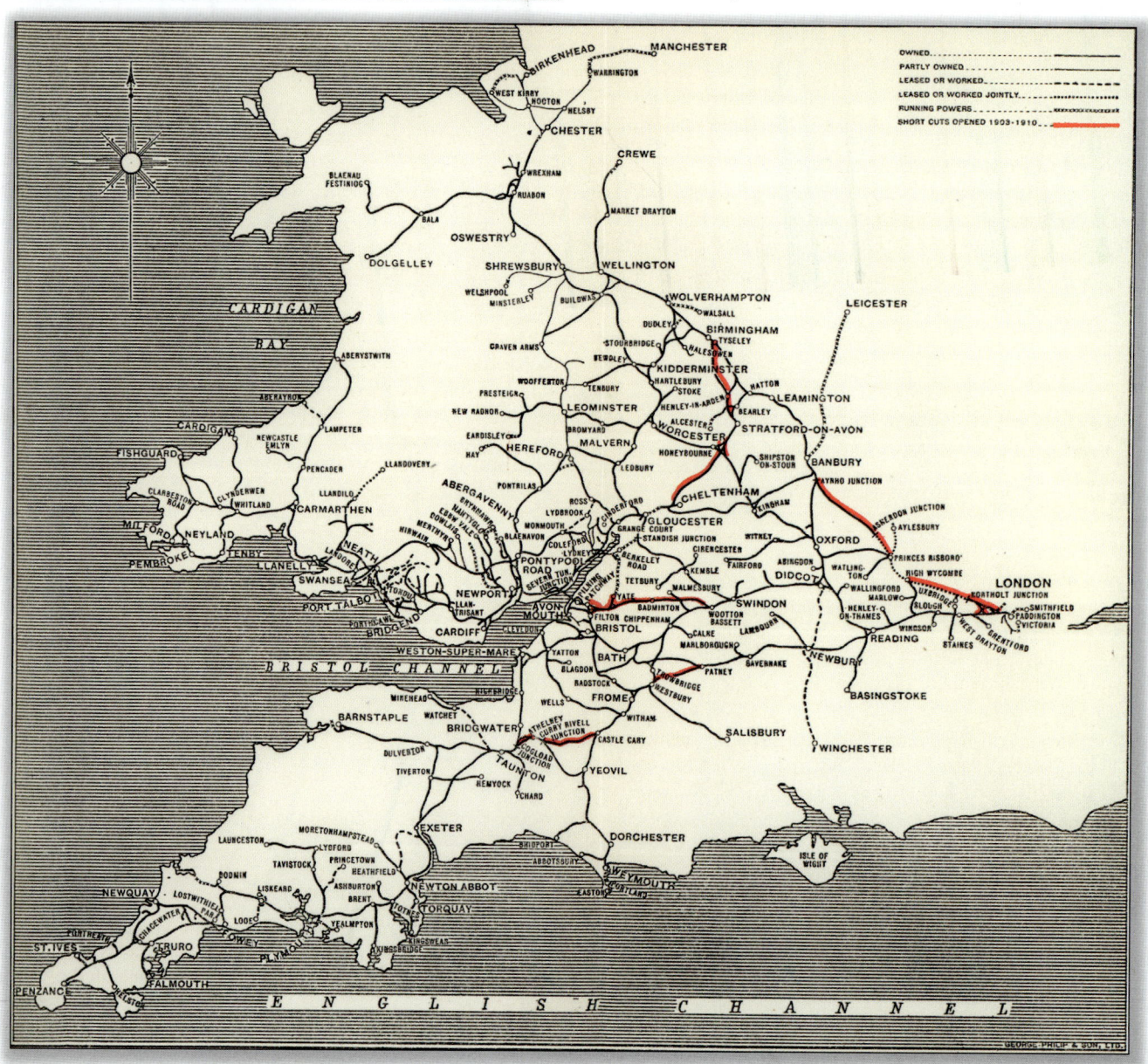

on the broad gauge and the host of narrow gauge companies, it would have been well to put some more practical men on the Commission.'

The Dalhousie Board and the Railway Mania, 1845

The demand for new railways also put great strain on Parliament's time, and with an increasing number of proposals to process, William Gladstone[16] set up an advisory board under Lord Dalhousie[17] to examine and report on every railway scheme laid before Parliament. Opposition to this intrusion into the free working of the market was strong and the Board only sat for a few months, ending in July 1845. It was the first and only serious attempt in Britain by government to provide a national strategic framework for the development of the railway network. After that, it was broadly left to the market until Dr Beeching's reshaping report of 1963[18] set out a strategy for the future development of the network but that was seeking to shrink it to what could be operated profitably, rather than control the location of new lines, and to plan for growth in passenger and freight demand. In Europe, some countries exercised much greater control on railway development, and in Belgium the network was entirely state controlled with concessions for construction and operation being sold. New lines were built for strategic military reasons as well as commercial ones, a quite different approach from that adopted in Britain.

The end of Dalhousie's board meant that there were no constraints to expansion and speculation, and Parliament was flooded with applications, with amazing scenes as promoters sought to deposit their plans before the deadline of noon on 30 November 1845. On 17 November, *The Times* had published figures showing that the capital value of the railways then in existence was some £70 million, but that the value of new lines for which powers were being sought was a staggering £563 million. The paper's leading article of 1 January 1846 talked of 'the recent mania', which effectively pricked the bubble of confidence and a terrible collapse ensued in which many speculators were ruined and some committed suicide. No fewer than 620 schemes valued at £543 million had been presented to Parliament, many of them uncommercial, and some simply fraudulent.

The political effect was significant, as Hamilton Ellis wrote in 1953:

What the Mania did, was not only to result in the building of some bad lines and the ruin of many investors, but to destroy much confidence in the railway and to make companies themselves unpopular.

The mania 'had left to the British railway industry a legacy of mutual suspicion, and a habit of power politics, which were to continue for many bitter years, never entirely departing from the nineteenth century business world, and persisting, in a more decorous form, even during the first part of the twentieth century'.[19]

Much of today's network was completed by 1865, and indeed occupied much Parliamentary time as the Bills for each line were scrutinised. As a response to this, a new form of authorisation for tramways was developed, based on delegating powers to the President of the Board of Trade to make an order, after due inquiry into the circumstances, and the Tramways Act, 1870 allowed a provisional order to be made, conferring the powers, while Parliament retained the right to approve or reject the provisional order.

Towards the end of the century, when only the most rural areas remained without connection to the railway network, this was encouraged further by the Light Railways Act, 1896, providing a simpler and cheaper process for authorising new lines, simpler construction standards, and in the case of the Mallaig extension of the West Highland Line, there was even a Treasury guarantee of 3 per cent on capital and a grant towards the harbour works at Mallaig. A number of lines in Ireland were funded through Treasury-guaranteed loans through the Public Works Loan Commissioners, and later, grants were made for railways in Ireland, such as the line from Stranorlar to Glenties in County Donegal, under the Light Railways (Ireland) Act, 1889.

The Great Central's London extension, authorised in 1893, was the last main line (until HS1), although some important cut-off lines remained to be authorised in the early twentieth century, notably the Great Western shortening their routes between London and Birmingham, Reading and Taunton and Cheltenham and Stratford-upon-Avon. So, for almost another hundred years new lines were authorised by Act of Parliament and throughout its existence, the British Railways Board promoted (almost annually) a private Parliamentary Bill for various spurs, new lines (like the Selby deviation line, where powers were given in 1979), and occasionally other issues such as revised by-laws. Eventually, the system was changed by the Transport

---

[16] William Gladstone (1809–98), four times Liberal Prime Minister between 1868 and 1894, serving a total of twelve years in all, and also a similar period as Chancellor of the Exchequer. Initially elected as a Conservative, he served as minister in Peel's government 1841–46, and as President of the Board of Trade was responsible for the Railways Act, 1844, – the first serious attempt to impose a degree of state regulation on what was then a new industry. In 1859 he became Chancellor of the Exchequer and joined the Liberal Party.

[17] Lord Dalhousie (1812–60) followed Gladstone as President of the Board of Trade 1845–46, and was then appointed Governor-General of India, where he served until 1856.

[18] *The Reshaping of British Railways*, HMSO 1963.

[19] *British Railway History, 1830–1876*, Hamilton Ellis. George Allen and Unwin Ltd, 1954.

and Works Act, 1992, which delegated the power of authorising new railways to the Secretary of State for Transport using an order-making procedure like that of the Light Railways Act, which it replaced in England and Wales. This procedure involves a public inquiry stage and the inspector's report informs the Secretary of State's decision.

The principles of the Transport and Works Act Order were the same as for the primary legislation it replaced, but for major projects where both public rights and private rights are affected, a hybrid Bill procedure is used, generally in relation to major schemes such as Crossrail and HS2. This is primary legislation and involves the usual stages of a public Bill, but effectively with the addition of a public inquiry at committee stage to allow petitions against the Bill to be heard. The Public Bill Office will decide whether a Bill is hybrid or not, and their use is quite rare. The process takes longer than a public Bill, and such Bills can be carried over between Parliamentary sessions, and from one Parliament to another.

Regulation of Railways

If we take the Liverpool and Manchester Railway of 1830 as the first 'conventional' railway for passengers and freight, then it was just eight years before the first Parliamentary select committee made recommendations on how the railways should conduct their affairs, in this first case in relation to the carriage of mails by train. This was followed later the same year by legislation compelling the companies to carry mails when called on to do so by the Royal Mail.

The following year, 1839 saw the first select committee inquiry into fares, goods rates and safety, which led to the Regulation of Railways Act, 1844. The first significant intervention by government though was on safety and the creation of Her Majesty's Railway Inspectorate under the Regulation of Railways Act, 1840. George Stephenson supported such a measure, but Brunel opposed any form of government intervention. In fact, the powers of the inspectorate were extended two years later, but remained those of persuasion rather than enforcement as the government wanted to leave safety management to the directors of the railway, rather than transfer it to the Board of Trade.

The concerns over public safety dominated, and were reflected by the comments of the Prime Minister, Sir Robert Peel[20] at the opening of the Trent Valley Railway in his constituency of Tamworth in 1845. If the privileges of the railway companies were to continue, he said, they had to show that they combined 'the greatest degree of

Isambard Kingdom Brunel, the supreme Victorian railway engineer who also built ships, docks, bridges and tunnels. *Published in* History of the Great Western Railway *by E. T. MacDermot; Peter Waller Collection*

velocity in travelling with the greatest safety to the traveller', that they had neglected no precaution which could tend to diminish the risk of accidents, the frequent occurrence of which could shake confidence in railway travelling; and they must 'make sacrifices of pecuniary gain for the sake of taking these precautions'.[21]

As the railways grew in strength and power, they progressively saw off the competition from canals, carriers by road and the stage coaches, and began to exercise monopoly powers in their own areas. This was mitigated by competition between the railway companies, but those such as the Great Western and the North Eastern had effectively market dominance in some areas such as between London and Bristol or Cardiff, and in County Durham, for example.

By the 1870s, the railways had market dominance in every area of inland transport for both goods and passengers, and maintained this until the end of the First World War. When people are dependent on a monopoly

---

[20] Sir Robert Peel 2nd baronet (1788–1850) entered the House of Commons in 1809 almost straight from Oxford University, as Conservative MP for the Irish rotten borough of Cashel, Tipperary. With just twenty-four electors on the rolls, he was elected unopposed. He subsequently represented Chippenham (1812–17) and Oxford University (1817–29), Westbury (1829–30) and then Tamworth until his death. He served twice as Prime Minister (1834–35 and 1841–46) and twice as Home Secretary (1822–27 and 1828–30). He was the founder of the modern police force, and gave his name to 'Bobbies' and 'Peelers'.

[21] *Railway Times*, 15 November 1845, quoted in The *Second Railway King; The Life and Times of Sir Edward Watkin, 1819–1901*, David Hodgkins, Merton Priory Press, 2002.

supplier, they become resentful of it and seek protection through regulation of its market power. This inevitably brought railways into conflict with the politicians who exercised this regulatory power. Public opinion tends to lag behind events, so the problem for the railway was that these constraints continued long after this monopoly power had been destroyed by the advance of the car, the lorry and the aeroplane.

The nineteenth century was a period of *laissez-faire* capitalism, but the regulation of safety by government is perhaps not so surprising. Regulation of fares, rates for goods traffic, and even industrial relations is not something normally associated with nineteenth-century governments, particularly Conservative administrations, but intervention grew throughout the century and by the beginning of the twentieth century, government was asking for a great deal of detail from the railway companies and exercising some control in all of these areas. Appendix 1 shows the number of returns required by various parts of government in 1901, an extraordinarily long list for a period when the railways were huge and powerful independent joint stock companies.

Most surprisingly, the Bill introduced by Gladstone as President of the Board of Trade, which became the Regulation of Railways Act, 1844, originally included powers for the state to take control of railways after an initial twenty-five-year period, during which it was assumed that the capital costs of construction would have been recovered. But this was a step too far, and these provisions did not appear in the final version of the Bill that received royal assent. Fares were regulated from as early as the the 1844 Act, which required the railways to provide at least one service a day on each line offering fares of a penny a mile – the so-called 'Parliamentary' trains. Today, the phrase has been adapted to refer to lines served by only a token service such as the Stalybridge Pullman, one train a week run on Saturdays from Stalybridge to Stockport in both directions (see earlier timetable on page 170). This minimal service avoids the official procedures of terminating a passenger service that has no support either from government or Transport for Greater Manchester.

Common carrier obligations predated the railways, but applied to them as they were built. Initially, goods traffic was so profitable that the obligation to carry awkward loads, or consignments to remote locations where costs were high, did not matter, but as road competition hit rail traffic after the First World War, it became an incubus that was not finally removed until the Transport Act, 1962. Before that though, freight rates and charges were regulated, the powers coming from a series of Railway and Canal Traffic Acts from 1854 to 1894 that established a system of classification of goods and the charges that could be levied for each. A Railway and Canal Commission was established in 1854, with powers to grant through rates between railways, compulsory control of agreements between railways and canals, and the requirement for railways to keep books for public inspection on a wide range of data, as required by the Commission.

While several other regulatory acts followed, the other principal piece of safety legislation was the Regulation of Railways Act, 1889, which required continuous automatic brakes on passenger trains and block signalling together with the interlocking of points and signals, following the Armagh accident on the Great Northern Railway of Ireland earlier that year with its eighty-nine deaths, many of them Sunday school children.

There was also government intervention on industrial relations, although this initially was triggered by public concern over railway accidents caused by fatigue resulting from excessive hours of work, particularly of drivers and signalmen. In some cases rostered turns for signalmen for the changeover between day and night shifts were 24 hours, and the basic day for many safety-critical staff was twelve hours. A step towards regulation was taken in the Hours of Labour Act, 1893, which required companies to provide details of duty rosters to the Board of Trade if any grade of railway staff complained that their hours of work were excessive, or their breaks were inadequate.

The legislation followed a select committee report on hours for work for railway servants, which brought a direct conflict between railway managers and the House of Commons. Evidence to the select committee was given by John Hood, the stationmaster at Montgomery, and the Cambrian Railways had dismissed him as a result, a decision that had been upheld on appeal. This was a breach of Parliamentary privilege, and the managers involved were called to the Bar of the House and suitably admonished by the Speaker. It was a clear reminder to railway managers that they could not seek to intimidate future witnesses and get away with it.

So, by the end of the nineteenth century, railways were already subject to considerable regulation and to extensive oversight with a statutory requirement to provide a great deal of information on a regular basis, which most private companies would have preferred to keep to themselves. It was a clear example of Parliament acting to correct a market failure in that the railways at that period had a clear monopoly on the movement of goods and passengers in much of Great Britain, which was not effectively mitigated by competition between railway companies, while other modes of transport had been effectively eliminated by the success of the railways. It also reflected the growing dissatisfaction with the railways that stemmed from their monopoly position, and, it has to be said, from the somewhat high-handed actions of some railway managers who took full advantage of this monopoly and the freedom from regulation they had previously enjoyed.

Appendix 3 lists primary legislation (public general acts) relating to railways and it is interesting to see that the rate of legislation is higher when the railways were in private hands than during the BR period. It dries up in 2005, although that is because most government direction these days is achieved through secondary legislation (regulations) made particularly under the 1993 and 2005 Acts.

The North Eastern Railway's Westminster office at 21 Cowley Street bears a marked resemblance to their headquarters offices at York, and both were indeed designed by the same architect. After a period as the HQ of the Liberal Democrat party, the building is now a private house. *Christopher Austin*

Westminster Offices and Early Lobbying

The larger railways had offices close to Parliament. The North Eastern Railway built a handsome office at 4 Cowley Street in Westminster in 1905. The architect was Horace Field, who also designed their headquarters building in York. For many years Cowley Street was the headquarters of the Liberal Democrat Party but is now a private house. The London and North Western Railway designed and built themselves a stunning suite of offices on the prime site of 1, Parliament Street, in 1888. It is now part of the Parliamentary Estate and contains offices and meeting rooms for MPs. At street level, it houses the Parliamentary bookshop. The 'lighthouse' top office was that of John Prescott[22] (now Lord Prescott) during his time as shadow Secretary of State for Transport in the early 1990s. Both buildings are now Grade II listed. The Midland Railway also had offices in Westminster, as, along with the NER, both railways had their headquarters outside London. The Midland offices were at 11, Great George Street, in a converted town house built in 1756, and now a Michel Roux restaurant, the building being incorporated into the adjacent Royal Institution of Chartered Surveyors.

It was here, in 1867, that the first moves toward a railway trade association were taken, as a basis for lobbying Parliament in the railway interest when the Great Northern, Lancashire and Yorkshire, LNWR, Midland and North Eastern railways met to form the United Railway Companies' Committee, which became the

---

[22] John – later Lord – Prescott (b 1938) Deputy Prime Minister 1997–2007 and First Secretary of State from 2001 to 2007. Labour MP for Kingston upon Hull East, 1970–2010. See Chapter 3.

Railway Companies' Association in 1870.[23] This remained a co-ordinating body for British railway companies until nationalisation in 1948.

We are indebted to *Grace's Guide* (the leading source of historical information on industry and manufacturing in Britain) for this description of the RCA's activities:

> Its purpose was to protect the interests of the companies and their shareholders, chiefly against parliamentary interference.
>
> The Association had its roots in a meeting of railway company chairmen, held at the Railway Clearing House (RCH) in March 1854, to discuss parliamentary matters of concern, but a properly constituted organisation developed only slowly. This was partly a result of the independent nature of the Victorian railway companies and the number of company chairmen and senior officers who were Lords or MPs in their own right, and partly a reflection of the gradually increasing role of government in regulating railway company actions and the need for an 'industry' response.
>
> By 1858 a United Railway Companies' Committee (URCC) had been formed, but it foundered after three years and was only re-constituted at a meeting on 26 June 1867, held at the Westminster office of the Midland Railway.

Detail for a drainpipe at the Cowley Street offices clearly showing the North Eastern Railway's monogram.
Christopher Austin

The splendid London & North Western Railway offices at 1, Parliament Street. Ideally placed at the corner of Parliament Square, they are now MPs' offices with the Parliamentary Bookshop on the ground floor.
Christopher Austin

The revived body's first achievement was to promulgate a standard format for the accounts of railway companies, drawn up by the chief accountants of five of the major companies. This was accepted by the Board of Trade and included as a Schedule in the Regulation of Railways Act, 1868 (31 & 32 Vict., cap. 119).

The URCC was renamed 'The Railway Companies' Association' in 1869. Its main task was to follow the progress of legislation which might affect railways, attempting to persuade MPs and Lords to vote in the 'railway interest', and giving evidence to Parliamentary committees. It also promoted legislation designed to assist railway companies. This finally left the RCH free of a political role and able to concentrate on the commercial organisation of inter-company services.

Membership of the Association received a boost with the arguments over the passing of the Railway and Canal Traffic Act, 1873 (36 & 37 Vict., cap. 48). The perceived threats to profitability, through regulation of the rates which the 'monopolist' railways could charge, led to several moderately large companies joining the major ones in the Association, finally giving it national coverage.

Chairmanship of the Association rotated amongst the chairmen of leading railway companies. Much of the actual lobbying work of the Association devolved on to its Parliamentary subcommittee, which consisted of Lords and MPs from the member companies' boards.

The Association had a small permanent secretariat, paid for by a precept of one or two shillings per £1000 of the gross revenue of each participating company. The first secretary of the association was Kenneth Morison, who was also the first secretary of the RCH, but by 1873 the honorary secretary was Henry Oakley[24] (knighted 1891), who was Secretary and then General Manager (1870–1898) of the Great Northern Railway. He remained in post at the Association for the rest of the nineteenth century, and the Association's activities were presumably co-ordinated from Oakley's offices at King's Cross.

In the aftermath of the Regulation of Railways Act, 1889 (52 & 53 Vict., cap. 57) and the industrial unrest of the 1890s, including the North Eastern Railway's unilateral recognition of the new trades union, the Amalgamated Society of Railway Servants, the ad-hoc nature of the Association came under increasing pressure, leading to a restructuring. This involved giving the secretariat a permanent base, in three rooms at 53 Parliament Street, leased from October 1900, and appointing a full-time paid secretary, the first being the rising barrister William Guy Granet,[25] appointed in November 1905. Later secretaries included barristers W. Temple Franks[26] (1905–1909) and Arthur Beresford Crane (1909–1929).

Sir Henry Oakley was General Manager of the Great Northern Railway from 1870 to 1898. Before joining the company in 1849, he had been an assistant clerk in the House of Commons. In 1873 he became chairman of the Railway Companies' Association. *Published in* The Railway Magazine; *Peter Waller Collection*

---

[24] Henry Oakley (1823–1914) began work as a clerk at Somerset House, moving on to be assistant at the House of Commons. In 1849 he joined the Great Northern Railway as clerk in the Secretary's Office. He progressed through the positions of Assistant Secretary, Accountant and Secretary, until he became General Manager in 1870. In 1873 he also became the Honorary Secretary of the Railway Companies' Association. In 1891 he was knighted. He left GNR in 1898 to retire, but went on to become Chairman of the Central London Railway. The first 4-4-2 or 'Atlantic' express locomotive built at Doncaster by the GNR was named *Henry Oakley*. It entered service in 1898, with the number 990. It is in the national collection and can be seen at the National Railway Museum in York.

[25] Sir William Guy Granet (1867–1943), general manager Midland Railway, 1905–18; deputy chairman of the London Midland and Scottish Railway (LMS), 1923–24; chairman, 1924–27. During the First World War he was successively deputy director of military railways and director-general of movements and railways.

[26] William Temple Franks (1863–1926) was an assistant librarian at the House of Commons before joining the RCA in 1905. He was a lawyer who became comptroller-general on merchandise marks, designs and trademarks.

The Midland Railway's Westminster offices at 11, Great George Street, where the first railway trade association met in 1867. *Christopher Austin*

Fielden House, the initial wartime Railway Executive headquarters and now offices for the House of Lords.
Christopher Austin

Fifty-three Parliament Street faces the Cenotaph and is a red-brick and terracotta building with an arts and crafts frieze built between 1893 and 1895. It may now be demolished to create a temporary replacement for the House of Commons while the Palace of Westminster is refurbished.

The Association's role was necessarily reduced during the First World War when Parliamentary interest in domestic transport matters was low, railways being managed for the war effort under the provisions of the Regulation of the Forces Act, 1871, but it gained in importance when the newly established post-war Ministry of Transport decided to deal with the railway companies jointly through the Association.

Because the Railways Act, 1921, during passage of which the Association lobbied for better compensation terms for shareholders, grouped British companies into four large concerns, another restructuring of the Association took place. The Parliamentary members' council was abolished, severing the direct link with Parliament, and the four new general managers constituted a standing committee of the Association. Briefings of independent railway-linked Lords and MPs continued, however, for example in the companies' 1938 'square deal' campaign for reform of freight rates' legislation in the face of road competition (which was overtaken by the onset of war in 1939), and in the run-up to the Transport Act, 1947, that nationalised the railways, canals, etc. With all railways then under a single management within the British Transport Commission, the Association was wound up at this point.

Another Parliamentary building with a significant railway history is Fielden House, which now houses offices for the House of Lords, and which played a crucial part in the history of Britain's railways in the run-up to the Second World War.

Sited on the wall in the entrance hall is a plaque that was unveiled by the Lord Speaker, The Rt Hon the Lord Fowler,[27] on 11 October 2016.

---

[27] Sir Norman Fowler, Lord Fowler (b 1938) was Conservative MP for Nottingham South, 1970–74, and for Sutton Coldfield, 1974–2001. After a long and distinguished ministerial career in the Commons, where he served successively as Secretary of State for Transport, Health and Social Services, and Employment, and Chairman of the Conservative Party, he joined the Lords in 2001

The plaque states that Fielden House was built in 1936–37 as the new headquarters for the London Midland and Scottish Railway property division and for the Railway Companies' Association. It became the HQ of the Railway Executive Committee in the build-up to the Second World War. The REC was responsible for co-ordinating Britain's private railway companies in time of war and were essential to the logistics of the war effort.

The building was named in honour of Edward Brocklehurst Fielden (1857–1942), who lived at 19 Great College Street, Westminster, from 1918 until his death. Fielden served as chairman of the board of directors of the Lancashire and Yorkshire Railway from 1919 to 1923 when it was absorbed into the LMS, of which he became subsequently deputy chairman. Fielden sat as Conservative MP for Middleton (1900–06), and later Manchester Exchange (1924–35).

It was originally intended that the entire wartime administration of the railways would be conducted from Fielden House, with the crucial telephone exchange in the basement. However, it was decided that the building would be vulnerable to bombing, so the Railway Executive Committee moved out to the disused Down Street underground station, which it shared with Churchill's wartime offices, on 3 September 1939.

In the event, Fielden House escaped unscathed and the Scottish Office moved there from 1941 to 1955 after they were bombed out of Whitehall. The Church Commissioners leased it from 1955 to 2001. Parliament purchased it on a very long lease in January 2002 and occupied it in 2005.

The House of Lords continues to commemorate the part Fielden House played in the story of Britain's railways by housing its remarkable – and valuable – collection of railway posters throughout the building.

In a more modest way, in 1990, British Rail established its own Parliamentary office as a base for discussion with politicians on the controversial Channel Tunnel Rail Link Bill (see Chapter 4). This was in the basement of Clutha House, 10 Storey's Gate, Westminster, where the fire escape conveniently led into the cellar bar of the adjacent Westminster Arms pub.

Lloyd George and the Railways

David Lloyd George had an interesting – and controversial – involvement with Britain's railways almost from the time he started in public life. In 1894 he campaigned against the policy of the London and North Western Railway of dismissing a number of employees who did not speak English and were Welsh speaking. He secured a debate in the Commons on 10 May 1895.

Against protestations that Parliament should have no involvement in an issue that related specifically to a privately owned company, *Hansard* reported Lloyd George as pointing out:

> that a Company which existed by virtue of statutory powers, was in a very different position from a private employer. The House had taken upon itself to regulate the rates which a Railway Company charged; it had now taken upon itself the function of regulating the charges of shopkeepers. The reason was that Parliament, having given Railway Companies a valuable monopoly, felt it necessary in the interests of the public to see that their powers were not used to the injury of any portion of the public.
>
> Yet the House had taken upon itself to protect traders against excessive rates, he submitted that it was also the duty of the House to see that the workmen employed by the Companies did not suffer. Against a private firm dealing unfairly with its workmen the public had a remedy; they could withdraw their custom.

David Lloyd George, first Earl Lloyd George of Dwyfor, OM PC, Prime Minister 1916-22. *Authors' Collection*

---

and was elected Lord Speaker in 2016 and served until 2021. He is now an independent cross-bench peer. Fowler's role as Transport Minister in resisting proposals for a second round of Beeching rail closures and approving a significant programme of electrification is described on pages 79–82 of *Holding the Line*. Before entering Parliament, he was a journalist on *The Times* from 1961, working as a Special Correspondent, 1962–66; and Home Affairs Correspondent, 1966–70. In *Holding the Line*, Chapter X, we recount how Fowler made an unequivocal comment that he would not authorise 'another Beeching', and wrote to Peter Parker on 8 November 1979 saying that it 'is my firm policy that there should be no substantial cuts in the passenger rail network'.

sum of money on this Company's line at Holyhead, and he maintained that the House, having conferred these powers, facilities, and exceptional advantages on the London and North-Western Company had, at any rate, some right to remonstrate with the Company if it acted unfairly towards its workmen.[28]

At the end of the debate, which was notable for some partisan speeches on both sides and a contribution by David Plunket[29] (chairman of the North London Railway) who had been put up to make the LNWR's case, Lloyd George said he was persuaded 'by the conciliatory speech of the President of the Board of Trade [James Bryce[30]] in meeting the complaints of the Welsh Members, and after the remarks the right hon. Gentleman had made as to the future, he did not intend to press the Motion'.

Lloyd George's next involvement with the railways came in 1907 when he was President of the Board of Trade, and led to one of his many biographers describing him 'as the saviour of the nation. This was, indeed, the first great triumph of his life.'[31] The 'triumph' was almost single-handedly to avert a national rail strike called by the Amalgamated Society of Railway Servants – later the National Union of Railwaymen, and later still the Rail, Maritime and Transport Workers Union – over demands for higher wages, shorter hours and, most important of all, recognition by the twelve main railway companies, eleven of which had refused it.

Writing to Prime Minister Henry Campbell-Bannerman,[32] he asked for a free hand in dealing with the railway company directors. 'There is a real danger of a strike being rushed owing to the ill-advised insolence of the directors – witness their dismissal of Union officials – unless something is done at once to get into contact with them.' He said that if the directors maintained their intransigence the government should immediately ask Parliament, when it reassembled in 1908, to approve a measure making arbitration in railway disputes compulsory in all cases where the Board of Trade considered it essential. Referring to the Conciliation Act of 1896, Lloyd George said it was 'a poor thing … It is only the knowledge that there is something behind it that will induce the directors to pay attention to it.'[33]

Praise from *Punch* for Lloyd George, after his successful intervention to settle the 1907 railway strike. The caption reads: 'LLOYD THE LUBRICATOR There's a sweet little cherub that floats up aloft to watch o'er the life of John Bull'. *Published in* Punch *magazine 23 November 1907*

But against a railway company they had no such remedy. They could not set up an opposition line without coming to the House of Commons, and the House of Commons was, after all, the ultimate tribunal which would try a question of this kind.

It was the statutory powers which had been conferred upon the London and North-Western Railway Company which had really enabled it to defy public opinion. The House had spent a large

---

[28] *Hansard*, vol. 33: debated on Friday, 10 May 1895.

[29] David Plunket (1838–1919), Conservative MP for Dublin University, 1870–95, served in the governments of Disraeli and Lord Salisbury. Became Lord Rathmore after leaving the Commons. Chairman of the North London Railway and later a director of the Central London Railway, and of the Suez Canal company. Practising lawyer on the Munster circuit, made QC 1868.

[30] James Bryce (1838–1922), Liberal MP, 1880–1907, for Tower Hamlets and then South Aberdeen. Served as minister in two positions under Gladstone, then President of the Board of Trade under Rosebery, 1894–95. Chief Secretary for Ireland, 1905–07, and then British ambassador to the United States, 1907–13. Ennobled as Viscount Bryce 1914. Awarded Order of Merit 1907. Author of report on German atrocities in Belgium published 1915.

[31] *Lloyd George,* by Peter Rowland, Barrie & Jenkins 1973, p.195.

[32] Henry Campbell-Bannerman (1836–1908), Liberal Prime Minister, 1905–08, and Leader of the party 1899–1908. MP for Stirling Burghs, 1868–1908. Father of the House, 1907–08 (the only MP to hold that position and be Prime Minister simultaneously). Served in the cabinets of Gladstone and Rosebery as secretary of state for war. Born and brought up Henry Campbell in Glasgow, he added the hyphen and Bannerman in order to inherit his uncle's Hunton Lodge estate in Kent.

[33] Campbell-Bannerman papers, B.M. Add. MSS 41240.

On 25 October 1907 Lloyd George put to the directors a conciliation plan for settling disputes with their employees based on those in place in the iron and steel industries. 'They left in a conciliatory frame of mind. What they will do when they meet next week in secret conclave I cannot tell. But I am very hopeful of a settlement after today's meeting.'[34]

Although the union's members had voted overwhelmingly for a strike, a settlement was reached that included the establishment of permanent boards in each company drawn from employees and management to consider questions of wages and hours. Recognition of the railway unions was not granted until the First World War had been declared, but the deal was an extraordinarily good one for them.

Praise was heaped on to Lloyd George's head by the leader of the ASRS, the railway directors, Campbell-Bannerman (who said that the country was 'largely indebted for so blessed a conclusion … to the knowledge, skill, astuteness and tact of the President of the Board of Trade'), and even by the King at a reception for Kaiser Wilhelm II at Windsor Castle.

Government and Industrial Relations: the Railway Strike of 1911

The summer of 1911 was notable for three things. First, it was the hottest in living memory with temperatures consistently in the high 20s and low 30s (80 to 90 degrees Fahrenheit) day after day; secondly Parliament was preoccupied with passing the final stages of the Parliament Act (which curbed the powers of the House of Lords) and there was much ill feeling in both houses of Parliament; and thirdly, there was an unprecedented amount of labour unrest through July and August, which brought the dockers and seamen out on strike, to be followed by the first-ever all-out railway strike, once it became clear that the conciliation machinery that Lloyd George had put in place in 1907 wasn't going to work this time.

Lloyd George had become Chancellor of the Exchequer in April 1908, and been succeeded as President of the Board of Trade by Winston Churchill (who had the job for two years) and then in 1910 by Sydney Buxton.[35] Campbell-Bannerman had died in 1908, and the new Prime Minister was Herbert Asquith.[36]

Buxton took an increasingly harder line, on 17 August offering the railway unions a Royal Commission, but making it clear that the government would do everything necessary to keep the railways running because the national interest mattered above everything else. His was a 'take it or leave it' approach, which didn't impress the union leaders, who said that they saw no good reason for postponing the strike.

Asquith was reported as saying, 'Then your blood be on your own head,'[37] and walked out of the meeting. The strike started at midnight the same day.

Lloyd George was appalled and was quoted by Lucy Masterman in the biography of her husband as saying: 'They are going to strike and I could have stopped it if I had been there.'[38] He promptly took charge of the dispute, set up an office in the Board of Trade, and restarted talks with the union leaders, saying that it had all been an unfortunate misunderstanding. The Royal Commission would be turned into a three-man committee – later increased to five – and with the railway companies and the unions now agreeable to taking part in the negotiations, a settlement was reached late at night on 19 August, just two days after the strike had started. The 1907 conciliation machinery would be investigated immediately and the other grievances examined.

Lloyd George wrote to his wife Margaret: 'Hardest struggle of my life but I won. I cannot even now realise quite how … The Railway Companies have agreed to something I thought quite impossible.'[39]

There are differing accounts of how the railway companies were won over. Frank Owen wrote:

> The German scare was still going strong, and the entire German High Seas Fleet was due to concentrate at Kiel early in September. That same day Lloyd George tackled the railway companies, who had hitherto point-blank refused to recognise the Railway Unions. There was one thing alone which might move them – Lloyd George appealed

---

[34] Ibid.

[35] Sydney Buxton (1853–1934), Liberal MP for Peterborough, 1883–85; Poplar, 1886–1914. President of the Board of Trade, 1910–14. From 1914 to 1920 he was the second Governor-General of South Africa. He became Viscount Buxton in 1914, and then Earl Buxton in 1920.

[36] Herbert Henry Asquith (1852–1928) Liberal MP for East Fife, 1886–1918; Paisley, 1920–24. Ennobled as Earl of Oxford and Asquith 1925. Served as Prime Minister 1908–16, previously Home Secretary (1892–95) and Chancellor of the Exchequer 1905–08. Leader of the Liberal Party, 1908–26; Leader of the Opposition, 1916–18, 1920–22. He became Prime Minister following the resignation of Campbell-Bannerman on health grounds (who died just three weeks later). Asquith was universally accepted as the natural successor. King Edward, who was on holiday in Biarritz, sent for Asquith, who took the boat train to France and kissed hands as Prime Minister in the Hôtel du Palais, Biarritz, on 8 April 1908. Asquith's premiership was notable for House of Lords reform (following their rejection of Lloyd-George's budget), for numerous social reforms, and for taking Great Britain and the British Empire into the First World War.

[37] *Lloyd George* by Peter Rowland, p.252.

[38] Lucy Masterman, *C F G Masterman, a Biography* (1939), p.204.

[39] Lloyd George Papers National Library of Wales 20430C (1375).

to their patriotism. The railway quarrel was paralysing the power of Britain to act if need be in this international crisis, and well the Germans knew it. The Unions, he understood, were anxious to come to terms. Why not try?

The two sides sat down to talk it over. Next day, the railways were working. The Red Tide ebbed.

From King George, came a telegram to the Chancellor of the Exchequer, 'Heartily congratulate you … for averting a most disastrous calamity.'

From the Prime Minister, came a letter acknowledging on behalf of all his colleagues, 'the indomitable purpose, the untiring energy and the matchless skill', which he declared Lloyd George had brought to the settling of the trouble.

Wrote Asquith: 'It is the latest, but by no means the least, of the loyal and invaluable services which you have rendered since I came to the head of the Government three-and-a-half years ago.'[40]

While Lloyd George won general acclamation for his intervention, this was not shared by the chairman of the Great Northern Railway, Sir Frederick Banbury. His hostility to Lloyd George was legendary, and he was to become a fanatical opponent of the Big Four Grouping. An intriguing 'railway whodunnit' centred on the relationship between Banbury and Lloyd George.

In 1917 the Great Central Railway unveiled the first of a new class of 4–6–0 express locomotives designed by their chief mechanical engineer, John G Robinson.[41] This was named *Lord Faringdon*[42] after the GCR's chairman. Five more followed in 1920, four with names associated with the First World War, three of them leaders, and a memorial engine named *Valour*, numbered 1165. No. 1167 was *Lloyd George*, renumbered by the LNER after the Grouping as 6165 (the others were *Beatty*[43] and *Haig*[44]).

For reasons that remain unclear to this day, the 'Lloyd George' nameplates were taken off the remarkably handsome locomotive that bore his name during 1923 – and disappeared. Two theories – both a little implausible – have been put forward for this strange decision. One was that the loco was rostered to head a special train carrying Queen Mary,[45] and was made anonymous to save her embarrassment (although Lloyd George was still a significant public figure in 1923 who had served as Prime Minister until the previous year, and was widely regarded as the politician who had won the war).

The second theory centres on Sir Frederick Banbury, although by 1923 he no longer had a railway connection, having declined to be part of the new LNER. The LNER Society, however states: 'No. 6167 Lloyd George lost its nameplates on the orders of Sir Frederick Banbury, during August 1923.'[46]

We have not been able to corroborate this assertion, and wonder whether Banbury still had enough influence to get the nameplates removed.

---

[40] *Tempestuous Journey. Lloyd George His Life and Times*, Frank Owen, 1954, pp.215–216.

[41] John G Robinson (1856–1943), Chief Mechanical Engineer Great Central Railway, 1900–22.

[42] Alexander Henderson, 1st Baron Faringdon (1850–1934), chairman of the Great Central Railway (GCR) from 5 May 1899 until the end of 1922, and then deputy chairman of the London and North Eastern Railway (LNER), from 1923 until his death. He was also a major shareholder in the Manchester Ship Canal. As Alexander Henderson, he was Liberal Unionist MP for West Staffordshire, 1898–1906, then for St George's Hanover Square, 1913–16. He was ennobled in 1916.

[43] Admiral of the Fleet David Beatty GCB OM GCVO DSO PC 1st Earl Beatty (1871–1936); First Sea Lord, 1919–27.

[44] Field Marshal Sir Douglas Haig KT, GCB, OM, GCVO, KCIE (1861–1928). During the First World War, he commanded the British Expeditionary Force (BEF) on the Western Front from late 1915 until the end of the war. He was commander during the Battle of the Somme, the Battle of Arras, the Third Battle of Ypres (Passchendaele), the German spring offensive, and the final Hundred Days Offensive.

[45] Queen Mary (1867–1953), Mary of Teck (Victoria Mary Augusta Louise Olga Pauline Claudine Agnes); Queen of the United Kingdom and the British Dominions, and Empress of India from 1910 until 1936 as the wife of King George V. Mother of Edward VIII and George VI, and grandmother of Elizabeth II.

[46] www.lner.info/locos/B/b3.php

Some exceptional politicians have had locomotives named after them. The Great Central named one of their new 'Director' class locomotives Lloyd George, although it did not carry the Prime Minister's name for long. The locomotive was withdrawn at the end of 1947, as LNER No 1498.
Authors' Collection

Whatever the truth, both plates remained lost until 1963, when they were discovered inside a partition wall at King's Cross Top Shed during demolition work. It seems likely that they were removed at Gorton Works and transferred to King's Cross in the expectation that they would be refitted there.

Happily they are now both safely in private hands, and one has been loaned to the excellent Lloyd George Museum at Llanystumdwy in North Wales.

The 1919 Railway Strike

While Lloyd George's efforts to avert and settle the 1907 and 1911 railway strikes rightly attracted much praise, his role in the dispute that led to an all-out stoppage lasting nine days from 26 September 1919 was significantly more controversial, and led to accusations that the coalition government that he led as Prime Minister deliberately and aggressively provoked the rail unions. Less than a year after signing the Armistice that ended the First World War, some felt that having defeated Germany in war, a similar all-out victory should be achieved over striking railwaymen.

To assess whether this is a fair judgment it is necessary to consider some pertinent political facts, the most important of which is the composition of the post-war coalition government. In 1907 Lloyd George had been a young ambitious President of the Board of Trade in a Cabinet made up entirely of Liberals who had one year earlier under Campbell-Bannerman's leadership won a stunning general election victory, getting 241 more MPs elected than the Conservative party.

David Lloyd George had taken over from Herbert Asquith as prime minister in acrimonious circumstances in December 1916. Asquith, however, retained the leadership of the party, and declined to serve in the coalition government headed by Lloyd George. Their falling out had catastrophic consequences for the Liberals, as some joined Lloyd George in government and others stuck with Asquith.

The turning point was a vote in the Commons on 9 May 1918, when Asquith led ninety-eight of his fellow Liberals in a division against the coalition on a motion which demanded:

> That a Select Committee of this House be appointed to inquire into the allegations of incorrectness in certain Statements of Ministers of the Crown to this House, contained in a letter of Major-General Maurice, late Director of Military Operations, published in the Press on the 7th day of May.

Although Asquith denied it was a vote of confidence, it looked pretty much like one, as Maurice had alleged that Lloyd George and Bonar Law[47] (the Conservative leader and Chancellor of the Exchequer) had lied about the strength of the British army in France.

Although he won the vote comfortably – by 293 to 106 – Lloyd George realised that if he were to remain Prime Minister for another term once the war was over, he would need to have a political machine under his control. His principal lieutenant in this venture was the coalition government's chief whip, Captain Freddie Guest,[48] who was charged with forming a pro-Lloyd George party of coalition Liberals, and negotiating with the Conservatives over which seats each would fight. Lloyd George wanted to field 150 coalition liberals, all of whom would avoid having to face Tory opponents in the election when it came.

Guest was also instructed to get agreement to a joint coalition manifesto, and by 20 July was able to put a draft agreement on candidates and policy to Lloyd George and Bonar Law. By 29 October he told Lloyd George that Bonar Law had agreed that there would be 150 Lloyd George Liberal candidates who would receive Conservative support. No one who voted for Asquith's amendment at the end of the Maurice debate would be on the list. All supporters of the coalition (Conservative Unionists, Lloyd George Liberals and eighteen members of the new National Democratic and Labour Party – a splinter group of former Labour politicians led by George Barnes[49]) received letters signed by Lloyd George and Bonar Law, confirming that they had the support of the coalition. It was this letter that became known as the 'coupon'.

Guest's other role was to raise money for what became known as the 'Lloyd George Political Fund'. The sale of honours was the principal route, with knighthoods costing £10,000 (between £210,000 and £250,000 in today's money), baronetcies £30,000 (today's £600,00–700,000), and peerages from £50,000 upwards (well over £1 million today).

In the summer of 1918 it was unclear when the election would be. The Parliament was already eight years old, and

---

[47] Andrew Bonar Law (1858–1923), Conservative Prime Minister, October 1922 to May 1923, MP successively for Glasgow Blackfriars, Dulwich, Bootle, and Glasgow Central. Born in New Brunswick, Canada, he served as a junior minister in Balfour's government, 1902–05, was Leader of the Opposition, 1911–15, and then in the wartime coalition Secretary of State for the Colonies, Chancellor of the Exchequer, and Lord Privy Seal. After Conservative MPs voted to end the Coalition in 1922, he again became party leader and, this time, Prime Minister. Bonar Law won a majority at the 1922 general election. His premiership was cut short by his throat cancer and he resigned in May 1923; he died later that year. He was the third shortest-serving Prime Minister of the United Kingdom (211 days in office).

[48] Frederick ('Freddie') Guest (1837–1945), Liberal MP for East Dorset, 1910–22; Stroud, 1923; Bristol North, 1924–29; and finally as a Conservative for Plymouth Drake, 1931–37. Secretary of State for Air, 1921–22 (following his time as chief whip). Winston Churchill was his first cousin.

[49] George Barnes (1859–1940), leader of the Labour Party, 1910–11; a Glasgow MP, 1906–22. Served under Lloyd George as Minister for Pensions, 1916–17, and then in the five-member War Cabinet as Minister without Portfolio, 1917–22. Refused to follow the Labour Party in opposition to Lloyd George in the 1918 Coupon election and was expelled. Retired from Parliament, 1922.

the electorate was three times as large as it had been in 1910, with the accession to the electoral roll of women over 30 and virtually all men over 21, so there was a strong argument for having the election sooner rather than later. There was, however, a fear that the war could go on until 1919 or even 1920, and there was a feeling that the Armistice should be signed before the country was convulsed in electioneering.

The issue was resolved by the breakthrough on the Western Front in the autumn of 1918, and the war came to an end in November.

Electioneering got under way almost immediately, but first Lloyd George had to decide what to do with Asquith. Following the Armistice he was offered a seat in the House of Lords and the position of Lord Chancellor, together with the right to nominate two secretaries of state, and six junior ministers. Asquith didn't respond, but his henchmen, John Simon[50] and Walter Runciman[51] declared 'relentless hostility', according to Lloyd George's biographer, Kenneth Morgan.

The election took place on 14 December 1918. Freddie Guest had succeeded in getting the number of coalition Liberals in receipt of the 'Coupon' up to 159, along with 364 (Conservative) Unionists and eighteen National Democratic and Labour candidates.

The outcome was a landslide of greater proportions than had ever been seen before or has happened since. 'coupon' supporters elected totalled 534, of whom 384 were Unionists, 136 Lloyd George Liberals, four Labour, and ten National Democrats. The Asquith Liberals were reduced to just twenty-seven, with Asquith himself defeated (even though the coalition did not run a coupon candidate against him), along with all of his senior colleagues.

Labour became the official opposition, with sixty-one seats – their ranks included five Liberals who joined them as soon as they were elected – the Irish Nationalists went down to seven, and there were five without party labels, thus making the number of active opposition MPs 100. The other victors of the election were Sinn Fein, who won seventy-three seats, including the first woman MP, but they had already announced that they had no intention of taking their seats at Westminster.

Even though Lloyd George had done well to get 136 coalition Liberals elected, and had benefited massively through his own popularity through leading the country to victory in the war, he was soon perceived as the prisoner of the Conservatives in his government, and there was an inevitability about the Tories' decision to pull out in 1922, following their historic meeting at the Carlton Club, and Lloyd George never held office again.

The NUR's principal demand in the spring of 1919 was the standardisation of grades and their rates of pay. It was estimated that there were 512 different grades in the railway service, and differences in the rate of pay in the same grade employed by different railway companies.

One group of railway workers who had few grounds for complaint were the locomotivemen in ASLEF, who reached a very favourable settlement on 20 August 1919 on the basis of 'standardisation upwards', which was described by their historian as 'a charter of service unparalleled in the history of British locomotivemen'.[52]

No similar or comparable offer was forthcoming for all the other grades of railway workers who were NUR members, and the union executive realised that they would not be able to hold them back from a series of local strikes unless there were a national agreement. As Philip Bagwell reported,[53] there was a conference of the Railway Executive (*ie* representatives from the railway companies), the President of the Board of Trade (Sir Auckland Geddes[54]), and the executive committee of the NUR on 16 September, at which the general secretary of the NUR, Jimmy Thomas,[55] urged that the discussions should be expedited.

'Do not let us have any more jumping off grounds,' he pleaded …'If you say a minimum of £4 a week or whatever it might be, say it rather than saying £3 leading up to £4. That is the kind of thing I have in mind.'

Geddes promised that they would have the government's response within a week, and delivered its proposals with a covering letter on 19 September. Geddes

---

[50] John Simon, 1st Viscount Simon (1873–1954), Liberal MP for Walthamstow, 1906–18, and then for Spen Valley, 1922–40. Home Secretary in Asquith's war coalition, 1915–16, when he resigned in protest over conscription. As an Asquithian Liberal opposed to Lloyd George he lost his seat in the 1918 election, but returned to the Commons in 1922 for Spen Valley, having initially lost the seat to Labour in a by-election in 1919. Deputy leader of the Liberal Party, 1922–24. Became a 'National Liberal' in 1931 and served as Foreign Secretary in MacDonald's National Government, 1931–35, Chancellor of the Exchequer under Chamberlain 1937–40, and then Lord Chancellor in Churchill's wartime government, 1940–45.

[51] Walter Runciman (1870–1949), Liberal MP for Oldham, 1899–1900; Dewsbury, 1902–18; Swansea West, 1924–29; St Ives, 1929–37. Education and then agriculture minister, 1908–14, President of the Board of Trade, 1914–16, and again 1931–37, when he became Viscount Runciman of Doxford. Implacable opponent of Lloyd George all his political life.

[52] N McKillop, *The Lighted Flame*, p.122.

[53] Philip Bagwell, *The Railwaymen*, p.382.

[54] Sir Auckland Geddes (1879–1954). British academic, soldier, politician and diplomat. He had a distinguished academic career at Edinburgh University, served as a major in the First World War and later brigadier general in the War Office, where he was director of recruiting, 1916–17, elected Unionist MP for Basingstoke in 1917, served under David Lloyd George as Director of National Service from 1917 to 1918, as President of the Local Government Board from 1918 to 1919, as Minister of Reconstruction in 1919 and as President of the Board of Trade (with a seat in the Cabinet) from 1919 to 1920. He was British Ambassador to the United States, 1920–24. Ennobled as Lord Geddes in 1942.

[55] James ('Jimmy') Henry Thomas (1874–1949), trade union leader and Labour politician. See Chapter 3 below.

wrote that 'the proposals contained in the attached memoranda are not put forward as a basis for negotiation, but as a definitive offer of the Government'.

The use of the word 'definitive' proved fatal to the prospects of industrial peace on the railways. *The Times* commented that it was 'a literary word used more often to give an impression of elegance than to express a precise meaning', and said it was a 'damning fault of the Minister to have used it – an impression borne out by Geddes's subsequent admission that the first draft of the letter had contained the word 'definite', not 'definitive'.

The NUR correctly interpreted it as meaning 'final' and said that the rates of pay put forward by the government were unacceptable because Bonar Law's promise on 22 March 1919 that standardisation would mean more money had clearly not been fulfilled. The offer did 'not contain a solitary case where the promise of more … materialised'.[56]

As Philip Bagwell points out: 'From the frequent negotiations on railwaymen's pay throughout the war Mr Thomas had never failed to produce a compromise settlement which, while not gaining for the men all they had asked for, had achieved enough to avoid a strike. Lloyd George had gained a great reputation as peacemaker for his part in the settlements of 1907 and 1911. How was it that neither of them was able to repeat the performance in 1919?'[57]

To obtain the answer to that question it's necessary to go back to the outcome of the 1918 election and composition of the ministry Lloyd George formed after it. Unlike the wartime coalition, it had a very strong Conservative bias in it, with their people taking many more ministerial places than any other group in Parliament. This was particularly important for the railways, because it meant that the ministers in charge – particularly Eric Geddes and his brother Auckland, Sir Robert Horne,[58] and Bonar Law – all took a much harder line in trade union disputes, and believed that it was necessary to restore Britain's competitive position by a reduction in wages. They told Lloyd George that if he made concessions to the railwaymen it would create a precedent that would make it difficult to stand up to the demands of other unions.

The unions had a particular problem with Sir Auckland Geddes, who had become President of the Board of Trade in 1919. Bagwell writes: 'it may be said that as a University Professor of Anatomy he found as much difficulty in finding any real point of contact with the railwaymen as they did with him'.[59] Kenneth Morgan writes that Geddes was 'out of his depth' when dealing with the unions and led to the hastening of the 1919 strike.[60]

Beatrice Webb[61] wrote in her diary that the strike 'had been desired, if not engineered, by the Geddes brothers, and subsequently desired by the Prime Minister. The Geddes brothers represent the universal determination of the capitalists to reduce wages to pre-war level, a possible pre-war money level but in any case pre-war commodity level.'[62]

Lloyd George, nonetheless, appeared to offer one last concession on Friday, 26 September – the very eve of the strike starting. He is reported as saying: 'The Government will not act on rigid lines, but will in the future, as in the past, be ready to consider and discuss anomalies and cases of hardship to any particular grades in the application of the percentage increase to be made.

'Mr Thomas clutched at the straw. He asked for clarification of this offer in the hope of finding a compromise which might justify calling off the strike. It was at this point that Sir Eric Geddes butted in with a "whispered" aside – "We could not do that" – which Mr Thomas heard quite clearly and which caused him to comment that in that case there was nothing further to be said.'[63]

Telegrams went out from NUR headquarters within minutes of the union's delegation returning from Downing Street 'Negotiations broken down; strike at midnight' [Friday/Saturday 26/27 September].

The ASLEF executive decided immediately to support their NUR colleagues, and the two executive committees met jointly every day until the strike was over. The government had attempted to divide the railwaymen and failed.

---

[56] *Daily Herald*, 29 September 1919.

[57] Philp Bagwell, *The Railwaymen*, p.384.

[58] Sir Robert Horne (1871–1940), Unionist politician who was MP for Glasgow Hillhead, 1918–37. Served under Lloyd George as Minister for Labour, 1919–20; President of the Board of Trade, 1920–21; and Chancellor of the Exchequer, 1921–22. In the First World War was Director of Railways on the Western Front with the honorary rank of lieutenant colonel in the Royal Engineers. Ennobled as 1st Viscount Horne of Slamannan (a village in Stirlingshire where his father was the Church of Scotland minister). From 1934–40 he was chairman of the Great Western Railway, which named two locomotives after him – *Viscount Horne*, Castle class locomotive No. 5086 built at Swindon Works in 1937 using components from the dismantled Star class engine *Sir Robert Horne*.

[59] Philip Bagwell, *The Railwaymen*, p.385.

[60] Kenneth O Morgan, *Consensus and Disunity: the Lloyd George Coalition Government 1918–1922* (Oxford, 1979), p.51.

[61] Martha Beatrice Webb (1858–1943) was a labour historian and social reformer. She played a major part in the formation of the Fabian Society and of the London School of Economics. Her husband, Sidney Webb, was ennobled in 1929 and sat in the House of Lords as Lord Passfield; she never referred to herself as 'Lady Passfield' and discouraged others from doing so. She was the author of the minority report to the Royal Commission on the Poor Laws and the Relief of Distress, 1905–09.

[62] *Beatrice Webb's Diaries 1918–24*, edited Margaret Cole, p.167.

[63] Philip Bagwell, *The Railwaymen*, p.385.

The government made a major effort to keep the railways running through the use of volunteers. As Bagwell writes: 'On no previous occasion had so many men and women whose names appeared in Debrett's Peerage offered their services for manual work on the railways. Lord Cholmondeley became a volunteer porter at Paddington where he might also have met the Earl of Portarlington, who was engaged in moving churns of milk or milking goats stranded for want of a train. The Duke of Manchester, the Earl of Latha, Lord Herbert Vane-Tempest and Lord Drogheda were also there to lend a hand with the movement of goods or the collection of the tickets. It was reported that Lord Grimthorpe was doing the work of two ordinary (sic) men in the provinder department at King's Cross where Admiral Sir Drury Wake and Sir Frederick Banbury also found employment. Lady Meux, wife of an Admiral of the Fleet, served as a ticket collector on the Great Eastern. On October 3rd, a band of volunteers from the Carlton Club went to Liverpool Street Station, offering to go out with the vans, and take whatever measures were necessary in case the drivers were attacked ... Lord Louis Mountbatten, then a sub-lieutenant at Osborne, drove engines for the Isle of Wight Central Railway, and ... Lord Montague of Beaulieu worked as an engine driver on the London–Bournemouth run.

'A favourite occupation with many of the volunteers was exercising the railway horses and cleaning out their stables.'[64]

When they weren't encouraging volunteers from social backgrounds as far removed from those of working railwaymen as could be imagined, ministers worked hard to get the mass media on their side. The Prime Minister – acting very differently from Lloyd George the conciliator in 1907 and 1911 – set the tone with a telegram to the chairman of Caernarvon County Council. He said the strike was not one 'for wages or better conditions. The Government have reason to believe that it has been engineered for some time by a small but active body of men who wrought tirelessly and insidiously to exploit the labour organisations of this country for subversive ends. I am convinced that the vast majority of trade unionists in the land are opposed to this anarchist conspiracy.'[65]

With the exception of the *Daily Herald* (which was edited by future Labour Party leader George Lansbury),[66] all national newspapers followed Lloyd George's lead. The *Daily Express* described the strikers as 'a little band of conspirators who forced their duped followers into a strike against the whole nation'. *The Times* said the strike 'was an attack on the community, an attempt to starve them into surrender ... Like the war with Germany it must be a fight to the finish.' The public 'were defending themselves now, as then, against an attack inspired by greed, ambition and lust for power'.

In the face of this hysteria, the joint executives of the NUR and ASLEF decided to fight back. They appointed the Labour Research Department (LRD)[67] to run a publicity campaign on their behalf. Although not formally part of the Labour Party, they had set up an office at party headquarters on 27 September 1919 as one of the first 'rebuttal' operations, and were active daily until the strike was over. Members included R Page Arnot,[68] William Mellor[69] (who succeeded Lansbury as editor of the *Daily Herald*) and the brilliant Australian-born cartoonist Will Dyson.[70]

The LRD team ignored Lloyd George's anarchist attacks and concentrated on one subject only: that the government intended to reduce the wages of railwaymen. This was the subject of an extraordinary exchange of full-page advertisements in *The Times* over three days when each side puts its case.

These were followed by a cinema advertisement on 2 October, when Lloyd George stated the case against

---

[64] Ibid., pp.288–289.

[65] *The Times*, 29 September 1919.

[66] George Lansbury (1859–1940), Labour MP for Bow and Bromley, 1910–12, 1922–40; Leader of the party, 1932–35. Co-founder of *Daily Herald* in 1912 and its editor. He was a pacifist and out of step with the mood of the 1930s, which was to oppose German rearmament. His grandchildren included the actor Angela Lansbury and Oliver Postgate, the animator, puppeteer and writer.

[67] Labour Research Department (LRD) is an independent left-wing organisation, separate from the Labour Party, which was founded in 1912 and played a major role in the 1919 railway strike. It claims to have over 4,000 trade union organisations and individuals, including fifty-one national unions, representing more than 99 per cent of total TUC membership, affiliated or subscribing to its services.

[68] Robert ('Robin') Page Arnot (1890–1986) was a foundation member of the Communist Party of Great Britain in 1920. He was a Guild Socialist who campaigned for closer co-operation between the Communist Party and Labour. In 1925 Arnot was among the twelve Communists charged under the Incitement to Mutiny Act, 1797. He was found guilty and jailed for six months, to be released on the eve of the 1926 General Strike. During the General Strike he helped to form the Northumberland and Durham Joint Strike Committee. After the failure of the strike, Arnot returned to the Labour Research Department as its Director of Research and wrote a book on the general strike.

[69] William Mellor (1888–1942) was a Guild Socialist and left-wing journalist. He joined the *Daily Herald* in 1913 and succeeded George Lansbury as its editor in 1926. Founder member of the Communist Party of Great Britain in 1920 but resigned in 1924. He was the first editor of *Tribune*, 1937–38, but sacked for opposing Sir Stafford Cripps's campaign for a Labour/Communist popular front . For the last ten years of his life, although married with a family, he conducted a passionate affair with the young Barbara Castle (*vide* biographical footnote in *Holding the Line*, Chapter II).

[70] William Dyson (1880–1938) cartoonist and artist who made his name in the First World War. He later became chief cartoonist for the *Daily Herald*.

the strike. It was shown on all cinema screens in the country, with him saying that the government was 'fighting to prevent the extremists of any industrial body from attempting to gain their ends by attacking the life of the community and so bringing untold misery on the lives of ordinary people'.

On the following day, cinemagoers were treated to a short film of Jimmy Thomas saying that 'the railwaymen were not fighting the community'. He reminded everyone he had 'always held back strikes' and was 'not captured by the extremists ... If the wages of railwaymen are reduced other trades will follow ... We are out to prevent a return to pre-war conditions and we mean to win. It is your fight as well as ours and we want you to help us.'

By then the tide of public opinion had turned towards the strikers. *The Times* said on 3 October that 'the wages question has not been well handled by the Government', and on the same day the *Daily Express* said: 'The railwaymen have a case.' The *Daily News* had said on 27 September that there was 'no shadow or semblance of excuse for a strike', but on 6 October said that the railwaymen's wages 'were not good enough ... The offer has got to be improved.' Similar expressions of support appeared in regional and local papers.

The public's appreciation of the government's case was not enhanced by an announcement by Sir Eric Geddes on 3 October that the pay the railwaymen had earned in the week the strike started would be withheld from them. The British sense of fair play strengthened against ministers.

Thanks to the efforts of volunteers – many drawn from the ranks of the aristocracy – some trains kept running during the strike, but it was clear that Lloyd George would need to find a solution with the union leaders. The accounts of the NUR published subsequently showed that a total of £251,860 had been spent on strike pay and £16,355 on publicity.[71] Philip Bagwell estimates that the union would have had sufficient funds to keep going for another three weeks, 'but not beyond that time unless the railway unions were prepared to accept help from other unions on a much larger scale'.[72]

The NUR leaders wisely turned down offers of support from other unions and Ernest Bevin[73] resisted pressure from within the Transport Workers Federation from London busmen, tramway workers and dockers to come out on strike in sympathy. There was though a conference of the Labour Party and the major unions in Caxton Hall on 1 October, which was addressed by Thomas and the ASLEF general secretary, John Bromley. They left the meeting, which then unanimously carried a resolution that declared the dispute was 'a purely trade union fight for wages and conditions', and decided to send an eleven-man deputation to see the Prime Minister that afternoon, which included Arthur Henderson,[74] Bevin and J R Clynes.[75] The delegation met Lloyd George, who repeated that the strike had to be called off before negotiations could be continued, but he did agree to meet the executive committees of the two railway unions. There was still deadlock by the Thursday evening (2nd), and the union believed that they would have to surrender before there could be a settlement.

In the face of this intransigence, those who had made up the Downing Street deputation decided to send the Prime Minister a statement that said unless the Cabinet adopted 'a more reasonable attitude ... it would be impossible to avert a widespread extension of the strike with all its consequences'. This had the desired effect. The trade union conference deputation met Bonar Law on the afternoon of Saturday (4th), and it was agreed that they and the rail unions' executives would meet the Prime Minister at 11.30 the following morning (Sunday, 5th). During discussions which lasted until 4.15 pm, an agreement to end the strike was reached, the terms of which were that wages would be stabilised at their existing level until 30 September 1920, and negotiations on the standardisation of wage rates would be completed before 31 December 1919. The arrears of wages that had been withheld were to be paid, the unions agreed to

---

[71] NUR Report and Financial Statement for 1919.

[72] Philp Bagwell, *The Railwaymen*, p.396.

[73] Ernest Bevin (1881–1951) was a towering political and trade union leader, who was one of the founders of the Transport and General Workers' Union and served as its general secretary for eighteen years from 1922 to 1940. Minister of Labour and National Service in the wartime coalition, and then Foreign Secretary in the 1945 Labour Government. As he was not an MP in 1940, a vacancy was created by persuading Harry Nathan, the member for Wandsworth Central, to resign his seat and accept a peerage. Bevin was elected unopposed in the subsequent by-election, re-elected in 1945 and retired at the 1950 election.

[74] Arthur Henderson (1863–1935) was the leader of the Labour Party in three different decades and represented five different constituencies between 1903 and 1935 (Barnard Castle, Widnes, Newcastle upon Tyne East, Burnley, and Clay Cross). He made more comebacks after losing his previous seat than any other politician in history. He was the first Labour Cabinet minister, serving as President of the Board of Education in Asquith's wartime coalition; Lloyd George appointed him to his small War Cabinet as Minister without Portfolio. He resigned in 1917 on an issue of principle and did not receive the 'coupon' for the 1918 election, losing his seat. He was awarded the Nobel Peace Prize in 1934, having served as Foreign Secretary in the 1929 Labour government. Away from politics, he was a powerful non-conformist preacher.

[75] John Robert Clynes (1869–1949). One of the founders of the Labour Party who had been a trade union official in Lancashire, he was elected MP for Manchester North East in 1906, and subsequently represented Manchester Platting until 1931 and then again from 1935 to 1945. He was leader of the party in 1921 but was defeated by Ramsay MacDonald after the election of 1922. He was Home Secretary in MacDonald's 1929 Labour Government, but refused to follow him into coalition with the Conservatives in 1931.

Lloyd George shown resting after his labours to end the 1919 railway strike is about to be awoken by the question of Irish home rule in this *Punch* cartoon of 1919. *Punch*

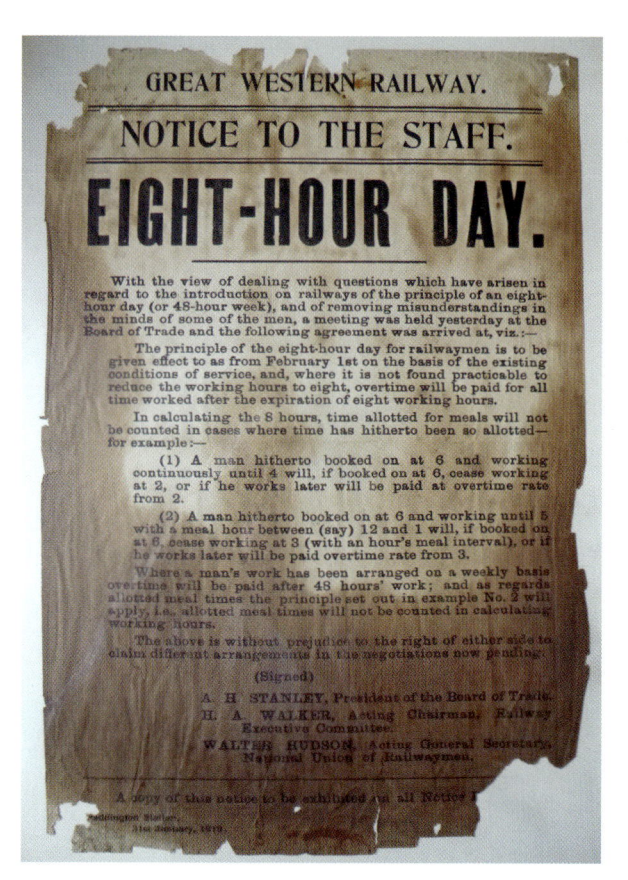

The GWR notice to staff about the introduction of the eight-hour day in 1919.
Richard Faulkner Collection

'work harmoniously with the railway servants who have remained at or returned to work',[76] and no man would be prejudiced in any way as a result of the strike.

The dispute had lasted nine days, and the unions at least felt the outcome was a victory for them. They had succeeded in winning over public opinion to their side by persuading much of the press that it was an industrial dispute about railwaymen's pay and conditions, and in so doing had laid to rest Prime Minister Lloyd George's attempts to blame anarchists and revolutionaries for fomenting the dispute.

In the words of *The Economist*, Sir Auckland Geddes's 'definitive' proposals were 'discreetly buried', and more people understood the difference between the use of the words 'definitive' and 'definite'.

The NUR was so appreciative of the efforts of Jimmy Thomas, their general secretary, that the executive set up a sub-committee to organise a special collection for him. The sum of £2,598 was raised, £2,000 of which was used to enable Thomas to buy his house in Dulwich, and the balance went to Mrs Thomas 'to be expended as and how she should think fit in the furnishing and decorating of their new house'.[77]

By 1919, the government had been running the railways directly for five years, controlling fares, freight rates and intervening directly in industrial relations to improve conditions for railway staff. Lloyd George had shown that intervention in railway industrial relations was politically popular and effective, while the railway directors had lost public support through their approach to working hours and wages. The public mood after the First World War was in favour of change and the creation of the Ministry of Transport that same year gave government the means to achieve that change. From 1919 onwards, the nature of railway policy and railway management had changed forever.

---

[76] It is hard to determine how true that turned out to be. The father of one of your authors had left school at the age of 14 in 1917 and joined the Great Western Railway as a booking clerk at Bordesley Junction. Still only 16, he worked through the strike and found that the attitude of his colleagues towards him after it was over was sufficiently hostile that he decided to leave the railway.

[77] Minutes of NUR special executive committee meetings, 15 and 24 October 1919.

3
Railwaymen in Parliament

'They also serve who only stand and wait.'
Milton, *Sonnet 16* (1678)

Railway Staff in Public Service

Railway staff from the earliest days had a high sense of public service and civic responsibility, and many have sought to serve their communities as councillors, or members of Parliament. Indeed, a large number rose to be council leaders, mayors or ministers. Their employers generally encouraged them, and the British Railways Board was particularly enlightened in giving time off for council service, and kept jobs open for staff who were elected to the House of Commons and subsequently sought to return to railway service if they ceased to be MPs. Several examples of former MPs who went back to work for the railway after membership of the House of Commons can be found later in this chapter.

In the Railway Interest: Railway Directors as Politicians

During the nineteenth century, many railway directors sat as members of Parliament, and some took an active interest in the promotion of lines proposed by their companies, or sought to mitigate the regulations being imposed by Parliament in response to public pressure to improve safety or constrain fares and freight charges.

The list of MPs 'in the railway interest' was a long and impressive one, including such well-known railway giants as George Stephenson, George Hudson,[78] Sir Daniel Gooch and Sir Edward Watkin.[79] There were 132 MPs 'in the railway interest' in the House of Commons by 1873, and scores of peers in the House of Lords.

The most egregious examples of the links between Parliament and the railway companies can be found in an analysis of the boards of the new companies formed following the 1923 Grouping.

---

[78] George Hudson (1800–71), the original 'Railway King' who played a huge part in the development of railways in the 1840s. He was responsible for developing his own city of York as a major railway centre, and served three times as Lord Mayor. He was involved in a number of railway companies, including the York and North Midland Railway, the Eastern Counties Railway, and the Midland Railway. He opposed the Great Northern Railway in its plans to bring their railway to York. Hudson was embroiled in a host of railway financial scandals after 1848 and imprisoned in York for debt in 1865, and then in London in 1866. It was alleged that shareholders in his companies were paid dividends out of capital rather than revenue (an early version of a 'Ponzi' scheme). For fourteen years he served as Conservative MP for Sunderland until his defeat in 1859, and lost his immunity from prosecution.

[79] Sir Edward William Watkin, 1st Baronet (1819–1901), Liberal MP for Great Yarmouth (1857–58), Stockport (1864–68), Hythe (1874–95, by which time he had become detached from the Liberals having voted against Irish Home Rule). He was chairman of nine different railway companies, the most notable of which were the Metropolitan and Great Central railways, which he envisaged would link to a Channel tunnel and the railways of France and continental Europe. Other railways included the Grand Trunk Railway of eastern Canada, the Athens–Piraeus Electric Railways, and he was a director of the Great Western Railway and the Great Eastern Railway and many others. He was responsible for 'Watkin's folly', an abortive attempt to recreate the Eiffel tower in the middle of Wembley Park. It was a financial failure and construction never got beyond the first stage. It was demolished in 1907 and the site later became the Empire (now Wembley) Stadium, and the home of the great exhibition of 1924.

Sir Edward Watkin was the visionary railway director who planned links from Manchester to Paris via his directorates on the Great Central, Metropolitan, South Eastern and Nord railway of France, and he was chairman of the Channel Tunnel Company. He was MP variously for Great Yarmouth, Stockport and Hythe and was the force that drove the Great Central extension to London in 1899. *Creative Commons (CC-BY-SA-4.0) via Wikipedia*

Sir Josiah Stamp was chairman of the LMSR under whose aegis Stanier was appointed CME in 1932. Stamp was tragically killed along with his wife and eldest son in 1941 following a Luftwaffe raid on the London area. *Published in* The Railway Magazine. *Peter Waller Collection*

Each one had a remarkable number of Parliamentarians – Commons and Lords – as directors. The LMS had the Hon. C N Lawrence, later to become Lord Kingsgate, as chairman, and directors included the Hon. A L Holland-Hibbert (the future Viscount Knutsford), and Sir E F Stockton, who served one year as MP for Manchester Exchange. In 1926 Sir Josiah Stamp (Lord Stamp from 1938) became chairman, serving until his death in an air raid in 1941.[80]

The LNER chairman was William Whitelaw, former MP for Perth[81] and grandfather of the Home Secretary with the same name in Margaret Thatcher's government over half a century later. Whitelaw senior chaired the LNER from 1923 to 1938; his deputy was Lord Faringdon, and other directors included Lord Joicey, who served as Liberal MP for Chester-le-Street for nineteen years and was described as 'the largest coal owner in the world'; Viscount Grey of Falloden, who was Foreign Secretary for a record nine years between 1905 and 1916 (it was he who said, 'The lamps are going out all over Europe, we shall not see them lit again in our life-time' on the outbreak of the First World War); M J Wilson MP; the Hon. Rupert Beckett; the Hon. E B Butler-Henderson, who was not only Lord Faringdon's son but he also had a whole class of Great Central express locomotives named after him; Lord Ailwyn (agriculture minister in

---

[80] Sir Josiah Stamp (1880–1941) was an English industrialist, economist, civil servant, statistician, writer, and banker. He became chairman of the London, Midland and Scottish Railway in 1926 and a director of the Bank of England in 1928. Stamp had left school at 16 and joined the Civil Service as a boy clerk in the Inland Revenue Department. With a brief interval in the Board of Trade, he rose to assistant inspector of taxes at Hereford in 1903, an inspector of taxes in London in 1909, and assistant secretary in 1916. In 1919 he changed career, leaving the Civil Service for business, to join as secretary and director of Nobel Industries Ltd, from which Imperial Chemical Industries developed. As chairman of the LMS, he was instrumental in getting William Stanier appointed in 1932 as Chief Mechanical Engineer to resolve the company's locomotive problems. From 1927 until his death, Stamp was colonel commanding the Royal Engineers Railway and Transport Corps and became honorary colonel of transportation units in the Royal Engineers Supplementary Reserve in 1938. Stamp, his wife, and eldest son all died instantly when their air-raid shelter at their home in Beckenham took a direct hit from a German bomb on 16 April 1941.

Butler Henderson. Great Central 'Director Class' locomotive. Built at Gorton works in 1919 and withdrawn in 1960, it is part of the national collection, and is currently on loan to Barrow Hill roundhouse. The Hon Eric Butler-Henderson was the son of Lord Faringdon, the Chairman of the Great Central Railway and was appointed a director of that company in 1918, becoming an LNER director on amalgamation in 1923. *Published in* The Railway Magazine; *Peter Waller Collection*

Balfour's short-lived government in 1905); and the Hon. A C Murray MP, who later became Viscount Elibank.

Even grander was the GWR: their chairman (continuously from 1908 to 1934) was Viscount Churchill, and the directors included the Hon. Lord Barrymore, Irish peer and MP; Lord Inchcape; the Rt Hon F B Mildmay, who served as both a Liberal and Conservative MP and later became a peer in 1922; J W Wilson, a Worcestershire Liberal MP; and Lieutenant Colonel David Davies MP.

Representation of the nobility on the Southern Railway board was more modest, but two of them made up for that by ancestry. The Rt Hon Sir Evelyn Cecil MP, later Lord Rockley, was a member of the family that had made its mark on English political life since the Tudors, and Lord Clinton's barony dated from 1298 and was the seventh oldest in England. In addition, Lord Pirrie was linked to Harland and Wolff, shipbuilders of the *Titanic*.

We are indebted to the *Railway Magazine* for the most comprehensive 'who's who' guide to all the senior railway industry figures in post at the time of the formation of the 'Big Four of the New Railway Era'.[82] Two observations: first, it would be hard to describe all these appointments, and hundreds of others, having been made on merit. All of the Big Four boards were made up of an agreed number of nominees from each of the constituent companies. And secondly – and this is an obvious point – there was not a single woman on any of the boards or in a senior management position, there was no representative of the passengers or the wider public interest, and despite some post-war flirtation with the idea, no one was appointed to represent the workers in the railway industry.

One name missing from all the new appointments was Sir Frederick Banbury, Conservative MP for Camberwell, Peckham from 1892 to 1906, and then for the City of London until 1924, when he became Lord Banbury of Southam. A stockbroker by profession, he was in the words of the *Railway Magazine*, a 'vigorous champion of railway interests both in and out of Parliament'.[83] He became chairman of the Great Northern Railway in 1917, and chairman of the Railway Companies Association in 1922. His opposition to the Grouping was unremitting, and he spoke in Parliament on virtually every occasion it was debated, often with angry interventions 'from a sedentary position'.

He was honoured by the GNR in September 1922 when it named its newest express passenger locomotive numbered 1471 *Sir Frederick Banbury*. This locomotive belonged to the GNR A1 class (later LNER A3, when it was numbered 4471), and remained in service until November 1961, eventually carrying the British Railways number 60102.

We have seen how much influence the nineteenth-century railway companies and their post-Grouping successors after 1923 were able to wield in Parliament as a result of the astonishing number of MPs and peers who had a direct financial interest as directors and shareholders. None of these, however, could be regarded as representing railway workers, and it needed the formation of the Labour Party (originally as the Labour Representation Committee, LRC) in 1900 before they had their own MPs.

---

[82] *Railway Magazine*, February 1923, pp.89–104.
[83] *Railway Magazine*, May 1922, p.367.

Sir Frederick Banbury. Built 1922, withdrawn 1961 loco 60102 is shown heading the up *South Yorkshireman.* Sir Frederick was chairman of the Great Northern Railway and became chairman of the Railway Companies Association in 1922. He was MP for Camberwell, Peckham and then for the City of London until 1924 when he became Lord Banbury of Southam. He was a strong opponent of Lloyd George. *John McCann/Online Transport Archive*

The Amalgamated Society of Railway Servants (the ASRS – the forerunner of the NUR and much later, RMT), played a crucial role in getting the LRC established by sponsoring the original TUC resolution at the Plymouth congress in 1899. A Doncaster member of the union, Thomas R Steels, proposed in his union branch that the Trade Union Congress call a special conference to bring together all left-wing organisations and form them into a single body that would sponsor Parliamentary candidates. The motion was passed at all stages by the TUC, and the proposed conference was held at the Memorial Hall on Farringdon Street in London on 26 and 27 February 1900. The meeting was attended by a broad spectrum of working-class and left-wing organisations – TUC represented about a half of the unions in the country and one third of the membership of the TUC delegates. The LRC was the direct predecessor of the modern British Labour Party.

The ASRS was at the heart of two major legal battles that took place in the first decade of the twentieth century. The first was the Taff Vale Judgement of 1901, which awarded huge damages and legal costs against the ASRS, which was held liable for the losses suffered by the Taff Vale Railway Company in South Wales in August 1900 in a brief but bitterly fought strike waged by the union. The company sued the ASRS and was awarded £23,000 in damages and £19,000 costs. This ruling threatened to destroy the unions' ability to take effective strike action; the need for political redress led to a sharp increase in the rate of trade union affiliations to the Labour Representation Committee. The Trades Disputes Act of 1906 overturned the court decision by legalising peaceful picketing and restoring union immunity against actions for damages caused by strikes.

The second legal case centred on Walter Victor Osborne, a railwayman who joined the Great Eastern Railway in about 1890 – becoming head porter at Clapton railway station by the turn of the century. He was an active member of the ASRS and objected to the compulsory payment by union members to a fund that was used to pay the salaries of Labour Members of Parliament, and for other political purposes.

In a ruling that became known as the Osborne Judgement, it was decided that unions had no power to collect or spend members' money for these purposes. It was not until 1913 that Asquith's Liberal government passed a law to reverse the Osborne Judgement, but with two conditions, first, that all union political funds had to be authorised by a majority ballot of the members and every individual had the right not to pay if he or she wished.

ASRS/NUR Representation, 1900–45

1900 general election

The very first railwayman to be elected to the House of Commons was **Richard Bell** (1859–1930), who had become the ASRS's general secretary in January 1898 following the dismissal of the previous incumbent, Edward Harford.

Bell had been put forward by the Derby Trades Council as their candidate for Derby in the 1900 general election, and served alongside the town's second MP, Sir Thomas Roe, a Liberal. Bell was technically not an LRC MP, and indeed was much closer to the Liberals than the only other Labour MP elected in 1900, Keir Hardie. Following a number of policy disagreements, and actions in the Commons that did not find favour with Labour MPs, Bell resigned as general secretary of the ASRS in December 1909 and stood down as MP for Derby at the January 1910 general election.

Bell's replacement as general secretary was the Assistant Secretary, James Williams, and in Derby another official of the ASRS, James (Jimmy) Thomas, was elected MP. Thomas became Assistant Secretary in September 1910, and then General Secretary in 1916, following Williams's resignation on health grounds. His subsequent career, with its highs (*eg* the 1919 railway strike) and lows (his eventual resignation from the government and public life in 1935), are described below.

Jimmy Thomas, MP for Derby, Cabinet minister and NUR General Secretary.
Library of Congress

1906 general election

In addition to **Richard Bell**, other ASRS MPs elected in 1906 were the following:

Walter Hudson (1852–1935) MP for Newcastle upon Tyne from 1906 to 1918. He worked as a guard with the North Eastern Railway for twenty-five years. He served as President of the ASRS for eight years, and in 1899 served on the Royal Commission on Accidents to Railwaymen.

From 1898 to 1906, Hudson was the Irish Secretary of the ASRS, and was President of the Irish Trades Union Congress (ITUC) in 1903. In the Commons he repeatedly introduced a private member's Bill between 1906 and 1910 that would have made mandatory an eight-hour day for railwaymen (one of the eventual outcomes of the 1919 railway strike – see Chapter 2). Hudson presided over the Labour Party's 1908 conference, and remained active in the ASRS and its successor, the National Union of Railwaymen (NUR), as chief of its movements department.

George Wardle CH (1865–1947) was editor of the union's journal *Railway Review* and MP for Stockport, 1906–20. He was chairman of the Labour Party, 1916–17, and served in Lloyd George's coalition government as Parliamentary Secretary at the Board of Trade. He received the 'coupon' in the 1918 election and was re-elected as Coalition Labour. He was a founding member of the Order of the Companions of Honour in 1917. He resigned as a Member of Parliament in 1920.

January and December 1910 elections

ASRS MPs returned in these two elections were **Walter Hudson, George Wardle,** and **James ('Jimmy') Henry Thomas** (1874–1949). Thomas was a trade union leader and Labour politician whose soaring successes leading the NUR and serving as a Cabinet member in Labour and coalition governments crashed to the ground over a 'cash for secrets' scandal that precipitated his sudden and total removal from public life. His railway career started in his native South Wales as a locomotive cleaner and he progressed upwards to become a driver. An active trade unionist, he promoted the merger of the Amalgamated Society of Railway Servants with two smaller unions to form the NUR and in 1916 became its general secretary, a position he held until 1931. Thomas combined his union role with Parliament and in 1910 became one of two MPs for Derby. He served as Secretary of State for the Colonies in Ramsay MacDonald's 1924 minority government, and was Lord Privy Seal in the 1929 ministry, Secretary of State for the Dominions, 1930–35 (combined with the Colonies for two and a half months in 1931), and then finally Secretary of State for the Colonies again in 1935–36. With his Labour colleagues Lord Sankey (Lord Chancellor), Philip Snowden (Chancellor of the Exchequer) and MacDonald himself, Thomas served in the National government, which was formed in August 1931, and re-elected by a landslide in the general election of November 1931 at which the Labour Party was the principal Opposition.

Thomas was expelled by the party and made to resign as NUR general secretary. The voters of Derby, however, continued to re-elect him standing as National Labour to Parliament with huge majorities at the 1931 and 1935 general elections (by which time Stanley Baldwin had replaced MacDonald as Prime Minister).

Thomas's career came to a sudden end in 1936. The *Hastings Press* reported: 'Jimmy Thomas held his government post until May 1936, when he was found guilty by a Tribunal of Inquiry of leaking budget secrets to his stockbroker son Leslie; to Sir Alfred Butt, the Conservative MP for Balham and Tooting; and to Alfred "Cosher" Bates, a wealthy businessman. In a Judicial Tribunal, Bates admitted giving Thomas £15,000 but tried to claim it was an advance for a proposed autobiography. Thomas was forced to resign from the government and left the House of Commons with his head bowed in shame.'

1918 'coupon' election

There were two NUR candidates elected: **Jimmy Thomas** as a Labour candidate for one of the two Parliamentary seats in Derby (the other was lost by the Liberals to a Unionist candidate who received the coupon), and **George Wardle** (who had the coupon).

1921 by-elections

Walter Halls (1871–1953) was very briefly Labour MP for Heywood and Radcliffe, which he won at a by-election, then lost it twice more in 1922 and 1923. Educated at a village school in Leicestershire, he worked on a farm until 18 years of age, then joined the Midland Railway service in the goods depot at Leicester for twenty years. He had joined the NUR/ASRS in 1896 and was secretary of the Leicester Branch for nine years. He had been elected as an organiser of the NUR in 1909.

James Wilson (1879–1943) was MP for Dudley, 1921–22, and then for Oldham, 1929–31. He left elementary school in Aberdeenshire to work as agricultural labourer at 13 years of age; joined the railway service in 1902 and was a member of the NUR Executive in 1916–19.

1922 general election

Henry Charleton (1870–1959) was MP for Leeds South from 1922 to 1931, and again from 1935 until he retired at the 1945 election. His father, also Henry Charleton, was an engine driver on the Midland Railway, and after a time as an assistant to a blacksmith, the younger Charleton worked his way up to a similar position, also with the Midland Railway. He had left board school at the age of 12.

While working on the railways, Charleton studied at the St Pancras Working Men's College, and became active in the NUR. In 1919 he compiled the *Locomotive Men's Conditions of Service* and later became a member of the NUR's executive committee.

Thomas Lowth (1858–1931) was MP for Manchester Ardwick from 1922 until his death. Born in Billingborough, Lincolnshire, he received elementary school education, entered the railway service in 1875 and moved to Manchester. He worked on the railway for twenty-three years, doing various jobs, then became the general secretary of the General Railway Workers' Union in 1898, a trade union he had helped to establish some years earlier primarily for low-paid workers on the railways. With a final membership of 20,000, it merged in 1913 with the ASRS and the United Pointsmen and Signalmen's Society to form the National Union of Railwaymen.

1923 general election

Jimmy Thomas won again in Derby, and was joined in the House of Commons by the first MP sponsored by the Railway Clerks' Association (which became the Transport Salaried Staffs' Association – TSSA – in 1951). He was **Herbert Romeril** (1881–1963), who had worked at the Railway Clearing House. He joined the Independent Labour Party (ILP), and became the chair of its Metropolitan Branch.

The ILP was affiliated to the Labour Party, and at the 1918 and 1922 UK general elections, he stood unsuccessfully for it in St Pancras South East. He finally won the seat in 1923, lost it in 1924, won it again in 1929, and then lost again in 1931.

Also elected in 1923 was **George Sherwood** (1878–1935) as MP for Wakefield. He lost the seat in 1924, won it back in 1929 and then finally lost it in 1931. The son of a miner, he was a railway employee (NUR) and for many years a councillor in Wakefield, serving as mayor in 1926–27.

1924 general election

The Associated Society of Locomotive Engineers and Firemen (ASLEF) had started sponsoring Labour candidates from 1906, but it was not until 1924 that **John Bromley** (1876–1945) was elected for Barrow-in-Furness. He was educated at elementary schools until the age of 12, when he began working successively as a country post boy, a chemist's errand boy, and assistant on W H Smith & Sons' bookstall at Shrewsbury railway station. At age 14 (1890) he began working for the Great Western Railway (GWR) as an engine cleaner at Shrewsbury. In 1892 he became an assistant fireman, and a regular fireman in 1896. He was a registered train driver in the GWR until 1905.

Becoming a fireman qualified him to join ASLEF. He became active in union branches in Shrewsbury and, as he moved employment in the GWR, at Worcester and Southall, Middlesex. In 1903 he joined the GWR locomotivemen's negotiating committee and in 1908 became ASLEF representative on the sectional conciliation board. In 1909 he became its organiser in the North of England, based in Manchester. In succession to Albert E Fox, he was elected with a clear majority as national general secretary in October 1914.

When the railway companies were brought under government control during the First World War, he was a railway unions' representative on the advisory committee to the Ministry of Transport. During the same period, as his union's head he campaigned for the interests of its trades against the claims of rival railway unions and secured an agreement in December 1918 for a standard eight-hour day for locomotive footplatemen.

Bromley contested Barrow in 1923, was elected in 1924 and re-elected in 1929. He retired at the 1931 election. He served as ASLEF's President from 1932 to 1933 and retired as ASLEF general secretary in 1936.

1925 by-election

Arnold Townend (1880–1968) joined his RCA colleague Herbert Romeril in the House at a by-election as MP for Stockport, a two-member constituency, and served until his defeat in 1931, holding the seat in 1929. He had contested it unsuccessfully in 1923 and 1924.

Townend joined the railway as a clerk in 1896. He was later unsuccessful at Carlisle in 1935. He relocated to Southport, where he served as mayor from 1955 to 1956.

1928 by-election

Albert Bellamy (1870–1931) was elected MP for Ashton-under-Lyne at a by-election in October 1928, after the sitting Conservative MP Cornelius Homan was disqualified when he was declared bankrupt.

Bellamy was born in Wigan, Lancashire, and took up employment as an engine driver for the London and North Western Railway. He became involved in trade union activities, rising to the presidency of the Amalgamated Society of Railway Servants. During the 1911 transport strike, he was prominent in leading the successful campaign for union recognition by the railway companies. When the ASRS was merged with the two other rail unions in 1913 to form the National Union of Railwaymen, Bellamy was its first President, serving until 1917.

He unsuccessfully contested Wakefield at the 1918 and 1922 general elections.

Re-elected at the 1929 general election. He was appointed Parliamentary Private Secretary to Frederick Roberts,[84] Minister of Pensions. Soon after entering government, Bellamy became ill and died in March 1931, aged 60.

1929 general election

The 1929 election, which was won by Labour and put Ramsay MacDonald back into Downing Street, saw a significant number of rail union MPs elected. From the Railway Clerks Association they were: **Herbert Romeril** (re-elected for St Pancras South-East), and **Arnold Townend** (who held Stockport).

And elected for the first time were:

Alexander Walkden (1873–1951) was MP for South Bristol, 1929–31 and 1935–45. He had contested four elections before winning in 1929, lost in 1931 and was returned again in 1935. On his retirement from the Commons he became Lord Walkden, and served as deputy chief whip in the House of Lords in 1945–49. He served for thirty years as General Secretary of the Railway Clerks' Association (1906–36), acted as Parliamentary Secretary to the RCA; Member of General Council of the Trades Union Congress, 1921–36, Chairman, 1932–33. He had started as a clerk on the Great Northern Railway in 1889; he was Goods Traffic Representative at Nottingham, then Agent at Peterborough. The TSSA's headquarters building adjacent to Euston station was named Walkden House in his honour. It was demolished to make way for High Speed Two's Euston terminus under an order dated June 2017 and the name was transferred to the union's new HQ in Devonshire Square.

George Mathers (1886–1965), MP for West Edinburgh 1929–31; Linlithgowshire 1935–50; West Lothian, 1950–51. From 1899 served as clerk with North British Railway; active in trade union and Labour movement from 1908; President of Carlisle Trades Council and Labour Party, 1917–20, transferred to Edinburgh, 1921; was Chairman of Edinburgh Central ILP and President Edinburgh Branch of Scottish Home Rule Association; elected to London and North Eastern Railway No. 1 Sectional Council and Railway Council. Government whip October 1944–May 1945; Scottish Labour whip, 1935–45; deputy chief whip, 1945–April 1946. Created Lord Mathers, 1951, and had the distinction of being the last hereditary peer nominated by a Labour Prime Minister. Lord High Commissioner to General Assembly of Church of Scotland, 1946, 1947, 1948 and 1951. Appointed Deputy Lieutenant of Edinburgh in 1946, and a Knight of the Thistle in 1956.

George Lathan (1875–1942) MP for Sheffield Park, 1929–31 and 1935 until his death. Entered service of the Midland and Great Northern Railway as clerk at Norwich, 1889; various positions in service until 1912; Member Board of Management of Railway Clearing System Superannuation Fund Corporation, 1906–12; President Railway Clerks' Association, 1908–12; Chief Assistant Secretary Railway Clerks' Association, 1912–37; Member National Wages Board for Railways, 1921–34; Member of Advisory Committee, International Labour Office, Geneva, 1923–37; Member National Executive Committee and Treasurer of Labour Party (Chairman, 1931–32).

---

[84] Frederick Owen Roberts (1876–1941), Labour MP for West Bromwich, 1918–31, 1935–41. Minister of Pensions under Ramsay MacDonald's first Labour Government and in the 1929–31 administration.

Frederick Charles Watkins (1883–1954), MP for Hackney South, 1929–31 and 1935–1945. He was a former railway clerk who was President of the RCA in 1937–43.

NUR MPs elected, in addition to **Jimmy Thomas, Albert Bellamy, George Sherwood, Henry Charleton, Thomas Louth** and **James Wilson** were:

Frederick George Burgess (1871–1951), MP for York, 1929–31. Worked on the railways for many years, and held prominent offices in the union, including secretary of the Maidstone branch for seventeen years. He also served on various government committees during the First World War. Left the railway industry in 1919 (refusing a post as night porter at NUR headquarters), and worked as a political agent and lecturer, also producing political cartoons and articles under the pseudonym of 'Battersea Bowser'. In 1937, he was elected to represent Camberwell North West on London County Council, serving until 1949. He also served on Camberwell Metropolitan Borough Council. He served as Camberwell's mayor from 1947 until 1949, taking over from his wife, Jessie Burgess, who held the role from 1945 to 1947, and after whom Burgess Park in Camberwell is named.

Arthur Law (1876–1933), MP for Rossendale, 1929–31, joined the railway in 1893 from Todmorden Council School as an engine driver; his father had been a railway signalman. Member of the NUR executive committee 1910 to 1912, 1918 to 1920, and 1925 to 1926.

The only ASLEF MP to be elected in 1929 was **John Bromley** (again for Barrow-in-Furness).

1931 by-election

The by-election in Manchester Ardwick was caused by the death of Thomas Lowth, and the NUR put up another of its candidates to succeed him. He was **Joseph Henderson** (1884–1950), who had been an employee of the LNER and had held official positions in the union that were to include NUR President 1933 to 1936. He had been the first Labour Mayor of Carlisle, 1927–28. He lost the seat in the 1931 general election, and then won it again in 1935, retaining it for the last time in 1945. He was ennobled as Lord Henderson of Ardwick in the 1950 dissolution honours, but died only five weeks later.

1931 general election

All the railwaymen seeking re-election as Labour candidates in the 1931 election – called by Ramsay MacDonald seeking a vote of confidence in his coalition government (made up almost entirely of Conservatives) – were defeated, with the exception of Jimmy Thomas, who stood as 'National Labour' and was re-elected with an increased majority in Derby. He had, however, been taken off the official NUR list, and was expelled from the Labour Party.

1933 by-election

William Dobbie CBE (1878–1950) became the first official NUR candidate to be elected in the 1930s, having successfully contested a by-election in Rotherham in February 1933. He was President of the NUR, 1925–28, and again from 1930 to 1933. Educated at a council school and son of a blacksmith, he was twice Lord Mayor of York, successfully defended his Parliamentary seat at the 1935 and 1945 general elections, and then died in office in January 1950.

1935 general election

A number of Labour MPs defeated in 1931 were re-elected in 1935. From the Railway Clerks' Association these were **Alexander Walkden, Fred Watkins, George Mathers**, and **George Lathan**. Joining them for the first time were:

Fred Simpson (1886–1939), MP for Ashton-under-Lyne, Chief Assistant Secretary, Railway Clerks' Association and its President, 1932–37. Ex-Alderman Leeds City Council and Lord Mayor, 1931–32. He had worked for the LNER in Leeds.

Frank Anderson (1889–1959), railway clerk. Contested four elections unsuccessfully until elected in Whitehaven in 1935, serving until his death, aged 69.

The NUR had significantly fewer MPs in 1935 than the Railway Clerks' Association. **William Dobbie** was re-elected in Rotherham, and **Adam Hills** (1880–1941) won Pontefract. Previously he had worked for the LNER. He was active in the union, serving on its national executive, and was elected a Newcastle City Councillor in 1934.

Jimmy Thomas was re-elected in Derby, but resigned from Parliament shortly afterwards.

1936 by-election

An additional RCA MP was elected at a by-election in Clay Cross, Derbyshire in 1936. He was **George Ridley** (1886–1944). He was a full-time union official from 1920 and edited the *Railway Service Journal*. He was Auditor to the Labour Party, 1934, 1935, and a member of the Labour Party Executive from 1936, serving as Vice-Chairman in 1942. He died in office at the age of 57 when he was Chairman of the Party.

1938 by-election

Cecil Charles Poole (1902–56) was elected Labour MP for Lichfield at a by-election in 1938, was re-elected in 1945, and moved to Birmingham Perry Barr when the Lichfield seat was abolished in boundary changes. He served there from 1950 until he retired in 1955.

He was a railway clerk with the LMS in South Wales, which he joined at the age of 16, and remained on the railway until his election. He was sponsored by the NUR. He served in the Royal Engineers in the Second World War, and reached the rank of major.

In 1951, Poole was Parliamentary Private Secretary to President of the Board of Trade (PBT), Harold Wilson. When Wilson resigned from the government in April 1951 in protest at the introduction of National Health Service charges to meet the financial demands imposed by the Korean War, Poole was offered the same role with the new PBT, Hartley Shawcross, but declined to serve, saying, 'I declined because I support the views of the three ministers who resigned in opposition to the dentures and spectacles charges and the general rearmament question.'

He retired from the House of Commons at the 1955 general election, and died the following year, aged 53.

1942 by-election

Thomas William Burden, 1st Baron Burden (1885–1970) was MP for Sheffield Park from 1942 to 1950, when he was appointed to the House of Lords. He was born in Mile End, and was educated at the London School of Economics. In 1909, he became the chair of the Poplar Labour League, then became its chair, serving until 1922. He joined the Railway Clerks' Association, and from 1916 served on its executive committee. From 1921, he was on the executive of the London Labour Party, and also of the Workers' Educational Association. He was also active in the Fabian Society and the Independent Labour Party. He was Second Church Estates Commissioner from 1945 to 1950 and a Member of the House of Laity of the Church Assembly from 1947 to 1950. From 1950–51 he was a government whip in the House of Lords.

1945 General Election

The 1945 election produced a Labour landslide of historic proportions, with the number of Labour MPs in the House up to 393, compared with 164 at the dissolution of the previous Parliament. Unsurprisingly there were more rail union-sponsored MPs than ever before (or have been seen since). There were twenty-eight of them on the Labour benches, with fourteen NUR members, twelve from the Railway Clerks' Association (which became TSSA in 1951) and two from ASLEF. The number of railway directors on the other side had shrunk to just two, compared with twelve between 1935 and 1945.

The NUR MPs were:

Joseph Henderson, MP for Manchester Ardwick since 1931 (see above).

John Hynd (1902–71), MP for Sheffield Attercliffe, 1944–70. Ex-LMS clerk in Perth, NUR clerk, 1925–44. Chancellor of the Duchy of Lancaster, and Minister for Germany and Austria, 1945–1947, and Minister of Pensions during 1947. Brother of Harry Hynd MP (see below).

William McAdam (1886–1952), MP for Salford North, 1945–50. His *Who's Who* entry described him as 'clerk, soldier, railway porter, goods guard, yard foreman'. He served on the National Executive Committee of the NUR, and the Scottish Executive Committee Labour Party. He was the author of *Birth, Growth and Eclipse of Glasgow and South Western Railway Company, 1923*.

Henry R Nicholls (1893–1952), MP Stratford division of West Ham, 1945–50. He worked for the London and North Eastern Railway painting coaches before his election.

Arthur Joseph Champion (known as Joe Champion) (1897–1985), Lord Champion from 1962. Worked on the railways after serving in the First World War. MP for South Derbyshire, 1945–50, then South Eastern Derbyshire until 1959, when he lost by twelve votes. From April to October 1951 Parliamentary Secretary to the Ministry of Agriculture and Fisheries. Deputy Leader House of Lords and Minister without Portfolio from 1964 to 1967 in Harold Wilson's government. NUR executive committee.

Tom Steele (1905–79), MP for Lanark, 1945–50 (when he lost to Lord Dunglass, the future Prime Minister Sir Alec Douglas-Home, whom he had unseated in the same seat in 1945). Elected in a by-election in 1950 for Dunbartonshire West, remaining there until his retirement in 1970. Steele previously worked as a stationmaster and was on the board of the Lanark Co-operative Society. He served as Parliamentary Secretary at the Ministry of National Insurance during the 1945–50 Labour government.

Percy Barstow (1883–1969) was MP for his home town of Pontefract from 1944 (when he was returned unopposed in a by-election) until his retirement in 1950. Like his father, Barstow was an engine driver and joined the National Union of Railwaymen. From 1906 he worked full-time as a clerk at the union's headquarters. In 1913, he was promoted to become a departmental manager at the union, then in 1934 became its office manager.

Joseph Sparkes (1901–81), MP for Acton 1945–59, having unsuccessfully contested the elections in 1929, 1931 and 1935. He joined the GWR as a clerk, and moved to London serving on Acton Borough Council and Middlesex County Council. He was mayor of Acton in 1957–58. He was also President of the London Region of the National Union of Railwaymen for ten years.

Alfred Balfour (1885–1963) was MP for Stirling and Clackmannan West from 1945 to 1959. Educated at elementary school, he began work as a baker's message boy and later worked in a sawmill, in a tannery, and as a carter before joining the railways at the age of 19. In his youth he was a keen amateur boxer, and was for a time the amateur bantamweight boxing champion of the north of Scotland.

Balfour continued his education in evening classes including through the Workers' Educational Association and the National Council of Labour Colleges, and he also became an active member of the National Union of Railwaymen. He was Secretary of the Aberdeen branch of the NUR for twenty years, and represented railwaymen on Aberdeen Trades Council. For many years, Balfour was a member of the NUR Executive. His final job on the railways was parcels foreman at Aberdeen railway station, and he was chairman of the employees' side of the sectional council of the London, Midland and Scottish Railway for twelve years.

His Parliamentary career was notable for the fact that in fourteen years he only made one speech – his maiden, and that after eight years. His loyalty to the whips was unstinting throughout.

William Thomas Proctor (1896–1967), MP for Eccles 1945–64. He worked as a railway guard, was secretary of the Pontypool branch of the National Union of Railwaymen and was a member of the Monmouthshire County Council.

David Thomas Jones (1899–1963), also known as **Dai Jones**, was MP for The Hartlepools, and held the seat until his defeat by only 182 votes at the 1959 general election. After leaving school at 12, he started on the railways at 14 and became a signalman. A member of Pontypridd urban district council for many years and active in the NUR.

Ernest Popplewell CBE (1899–1977), MP for Newcastle upon Tyne, West 1945–66. Created a life peer as Lord Popplewell in 1966. Railway signalman; NUR Branch Secretary. Government whip, 1946–51; Opposition whip, 1951; deputy chief whip, 1955–1959. Chairman: Labour Parliamentary Transport Group, 1959–65; Parliamentary Nationalised Industries Committee, 1964–66. Served in First World War and was awarded the RMA (Belgian Croix de Guerre).

James Harrison (1899–1959), MP for Nottingham East from 1945 until the seat's abolition for the 1955 general election. He was then returned for the new Nottingham North constituency, and died in office in May 1959, aged 59. He was an engine driver and member of the NUR's executive committee.

Ivor Owen Thomas (1898–1982) was MP for The Wrekin, 1945–55. He was from Briton Ferry in South Wales, and his first job was as a barber's lather boy, and then at Gwalia Tinplate Works from 1912 to 1918, when he was called up for military service. As a conscientious objector, he refused, and spent a year in prison. Thomas became an engine cleaner on the Great Western Railway from 1919 to 1923. He won a scholarship to the Central Labour College in London, where he studied from 1923 to 1925, then worked at the head office of the NUR until 1945.

After he lost his seat in 1955, he returned to work at the NUR headquarters until 1958, and for British Rail at London Waterloo station from 1960 to 1965.

There is a road named after him in the village of St George's, situated in Telford in his old constituency – Ivor Thomas Road, St George's, Telford, TF2 9EZ.

The Railway Clerks' Association's MPs (TSSA from 1951)

Thomas W Burden (MP for Sheffield Park), see above.

Frank Anderson (1889–1959), MP for Whitehaven since 1935. See above.

George Mathers (1886–1965). Elected in 1929 for Edinburgh West, and then Linlithgowshire – see above.

Albert E Davies (1900–53), MP for Stoke Burslem, 1945–1950; Stoke on Trent North, 1950–53. Started work aged 14 on the railway. He continued as a clerk at the railway until he was elected at the 1945 general election. Davies was on his way to Jamaica as member of a delegation from the Commonwealth Parliamentary Association on board the SS *Bayano* when he died, aged 52, and was buried at sea.

Clarence Barton (1892–1957), MP for Wembley South, 1945–50. Clerk with the London and North Eastern Railway. Served on Wembley Borough Council, 1934–49; Mayor of Wembley, 1942–43.

Ray Gunter (1909–77), MP for South East Essex, 1945–50; Doncaster, 1950–51; Southwark, 1959–72. Commissioned and served as a captain in the Second World War, having enlisted in the Royal Engineers. He was a backbencher throughout the six-year Labour government of Clement Attlee. Gunter was a member of the Labour Party's National Executive Committee (NEC) from 1955 to 1966 and was President of his union, TSSA, 1956–64. After the 1964 general election Harold Wilson made Gunter Minister of Labour. He famously described the job as a 'bed of nails', particularly after the seamen's strike of 1966, and he was frustrated in his efforts to reform trade union law based on the Donovan Commission report by being reshuffled to the post of Minister for Power in April 1968. He resigned from government on 1 July, stating that he could no longer work in a Wilson government, and was 'going back to the people from whence (*sic*) I came'. Gunter was re-elected in his Southwark constituency at the 1970 general election that saw the Labour government replaced by a Conservative one led by Edward Heath. He was by now a senior opposition backbencher and resigned from Parliament in 1972.

Percy Morris (1893–1967), unsuccessfully contested Swansea West in 1935, then was elected in 1945 serving as its MP until he was defeated in 1959. Joined the Great Western Railway in an administrative role at the age of 15, and became an active trade unionist. He served as treasurer of the Railways Clerks' Association, 1937–43 and as its President, 1943–53. Member of Swansea Borough Council from 1927, became a council alderman, deputy mayor in 1944–45 and mayor in 1955–56.

John Belcher (1905–1964) was MP for Sowerby from 1945 to 1949. He worked as a clerk for the GWR at its Smithfield goods depot from 1921, and was active in the Railway Clerks Association, becoming branch secretary in 1929. Parliamentary Secretary at the Board of Trade. He saw his job as promoting relationships between government and business, but became too close to a number of individuals who felt they could corrupt him with gifts, holidays and other largesse, the most prominent of whom was Sidney Stanley, a Polish émigré to the UK.

The rumours became allegations and were the subject of a tribunal of inquiry under the chairmanship of a high court judge, Sir George Lynskey.[85] Belcher took leave of absence from his ministerial office once the tribunal started work. He and his wife were subjected to particularly brutal cross-examination by Sir Hartley

---

[85] Sir George Justin Lynskey (1888–1957) was an English judge chiefly remembered for presiding over the tribunal that bore his name.

Shawcross,[86] the Attorney General, who had conducted prosecutions of Nazi war criminals at Nuremburg. While no criminal charges were brought, Belcher decided he had no choice but to resign his Parliamentary seat, which he did in February 1949. He returned to the railways as a ticket clerk, and eventually retired through ill health in 1963, dying a year later at the age of 59.

Henry (Harry) Hynd (1900–85), MP for Hackney Central, 1945–50; Accrington, 1950–66. Brother of John Hynd MP. Railway clerk with LMS, 1915–20; Railway Clerks Association official, 1920–45; Member Hornsey Borough Council, 1939–52. Commander of Belgian Order of the Crown and Officer of Luxembourg Order of the Oak Crown.

George Rogers (1906–83), MP for North Kensington 1945–70. Councillor on Wembley Borough Council, 1937–41, and worked as a railway clerk, then an industrial consultant with London Transport. He was a member of the TSSA. During the Second World War, he was a corporal in the Royal Signals.

He was Secretary of the Parliamentary Painting Group, 1950–1970, and Parliamentary Private Secretary to George Strauss, Minister of Supply from 1947 to 1949, and to Kenneth Younger, Minister of State for Foreign Affairs in 1950. He was a delegate to the United Nations Assembly in 1950, and to the Council of Europe and Western European Union from 1961 to 1963.

He served as an opposition whip, 1954–1964, and as Member of the Commons Chairmen's Panel, 1952–54 and 1966. He was a Lord Commissioner of the Treasury and government whip, October 1964–January 1966. Rogers was appointed a CBE in 1965.

James Haworth (1896–1976), MP for Liverpool Walton, 1945–50. He was a railwayman living in Oswaldtwistle, Lancashire, and national treasurer of the Railway Clerks Association. Refused recognition as a conscientious objector in the First World War, he was in Preston prison and then went to Princetown Work Centre in Dartmoor Prison. He lost Liverpool Walton in 1950, and was defeated standing for Chelmsford in the 1951 general election, and for Bolton West in the 1955 general election.

George Samuel Lindgren, Baron Lindgren, JP, DL (1900–71) was MP for Wellingborough, 1945–59. LNER Railway clerk, member National Executive Committee of Railway Clerks' Association, 1933–46; Treasurer, Transport Salaried Staffs Association, 1956–61.

Junior minister in the Labour government, serving as Parliamentary Secretary to the Minister of National Insurance from 1945–46, to the Minister of Civil Aviation from 1946–1950, and to the Minister of Town and Country Planning from 1950–1951.

On losing his seat in 1959 general election he returned to his former occupation as a railway clerk, working in the Eastern Region Chief Civil Engineer's Office at King's Cross station.

He was made a life peer on 9 February 1961 as Lord Lindgren, and in Harold Wilson's Labour government he served from 1964 to 1966 as Parliamentary Secretary at the ministries of transport and power.

ASLEF MPs

The Associated Society of Locomotive Engineers and Firemen had no MPs in the Commons between 1931 and 1945, when two were elected.

Walter Monslow, Baron Monslow (1895–1966) won back Barrow in 1945 (having fought Newcastle upon Tyne Central unsuccessfully in 1935) and held it until his retirement in 1966. He served as Parliamentary Private Secretary at the Ministry of Civil Aviation, 1949–50, and the Ministry of Food, 1950–51. He was Organising Secretary of ASLEF. He was made a life peer in June 1966, but died four months later.

Percy Collick (1897–1984) was MP for Birkenhead West, 1945–50, and then for Birkenhead until 1964.

Originally a fireman with the Southern Railway, he was a member of the ASLEF, serving as organising secretary from 1934 to 1940 and assistant general secretary from 1940 to his retirement in 1957.

In Clement Attlee's post-war Labour government, he served as Parliamentary Secretary to the Ministry of Agriculture and Fisheries from 1945 to 1947.

Union Representation, 1946–92

1950 general election

The 1950 general election saw a significant swing to the Conservatives and Labour suffered a net loss of sixty-nine seats. A number of those were railway union MPs who had been elected in 1945. New rail MPs were:

Alex Hargreaves (1899–1978) was elected as MP for Carlisle. He held the seat in 1951, but was defeated in 1955 and failed to regain the seat in 1959.

He had worked as a railway clerk and was a member of the Railway Clerks' Association. Elected to Liverpool City Council in 1928, he served until 1950. In 1945, he was the President of Liverpool Trades Council and Labour Party. In 1949, he was appointed to the Mersey Docks and Harbour Board as a nominee of the Ministry of Transport.

---

[86] Hartley William Shawcross, Baron Shawcross, GBE, PC, QC (1902–2003), known from 1945 to 1959 as Sir Hartley Shawcross, was an English barrister and Labour politician who served as the lead British prosecutor at the Nuremberg War Crimes tribunal. He was also Britain's principal delegate to the United Nations immediately after the Second World War and Attorney General for England and Wales. Labour MP for St Helens, 1945–58. He is remembered as allegedly saying in the House of Commons in 1946, when debating the repeal of laws against trade unions, 'We are the masters now.' He was one of the first life peers to be appointed to the House of Lords, and sat as a cross-bencher. He never joined another political party and the insulting description of him as 'Sir Shortly Floorcross' was unjustified and unfair.

Archibald Clark Manuel (1901–1976) was elected as MP for Central Ayrshire. Manuel only had an elementary school education, but later in life went to classes through the National Council of Labour. He worked on the railways as an engine driver, and was a member of ASLEF.

Originally from Morvern, in Argyll, he lived in Ardrossan, where he joined the Labour Party in 1927. He became a member of the Town Council, and was later elected to Ayrshire County Council. He was appointed to the Western Regional Hospital Board and to the Ayrshire Executive Council of the National Health Service.

He was re-elected in 1951 but lost the seat in 1955. Persisting despite this rejection, he was re-elected in 1959 and eventually retired in 1970.

A great friend of the Secretary of State for Scotland Willie Ross, Manuel was (like Ross) a ferocious opponent of the Scottish National Party. In an adjournment debate in the Commons in November 1969, Manuel joined in the general attack on the sole SNP MP Winnie Ewing, calling her 'a Tory in disguise' and 'a parasite'.

1951 and 1955 general elections

There were no fresh rail union MPs elected in 1951, and just one (from the NUR) in 1955. He was:

Charles Howell OBE (1905–74), MP for Birmingham Perry Barr, 1955–64, which he lost against the national pro-Labour trend. He was an Opposition whip, 1959–64. He had been a railway guard on the LMS in Derby, secretary of the NUR Derby No. 1 branch, member of LM Region Sectional Council No. 3 (Traffic Grades), 1943–55; Member of the National Executive Committee, NUR, 1951–53; Voluntary Tutor, National Council of Labour Colleges; Member of Derby County Borough Council, 1943–53; Secretary of Derby Trades Council, 1945–56, and from 1966. Chairman of Derby Borough Labour Party, 1950–51.

His final job back on the railways was as clerical officer, National Carriers Ltd (formerly British Railways).

1958 by-election

Leslie Spriggs (1910–90) was MP for St Helens from 1958 (the by-election was caused by the resignation of Sir Hartley Shawcross) until 1983. After service in the Merchant Navy, he joined the railways as a goods guard. He was President, North West (NUR) District Council, Political Section, 1954; Vice-President, Industrial Section, 1955. Formerly Lecturer, National Council of Labour Colleges on Industrial Law, Economics, Foreign Affairs, Local Government, Trade Union History. He was a member of numerous parliamentary groups: Employment, Environment, Health, Industry, Transport, and Trade, including aviation, shipping, textiles, clothing and footwear.

1959 general election

Although Labour were heavily defeated in the 1959 election, most of the rail union-sponsored MPs held on to their seats.

The three **ASLEF** MPs were all re-elected – **Walter Monslow** (Barrow-in-Furness), **Percy Collick** (Birkenhead) and **Archie Manuel** (Central Ayrshire).

TSSA members had mixed fortunes. Re-elected were **Harry Hynd** (Accrington), **George Rogers** (Kensington North), **Ray Gunter** (for Southwark, having moved from Doncaster) and **Tom Steele** (West Dunbartonshire). George Lindgren lost his Wellingborough seat, and Alex Hargreaves again failed to win Carlisle, which he last represented in 1955.

Elected for the first time was:

Charles Mapp (1903–78), MP for Oldham East, 1959–1970. This was the only seat in England that was lost by the Conservatives to Labour: this was attributed to the decline in the local textile industry. Mapp had fought it unsuccessfully in 1955. He was a railway goods agent and was elected to Sale Borough Council in 1932 (serving until 1935) and 1945–46. He retired at the 1970 general election.

There were no fresh **NUR** MPs elected in 1959. **John Hynd** (Sheffield Attercliffe), **Ernest Popplewell** (Newcastle upon Tyne West), **Charles Howell** (Birmingham Perry Barr), **William Proctor** (Eccles), and **Leslie Spriggs** (St Helens) were all re-elected. Two lost their seats by tiny majorities – **Joe Champion** by twelve in South East Derbyshire, and **Dai Jones** by 182 in The Hartlepools.

1962 by-election

The ranks of TSSA MPs were increased by a by-election victor in 1962, who was to play a significant but ultimately unsuccessful national political role.

Tom Bradley (1926–2002), MP for Leicester North East 1962–74, then Leicester East 1974–83. Kettering-born, Bradley was educated at Kettering Central School and worked in the mines during the Second World War. He joined the London Midland and Scottish Railway and had clerical jobs in the goods depots at Kettering and Oundle. He joined the TSSA in 1942, and served as its Treasurer 1961–64, President, 1964–77, and Acting General Secretary in 1976–77.

Bradley contested Rutland and Stamford in 1950, 1951 and 1955, and Preston South in 1959. He was a member of the Labour Party's national executive committee, 1965–82 (also its chairman in 1976). Bradley chaired the party's transport sub-committee, some of whose deliberations (and Bradley's role in them) are described in Chapter XV of *Holding the Line*. His political career was on the right of the Labour Party and he served as Parliamentary Private Secretary to Roy Jenkins, 1964–70, to whom he was devoted, even adopting some of Jenkins's mannerisms of speech. Bradley was passionately pro-EEC, left Labour to join the SDP in 1981 but subsequently came third in his Leicester East constituency at the 1983 election. Disappointed by politics, Bradley threw himself into non-league football, becoming chairman of Kettering Town FC, but failing in his ambition to see them elected to the Football League.

1964 General Election

There were a number of new rail union MPs elected in the 1964 election, which was narrowly won by Labour under the leadership of Harold Wilson.

The following came into the House from the **NUR**:

Gordon Bagier (1924–2012), MP for Sunderland South, 1964–87. He was a signals inspector on British Railways. He served in the Royal Marines from 1941 to 1945, as a gunner aboard the light cruiser HMS *Belfast*, and later played a part in her preservation. Councillor on Keighley Borough Council, 1956–60, and Sowerby Bridge Urban Council from 1962. President of the Yorkshire District Council of the NUR. Later, chairman of the NUR group of Labour MPs.

Richard Buchanan (1912–2003), MP for Glasgow Springburn ,1964–79. He worked as an engineer and toolfitter and was a councillor on the Glasgow Corporation from 1949. He joined the NUR in 1928, and in later years was secretary of its political committee.

Ronald Lewis (1909–90), MP for Carlisle, 1964–87. Left school at 14 and worked in coal mines (Somerset and Derbyshire, 1930–36); then railways (LNER Sheds, Langwith Junction); left that employment on being elected to Parliament. Member Derbyshire County Council, 1949–74. Vice-Chairman House of Commons Trades Union Group, 1979–82. Methodist local preacher.

NUR-sponsored **Leslie Spriggs** (St Helens) and **John Hynd** (Sheffield Attercliffe) were both re-elected in 1964.

The only **ASLEF** MP elected in 1964 was **Archie Manuel** (Central Ayrshire).

TSSA had **Tom Bradley** (Leicester North East), **Ray Gunter** (Southwark), **Harry Hynd** (Accrington), **Charles Mapp** (Oldham East), **George Rogers** (North Kensington), and **Tom Steele** (Dunbartonshire West) all re-elected.

They were joined by **Harry Howarth** (1916–69), who won back Wellingborough, which he retained in 1966. He worked on the railways as a clerk, and was a member of the TSSA. He joined the Royal Air Force on the outbreak of the Second World War; after demobilisation he returned to his old job.

He served on the National Executive Committee of his union from 1954 to 1960, and was elected to Wembley Borough Council from 1953 to 1956 and 1957 to 1960.

1966 general election

Again **Archie Manuel** (Central Ayrshire) was the one **ASLEF**-sponsored candidate re-elected.

The **NUR** had five of their MPs re-elected: **Gordon Bagier** (Sunderland South), **John Hynd** (Sheffield Attercliffe), **Leslie Spriggs** (St Helens), **Richard Buchanan** (Glasgow Springburn), and **Ronald Lewis** (Carlisle).

Ernest Popplewell (Newcastle upon Tyne West) retired and went to the House of Lords. There was one new NUR-sponsored MP:

Tom McMillan (1919–80) was MP for Glasgow Central from 1966 until 1980, when he died in a hospital in London due to injuries sustained falling from a bus two weeks previously. McMillan was a wood machinist at Cowlairs railway workshops. He was a councillor on Glasgow City Council from 1962.

The **TSSA** had six of their MPs re-elected in 1966 – **Tom Bradley** (Leicester North East), **Ray Gunter** (Southwark), **Charles Mapp** (Oldham East), **George Rogers** (North Kensington), **Tom Steele** (Dunbartonshire West) and **Harry Howarth (**Wellingborough**). Harry Hynd** (Accrington) retired at the election.

1970 general election

Representation of the **TSSA** changed at the 1970 election. George Rogers and Tom Steele retired, **Ray Gunter** (Southwark) and **Tom Bradley** (Leicester North East) were re-elected, and were joined by two new colleagues. They were:

Walter Johnson (1917–2003) succeeded Philip Noel-Baker as MP for Derby South. He was an assistant government whip from 1974 to 1975. He stood down as an MP at the 1983 election. Chairman of the PLP Aviation Committee, 1979–83. Particularly interested in welfare services, transport, labour relations and aviation matters. He was treasurer of the TSSA, 1965–1977, and president, 1977–81. Worked for London Transport as principal executive assistant (formerly a senior executive, staff training). Governor, Ruskin College, Oxford, 1966–85.

Stan Cohen (1927–2004), MP for Leeds South East 1970–83. Served in the Royal Navy, 1947–49. Employed in clothing industry, 1943–47 and 1949–51; Clerical Officer with British Railways, 1951–70. Member Leeds City Council, 1952–71; elected Alderman, 1968. PPS to Minister of State, Department for Education and Science, 1976–79.

ASLEF's one MP, Archie Manuel, retired at the 1970 election, and there have been no members of the Association who were working railwaymen serving in the House of Commons since then.

NUR representation continued to consist of **Gordon Bagier** (Sunderland South), **Leslie Spriggs** (St Helens), **Richard Buchanan** (Glasgow Springburn), **Ronald Lewis** (Carlisle), and **Tom McMillan** (Glasgow Central). **John Hynd** retired at the 1970 election.

February and October 1974 general elections

The same five NUR MPs were elected in both elections held in 1974: **Gordon Bagier** (Sunderland South), **Leslie Spriggs** (St Helens), **Richard Buchanan** (Glasgow Springburn), **Ronald Lewis** (Carlisle), and **Tom McMillan** (Glasgow Central).

They were joined by **Peter Snape,** (later **Lord Snape)** (b 1942), who was elected for West Bromwich East in the February election and served as its MP until 2001. He was ennobled in that year and is an active member of the House of Lords, a powerful and effective advocate for the railway. He was a signalman at Stockport, 1957–61; regular soldier, 1961–67; goods guard, 1967–70; clerical officer BR, 1970–74. Non-executive. Director, West Midlands Travel, 1992–97; Chairman, Travel West Midlands, 1997–2000. Government whip, 1975–79; opposition spokesman for Defence, 1979–82, for Home Affairs, 1982–83, for

Ray Gunter in 1972. The Association's general secretary, Richard Rosser,[87] was narrowly defeated in the new constituency of Croydon Central.

1976 by-election

The by-election in Newcastle Central in 1976 brought the last NUR-sponsored Labour candidate who had worked in the railway industry to Parliament.

Harry Cowans (1932–85) had been a Signals and Telecommunications technician officer with British Rail. Branch Secretary with the NUR, he was a member of the Executive Committee of the Labour Party Northern Region. He was a member of Gateshead Metropolitan Council (chairman of its Housing Committee), and of Tyne and Wear Metropolitan County Council. In the Commons he was a member of the Transport Select Committee from 1984 until his untimely death at the age of 53. He was also Opposition whip for the Northern Region and transport, and secretary of the Northern Group Labour MPs. He represented Newcastle Central in November 1976–83, and after boundary changes, Tyne Bridge, 1983–85.

Expanding the Rail Unions' Group

By the early 1970s it became evident that following the decline in the number of NUR branches and members as a consequence of the Beeching cuts and other contractions in the railway workforce, the union was facing a serious decline in the number of Labour MPs it sponsored. Two further factors were, first, that increasing numbers of NUR members, disillusioned by the 1964 Labour government's failure to honour its election manifesto commitment to halt the Beeching closures,[88] were less inclined to pay the political levy that provided the union with the funds it needed for political campaigning; and, secondly, fewer NUR branches were affiliated to constituency Labour parties. The problem was exacerbated by the existence of a union rule that its MPs had to retire at the age of 65 (which had required **John Hynd** to stand down as MP for Sheffield Attercliffe in 1970).

Under the leadership of Assistant General Secretary, Sidney Weighell, the NUR tackled all these issues. The Derby No. 3 branch submitted a resolution for consideration by the union's executive that called for an examination of 'every aspect of the union's political activities, with a view to increasing our representation in the House of Commons. Such examination to take into account the way we select our candidates and the possibility of sponsoring selected nominees other than

Peter Snape MP was a former signalman and Goods Guard who was seconded by BR when he was elected at Labour MP for West Bromwich East from 1974 to 2001. Now in the House of Lords, where he frequently speaks with authority on railway matters. *UK Parliament*

Transport, 1983–92. Member: Council of Europe and WEU, May–November 1975; North Atlantic Assembly, 1980–83. Consultant: National Express Group, 2001–07; First Group plc, 2007–09. Chairman., Bus Appeals Body, 2009–13; National Patron, Community Transport, 2008–13. Fellow, Institute of Travel and Tourism, 2008–. Member, Bredbury and Romiley UDC, 1971–74 (Chairman, Finance Committee). Chairman, Stockport County AFC, 2011–13 (Director, 2010–13). FCILT 2020. Honorary Freeman, Borough of Sandwell, 2010. He was also secretary of the NUR group of Labour MPs.

Snape features prominently in our Chapter XIV on Railway Conversion in *Holding the Line*. His opposition to the madcap ideas of Thatcher's guru, Alf Sherman, is fully described.

TSSA's representation after the two 1974 elections was reduced to three: **Tom Bradley** (Leicester East), **Walter Johnson** (Derby South), and **Stan Cohen** (Leeds South East), following the resignation from Parliament of

---

[87] Richard Rosser, Lord Rosser (b 1944) is one of Labour's most effective front-bench spokespeople, speaking on transport and home affairs, in the House of Lords, which he joined in 2004 following his retirement as general secretary of TSSA. Appointed in 1989. he was the Association's second-longest serving holder of that post (only Alexander Walkden served longer). He had joined as a full-time staff member in 1966, after four years' working at London Transport. As a union leader he served on the General Council of the TUC, and the National Executive Committee of the Labour Party, culminating in a year as its chairman in 1997–98.

[88] Labour's 1964 election manifesto said: 'Labour will draw up a national plan for transport covering the national networks of road, rail and canal communications, properly co-ordinated with air, coastal shipping and port services. The new regional authorities will be asked to draw up transport plans for their own areas. While these are being prepared, major rail closures will be halted.'

those on List 'B'[89] of the Labour Party. Further to consider the sponsorship of existing MPs who represent 'railway' constituencies ie York, Crewe, Swindon, Derby etc.'

These proposals were endorsed by the NUR's executive and approved at the AGM held in St Helier, Jersey in July 1975,[90] which at the same time abolished the 'retire at 65' rule.

The first MPs to receive the new form of NUR sponsorship were:

Robin Cook (1946–2005), MP for Edinburgh Central February, 1974–83; Livingston, 1983 until his death. Served in the 1997 Labour government as Foreign Secretary in 1997–2001, when he was moved against his will to become Leader of the House of Commons until he resigned in March 2003 over the decision to invade Iraq, saying, 'I can't accept collective responsibility for the decision to commit Britain now to military action in Iraq without international agreement or domestic support.' A brilliant orator and debater, Cook's resignation speech in the House of Commons was seen as one of the most devastating in recent times. He died of a heart attack while on a walking holiday in Scotland.

Tam Dalyell (1932–2017) MP for West Lothian, 1962–83; Linlithgow, 1983–2005. As the member of the Commons with the longest unbroken service, he was 'Father of the House' in 2001–05. A serial rebel who voted against his own government 100 times in 1978–79, Dalyell was one of the most colourful politicians of his time. Educated at Eton, he was chairman of the Cambridge University Conservative Association and switched to Labour in 1956 in protest over the Suez invasion – one of many British military interventions that he opposed during his political lifetime, including the Falklands War, for which he acquired national fame for his harrying of Prime Minister Margaret Thatcher over the sinking of the *Belgrano*. A fervent opponent of Scottish devolution, he is remembered for inventing the 'West Lothian Question'.

Although he never used the title, he was 'Sir Thomas Dalyell' as the holder of a baronetcy dating back to 1685 that he inherited from his mother, along with his surname and a stately home, the House of the Binns. The NUR's decision to adopt Dalyell as a sponsored MP raised many eyebrows – he was the first and likely to remain the only old Etonian to achieve that status.

Michael O'Halloran (1933–99), MP for Islington North, 1969–83 (Labour, 1969–81; SDP 1981–2; Independent Labour, 1983). Born in Ireland, he was self-educated, worked on the railway, 1948–63, and as a building works manager, 1963–69, and after he left the Commons.

Phillip Whitehead (1937–2005), MP for Derby North, 1970–83; spokesman on higher education, 1980–83; and on the arts, 1982–83. He was a member of the European Parliament from 1994 to his death, first serving as MEP for Staffordshire East and Derby, and later as one of the members for the East Midlands. Chair of the Parliamentary committee on the Internal Market and Consumer Protection. He was chair of the European Parliamentary Labour Party. He was a much-respected and popular writer and television producer, winning numerous awards.

1979 general election

After the 1979 election additional MPs were sponsored by the NUR. They were:

Donald Anderson, Lord Anderson of Swansea (b 1939), MP for Monmouth, 1966–70; Swansea East, October 1974–2005, when he was appointed to the House of Lords. Member of HM Foreign Service, 1960–64: Foreign Office, 1960–63; 3rd Secretary, British Embassy, Budapest, 1963–64. Barrister; called to Bar, Inner Temple, 1969. Front-bench spokesman on foreign affairs, 1983–92, on defence, 1993–94; Shadow Solicitor General, 1994–95. Member: Select Committee on Welsh Affairs, 1980–83 (Chairman, 1981–83); Select Committee on Home Affairs, 1992–93; Speaker's Panel of Chairmen, 1995–99; Chairman, Foreign Affairs Committee, 1997–2005. Chairman: PLP Environment Group, 1974–79; Welsh Labour Group, 1977–78. Commander's Cross, Order of Merit (Federal Republic of Germany), 1986; Foreign Minister's Medal (Republic of Slovakia), 2004; Chevalier, Légion d'Honneur (France), 2005; Officer's Cross, Order of Merit (Hungary), 2007.

Gwyneth Dunwoody (1930–2008), MP for Exeter, 1966–70; Crewe, February 1974–1983, Crewe and Nantwich from 1983 until her death. She served as a junior minister at the Board of Trade 1967–70, and was an appointed member of the European Parliament, 1975–79; spokesman on foreign affairs, 1980; on health, 1980–83, on transport, 1984–85.

Dunwoody was the daughter of Labour's long-serving general secretary, Morgan Phillips, and Nora – later Baroness – Phillips. She is best remembered as the chair of the Transport Select Committee, for her astute and questioning style; she was appointed to that position in 1997 and served until her death eleven years later. In her earlier career she was a journalist and acted in repertory.

Frank Dobson (1940–2019), MP Holborn and St Pancras South, 1979–83; Holborn and St Pancras, 1983–2015. Held administrative jobs with Central Electricity Generating Board, 1962–70, and Electricity Council, 1970–75; Assistant Secretary, Commission for Local Administration (local Ombudsman's office), 1975–79. Member, Camden Borough Council, 1971–76 (Leader of Council, 1973–75). Front-bench spokesman on Education, 1981–83, on health, 1983–87; Shadow Leader of the Commons and Party Campaign Co-ordinator,

---

[89] List 'B' consisted of people nominated by any constituency party or affiliated organisation. The NUR's political sub-committee recommended that the EC should select candidates from List 'B' to the Labour Party's List 'A' whom trade unions were willing to sponsor.

[90] Among those placed on the 'A' list of sponsored candidates was your co-author, Richard Faulkner, who was subsequently selected to contest Huddersfield West (sadly unsuccessfully) at the 1979 general election.

1987–89; opposition front-bench spokesman on energy, 1989–92; on employment, 1992–93; on transport, 1993–94; on London, 1993–97, and on the environment, 1994–97; Secretary of State for Health, 1997–99. He resigned as a minister in order to contest the London mayoral election. He defeated Ken Livingstone for the Labour nomination, but was defeated by him when Livingstone stood as an independent, and disappointingly came third.

John Marek (b 1940), MP for Wrexham, 1983–2001, and also represented Wrexham in the National Assembly for Wales, 1999–2007. He sat as Labour, 1999–2003, and was Independent, 2003–07. He was opposition frontbench spokesman: on health, 1985–87; on treasury and economic affairs, and on the Civil Service, 1987–92. He was Deputy Presiding Officer of the Welsh Assembly, 2000–07. He was deselected as the Labour candidate for the Assembly election in 2003, and stood as the John Marek Independent Party, defeating the Labour candidate. He then founded and led Forward Wales from 2003 until 2010, when the party was disbanded and he joined the Conservatives. Prior to entering Parliament he was an academic, lecturing in Applied Mathematics at the University College of Wales, Aberystwyth, 1966–83. Born in London and of Czech descent, Marek was the only Czech-speaking MP in the House of Commons.

Donald Dewar (1937–2000), MP for South Aberdeen, 1966–70, and for Glasgow, Garscadden, April 1978–97, and then Glasgow Anniesland from 1997 until his death. He also represented Anniesland in the Scottish Parliament from 1999. He was the inaugural First Minister of Scotland and leader of the Scottish Labour Party, 1999–2000. He was Secretary of State for Scotland in the first Blair government from 1997, and is regarded as the 'father of the Scottish nation'. He was a solicitor by profession and had studied law at Glasgow university, where he met several future politicians at the university Dialectic Society, including John Smith (future leader of the Labour Party), Menzies Campbell (future leader of the Liberal Democrats) and Lord Irvine of Lairg (Lord Chancellor in Tony Blair's Labour government). In May 2002, then Prime Minister Tony Blair unveiled a statue of Dewar at the top of Glasgow's Buchanan Street in Glasgow city centre. In keeping with his famous unkempt appearance, it showed Dewar wearing a slightly crushed jacket. On the base of the statue were inscribed the opening words of the Scotland Act: 'There Shall Be A Scottish Parliament', a phrase to which Dewar himself famously said, 'I like that!'

ASLEF and TSSA-sponsored MPs

Following the lead of the NUR in extending its list of sponsored MPs to those who were not members of the union but were considered useful and supportive of its policies, ASLEF and the TSSA followed suit, but in a more modest way.

ASLEF sponsored:

Les Huckfield (b 1942). Elected for Nuneaton at the age of 24 in a by-election caused by the resignation of Frank Cousins in March 1967, he remained an MP until 1983. He was an MEP for Merseyside East, 1984–89. Junior minister, Department of Industry, 1976–79. He was a former lecturer in Economics at the City of Birmingham College of Commerce, 1963–67. Member of the National Executive Committee of the Labour Party, 1978–82; chairman of the party's Transport Group, 1974–76.

Huckfield was also sponsored by the Transport & General Workers Union. In April 1975 he chaired a transport policy study group for the *Socialist Commentary* magazine. In the chapter on railway policy, the report questioned whether subsidies for the passenger railway were in the community's interest, 'since resources used to support an unprofitable railway system must inevitably be diverted from other, perhaps more economically and socially worthwhile, uses within the economy'.

Glenda Jackson (b 1936), MP Hampstead and Highgate, 1992–2010; Hampstead and Kilburn, 2010–15. Junior minister at the Department for Environment Transport and the Regions (DETR), 1997–99. Jackson is one of the UK's most stellar actors, with a career that started in 1957.

TSSA extended their sponsorship to:

John Home Robertson (b 1948) MP Berwick and East Lothian, October 1978–83; East Lothian, 1983–2001; and Member of the Scottish Parliament for East Lothian, 1999–2007. Opposition Scottish whip, 1983–84; opposition spokesman on agriculture, 1984–87, 1988–90, on Scotland, 1987–88. Member, Select Committee on Scottish affairs, 1980–83; Select Committee on Defence, 1990–97; British–Irish Parliamentary Body, 1993–99. Chairman, Scottish Group of Labour MPs, 1983. Deputy Minister for Rural Affairs, Scottish Executive, 1999–2000. He is a farmer who is related to the Earls of Home.

Alan Williams (1930–2014), MP Swansea West, 1964–2010. Father of the House, 2005–10. Junior minister in two departments, 1967–70, and held a succession of front-bench posts during Labour's years of opposition, 1979–97, including shadow secretary of state for Wales, 1987–88. Member: Public Accounts Committee, 1966–67, 1990–2010 (Senior Member 1997–2010); Standards and Privileges Committee, 1994–95, 1997–2003; Chairman: Public Accounts Commission, 1997–2010; Liaison Committee, 2001–10; Secretary British American Parliamentary Group, 2001–08; Chairman, Welsh PLP, 1966–67; Delegate, Council of Europe and Western European Union 1966–67.

NUR/NUS Merger

One consequence of the merger in 1990 of the National Union of Railwaymen and the National Union of Seamen to form the National Union of Rail Maritime and Transport Workers was that John Prescott, the NUS's most prominent sponsored MP, became RMT sponsored.

John – later Lord – Prescott (b 1938), Deputy Prime Minister, 1997–2007 and First Secretary of State from 2001 to 2007. Labour MP for Kingston upon Hull East, 1970–2010. Appointed to the Lords 2010. Born in Prestatyn, North Wales, the son of a railway signaller, he worked as a steward on passenger liners, and was active in the National Union of Seamen. Educated at Ruskin College, Oxford, and the University of Hull. Nominated member of the European Parliament, 1975–79, and Leader of the Labour group while a member of the House of Commons. Elected Deputy Leader of the Labour Party following the death of John Smith in 1994, serving until 2007. On Labour's election to government in 1997, Prescott became Secretary of State for Environment, Transport and the Regions, and among his achievements was the establishment of the Strategic Rail Authority under the chairmanship of Sir Alastair Morton[91] in 1999, and the overruling of a government planning inspector's recommendation to block the reconstruction of the 25-mile Welsh Highland Railway, which runs from Porthmadog to Caernarfon. See Chapter 8 for an appraisal of the Labour government's railways policy.

1987 General Election

Sir Alan Meale (b 1949) was Labour MP for Mansfield, 1987–2017. Assistant to General Secretary ASLEF, 1980–83; Political Adviser to Rt Hon. Barbara Castle, MP, 1977–79, to Rt Hon. Tony Benn, MP, 1980–86; Parliamentary and Political Adviser to Michael Meacher, MP, 1983–87; Secretary, Socialist Campaign Group of Labour MPs, 1981–87. He supported BR's 1989 private Bill authorising reopening the Robin Hood line, which served his constituency. An Opposition whip, 1992–94; PPS to John Prescott, 1994–98. Junior minister Department of the Environment Transport and the Regions, 1998–99. Knighted 2011.

1992 General Election

Keith Hill (b 1943) was MP for Streatham, 1992–2010. In government he was an assistant government whip, 1998–99; junior minister at the Department for the Environment Transport and the Regions, 1999–2001; government deputy chief whip, 2001–03; Minister of State (Minister for Housing and Planning), Office of the Deputy Prime Minister, 2003–05; PPS to Prime Minister, 2005–07.

Hill's most important role as far as the subject matter of this book is concerned is that from 1976 until 1992 he was the political research officer of the NUR (later National Union of Rail, Maritime and Transport Workers). A request had been made to the NUR's political sub-committee by Peter Snape in June 1976 for 'specialised assistance to enable the enlarged group to work as a more effective and cohesive force'.

As Philip Bagwell writes: 'Among Keith Hill's many activities were the drafting of House of Commons questions to the Secretary of State for Transport and to junior ministers; the provision of research backing for MPs' speeches; the briefing of the General Secretary on political issues; the preparation of proposed amendments to transport Bills and MPs' briefing on them; attendance at standing committees of the House to provide on-the-spot assistance to members of the group; the organisation of meetings with members of the BRB and with the board members of other public transport bodies; preparation of newspaper articles and letters and the organisation of a political course at Frant Place, Tunbridge Wells (the NUR education centre) for potential Parliamentary candidates.'[92]

His background had been in academe and political research, having been a research assistant in politics at the University of Leicester 1966–68; Belgian government Scholar, Brussels, 1968–69; lecturer in politics, University of Strathclyde, 1969–73; research officer, Labour Party International Department, 1974–76. Since leaving Parliament he has been chairman of the regulatory panel for the association of Residential Managing Agents, 2013–16, and of the London Borough of Hammersmith and Fulham Residents' Commission on Council Housing, 2015–16.

Hill was offered a knighthood in the 2010 resignation honours list, but declined it, even though the Parliamentary website had announced it three weeks previously.[93]

Ending of Union Sponsorship

Sponsorship of Labour MPs ceased in 1996 following publication of the first Nolan Report on standards in public life in 1995.

Trade unions still, however, affiliate to the Labour Party and contribute significantly to it from their political fund. Still affiliated in 2022 are the TSSA and ASLEF; the RMT, however, broke their link with the party in 2004, following their decision to support the Scottish Socialist Party, which stood candidates against Labour in Scotland.

At the time, Ian McCartney MP, then chair of the Labour Party, said of the RMT's general secretary Bob Crow: 'He has taken the RMT out of Labour's annual conference and Labour's National Policy Forum which will shape Labour's next manifesto and he has taken his union outside the NEC, which gives the RMT a seat at the table with the prime minister and the deputy prime minister.

'And for what? To have the privilege of sitting around the table with a small Trotskyite splinter group.'

He could have added that the RMT's predecessors had played a crucial role in the formation of the Labour Party in 1899 – something that Sid Weighell referred to repeatedly in his many attempts to keep Labour Party

---

[91] Sir Alastair Morton (1938–2004), Johannesburg-born industrialist who came to Britain to study law at Worcester College, Oxford. He was managing director of the British National Oil Corporation, 1976–80; chief executive of Guinness Peat Group, 1982–87, and chairman in 1987; co-chairman of Eurotunnel, 1987–96; chairman of the Strategic Rail Authority, 1999–2001. Knighted in 1992.

[92] *The Railwaymen*, vol. 2, pp.384–5.

[93] 'Former Streatham MP turns down knighthood', *Streatham Guardian*, 18 June 2010.

policy firmly on a pro-railways track, including the occasion when he was reported as saying in 1975 that the NUR would instruct its sponsored MPs to withdraw their support from the Labour government if it went ahead with large cuts in the network.[94]

Looking back on over 120 years of railway union MPs in Parliament, the notable feature is the breadth of experience offered compared to today's MPs, so many of whom have little experience of life outside the Westminster bubble. From school to a degree in politics and economics, followed by a stint as a political researcher and then a Parliamentary candidate is a path many have taken. But for almost the whole of the twentieth century, membership of the House of Commons for railwaymen came after experience as a fireman, signalman or railway clerk. These men (and they were all men) mixed this experience with active unionism and often local government service, so they understood how to manage meetings, rally support and run campaigns. And they brought a rich variety of experience to the deliberations of the House of Commons, and in a number of cases, to the House of Lords, too.

Special Advisers

In the latter days of BR, special advisers played an increasingly important role in the relationships between the railway and the government. Special Advisers (with the unfortunate acronym of SPADs) were appointed as personal assistants to ministers to advise them on policy and media issues and generally to marshal support for their minister and the government. Most SPADs were and are young graduates with little experience of the world outside Westminster and many go on to become MPs themselves.

Examples of those who have been involved with railway issues are:

Elizabeth Buchanan, special adviser to Cecil Parkinson and Paul Channon, subsequently becoming private secretary to the Prince of Wales from 2002 to 2005. She was Margaret Thatcher's press secretary and went on to work for lobbyists Lowe Bell. Her father, Bill Buchanan, was adviser on disability to the BR Board, appointed by Sir Peter Parker.

Eleanor Laing was adviser to John MacGregor[95] during the run-up to privatisation. She had advised him as Education Secretary, as Leader of the House, and Transport (1992–94). Dame Eleanor Laing (b 1958) has been Conservative MP for Epping Forest since 1997, and since 2020 First Deputy Speaker and Chairman of Ways and Means – the first woman to hold that post. She played an influential role in the railway privatisation debate and was critical of the British Railways Board's alleged lack of co-operation during the process. Your co-author, Chris Austin, recalls how he and his Director, Jerry Evans, were 'ticked off' by her for apparently supporting the Opposition in seeking to promote BR's achievements during privatisation.

Rosie Winterton was head of John Prescott's private office, 1994–97, leaving to become Labour MP for Doncaster Central. She held a series of ministerial roles during the Labour government, including Minister of State for Transport, 2007–08, and Opposition chief whip, 2010–16. Before going to work for John Prescott she was managing director of Connect Public Affairs for four years. Dame Rosalie Winterton (b 1958) has been Labour MP for Doncaster Central since 1997. Since 2020 she has been Deputy Speaker and Deputy Chairman of Ways and Means.

Joe Irvin was adviser to John Prescott when he became Deputy Prime Minister. He went on to advise Gordon Brown[96] during his term as Prime Minister, and then became CEO of the campaigning group for pedestrians, Living Streets. He was involved in writing the 1998 white paper on transport, which we cover in Chapter 8.

Dan Corry was adviser to Stephen Byers during the period that Railtrack was placed in railway administration and while its replacement, Network Rail, was created. Subsequently he became head of the No. 10 Policy Unit under Gordon Brown and is now Chief Executive of New Philanthropy Capital, a charity sector think tank.

More controversially, **Ian Heggie** was employed as special adviser for two days a week in the Department of Transport by Norman Fowler from 1979 to 1981, but left hurriedly after *New Scientist* magazine in its issue dated 29 January 1981 published a letter from Heggie, written on the Transport Minister's writing paper on 18 March 1980, to Dr Phil Goodwin, acting director of Oxford University's Transport Studies Unit (TSU), implying that if the university did not employ him as a reader it would not get valuable research contracts that were in his gift. Heggie said that: 'The sensible solution would be for you [Goodwin] perhaps to become nominal Director and for me to become reader.' But if the university did not offer

---

[94] See *Holding the Line*, Chapter VIII.

[95] John MacGregor (b 1937), Conservative MP for South Norfolk, 1974–2001, when he became Lord MacGregor of Pulham Market. He held a series of senior appointments in the Thatcher and Major governments including Chief Secretary to HM Treasury, 1985–87; Minister of Agriculture, Fisheries and Food, 1987–89; Secretary of State for Education and Science, 1989–90; Lord President of the Council and Leader of the House of Commons, 1990–92; then finally Secretary of State for Transport, 1992–94. Retired from the House of Lords in 2019. MacGregor joined the Magic Circle as a member in 1989, and the Inner Magic Circle in 2000.

[96] Gordon Brown (b 1951) was Labour MP for Dunfermline East, 1983–2005; Kirkcaldy and Cowdenbeath, 2005–15; Chancellor of the Exchequer, 1997–2007; Prime Minister and First Lord of the Treasury, 2007–10. He is a major political figure who since 2012 has been Special Envoy for the UN Secretary-General for Global Education. He was the youngest ever Rector, Edinburgh University, 1972–75. Journalist and Current Affairs Editor, Scottish TV, 1980–83.

Heggie a job, 'I shall have to actively try and secure research contracts for RPT Economic Studies Group ... There are at least two important contracts in the DTp pipeline which would have ordinarily gone to TSU.' RPT employed Heggie as a consultant.

The article, which was written by Mick Hamer, went on to carry a quote from a spokesman for the Civil Service Department confirming that the Civil Service code applied equally to special advisers as to ministers. They should be 'like Caesar's wife: above suspicion. They should avoid conflicts of interest and not use their position to give advantage to someone else. Nor can you accept a reward for doing something or for refraining from doing something.'

Heggie was not popular at the British Railways Board, and no tears were shed over his sudden departure.[97]

---

[97] *New Scientist*, 29 January 1981.

4
Wartime Control and the Big Four, 1921–47

'The four great railways seemed part of the settled order of things ...'
Michael Bonavia, 1980

Prior to 1914, most railways in Great Britain were strong financially, technically advanced compared with other systems abroad, and provided a generally good service for both passengers and freight forwarders. These were 'the proud years', as Hamilton Ellis called them.[98] The biggest and best of the railways were mighty joint stock companies, vertically integrated, running ships, harbours, hotels, workshops, laundries and quarries as well as railways. They were the lifeblood of the economy, had liberated millions of people who had previously been unable to travel, and were major employers in their own right. Together with the steamship and the telegraph, the railways had conquered the world.

Wartime Control

In 1921, after seven years of government control, they emerged impoverished, with a backlog of maintenance and a desperate need for investment to meet the challenges of a new age. Their public reputation was tarnished, as the service was poorer than pre-war, and there was an understandable reaction to massive increases in fares, rates and charges, made late in the day by the government in 1917.

Sir Felix Pole,[99] General Manager of the GWR, in a very restrained comment some years later, wrote that: 'seven years of Government control had reduced the railways from relatively prosperous commercial concerns to a precarious financial position.'[100]

It is true that the Great War changed everything and the railway would have had to change with it and adapt to a more competitive environment anyway, but the financial mismanagement of the railways was a prime cause of

Sir Felix Pole. Son of a Wiltshire village schoolmaster, Felix Pole entered the GWR's telegraph department at Swindon in 1891 at the age of 14 and subsequently became the company's General Manager from 1921 to 1929. He was knighted in 1924. *Published in* The Railway Magazine; *Peter Waller Collection*

---

[98] *British Railway History*, vol. 2.
[99] Sir Felix Pole (1877–1956) was the General Manager of the Great Western Railway, 1921–29; knighted, 1924, and Chairman of Associated Electrical Industries Ltd, 1929–45; Director, 1945–55. Pole had an ex-GWR Castle class 4–6–0 locomotive, No. 5066, named after him in April 1956.
[100] Quoted in *The Four Great Railways*, Michael Bonavia, David & Charles, 1980.

the problems and government's shameful refusal to pay for the wear and tear of serving the nation in the exceptional conditions of the war, in which thousands of railway staff had made the ultimate sacrifice, was a source of mistrust between the industry and politicians, and particularly the first Minister of Transport, Sir Eric Geddes.

The railways were the logistical backbone of the war effort and served their passengers and freight customers well, in addition to providing trained men and equipment for the war effort, including sending rolling stock and track to France to support the army. Railway workshops turned out armaments as well as ambulance trains, and railway ships supported the war effort as well. The human sacrifice for railway staff and families was huge, and the execution of Captain Charles Fryatt[101] of the Great Eastern's steamship *Brussels* following its capture by the Germans was a particularly dark moment in the war.

This sacrifice is commemorated by war memorials at many stations today and in the imposing memorial in front of the North Eastern Railway headquarters in York.[102]

Lord Kitchener himself had congratulated the railway companies for their success in moving the British Expeditionary Force to France during sixteen days at the start of the war, which, he said, had more than justified the complete confidence reposed in them by the War Office.[103]

And in a Commons debate on Railway Agreements on 28 February 1921, Andrew Bonar Law, Leader of the House of Commons, said: 'As my right hon. Friend the Minister of Transport (Sir Eric Geddes) has said, there is no industry which is more essential to the country than the railway industry of the United Kingdom, and I repeat what he has said, namely, that any action which we take as a government, or which the House of Commons takes, will certainly be fair to the railway interests in this matter.'[104]

Even the select committee meeting at the end of the war affirmed the success that attended the operation of the railways throughout it. They particularly commended the railways for managing with many inexperienced staff, higher traffic volumes, including heavy government traffic, and the requirement for rolling stock and other equipment to be sent abroad for army use, noting that 'there has been little dislocation'.[105]

Yet, under the seven years of government control, labour costs had risen by 268 per cent, while fares and freight rates and charges had been held down with

Sir Eric Geddes, former North Eastern Railway director and first Minister of Transport. *Library of Congress*

inevitable and disastrous effects on the financial state of the companies. Then in 1917, ordinary fares were increased by 50 per cent in one hit and most reduced fares withdrawn, and in 1920 freight rates rose by between 75 per cent and 200 per cent, with the inevitable customer resistance reducing traffic volumes.

At the same time, thousands of men were demobbed and the surplus of army lorries was sold off, many being bought by former soldiers who started in business on their own account as hauliers, or converted them to buses. With roads provided then (as now) by the state, and no regulation, competition started to bite and soon resulted in serious losses of traffic and a progressive shift of goods to road that continued for a further half century.

---

[101] Charles Algernon Fryatt (1862–1916), Great Eastern Railway ship's captain whose ship, SS *Brussels*, was captured by five German destroyers off the Belgian coast in 1916. Fryatt was court-marshalled and executed by firing squad for allegedly ramming and sinking a German submarine. In 1919 his body was brought back to England and he was given a state funeral in St Paul's Cathedral. His remains were carried in the prototype PMV (parcels and miscellaneous van) of the South Eastern and Chatham Railway from Dover. This same vehicle was also used to convey the remains of Nurse Edith Cavell and the Unknown Warrior. The van has been preserved and is to be found on the Kent and East Sussex heritage railway.

[102] Now the Grand Hotel, York.

[103] *British Railway History*, vol. 2, Hamilton Ellis, George Allan & Unwin, 1953.

[104] HC Deb 28 February 1921, vol. 138 cc. 1463–570.

[105] Quoted in *The Ministry of Transport Act, 1919*, W A Robertson, Stevens & Sons Ltd, 1919.

The period of government control had also given politicians a reason for intervention that they were unwilling to give up with the end of hostilities.

During the First World War, the government had taken control of the railways under the provisions of the Regulation of the Forces Act, 1871. Control was exercised by the President of the Board of Trade working through a Railway Executive Committee formed of chief officers of twelve of the principal railway companies, under the Chairmanship of Sir Herbert Walker,[106] General Manager of the London & South Western Railway.

In political terms the objective was to ensure the railways did not profit from the additional wartime traffic and the government took on the financial risk directly. Shareholders were guaranteed roughly the 1913 net revenues. This was to be paid monthly, with an allowance (from 1915) for deferred maintenance,[107] these grants continuing until the railways were decontrolled (which did not happen until 1921).

Relations between railways and government were soured by the latter's refusal to pay, the test case being that of the North British Railway (NBR), the northern link in the East Coast Main Line serving the dockyard at Rosyth and the railway that handled much of the traffic to support the fleet at Scapa Flow. The NBR claimed an instalment of £616,194 due early in 1920, but the newly formed Ministry of Transport withheld payment pending investigation. The dispute was referred to the Railway & Canal Commission, which made an interim award of £430,000 that was also denied. The Treasury was taken before the Court of Sessions, which reversed the Commission's decision, saying that the Ministry was able to withhold payment until the railways were decontrolled. After decontrol, the NBR submitted a total claim for unpaid compensation of £10,681,243 and the Treasury settled at £9,790,545.

The battle was fought between Eric Geddes as Transport Minister (and a former North Eastern Railway director) and William Whitelaw, North British Chairman. Whitelaw emerged with great credit from this bruising encounter, and shortly after became chairman of the newly formed London & North Eastern Railway.

Post-War Uncertainty and the Grouping

A period of great uncertainty followed the Armistice, with debate on the future of the railways embracing nationalisation, which was supported by Winston Churchill (then a Liberal) in a speech in Dundee, saying: 'Railways in private hands must be used for immediate direct profit, but it might pay the state to run railways at a loss to develop industries and agriculture.'[108]

At the 1918 general election the manifesto of the Lloyd George/Bonar Law Coalition had little to say about railways:

> Active measures will be needed to secure employment for the workers of the country. Industry will rightly claim to be liberated at the earliest possible moment from Government control. By the development and control in the best interest of the State of the economical production of power and light, of the railways and the means of communication, by the improvement of the Consular Service, and by the establishment of regular machinery for consultation with representative trade and industrial organisations on matters affecting their interest and prosperity, output will be increased, new markets opened out, and great economies effected in industrial production.

There was no hint there of the massive reorganisation that would come with the creation of the Big Four.

In August 1918 the House of Commons appointed a select committee to report on internal transport and its report was published just two weeks after the Armistice was signed. It too thought the railways had performed well during the war but reported, *inter alia*: 'That the organisation of the transport agencies of this country – and particularly the railways – cannot be allowed to return to its pre-war position.

'That the temporary arrangements for the control of railways and canals during the war would not be satisfactory as a permanent settlement,' and: 'That unification of the railway system is desirable under suitable safeguards, whether the ownership be in public or private hands.'

This was followed by a white paper in 1920 that proposed, *inter alia*, that there should be worker representation on the board of the new railway companies. This was an unprecedented interference in the running of private companies and neither the railways nor the trades unions liked it, the latter because they wanted to see nationalisation, not the creation of fewer companies. This proposal was dropped before the 1921 Act grouped the 123 most significant companies into the Big Four.

Indeed, the government's proposals in 1920[109] were significantly different from those enacted in 1921 and are

---

[106] Sir Herbert Ashcombe Walker (1868–1949) General Manager of the London and South Western Railway from 1912 to 1923, and then of the Southern Railway, 1923–37. He was responsible for the very extensive programme of third-rail electrification, and he oversaw the rebuilding of Waterloo station completed in 1922, where a stone cameo portrait commemorating his immense achievements can still be seen today.

[107] *British Transport since 1914*, Derek H Aldcroft, David & Charles, 1975.

[108] The *Four Great Railways*, Michael Bonavia, David & Charles, 1980.

[109] *Outline of proposals as to the future of transport undertakings in Great Britain and their relation to the state*, Cmd 787, 1920.

an indication of political views changing, even as the new structure was being forged. This was very different from the government's clear vision in 1947 when the railways were nationalised, but very similar to the uncertainty evident from the discussions between 1988 and 1992 prior to privatisation. The command paper is a slim five-page document that is, to say the least, superficial. It proposed grouping the railways into seven companies:

- Southern
- Western
- North Western
- Eastern
- North Eastern
- London Group (local lines)
- Scottish Group

Light Railways were to be excluded, and the government would offer further assistance to local authorities or private companies to open further light railways 'for the benefit of agriculture and other industries', stating: 'It should be the policy of the ministry to stimulate the development of light railways, constructed, equipped and worked on the cheapest possible lines.'

In 1920, it was perhaps a little late to seek to promote many more new lines at the dawn of the motoring age, although some indeed were opened as a result of this policy, including the Totton to Fawley and Halwill Junction to Torrington lines in 1925 and the Romney, Hythe & Dymchurch in 1927 (although with its ultra-narrow gauge, the latter was not the sort of light railway envisaged by the drafters of the command paper).

The paper also asserted the government's right to intervene in railway management: 'For the protection of the public, including the right to require the railways to provide adequate services and facilities, including minor extensions of their networks, or for safety improvements; for economical working, including the right to impose technical standards, enforce common user of rolling stock and facilities, and to pool traffic receipts "where competition is causing waste".

'To safeguard the national interest, which included requiring Government approval for capital projects (even though the companies raised the capital) and the right for Government to determine the level of reserves for depreciation and renewals before dividends are paid.'

In retrospect, such sweeping powers, had they been granted, would have been analogous to those exercised over BR, and were quite inappropriate for private companies owned by shareholders. The rationale in the command paper was that such powers were necessary as government had the duty to set rates and charges at such a level as to provide adequate income for the railways, so this level of regulation was required.

Ministry of Transport

The white paper was the first statement of government policy by the newly created Ministry of Transport, established in 1919. It too marked a stage in the exercise of closer government control of the railway. Following the enactment of the primary legislation, the role of three departments in relation to transport were transferred to the new ministry. These were:

- The Board of Trade
- The Ministry of Health
  (formerly the Local Government Board) and
- The Roads Board.

The intention of the 1919 Act was that the new Minister of Transport should 'exercise a general control, and will give his directions, leaving those responsible for the undertaking to carry them out in their own way'.[110] However, he was enabled to give directions as to rates, wages, standardisation of works and rolling stock and co-operation between companies, as well as being able to require alterations and additions to be made, and even jobs to be abolished.

The 1919 Act continued the wartime provisions for control of the railways for two years. It also provided for a separate roads division, even though the minister's duties were expected to be within a general scheme of co-ordinated transport. This was to lead to the ministry in later years becoming a champion of roads and motorway construction, while remaining as a regulator for railways, until nationalisation.

In 1900, there were 653,571 wagons operating on the railways of Great Britain, and many of these were privately owned. A major inefficiency was that private owner wagons were generally returned empty to their owner to reload rather than deployed to best advantage. Under wartime control, these wagons became common user, and so could be used more efficiently with a reduction in empty wagon mileage. To retain these benefits, the 1919 Act included powers for the minister to purchase these wagons, but this was not pursued and it was only with the Transport Act, 1947 that they came together under the control of British Railways.

Under the 1919 Act, the Minister was empowered by order to require the railways:

a) to conform gradually to measures of general standardisation of ways, plant and equipment (including methods of electrical operation, type, frequency, and pressure of current)

b) to adopt schemes for the co-operative working or common user of rolling stock, workshops, manufactories, plant and other facilities.[111]

The Act enforced collective bargaining. It also required railways to handle traffic to and from connecting railways

---

[110] *The Ministry of Transport Act, 1919*, W A Robertson, Stevens & Sons Ltd, 1919.

[111] Railways Act, 1921, clause 16(2).

efficiently and not to give priority to their own traffics.[112] Such transfers had to satisfy the 'reasonable requirements of the public'.

Geddes did not have the universal admiration of his former colleagues, the chairmen and general managers of the great railway companies. He was a formidable administrator with a great intellect and a lot of experience. In 1916 Lloyd George had plucked him from his job as general manager of the North Eastern Railway to make him director-general of munitions 'who possessed the drive as well as the make of one of the NER's own powerful locomotives'.[113] In this role Geddes enthusiastically built railways behind the British lines in France, until Lloyd George made him First Lord of the Admiralty, replacing the less than successful Sir Edward Carson.[114] Field-Marshal Sir Douglas Haig greatly admired Geddes and made him a temporary major general, and the Prime Minister decided he wanted him to take charge of naval construction including mercantile shipbuilding as well, acquiring the additional rank of vice admiral.

So it was that Geddes became the first Minister of Transport in 1919. At the time some thought it was a mistake to appoint a former general manager who wanted to manage the railways and was quite capable of doing so, rather than a policy expert who would set the strategic framework and leave the railwaymen to get on with it.

In retrospect, this was massive and heavy-handed interference with major joint stock companies that, before the war, had operated successfully and profitably. The interests of shareholders were pushed aside (but not overruled) and a clear public interest element introduced in the operation of the railways. Henceforward, the government would be able to interfere much more in the provision of railway services, while leaving the commercial risk with the railways. The seeds were sown that led to the Square Deal campaign of 1938 and the crippling obligations imposed on the railways in terms of common carrier liability that were not finally removed until 1962.

Introducing the Railways Bill 1921, Geddes made much of the high capital cost of British lines – £56,000 per mile here, compared with £26,000 in Prussia and £16,000 in the USA. He also said that British railway track was worked far less hard than that elsewhere – in the US the average wagon load was 23.5 tons, in Prussia 8.8 tons and just 5.4 tons in Great Britain. The *Railway Magazine*, however, was not impressed by these figures and said:

'such argument is dangerously specious; it is the sort of argument beloved by the pre-war advocate of nationalisation, as it may prove anything or nothing, according to the point of view, and the extent of the knowledge of hearers and readers.

'High capital cost is the "millstone" round the neck of British railways, partly the penalty of our pioneer position, but largely due to legislative action in the past, the virtually entire absence of anything in the nature of state assistance and the high valuation of land and property which had necessarily had to be secured in the past ... High capital cost is therefore a legacy from the past which cannot be evaded, and it is reflected in every section of railway working so that in one way or another it accounts for a substantial percentage of the excess transit costs of the United Kingdom over the other countries cited.'[115]

Although many commentators took the view that the Grouping of the Big Four, which took effect from 1 January 1923, was a reasonable compromise, as it steered a middle way between nationalisation and a continuation of the pre–1914 *laissez-faire*[116] approach, there was still some substantial opposition (in addition to that of railwaymen politicians such as Sir Frederick Banbury). In June 1921 the *Railway Magazine* said that 'the government's proposals for the grouping of railways met with very limited approval and were condemned in nearly every quarter of importance.

'As an alternative, the Railway Companies' Association produced a four-group scheme. The new proposals of the government Bill represent in some degree a compromise between the two, by combining the Eastern with the North Eastern instead of isolating the North Eastern and Hull & Barnsley Railways into a group by themselves.

'There will be four English groups: Southern (L&SW, LB&SC, SE and LC&D), Western (GW and Welsh railways), North Western and Midland (L&NW, L&Y, Midland, North Staffs, Furness and Maryport & Carlisle, and North Eastern and Eastern (GE, GC, GN, NE, and H&B Railways). Two Scottish groups are proposed, West Scottish (Caledonian, G&SW and Highland) and East Scottish (North British and Great North of Scotland). The separation of the Scottish lines from their English associates remains, however, a bone of contention.

'The Scottish companies claim they are most seriously placed by the changed conditions, and the general view of the companies seems to be that the only logical course is to associate them with the appropriate English companies.'

---

[112] Clause 75.

[113] Quoted in *Tempestuous Journey – Lloyd George His Life and Times* by Frank Owen, p.293.

[114] Sir Edward – later Lord – Carson (1854–1935), Irish unionist politician, barrister and judge. From 1892 to 1918 Carson was Irish Unionist Alliance MP for the University of Dublin. In 1915 he entered Asquith's war Cabinet as Attorney General. He played a major role in forcing the resignation of Asquith as Prime Minister, returning to office on 10 December 1916 as First Lord of the Admiralty, and appointed as a Minister without Portfolio on 17 July 1917. Served as MP for Belfast Duncairn, 1918–29. Virulent opponent of Irish Home Rule, and although not supporting partition, he played a significant part in ensuring that the six counties remained part of the UK.

[115] Pertinent Paragraphs *Railway Magazine*, 1921.

[116] *Railway Magazine*, June 1921.

That pragmatic approach was adopted and the LMS and the LNER encompassed the railways from the west and east of Scotland respectively. There had been the stirrings of a Scottish independence movement immediately before the First World War, when the House of Commons gave a second reading to the Government of Scotland Bill 1913 (also referred to as the Scottish Home Rule Bill) by 204 votes to 159. The Bill was supported by Liberals and opposed by Unionists. The outbreak of war stopped it proceeding further.

Scottish railways remained part of the national network right through nationalisation (as part of British Railways, with its own Scottish Region) and up to the time of privatisation. Even today, notwithstanding the creation of the Scottish Parliament and government, railway safety and the role of ORR are not devolved matters and Network Rail operates north of the border stating on its website:

> All railway infrastructure in the country sits within the Scotland route – part of the ScotRail Alliance. Network Rail Scotland looks after Scotland's Railway infrastructure, and together with Abellio ScotRail, our partners in the ScotRail Alliance, we are committed to putting passengers and freight customers at the heart of how we run Scotland's Railway.[117]

British Transport Police

By contrast, the status of the British Transport Police (BTP) in Scotland was the subject of heated debate in the House of Lords following the publication of the report of the Smith Commission in 2014 and during the passage of the Scotland Bill.[118] The Commission had been set up under the chairmanship of Lord Smith of Kelvin[119] following the 'No' vote in the Scottish independence referendum. Its purpose was to fulfil what was called 'The Vow', which promised the devolution of more powers from the UK Parliament to the Scottish Parliament. Paragraph 67 of the report said curtly: 'The functions of the British Transport Police in Scotland will be a devolved matter.'

There is evidence to suggest that this recommendation was arrived at in the Commission after the most minimal debate.[120] It ignored the unique role of BTP as a genuinely national police force, responsible for policing the railways of the whole of Great Britain, having been established at the time of the dawn of railways in 1826. The first mention of railway police anywhere was in a regulation of the Stockton and Darlington Railway, which contained a description of railway employees as 'police' with an establishment of 'One Superintendent, four officers and numerous gate-keepers'. This was three years before the Metropolitan Police Act was passed.

The proposal to transfer BTP Scotland to Police Scotland was contained in the Scotland Act, but has not been implemented. Powerful representations by the British Transport Police Authority and many others who know rather more about the BTP than was demonstrated by the members of the Smith Commission appear to have persuaded the Scottish government not to proceed with this change.

Herbert Morrison and the Creation of London Transport

The 1929 general election saw Labour's return to power as a minority government. Their minister of transport was Herbert Morrison,[121] who had been elected MP for Hackney South in the 1923 general election. He then lost his seat in 1924 when Ramsay MacDonald's first Labour government was defeated in the general election, and then won it back in 1929.

During Morrison's two years as Transport Minister, world events such as the international financial crisis and the rise of fascism in Europe meant that the public's attention was not focused on Britain's railways. When MacDonald responded to the national emergency by forming a 'national' – Conservative-dominated –

---

[117] www.networkrail.co.uk/running-the-railway/our-routes/scotland (ScotRail was taken into public ownership by the Scottish Government in April 2022.

[118] See particularly *Hansard*, cols 369–385, 24 February 2016.

[119] Robert Haldane Smith, Lord Smith of Kelvin (b 1944), Scottish businessman who trained as a chartered accountant. Chairman: Forth Ports, since 2015; IMI plc, since 2015; British Business Bank, since 2017; Scottish Enterprise, since 2019, and numerous enquiries, commissions and public bodies over the past thirty years including Commonwealth Games Organising Committee, Glasgow 2014 Ltd, 2008–15; and the Board of Trustees, National Museums of Scotland, 1993–2002.

[120] In a private conversation between a member of the Commission and one of the authors of this book

[121] Herbert Morrison, Lord Morrison of Lambeth (1888–1965), Labour MP for South Hackney. 1923–24, 1929–31 and 1935–45; East Lewisham, 1945–51; South Lewisham, 1951–59. Minister of Transport, 1929–31; Minister of Supply, 1940; Home Secretary and Minister of Home Security, 1940–45; Member of War Cabinet, 1942–45; Deputy Prime Minister, 1945–51; Lord President of the Council and Leader of House of Commons, 1945–51; Secretary of State for Foreign Affairs, March–October 1951; Deputy Leader of Opposition, 1951–55. On his return to the Commons in 1935 Morrison stood for the leadership of the Labour Party, but was defeated by Clement Attlee. His principal supporter was Hugh Dalton (*qv*): between them they alleged that the Masonic New Welcome Lodge had backed the third-place leadership candidate Arthur Greenwood and then switched their votes to Attlee. There were strong rumours of a plot, orchestrated by Harold Laski, to install Morrison as Prime Minister after Attlee had led Labour to victory in the 1945 general election. That came to nothing, and Attlee remained as leader until after the 1955 election, by which time Morrison was felt to be too old at 67, and he came third in the poll. He retired from the Commons in 1959 and was appointed to the House of Lords. A further connection with the railway was that his first wife, Margaret Kent, was the daughter of a railway clerk; Peter, Lord Mandelson, is Morrison's grandson.

Herbert Morrison MP, Minister of Transport 1929 to 1931 and founder of London Transport. *CC BY-SA 3.0 nl*

coalition, Morrison stood as a Labour candidate in the election called in 1931, and again lost his seat.

Morrison put his four years out of the Commons to good use. He had always been a London local government politician first and foremost. He had been elected to the Metropolitan Borough of Hackney in 1919 when the Labour Party won control of the borough, and he was Mayor in 1920–21. In 1922 he won the Woolwich seat on the London County Council, and was elected leader of the Labour group in 1934 (which won control that year) and served until 1940, when he joined Churchill's wartime coalition.

In 1933 he wrote a book, *Socialisation and Transport: the Organisation of Socialised Industries with Particular Reference to the London Passenger Transport Bill*. He had worked on these plans during his two years as Transport Minister and was able in 1933 to create the London Passenger Transport Board (LPTB, universally known as London Transport), which unified bus, tram and trolleybus services with the Underground. Interestingly, the Bill to achieve this was a hybrid Bill (see Chapter 2) and so could carry over from the Labour government to the National government, which, despite Conservative domination, voted through this measure to take a number of private railway, tramway and bus companies into public ownership.

Lord Ashfield

The first chairman of the LPTB was Lord Ashfield, whom the London Transport Museum describes on its website as the 'founder of the London Underground'. Born Albert Knatriess in Derby in 1874, he emigrated as a child to the USA and joined the Detroit Street Railway as a messenger boy. The family changed their name to Stanley in 1897, and at 29 Albert Stanley became general manager of New Jersey Tramways. He was sent to London in 1907 by the American shareholders to keep an eye on George Gibb in the financially troubled Underground Electric Railways of London, and succeeded him as general manager in 1910.

The UERL was the holding company of four underground railways in central London. Three of these (the District Railway, the Baker Street and Waterloo Railway and the Great Northern, Piccadilly and Brompton Railway) were already in operation and the fourth (the Charing Cross, Euston and Hampstead Railway) was about to open. The UERL had been established by American financier Charles Yerkes and much of the finance and equipment had been brought from the United States, so Stanley's experience of managing urban transit systems in that country made him an ideal candidate for the position. The cost of constructing three new lines in just a few years had put the company in a precarious monetary position and income was not sufficient to pay the interest on its loans.

With Commercial Manager Frank Pick,[122] Stanley devised a plan to increase passenger numbers: developing

---

[122] Frank Pick (1878–1941) was one of the twentieth century's most outstanding administrators, who was responsible for the successful expansion of London's public transport services and for the adoption of an iconic design and corporate house style that is still used extensively by Transport for London today. Writing in 1968, Nikolaus Pevsner described Pick as 'the greatest patron of the arts whom this century has so far produced in England, and indeed the ideal patron of our age'. Writing in *The Subterranean Railway: How the London Underground was Built and How it Changed the City Forever*, Christian Wolmar said it is 'almost impossible to exaggerate the high regard in which [London Transport] was held during its all too brief heyday, attracting official visitors from around the world eager to learn the lessons of its success and apply them in their own countries' and that 'it represented the apogee of a type of confident public administration ... with a reputation that any state organisation today would envy ... only made possible by the brilliance of its two famous leaders, Ashfield and Pick.'

Having qualified as a solicitor, Pick began working for the North Eastern Railway in 1902. He worked first in the company's traffic statistics department before becoming assistant to the company's general manager, Sir George Gibb, in 1904. Gibb became managing director of UERL in 1906 and took Pick with him to London. By 1908, Pick had become publicity officer responsible for marketing and it was at this time that, working with Albert Stanley, he began developing the strong corporate identity and visual style for which the London Underground later became famous. Pick's philosophy on design was that 'the test of the goodness of a thing is its fitness for use. If it fails on this first test, no amount of ornamentation or finish will make it any better; it will only make it more expensive, more foolish.'

the 'Underground' brand and establishing a joint booking system and co-ordinated fares throughout all of London's underground railways, including those not controlled by the UERL. In July 1910, Stanley took the integration of the group further, when he persuaded previously reluctant American investors to approve the merger of the three tube railways into a single company.

Further consolidation came with the UERL's take-over of London General Omnibus Company (LGOC) in 1912 and the Central London Railway and the City & South London Railway on 1 January 1913. By then only the Waterloo & City Railway and the Metropolitan Railway (and its subsidiaries the Great Northern & City Railway and the East London Railway) remained outside the Underground Group's control.

Stanley was knighted for services to transport in 1914, In 1915, he was given a wartime role as Director-General of Mechanical Transport at the Ministry of Munitions. In 1916, he was selected by Prime Minister David Lloyd George to become President of the Board of Trade. He was elected to parliament unopposed for Ashton-under-Lyne on 23 December 1916 as a Conservative Unionist. At 42 years old, he was the youngest member of Lloyd George's coalition government.

He was re-elected in 1918, but returned to the London Underground Group, this time as both managing director and chairman. He left the Commons on being ennobled as Lord Ashfield in 1920. He was the natural choice for chairman of the LPTB, and Frank Pick was the first chief executive.

There was one railway locomotive named *Lord Ashfield*, a fireless tank engine built in 1931 by Andrew Barclay Sons & Co., Kilmarnock, with the works number 1989 for the Brimsdown A power station on the Lee Navigation in the London Borough of Enfield, and which had initially supplied tramways in north London. It still exists and is being restored by the Scottish Railway Preservation Society at Bo'ness.

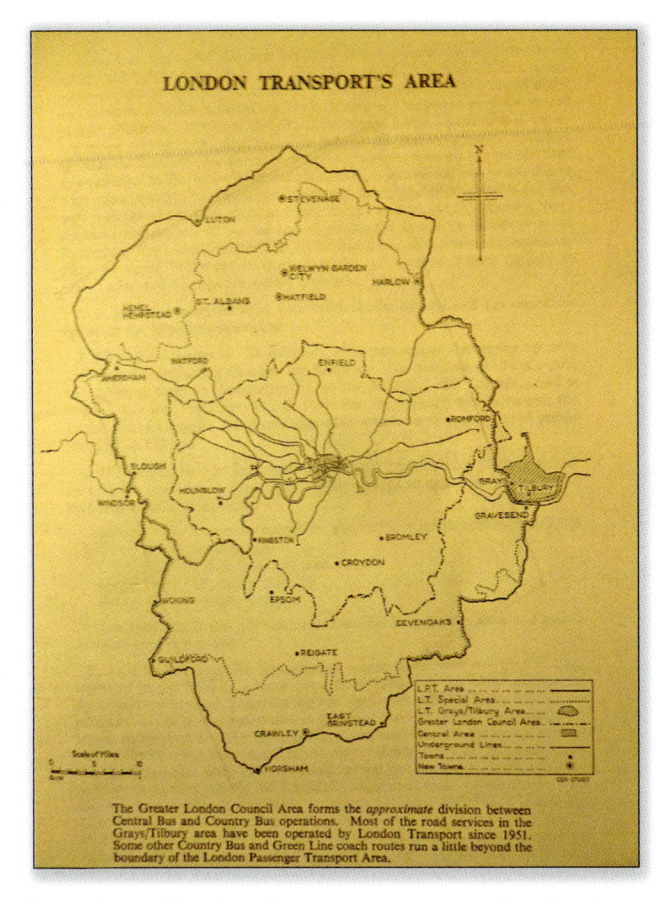

Working with the Main Line Companies

One profound effect of the formation of London Transport was the creation of the London Passenger Transport Board area of some 2,000 square miles, stretching from Stevenage and Luton in the north to Horsham and Sevenoaks, as well as west to east from Slough and Guildford to Gravesend and Harlow (the London County Council area had only been 117 square miles). Within this wider area, fares were pooled between London Transport and the main-line railways, avoiding competition for passengers between parallel main-line rail, Underground, tram, trolley bus and motor bus services.

The enlarged London Transport area created under the 1933 Act encompassed almost the entire Underground network as well as the area served by London's green buses. Within the area, charging between LT and the main line railways was coordinated.
London Transport annual report 1966

The Underground railways that came to be part of London Transport had a long history of working with the main-line companies, and indeed, London's first underground railway, the Metropolitan, was built to mixed gauge in 1863 to accommodate Great Western trains as well between Paddington and Moorgate. The GWR was also joint owner of the Hammersmith and City Line over which trains ran to Kensington (Addison Road) as well as to Hammersmith. The Metropolitan and Great Central joint line from Aylesbury allowed the GC to reach the capital from Manchester and Yorkshire and the LNER and Met jointly built their own branch to Watford in 1925, while the London and South Western Railway accommodated Metropolitan District Railway trains over its lines to Richmond and Wimbledon. The East London Line carried Great Eastern trains from Liverpool Street to points south via New Cross and New Cross Gate.

The LT Museum website reports that: 'Pick left London Transport in 1940, after a technical disagreement with Lord Ashfield over government interference in LT finances. For a short but unhappy time he was Director General of the Ministry of Information. However, Pick clashed with Prime Minister Winston Churchill on another point of principle when he refused to distribute false propaganda in Germany. He moved to the Ministry of Transport, studying the usage of Britain's canals and rivers.'

During his career he was offered a knighthood and a peerage, but declined both He did, however, accept, in 1932, the Soviet Union's Honorary Badge of Merit for his advice on the construction of the Moscow Metro.

The Metropolitan Railway only – reluctantly – became part of the London Underground in 1933. By virtue of its relationship with the Great Central Railway (previously known as the Manchester, Sheffield and Lincolnshire Railway), and sharing Sir Edward Watkin as its chairman, it was seen as part of a uniquely ambitious project not only to build a brand new main line to London and on to the Continent by way of a Channel tunnel, but also transform the neighbourhoods through which its trains ran by creating and promoting a residential property company that built housing estates on surplus land acquired before the railway arrived. Thus came about the Willesden Park Estate in the 1880s and '90s, followed by those in Pinner and Wembley Park a decade later.

The full-scale development of what was christened 'Metro-Land' (sometimes spelt as one word) came in the 1920s, following the creation of the Metropolitan Railway Country Estates Ltd in 1919, which first built houses itself at locations down the line from Neasden to Amersham, and then later laid out the estates, giving individual purchasers the opportunity to build on their own plots to their own specification. As Oliver Green, then curator of the London Transport Museum, wrote in 1987 in his introduction to the reprint of the 1932 edition of *Metro-Land* (the annual guidebook produced annually by the company between 1915 and 1932):

> In 1929 the Metropolitan Railway's Commercial Manager estimated that between 1919 and 1928 some 12,000 houses had been built within half a mile of the stations between Willesden Green and Rickmansworth, Uxbridge and Watford, and that a further 17,000 were planned.

The development ambitions of the Metropolitan Railway appeared almost limitless, and it was only when they went as far as north Buckinghamshire, well beyond Aylesbury, that they found they had overreached themselves as they were prevented from building houses in unspoilt rural countryside. In 1935 and 1936 the two furthest outposts of the Met – the branch lines from Quainton Road to Brill and to Verney Junction – were closed to passengers forever. In his BBC film *Metroland*, broadcast in 1973, Sir John Betjeman commented: 'The houses of Metroland never got as far as Verney Junction. Grass triumphs and I have to say I am rather glad.'

South of the River Thames, the District's proposed extension of their Wimbledon line to Sutton was, for the Southern, a step too far, particularly as the Northern Line was being extended to Morden at the same time. The agreement reached provided for the Wimbledon and Sutton Railway to be built by the Southern, which opened to Sutton in 1930, while the Underground Electric Railway Ltd was allowed to build the extension to Morden, but not to link to the Wimbledon and Sutton (even though the means existed for a simple connection from the Northern Line's carriage sidings to Morden South station on the Sutton line).

Following the formation of LPTB, an ambitious new works programme was put together by Frank Pick in 1935 to extend the network by:

1. Electrification to Aylesbury.
2. Incorporating the Ongar and Fairlop loop lines in the eastward extension of the Central Line.
3. Replacing Great Western local train services between Old Oak Common and Denham by a westward extension of the Central Line.
4. The Northern Heights scheme, which would have extended the Great Northern and City branch (Moorgate to Finsbury Park) and taken over the LNER suburban branches to Alexandra Palace, High Barnet and Edgware and onwards to Bushey Heath.

The onset of war delayed some of these schemes and Underground trains did not reach Ongar until 1957,[123] while electrification to Amersham and Chesham was achieved in 1960 (thus bringing to an end the change of locomotives at Rickmansworth from steam to electric, which was often achieved in as little as 4 minutes). The LNER provided the tank engines, latterly 2-6-4s of the L1 class designed by Thompson and introduced from 1945, for the Rickmansworth to Aylesbury service.

The line from Amersham to Aylesbury remains unelectrified, and is now served by Chiltern Trains' DMUs from Marylebone, as is the former GWR line from Princes Risborough to Aylesbury.

It was the drive of Lord Ashfield and Frank Pick with political support from Morrison that allowed this ambitious programme to be put forward. So, it is perhaps ironic that a number of extensions were cancelled because the expected new housing was not built after the Second World War due to green belt restrictions, for which, as leader of the London County Council, Morrison had pushed hard during the passage of the legislation in 1938. The cutbacks were:

- The planned extension of the Edgware branch to Bushey Heath. The workshop already built at Aldenham was used initially for wartime aircraft production, and then as the main workshop for London buses until 1986.
- The LNER Edgware branch was only electrified to Mill Hill East, and the remainder of the branch, which had lost its passenger service between Edgware and Finchley (Church End)[124] in 1939, stayed open for freight until 1964.
- The Central Line western extension was planned to run to Denham, but was cut back to West Ruislip. There was one intermediate station opened by the Great Western at South Harefield. It was used briefly between 1928 and 1931 and served by trains to both Marylebone and Paddington.

---

[123] The single line between Epping and Ongar was closed by London Transport in 1994, but is now a popular heritage railway.

[124] Renamed Finchley Central in 1940.

Separately, it was decided not to provide the extension of the Great Northern and City line, although the unfinished construction at Finsbury Park, halted at the outbreak of war, remained an eyesore on the up side entrance to the station until the 1980s, when a joint BR/LT scheme with GLC funding (and planned by one of your authors with his LT counterpart) cleared it away and provided a proper bus interchange in its place. Similarly, the line between Finsbury Park and Alexandra Palace did not become part of the Underground, but was closed in 1954.

The Waterloo and City (unflatteringly known as 'The Drain') managed to escape the clutches of London Transport until the last decade of the twentieth century. It was opened by the London and South Western Railway in 1898 to bring its commuters arriving at Waterloo directly to Bank station in the City of London. Its ownership passed to the Southern Railway on Grouping and then to British Railways on nationalisation. London Underground finally took it over in 1994, removed all traces of SR/BR branding and introduced its own rolling stock.

The Square Deal Campaign

The Big Four had accepted their public service obligations with few complaints and had made the most of their obligations with generally good services on even the quieter parts of their networks, although with some modest retrenchment, particularly by the LNER, which had closed many local stations on some of their main lines in the 1930s. In return, they had expected some relief from their common carrier obligations for freight, to allow them to select or reject traffic and the freedom of pricing that road hauliers enjoyed. When this did not happen and the railways continued to suffer from the trade depression of the later 1930s, they launched together their 'Square Deal' campaign in November 1938 to lobby for equitable treatment with road. While the government had some sympathy with this, it would have led to fundamental change for which there was no appetite by politicians or public, and before any progress was made, the onset of war just ten months later ended the issue as government again took over responsibility for railways. After the war, the companies returned to the issue in setting out their alternatives to nationalisation, but the die was cast as the politicians' answer after 1945 was nationalisation. This did not resolve the problem though, and it was not until the 1953 Transport Act that greater freedom was given to the railway (of which the Commission failed to take advantage), and 1962 before the final obligations were removed and a clear commercial, rather than a public service, remit was set for freight.

Big Four Achievements

Nevertheless, over the brief span of twenty-five years, the Big Four built a formidable reputation for innovation, investment and customer service, and principally over sixteen short years from 1923 to 1939 when war again meant government control of the railways: the Southern, with its electrification programme, the LNER with its streamlined expresses, the GWR for speed (*The Cheltenham Flyer* was, when introduced in 1929, the fastest train in the world), while the LMS became the largest railway company in the world at the time.[125]

That is not to say there were not complaints, and indeed, the Southern was so concerned about them that they appointed the young John Elliot[126] as public relations and advertising assistant to Sir Herbert Walker. They capitalised on success as well, through the imaginative use of locomotive naming, some excellent railway publications and tourist guides as well and some high-profile named trains. Perhaps the Great Western was most successful, but they did serve the great holiday destinations, while the Southern's core traffic remained London commuters for whom the train was regarded with the same distaste as the work to which they were travelling.

The Big Four in that short period built reputations that survive to this day and still generate loyalties among generations that never knew them. Their memorial is far more positive than BR's, even though they had only half the time in which to create it.

The Big Four offered an amazing network of services to the public, not just passenger trains and the delivery of goods, parcels and mail to a local station, but a huge fleet of ferries serving the Channel Islands, Ireland, the Clyde and the Western Isles, Harwich–Hook of Holland, the short sea routes to Belgium and France, the Isle of Wight and on Lake Windermere. Many years earlier, the Furness Railway Company realised the potential for attracting tourists on to their branch line to Coniston, and in 1859 had built the Steam Yacht *Gondola*, which is the oldest steam yacht in the North of England. Now fully restored, she once again provides cruises and boat trips on beautiful Coniston Water.

In retrospect, it is interesting that today's train operators have chosen to embrace the reputations of the historic companies for good commercial reasons, and that LNER, London Northwestern and Great Western Railway use the names of the old companies to promote their part of today's railway. Southern was also used in recent years, as was London Midland. It seems that passengers are still attracted by the names and the connection with stylish service and good value.

Apart from conventional steamers, the companies ran train ferries to Belgium and France and they pioneered car ferries and ran many of the ferry ports and major docks such as Southampton, Hull and Cardiff. They also had a substantial stake in bus companies, too, and in many cases

---

[125] *British Railway History*, vol. 2, Hamilton Ellis, George, Allen & Unwin, 1953.

[126] Sir John Elliot (1898–1988) was the Southern Railway's first public relations officer, before becoming chairman of the Railway Executive and later of London Transport. Born John Elliot Blumenfeld, son of the *Daily Mail's* news editor, he changed his name to John Elliot in 1923 and was knighted in 1954.

LNER No 2509 *Silver Link* heads the 'Silver Jubilee' streamlined set on the East Coast Main Line. This train achieved 112mph on a demonstration run in 1935, later exceeded by *Mallard*.
Neil Davenport Collection/Online Transport Archive

In response to the 'Silver Jubilee', the LMS introduced their own streamlined train, the 'Coronation Scot' in 1937, marking the coronation of King George VI. The train ran until 1939 and inspired a popular piece of light music by Vivian Ellis. *Neil Davenport Collection/Online Transport Archive*

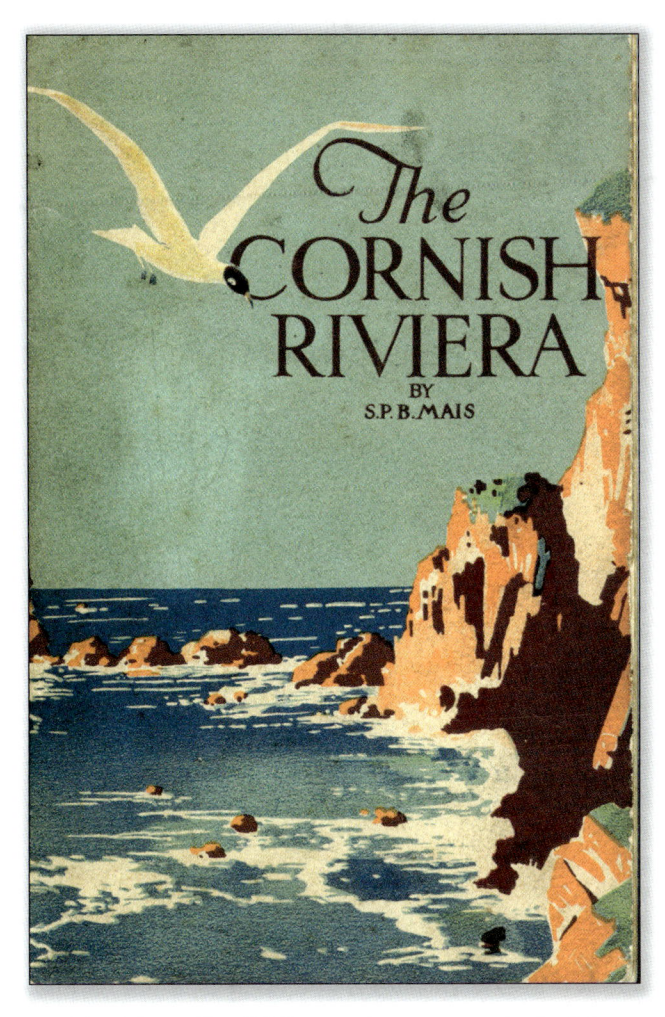

Cornish Riviera. The GWR served many popular holiday destinations in the West Country and promoted summer holidays actively through a series of popular guidebooks and posters, the Cornish example being written and illustrated by the prolific travel writer and broadcaster, Stuart (SPB) Mais. Cornwall was promoted as the Cornish Riviera, with associations of glamour with the popular French Riviera (Cote d' Azur). *Peter Waller Collection*

Sands Across The Sea. 2nd edition, 1938. Southern Railway promotion of their shipping routes to France and connecting boat trains. BR continued to publish the guide until 1962. *Peter Waller Collection*

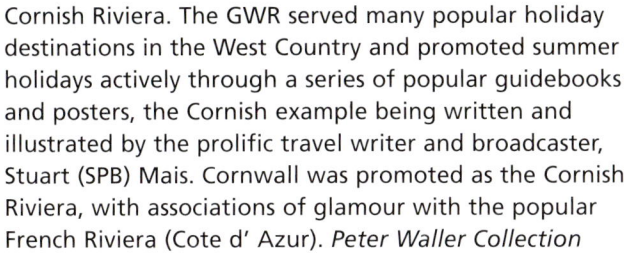

a controlling interest. The portfolio was completed with hotels, some of which like Gleneagles were (and remain) world class. They owned refreshment rooms and ran restaurant cars and sleeping cars. Highly vertically integrated, they built and maintained their own locomotives and rolling stock, ran quarries, concrete works, laundries and owned several toll bridges and toll roads.

Most imaginatively though, they embraced the new transport mode, aviation, through Railway Air Services Ltd, formed in 1934 by the Big Four, together with Imperial Airways. Services linked Birmingham and South Wales with the West Country and the Isle of Wight, as well as with Manchester, Liverpool, the Isle of Man, Belfast and Glasgow. This brought the companies into close contact with government on aviation strategy in the 1930s. The government, however, adopted a 'hands off' approach that eventually meant the railways left the stage.

The Southern was particularly involved in London airport policy through its planned purchase of a site for a potential international airport at Lullingstone in Kent. A station was built between Swanley and Eynsford on the Maidstone East line, some traces of which can still be seen today from the train. A short spur was to be constructed into the airport, and in 1935, the Southern board was prepared to purchase the land and develop the airport at its own expense. Even though this would be a major international airport for London, decisions were not taken by government, but left to the company, as described by the Minister Sir Philip Sassoon in a 1937 Parliamentary Answer:

> any decision in regard to the establishment of the Airport will be one to be taken by the Southern Railway and will not rest with the Air Ministry.[127]

---

[127] *Hansard*, HC debates, 14 April 1937, vol. 322, c. 998.

Railway Air Services were part of the Big Four's joined-up approach to transport. Here is a De Havilland four engine bi-plane (DH 36B) aircraft at Croydon airport on the Belfast or Glasgow route. Its capacity was 10 passengers.
Malcolm Knight Collection/Online Transport Archive

The plan foundered following detailed evaluation by the Southern, principally on the uncertainty over the future of London airport developments, and the lack of any coherent government strategy. In particular, Croydon Airport was open, but was constrained by its site, Heston airport was being developed, Gatwick had originally been served by train, but had been closed to passengers in 1937, while the City of London was looking at the possibility of an airport at Fairlop in Essex. All this was against the background of an aviation sector that was growing, but which remained unprofitable.

The Southern's inevitable conclusion was that they could not justify investment in such a venture that in their view was more of a national project than one for private enterprise. The General Manager, Gilbert Szlumper[128] explained this to Sir Francis Shelmerdine,[129] the Director General for Aviation at the Air Ministry. The railway was, however, prepared to build a spur line into the airport, if it were built, at their own expense. It was also still considering buying the land as even if the airport did not go ahead, it could be used for housing. The Secretary of State for Air was unhappy with the decision but no further

---

[128] Gilbert Szlumper (1884–1969) was the Southern Railway's penultimate general manager, 1937–39, when he left for war service becoming Director-General of Transportation & Movements, War Office (1939–40); Railway Control Officer, Ministry of Transport, 1940–41, and Director-General of Supply Services, Ministry of Supply, 1942–45. His father had been Chief Engineer of the London and South Western Railway.

[129] Sir Francis Shelmerdine (1881–1945) served in the European War in France and Egypt; seconded to the Royal Flying Corps, 1915; Senior Assistant, Directorate of Civil Aviation, Air Ministry, 1919; Director of Civil Aviation in India, 1927–31; Director of Civil Aviation, Air Ministry, 1931–34; Director General of Civil Aviation, 1934–41.

London's principal airport could have been at Lullingstone in Kent instead of at Heathrow. The remains of the platform can be seen behind this northbound Thameslink train in 2020. The runway would have been on the top of the hill in the background and the terminal would have been served by a double track branch from the south end of the new station. *Christopher Austin*

action was taken, the ministry declined to reimburse the money the Southern had spent on planning the airport and then the war supervened. After the war, the decision was made to develop Heathrow, as some work had already been done to prepare it as an RAF station and this meant that its development would be a little cheaper. So, with this tactical decision, based on the cheapest option, the strategic future of London's airports was decided.

In the event, Lullingstone station was built, and even appeared in *Bradshaw*, but no trains ever called there and after the war, green belt legislation precluded housing developments nearby and the station was abandoned and much of it was demolished in 1955. The canopies still exist as they were moved to Canterbury East in 1960.

Government Control in War

The railways again came under government control from September 1939. This time, the Railway Executive Committee was based in Fielden House in Westminster (see Chapter 2).

During the Second World War, Gilbert Szlumper was seconded to the Ministry of War Transport and helped smooth relationships between the ministry and the Railway Executive Committee. As he explained to Sir Cyril Hurcombe[130] in 1941, even

---

[130] Cyril William Hurcomb, 1st Baron Hurcomb GCB KBE (1883–1975), was Permanent Under-Secretary of the Ministry of Transport from 1927 to 1937; of the Ministry of Shipping from 1939; and then of its successor the Ministry of War Transport from 1941 until 1947. He was the first chairman of the British Transport Commission between 1948 and 1953. He was also a keen ornithologist and conservationist, and played a key role in the 1954 Protection of Birds Act. He served as chairman of the Royal Society for the Protection of Birds' council, as president of the RSPB. He was a Grand Officer of the Order of the Crown (Belgium) and Grand Cross of the Order of St Olav. The BR Standard Britannia class locomotive number 70001 was named *Lord Hurcomb* in his honour.

Bradshaw's guide, 1939. Founded 100 years before by a printer and mapmaker, George Bradshaw, based in Manchester. His name became a household word for railway timetables in an age when 150 railway companies each produced their own. Publication ceased in 1961, but reprints have been produced, inspired by the television series by Michael Portillo, based on the 1863 edition, which started in 2010. *Peter Waller Collection*

Armoured train. 26 men, bren guns and two three-inch guns are shown on this armoured train provided by the LNER and shown here near Saxmundham in 1940. Class F4 tank locomotive. *Reproduced in* It Can Now Be Revealed *(published in 1945); Peter Waller Collection*

titles could touch a raw nerve. They were discussing the role of a senior civil servant, whom Hurcombe wanted to call 'Railway Control Officer'. Szlumper counselled against this, and in his diary reflects: 'I wonder why every civil servant wants to control something. I suppose it is a natural desire to "spread themselves" in wartime and exercise a brief authority in wartime that they do not possess in peacetime.'

The REC had objected to the appointment of a civil servant as Railway Control Officer, and resented 'putting in charge of the railways someone without railway knowledge'.

Whilst the relationships between railway and civil servants were somewhat strained, at working level and with the armed services, there was effective co-operation and a lot of effort went into improving co-ordination. The railways were disciplined and hierarchical organisations, and performed well once the task was clear. To help this, the army appointed 'rail transport officers' around the country to liaise with stationmasters and control offices in relation to military requirements. The railways followed suit with 'railway liaison officers' appointed to work with the forces, and much was achieved, mostly delegated to local level.

The railways' efforts were prodigious, from the faultless evacuation plans mainly for children from the big cities to the railway steamers that rescued troops from Dunkirk and the trains that took them away from Dover, and the amazing logistical achievement of getting vast numbers of troops and equipment to the south coast ports for D-Day. Between this the railway continued to take people to work and to deliver the goods, while under attack from aircraft. The workshops were turning out everything from tank traps to landing craft as well as rolling stock for use overseas, and many of the regular men had gone off to fight, with many women stepping into the gap they left, particularly those from railway families. As if that wasn't enough, railway staff found time to raise funds to build aircraft, join the Home Guard, act as fire wardens and 'dig for victory' in lineside allotments.

More capacity for war traffic. Capacity was limited by the double track section between Cheltenham and Gloucester shared by GWR and LMS trains. The line was quadrupled in 1941/2 to provide the capacity required, particularly to and from South Wales. The picture shows Lansdown Junction at Cheltenham with its new signal box (still visible). On the left is the line for Kingham and Banbury and to Southampton via Marlborough. *Reproduced in* British Railways in Peace and War *(published in 1944); Peter Waller Collection*

Cold Meece station, Staffordshire. Built in 1941 by the LMS to serve the Royal Ordnance Filling Factory at Swynnerton where the number of staff had risen to 18,500. It had four platforms and was at the end of a new two mile branch from Swynnerton Junction on the Norton Bridge to Stone line. 19 trains daily ran to and from Blythe Bridge, Newchapel and Silverdale. The factory closed in 1958 and trains ceased, with the station being closed in 1959. Neither trains nor station appeared in the public timetable. *Reproduced in* It Can Now Be Revealed *(published in 1945); Peter Waller Collection*

Left: Train of tanks. Larger tanks were too large for the restricted British loading gauge, but trains could carry smaller ones, armoured cars and guns. *Reproduced in* It Can Now Be Revealed *(published in 1945); Peter Waller Collection*

Bomb damage. Bombing caused extensive damage, particularly on the Southern and on the elevated sections of line in South London. Loss of bridges meant loss of signalling, traction current cables and often other services such as water pipes. Engineers worked miracles to restore services within hours of major damage. *Reproduced in* It Can Now Be Revealed *(published in 1945); Peter Waller Collection*

Timetables. In addition to Bradshaw, the Big Four produced their own timetables and the ones shown are the penultimate publications covering the summer of 1947 and just before nationalisation. *Peter Waller Collection*

The government established 'buffer depots' around the country to stockpile supplies in case of invasion or blockade as well as coal dumps in case coal supplies were disrupted. All these were rail connected and the railways had the job of filling them up and, at times, moving supplies between them as well. For a brief period, while the invasion threat seemed imminent, armoured trains were in steam day and night at depots around the country, patrolling lines, protecting vulnerable points and capable of moving rapidly in the event of invasion.

All this was achieved without reorganisation, and by leaving the railway management to the professionals within general directions issued by ministers. At crucial stages of the war, such as the evacuation from Dunkirk, the military were in charge but implementation was still left to the railway managers and the railway staff themselves with decisions taken at a relatively modest (and appropriate) level in the command structure by such individuals as timetable planners, controllers, and locomotive inspectors.

5
British Railways, 1948–94

'We had the best trains in the world, it was only natural that kids took an interest.'
Platform Souls, Nicholas Whittaker, Victor Gollancz, 1995

Nationalisation

In a story of the relationship between government and railways, one might have thought that the biggest milestone was nationalisation. In the event, it was perhaps privatisation that was more significant and established a system of closer control on the detailed management of the railway by government than was ever achieved when the railway was state owned.

Somewhat surprisingly, given the unremitting war pressures on the railway, post-war planning started as early as 1942 when the companies met at the Railway Companies Association, under the chairmanship of Sir Eric Gore-Brown.[131] Their conclusion relating to a financial merger between the railways was rejected, however. While the war was still at its height, the Beveridge report on social insurance and the creation of the NHS was published, while the railways developed plans for a return to private ownership, with the benefits they had sought in the Square Deal campaign of 1938 particularly in relation to ending their common carrier obligations.

At the same time, senior civil servants in the Ministry of War Transport were coming to the conclusion that a return to the position of 1939 would not be satisfactory. The Permanent Secretary, Sir Cyril Hurcombe, suggested that some form of public control board would be needed. The concern was that any functional transport board would be dominated by the railways, which the civil servants did not want.[132]

At senior level the working relationship between the senior civil servant, Sir Cyril Hurcombe, and Sir William Wood,[133] President of the LMS, was good, but the same was not consistently true at working level. Michael Bonavia put this down to a failure to appreciate each other's problems and a 'resentment from time to time among professional railwaymen at receiving instructions from those they considered amateurs. And civil servants sometimes felt that that they were being faced with

---

[131] Colonel Sir Eric Gore-Browne (1885–1964) was a director of the Southern Railway 1930–48, deputy chairman from 1935; chairman from 1944. He remained chairman until the railways were nationalised in 1948. He had a distinguished war record, winning the Croix de Guerre in 1917 and the Distinguished Service Order in 1918. He was a partner, and later director, of Glyn, Mills & Co. bank from 1922 until his death.

[132] *The Four Great Railways*, Michael R Bonavia, David & Charles, 1980.

[133] Sir William Valentine Wood (1883–1959) spent almost all his working life on the railways, initially as an accountant with the Northern Counties Committee in his native Ireland. He worked for the government during the First World War and became the first director of finance when the Ministry of Transport was created in 1919. He returned to railway work on the LMS and became vice president (finance and services). When Josiah Stamp was killed in 1941, Wood was asked to take over as President, a post that he held until the nationalisation of the Railways in 1948. He then worked for five years with the British Transport Commission (BTC).

Electrification of the LNER's Ongar line involved transferring it, along with the Ilford to Woodford line to London Transport to become part of the Central Line. At Epping, a train for West Ruislip connects with the steam shuttle from Ongar worked by a class F5 tank engine which continued to run until fourth rail electrification in 1957.
Marcus Eavis/Online Transport Archive

demands from the Railway Executive Committee without the kind of supporting evidence that their training had led them to expect.'[134] This theme recurs later in our story, but is well described at this relatively early point by Bonavia.

The views of the railwaymen were well expressed by Gilbert Szlumper in his diary in 1944: 'a disastrous course, with a horde of black-coated, stripe-trousered young men, full of theory and playing at trains and lorries when their knowledge of transport was limited to the cost of a season ticket from their home towns to Whitehall'.[135]

Unsurprisingly, the Big Four railways opposed the policy, but left their lobbying a bit late, and were clearly swimming against the tide of public opinion. On 12 October 1946, they published their views on nationalisation in a booklet called *British Railways and the Future*,[136] published from their joint Westminster office at 22 Palace Chambers, where Portcullis House is today.

It was presented as a factual analysis of the railways in 1946, and could have been seen as a 'soft sell' in today's phraseology, but some of the conclusions were hard hitting and showed the railways very unhappy with the prospect of government control. The booklet points to the achievements of the Big Four since their establishment in 1923, and in particular to their proud war record and their role in moving men and supplies, of the Dunkirk evacuation trains, their role in preparing for D-Day and in the production of armaments for the government, saying: 'The Railway Companies believe that their record amply justifies their claim to have met in full their obligation to the public in times of both peace and war.'

Drawing on their own experience, they estimated it took ten years from their creation in 1923 before the economies expected were realised: 'It is a matter of record that the amalgamations under the Railways Act of 1921 involved an administrative upheaval which was much more prolonged and disrupting and far less productive of economies than was anticipated when the Railways Bill of 1921 was introduced.'

This has a striking parallel with the later experience of privatisation, which resulted in a planning hiatus of eight years from 1992 to 2000, including a five-year period when no new rolling stock orders at all were placed (see Chapter 7).

---

[134] *The Four Great Railways*, Michael R Bonavia, David & Charles, 1980.

[135] 25 January 1944 in a speech to the Engineering Industries Association, while he was with the Ministry of Supply. It led to questions in the House and an admonition from his Permanent Secretary. Quoted in *Gilbert Szlumper and Leo Amery of the Southern Railway*, edited by John King, Pen & Sword, 2018.

[136] Held by TNA MT 74/167.

The booklet accepted the need for closer working between the companies, including transferring joint lines to a single operating company, along with operations or ownership of penetrating lines. They also proposed the continuation of the common use of privately owned wagons, introduced as a wartime efficiency measure, but they warned that: 'There is, however, a practical limitation to unification and centralisation. Beyond that limit, simplicity is not found, it is lost. The machine becomes unwieldy, soulless and sluggish and may become unworkable.'

The history of the first fifteen years of nationalisation suggests they were right, and the British Transport Commission appears to have been unmanageable.

The booklet included a tempting list of new projects being promised by the Big Four if they continued without state intervention. This included electrification of the Oxted line, where work was expected to commence 'shortly'. In the event, it was to be another forty-two years before the third rail was energised on this route. However, the Shenfield electrification and Manchester–Sheffield–Wath were also included and these had been started by the LNER and were completed by the newly formed British Railways, while the LNER suburban route to Ongar was electrified by London Transport as part of the Central Line extension, and was later closed by them in 1994. It is now run as a heritage railway.

New hotels planned by the GWR at Swindon, Cardiff, Swansea and Looe were never built, however, nor were the proposed holiday camps developed through the British Transport Commission's ownership of Thomas Cook & Son.

The government was having none of it, however, and in an internal memo, ministry official Mr S S Wilson, the Assistant Secretary responsible for drafting the Bill, and who was closely involved in setting up the British Transport Commission, referred to it as 'a self-commendatory publication of the Four Main Lines …' and judged that: 'The reference on page 16 to £2,000,000,000 as the value of the railway assets presumably is intended as a bargaining point on compensation.'

British Railways and the Future was reported extensively in the press and the *Financial Times*, in particular devoted a lot of space to analysis and comment. It asked why the proposals had not received more support, and reviewed some of the underlying issues, principally around the unresolved conflict between an unregulated road haulage industry operating on a publicly funded infrastructure and the railways having to pay for their track as well as being tightly regulated with their common carrier liabilities and requirement to publish rates. The resulting inherent unprofitability of the railways was seen as making nationalisation inevitable, particularly as traffic was continuing to be lost steadily to road.

The LNER's Track Authority Proposal

While supporting the arguments set out in *British Railways and the Future*, the LNER went much further and published its own document, *The State and the Railways, an Alternative to Nationalisation*, which was sent to the Minister, Alfred Barnes, by its chairman, Sir Ronald Matthews[137] from his office at Marylebone. It was drafted by Michael Bonavia, who was Assistant (Public Liaison) to Sir Charles Newton, Chief General Manager of the LNER at the time.[138]

Referring to it as their 'landlord and tenant scheme,' the LNER's proposal was that the government should buy the track and signalling from the Big Four and lease it back to them at a discounted rate. The railways would continue to maintain the infrastructure. The capital value of the assets would be used by the railways to deal with the backlog of improvements and modernisation projects, while the discounted leaseback rate would allow comparability between road and rail infrastructure costs.

But following a landslide victory for Labour and a manifesto with a clear commitment to nationalise the railways, such a proposal was rejected out of hand. On transport, *Let Us Face The Future: A Declaration of Labour Policy for the Consideration of the Nation*, had said this: '**Public ownership of inland transport**. Co-ordination of transport services by rail, road, air and canal cannot be achieved without unification. And unification without public ownership means a steady struggle with sectional interests or the enthronement of a private monopoly, which would be a menace to the rest of industry.'

The Minister, Alfred Barnes, declined to even meet the LNER Chairman, Sir Ronald Matthews, saying their scheme was 'unworkable.' In the aggressively polite language of the civil servants of the time, his letter concluded: 'In these circumstances, I do not think that I should be justified in talking up your time to discuss the many difficulties …'[139]

Mr S S Wilson's comment in his internal memo was quite clear about the problem with such a proposal: 'The cloven hoof of a subsidy is developed in the LNER pamphlet.'

The Devil's work indeed! It was another decade before subsidy became inevitable and another thirty years before

---

[137] Sir Ronald Matthews (1885–1959) was the final chairman of the LNER, serving from 1938 (when he succeeded William Whitelaw) to nationalisation in 1948. He was knighted in 1934 for political and public services in Sheffield, and was deputy chairman of the Independent Television Authority from 1955.

[138] Michael Robert Bonavia, 1909–99. Following a spell working as an economist for N M Rothschild, he joined the LNER in 1945. Chief Officer New Works, Railway Executive and BTC. British Transport Staff College, Woking, Director of Training & Education, BRB. Chief Officer (Special Duties), BRB. Director, Channel Tunnel. Retired 1974. Your co-author, Chris Austin, was interviewed by Michael Bonavia prior to joining BR as a management trainee in 1967.

[139] Letter from the Minister to Sir Ronald Matthews, 15 October 1946. TNA MT 74/167.

The Liverpool Overhead Railway escaped the net of lines to be nationalised. The elevated line along Liverpool's waterfront opened in 1893 and was Europe's first overhead electric railway, a pioneer of automatic signalling and in the use of escalators. The line closed at the end of 1956, the year in which this photograph of Alexandra Dock station was taken. *Phil Tatt/Online Transport Archive*

Sir Peter Parker[140] articulated the rationale for it as a payment for services that the government wished to retain.

The Minor Railways

The railways to be nationalised were those subject to the Control Order made by the government in 1939 for the duration of the Second World War. It covered the Big Four and London Transport, the joint committees and a number of smaller railways, but many minor railways were omitted. Some like the Edge Hill Light Railway were moribund, others such as the Ffestiniog, barely used. The Liverpool Overhead was separate and locally managed, while others like the Barrington Light Railway in Cambridgeshire were essentially private sidings. The Manchester Ship Canal Railway was a substantial concern with 180 miles of route, while others were going concerns, but quite small: the Easingwold Railway in Yorkshire, just 2½ miles long, was one example. The government resisted all attempts to breach the principle that only those railways subject to the control order should be included in the Bill. The civil servants (probably rightly) took the view that these small concerns were either losing money, or were about to become loss making, and were a distraction to the major task of fusing the railways into a single entity, fully co-ordinated with other means of transport.[141]

The Derwent Valley Railway in Yorkshire had been an important independent line during the Second World War, even though passenger services had ceased back in 1926. It had supplied the airfields in the area with fuel oil, asphalt for runway construction, bombs and timber. More generally, it had delivered coal to the area and had carried local farm produce. It was linked to the LNER at both the York end and at Cliff Common on the Selby to Market Weighton and Driffield line. It hosted the Association of Minor Railway Companies, which included the Easingwold and the North Sunderland Light Railway in Northumberland. The railways were worried that increased wages for staff of the new BR would have the effect of increasing their costs, too. The Derwent Valley tried valiantly to be included in the list of lines to be nationalised because, as an independent railway,

---

[140] Sir Peter Parker (1924–2002) was Chairman of the British Railways Board, 1976–83. We attempt in Chapter XIII of *Holding the Line* to offer a fair appraisal of what he achieved. There we quote from Geoffrey Goodman's obituary of Parker published in *The Guardian* on 1 May 2002: 'one of the outstanding industrial leaders in post-war Britain. Had he continued to run British Rail after 1983, he would – given essential Government financial support – have turned it into the finest railway system in the world … Parker was a prophet in advance of his time. His fertile, artistic, imaginative and, yes sometimes, eccentric brilliance put him well ahead of virtually every other industrial chief in the land.'

[141] Internal memo to SS Wilson, Ministry of Transport. MT 74/94.

Minor railways. Several smaller lines escaped nationalisation in 1948, including the Derwent Valley Light Railway from the Layerthorpe station (shown here) at York to Cliffe Common on the York to Market Weighton line. Despite pleas to be included the DVLR was not but managed to survive in a truncated form until 1981.
John McCann/Online Transport Archive

it suffered from the charging system in place, which provided for a Derwent Valley add-on to the LNER rates to the junction points at either end of the line, so that rates would be higher for DVLR customers than for others served by the nearby BR goods stations. Not for the last time, the method of cost allocation worked against branch line economics when the railway was split and not treated as a network.

The request was declined, although the civil servant involved, S S Wilson, again suggested that they might want to get the LNER to buy them out prior to the Act coming into force, and went so far as to suggest that their local MP could sponsor an amendment to the Bill at committee stage to seek to include the railway.

In the event, the railway remained independent for a remarkably long period, and while the line was progressively cut back, it clung on until finally closed in 1981. A heritage railway operates over a short part of the line, based at Murton Park.

In November 1948, a review was undertaken by Railway Executive staff for the British Transport Commission, looking in detail at the railways not covered by the 1947 Act (342 miles in total), and none was recommended for inclusion within the BR portfolio.[142] They are listed in Appendix 7.

The Transport Act, 1947, had 128 clauses and fifteen schedules, and was debated extensively, with 18¼ hours of the time of the House being taken up in the Commons second reading debate and 77½ hours spent in committee. The government applied the guillotine to ensure the implementation date of 1 January 1948 was maintained, including (unusually for the time), in committee where some thirty-seven clauses remained undebated.

---

[142] TNA AN/88/13.

The scale of the changes proposed were huge, and proved to be quite unmanageable. Sixty railway undertakings were transferred to public ownership, comprising 52,000 miles of track, 20,000 locomotives, 1.23 million wagons, 45,000 passenger coaches, 25,000 horse-drawn vehicles and 50,000 houses. Seventy hotels were transferred along with 1,640 miles of canals and waterways and 100 ships grossing 150,000 tons. Some 34,000 commercial lorries were to pass into the hands of the Commission and staff numbers would total 692,000.[143]

All of this would change ownership in a single day, just five months after the Bill had received Royal Assent. Compare this with privatisation almost fifty years later, where it took nearly two years between letting the first franchise (SWT in February 1996) to completion of the programme with the sale of Railfreight Distribution in November 1997.

In making the case for nationalisation, the Labour government made the same mistake that the Conservatives did in proposing privatisation in the early 1990s. To soften up the electorate and bolster their case, they talked down the railways and their staff and depressed morale as well as the reputation of the railway as a whole. The Chancellor, Hugh Dalton,[144] in introducing the second reading of the Railways Bill on 17 December 1946, revealed a contempt for the railways that still stands as a memorial of shame today. To be fair to Dalton, he was dealing with Conservative claims that compensation to shareholders was inadequate, and making the case for nationalising the railways on the basis that they could not survive in competition with an uncontrolled road network, but his comments still rankle.

The railways had been, he said, 'sheltered for many years by legislative and administrative action'. He went on to add: 'Let us look at the railway system now. It is in very poor shape. Partly that is due to the strain of six years of war; partly, but not wholly. Those dingy railway stations, those miserable, unprepossessing restaurants, all the out-of-date apparatus for sleeping and eating, make one ashamed as an Englishman when one is travelling abroad and sees how well the thing is done in Continental Europe, Western Europe, in Sweden and France. [An Hon. Member: 'In Russia.'] We must get our geography right. I said 'Western Europe'. Still more do we feel that if we go to America and Canada. One feels very much ashamed in Canada of this branch of private enterprise in the old country. That is one reason why the tourist traffic is not so easily attracted here. The railways are in very poor physical shape.'[145]

And then the final twist of the knife: 'I am saying that this railway system of ours is a very poor bag of physical assets. The permanent way is badly worn. The rolling stock is in a state of great dilapidation. The railways are a disgrace to the country. The railway stations and their equipment are a disgrace to the country. [Interruption]. We are talking about the values of these things and I am saying that they are a pretty poor bag of physical assets.'

Of course, the railways were looking run-down and tired in 1946, but that was because they had been under government control during wartime for seven years,

---

[143] *Hansard*, third reading debate, 5 May 1947, vol. 437, col. 36.

[144] Hugh Dalton (Edward Hugh John Neale Dalton, Lord Dalton) (1887–1962) was a Labour politician who had served in Churchill's wartime coalition as Minister of Economic Warfare and founded the Special Operations Executive. He was MP for Peckham, 1924–29, and Bishop Auckland, 1929–31 and from 1935 to 1959. He was Chancellor of the Exchequer, 1945–47, resigning in 1947 over a budget leak to an evening newspaper that was published before Dalton began his speech. That leak established an informal Whitehall rule that no unauthorised domestic policy revelation was more serious than a budget leak.

As Martin Kettle reported in *The Guardian* on 20 March 2013, following a major political row over leaked budget proposals then: 'The Dalton leak came when the chancellor, on his way into the Commons chamber before the budget in November 1947, indiscreetly told the Star's John Carvel, whose son Robert and grandson John were both distinguished political journalists: "No more on tobacco; a penny on beer; something on dogs and pools but not on horses; increase in purchase tax, but only on articles now taxable; profits tax doubled." Carvel's story, with its market-sensitive information, was on the streets approximately 20 minutes before Dalton began speaking in the Commons.

'Initially, it looked as if Dalton would not suffer for his indiscretion, though he immediately offered his resignation to the prime minister at the time, Clement Attlee. Attlee, who rarely gave interviews and never briefed the press, was astounded at what had happened. "Talked to the press?" he said when his adviser Francis Williams explained the facts to him. "Why on Earth did he want to talk to the press?"

'On the day after the budget, Dalton apologised to the Commons for his "grave indiscretion". Winston Churchill, then leader of the opposition, offered him sympathy and commended Dalton's "very frank manner". Later in the evening, however, Dalton offered his resignation again, and this time Attlee accepted it. Dalton was replaced by Sir Stafford Cripps.

'In his retirement, Attlee was more forthcoming about the incident. "Perfect ass," he said of Dalton in a Granada TV interview. "His trouble was that he would talk. He always liked to have a secret to confide to somebody else to please him. He did it once too often."

'The Dalton leak would probably never have happened but for two unusual factors. The first was that MPs were still sitting in the House of Lords chamber in 1947 because the House of Commons, badly bombed in the wartime blitz, was still being rebuilt. As a result the chancellor had to walk past lobby journalists on the way to the Lords. The second was that Dalton's political minder, Douglas Jay, who would normally have been on hand to fend off the journalist, had been sent on ahead to check that there was a glass of water at the dispatch box for Dalton during his speech.'

Dalton returned to the Cabinet in 1948 as Chancellor of the Duchy of Lancaster. After the 1950 general election he was made Minister of Town and Country Planning (later expanded to Local Government and Planning). He was awarded a peerage in the January 1960 New Year's honours list.

[145] *Hansard*, vol. 431, col. 1809.

subject to widespread damage from aerial bombardment, underinvested and inadequately funded during a period of austerity. But the description would have struck a chord with rail users of the time, and 1946 had been a record year for passenger numbers as people enjoyed their new freedom, while petrol remained on ration and motoring was expensive.

The structure established in 1948 was destined to last only eight years. The weakness was that the government attempted at one go to nationalise and co-ordinate the entire transport system of Britain. It was a massive undertaking but there was no strategy to define the objectives, or what 'integration' meant in practice. The structure chosen continued the modal separation reflected in the 'Executives' set up for railways, road passenger, road haulage, docks and inland waterways, London transport, and hotels. While the docks and catering had been separated from the railways that owned them before, the principal areas where useful change might have occurred, rail and road, remained separately managed. The world's largest fleet of ferries remained in railway ownership, as did the packet ports of Newhaven, Folkestone, Harwich and Holyhead.

British Transport Commission

The BTC was one of the largest employers in the country with a total at the start of 649,000 railway staff. It was an unmanageable behemoth and, again, the objective in creating it had been to deliver on the manifesto pledge on 'nationalisation of the means of production and distribution', while the requirement of 'integration' had not been defined, nor had the role of the railway. The government also wanted to see representation of the trades unions on the boards of the new organisations. So, the objectives were several and varied, but not generally related to the needs of the passenger or the freight customer.

At the same time, the structure of the organisation was complicated and resulted in many points of conflict, not just between government and BTC, but also between BTC and the Railway Executive and the Executive and the railway regions. In theory, the key policy decisions were made by the Executive and the regional chief officers were not intended to be general managers of their patch, but administrators working within the framework set by the Executive. Again, the separation of responsibilities between the Executive and the BTC was also unclear.

The Board of the BTC was dominated by Sir Cyril Hurcomb, who was a former civil servant and an excellent administrator with a strong personality, but with little practical experience in running transport undertakings, and supported by a relatively weak board that he dominated. Most of the experienced railway managers went to the Railway Executive, chaired by Sir Eustace Missenden,[146] previously Chairman of the Southern Railway.

With such complexity, conflicting objectives and with no clear strategic objectives, the arrangement could not succeed and therefore did not survive. The incoming Conservative government of 1951 was elected on a pledge to denationalise road transport.[147] The objective behind the new Transport Act, 1953, was to provide for competition and the pursuit of 'integration' ceased. It was a radical reversal of the policy of just six years beforehand, and again was driven by political imperatives and economic theory rather than by the rapidly changing nature of the market for both inland freight and passenger movement.

A main plank of the policy was the de-nationalisation of road haulage, which took some time as buyers proved to be reluctant, reflecting the lack of understanding by government of the nature of the market and how it was served. A similar lack of understanding was evident fifty years later when another Conservative government divided rail freight operations between five companies for sale, only to see four of them bought and combined as EWS. Their enthusiasm for competition was not shared by the market at the time, and ignored the real competition from road haulage, whose infrastructure was provided at public expense.

The 1953 Act saw the end of the Railway Executive, and the conflicts and jostling for authority between the Executive and the Commission stopped, but were replaced by tensions between the regions and the Commission, with the latter nominally in control of policy and the former there to run the railway. The regions became much more powerful, partly because the Commission had more on its plate than it could reasonably handle, and partly because the regional structure fitted well with the 'command and control' structure that both the Big Four and BR adopted for the management of the railway. It also reflected the calibre of many of the general managers of the period and the skills and experience gained through six years of war. The principal problem was that it failed to bring together income and costs at any level, other than the national level of BR as a whole.

The Big Four were financially discrete, with an army of

---

[146] Sir Eustace Missenden (1886–1973) was a career railwayman who left school at the age of 13 to work as a clerk on the South Eastern and Chatham Railway. His father had been a stationmaster on the South Eastern Railway. After Grouping he remained with the Southern Railway, rising to be Docks and Marine Manager and in 1941 General Manager. With the passing of the Transport Act, 1947, Missenden became the first Chairman of the Railway Executive later that year, accountable to the British Transport Commission for the running of British Railways. In 1949 BR named locomotive numbered 34090 *Sir Eustace Missenden Southern Railway* after him and his former company.

[147] The Conservative manifesto said: 'publicly-owned rail and road transport will be reorganised into regional groups of workable size. Private road hauliers will be given the chance to return to business and private lorries will no longer be crippled by the twenty-five mile limit.'

Hump shunting. Tinsley Yard near Sheffield was the most up to date yard in Britain when built in 1965, combining the work of several other local yards. Movements were controlled from the tower in the picture and wagons were slowed to the correct speed by the Dowty retarders, which the 16t mineral wagon is just passing over.
John Meredith/Online Transport Archive

Railway Clearing House clerks to divide revenue according to mileage so that each company could produce a profit and loss account. But with a single operator after nationalisation, the revenue allocation function was no longer required, and the functions of the RCH were transferred to the BTC in 1954. As a consequence, it was no longer possible to match revenue and costs in a meaningful way. So revenue taken in Manchester for a journey to Plymouth would all accrue to the London Midland region, but the costs, at least from Bristol to Plymouth, would be largely borne by the Western region. Only in 1990 was this issue resolved by Sir Robert Reid, when his sector management structure was fully implemented (see below).

The principal task during this period was the belated decision by the Commission to replace steam with electric and diesel traction, and to invest in rolling stock renewal, both wagons and carriages, as well as signalling, stations and some electrification (see Chapter 10). This came together in the modernisation plan of 1955,[148] and while radical in some ways, in others it perpetuated a method of operation that was already obsolete, with investment in branch lines that within a decade had been closed, and in short wheelbase, low-capacity wagons and marshalling yards. Also criticised were the decisions by BTC at this time to standardise on the vacuum brake and the continued use of steam heat in the new carriages being built, and the consequent need to retain steam heat boilers on diesel locomotives with second men to operate them. There is no doubt that much of the investment was misdirected, and this was highlighted in a report of the House of Commons Select Committee on Nationalised Industries, *British Railways in 1960*, and immediately after that, the government set up their own inquiry into the way the Commission was managing the railways, under the industrialist Sir Ivan Stedeford,[149] which included Dr Richard Beeching[150] as a member, as well as the accountant Henry Benson,[151] whose 1962 report to Stormont recommended

---

[148] *Modernisation and Re-equipment of British Railways*, British Transport Commission, 1955.

[149] Sir Ivan Stedeford (1897–1975) had a background in the motor industry, having set up a dealership in Birmingham specialising in sports cars and limousines after returning from service in the First World War with the Royal Naval Air Service. Later he became chairman and managing director of Tube Investments. The Stedeford Committee was described as 'The Special Advisory Committee to examine structure, finance and working of organisations controlled by British Transport Commission'.

[150] Dr Richard Beeching (Lord Beeching from 1965) (1913–85) was chairman of the British Railways Board 1961–65, when the incoming Labour government declined to renew his appointment. He returned to ICI, his former employer.

From 1963 to 1965, the North Eastern Region summer timetable with its distinctive orange covers featured a Deltic (class 55) locomotive which by then was providing most of the power for East Coast Main Line services. The North Eastern Region was merged with the Eastern Region in 1967, only to be split again when the Anglia Region was created 20 years later. *Peter Waller Collection*

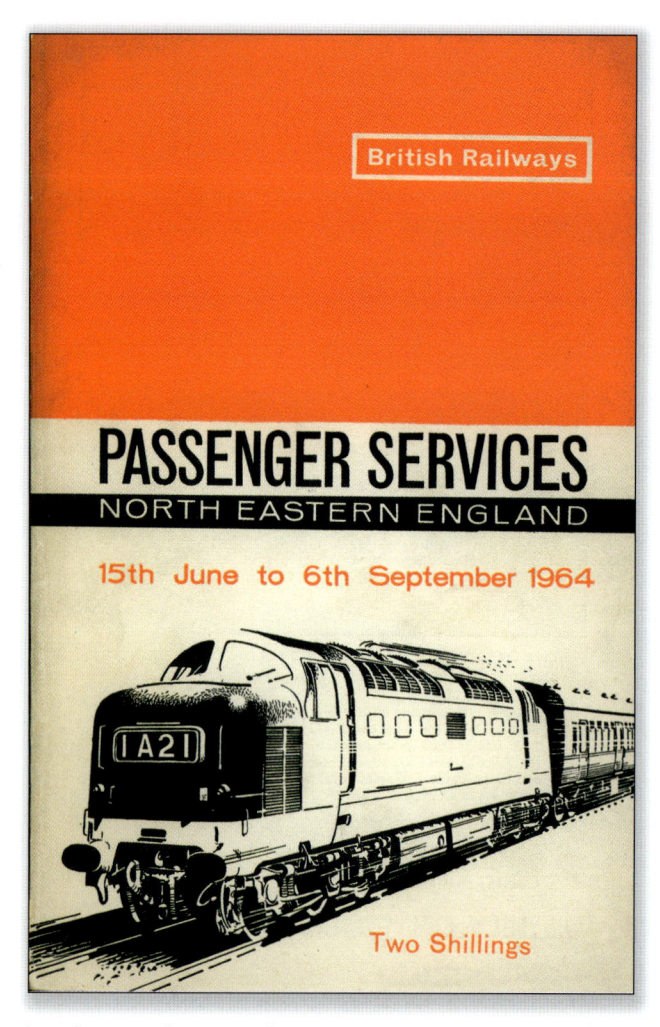

the closure of much of the rail network operated by the Ulster Transport Authority. The Committee's secretary was David Serpell,[152] who produced his own ill-fated report on BR network size options in 1982.

This was a low point in relationships between railway managers and government. The Commission's plans failed to tackle the cost base of the railway, while ill-conceived investment plans of 1955 added to the interest burdens without producing the cost savings or revenue benefits required to meet the government's financial objectives.

Following a critical select committee report, the formation of the Stedeford Committee marked a complete loss of faith in railway management, and resulted in the replacement of the Commission by the British Railways Board with Beeching as chairman, which had far-reaching consequences. The railway managers were not to be trusted again by the civil servants for another twenty-five years until Sir Robert Reid[153] showed that the railway could manage its own financial objectives properly again.

Stewart Joy was an abrasive Australian who joined BR as the Board's Chief Economist in 1968, having worked as a consultant to the Ministry of Transport, and after writing his doctoral thesis for the London School of Economics on the issue of track costs. He was scathing about the management of the British Transport Commission and its failure both to grasp the cost problem, and to do anything effective about it. In particular, he was critical of the Modernisation Plan and the huge investment in diesel multiple units for branch lines where, even after the investment, revenue covered only half the direct movement costs of the trains, without providing for infrastructure costs or depreciation.[154]

---

[151] Henry Benson (1909–95) (Lord Benson from 1981) was born and educated in Johannesburg, South Africa. He worked for Coopers and Lybrand Chartered Accountants until 1975, having joined in 1926. In addition to his membership of the Stedeford Committee, he was appointed in 1962 by the Minister of Commerce, Northern Ireland, on Beeching's recommendation 'to investigate position of railways, to make recommendations about their future, and to report on effect which recommendations will have on transport system of Ulster Transport Authority'. In 1963 Benson submitted his report, which recommended closing all railways in Northern Ireland except the Belfast commuter lines to Bangor, County Down and Larne and the main line between Belfast and the Republic of Ireland, and the reduction of the main line between Portadown and the Republic to single track.

[152] Sir David Serpell (1911–2008) joined the Ministry of Transport in 1960 as Deputy Secretary responsible for railways and roads; Permanent Secretary, 1968–72; member of the British Railways Board, 1974–82. Chairman of the report bearing his name in 1982. See *Holding the Line*, Chapter XII.

[153] Sir Robert (Bob) Reid (1921–93) was a career railwayman who rose to become Chairman of the British Railways Board from 1983 to 1990, succeeding Sir Peter Parker. He joined the LNER as a traffic apprentice in 1947, having seen war service as a captain in the Royal Tank Regiment. His career took him to York as Goods Agent in 1958; to Glasgow as Assistant District Goods Manager in 1960; he was a District Passenger Manager in 1961; Divisional Commercial Manager, 1963; Planning Manager, Scottish Region, 1967; Divisional Manager, Doncaster, 1968; Deputy General Manager, Eastern Region, back in York, 1972; General Manager, Southern Region, 1974–76. At the British Railways Board he was Executive Member for Marketing, 1977–80; Chief Executive (Railways), 1980–83; a Vice-Chairman, 1983. Director: British Transport Hotels Ltd, 1977–83; Chairman, Nationalised Industries Chairmen's Group, 1987–88; President, European Community Railways Directors General, 1988–89, and President of the Chartered Institute of Transport, 1982–83. His achievements included the successful sector management reorganisation of the railways business and establishing a rapport with Conservative ministers by convincing them that under his leadership BR could accept cash limits and reduce costs. His reward was approval for East Coast Main Line electrification, completed in 1991.

[154] Stewart Joy, *The Train that Ran Away*, 1973.

The Western Region winter 1961/62 timetable in its brown cover (summer timetables were cream – the Western clung to their traditions!). This timetable was the last before the big boundary changes of 1962 which transferred the West Midlands services to the London Midland Region and the Southern's services over the 'withered arm' in Devon and Cornwall to the Western. September 11 1961 also saw the closure of the Midland & South Western Junction line from Andoversford Junction near Cheltenham to Andover Junction in Hampshire which carried trains from Cheltenham to Southampton. *Peter Waller Collection*

Similarly, on the freight side investment continued in traditional short-wheelbase wagons and no attempt was made to get out of unprofitable traffic, or to price up.

The Beeching Whirlwind

Dr Richard Beeching first appears in our story when he joins the Stedeford Committee in 1960. He is best remembered for the branch line closures included in his first report, *The Reshaping of British Railways*, published in 1963, and we covered this and an assessment of his contribution to the development of the railway in our first book, *Holding the Line*, in 2012. In the context of the relationship between railway and government though, his role is rather different. He was the first to bring a business approach to railway management and to identify the strong points of the railway (InterCity and trainload freight) as well as identifying the financially less successful areas (rural lines and commuter services outside London as well as the general freight operation that was already (in the early 1960s) being rapidly overtaken by a new approach to logistics that did not involve rail haulage at all.

In terms of the relationship with government, he had the advantage of being the appointment of the Transport Minister, rather than being a career railwayman, and he was focused on delivering the government's rather narrow financial objectives, uncluttered by notions of public service. To be fair to Beeching, he did, in the report, identify that there might be other social objectives that the railway performed (like relief of traffic congestion in major cities outside London) and that these could be identified and paid for by local or central government, but not by BR if it was to be held to its financial targets.

Not only was Beeching the government's man, but the new organisation, the British Railways Board, was also a creation of government, stemming from the work of the Stedeford Committee, and together this should have been the opportunity for a new era of understanding and co-operation between the industry and government. But this did not happen, even though Beeching worked quickly to produce his report and to implement it. The first passenger closure, the lines to Wetherby, took place in January 1964, just ten months after publication of the report, and others quickly followed. But in October 1964, there was a change of government with a manifesto commitment to 'halt major

In November 1964, the BRB agreed to a series of proposals on corporate identity which were illustrated at an exhibition opened in January 1965 by Dr Beeching. A new corporate identity was the start of the long process of changing the image of the industry. *Crécy Archive*

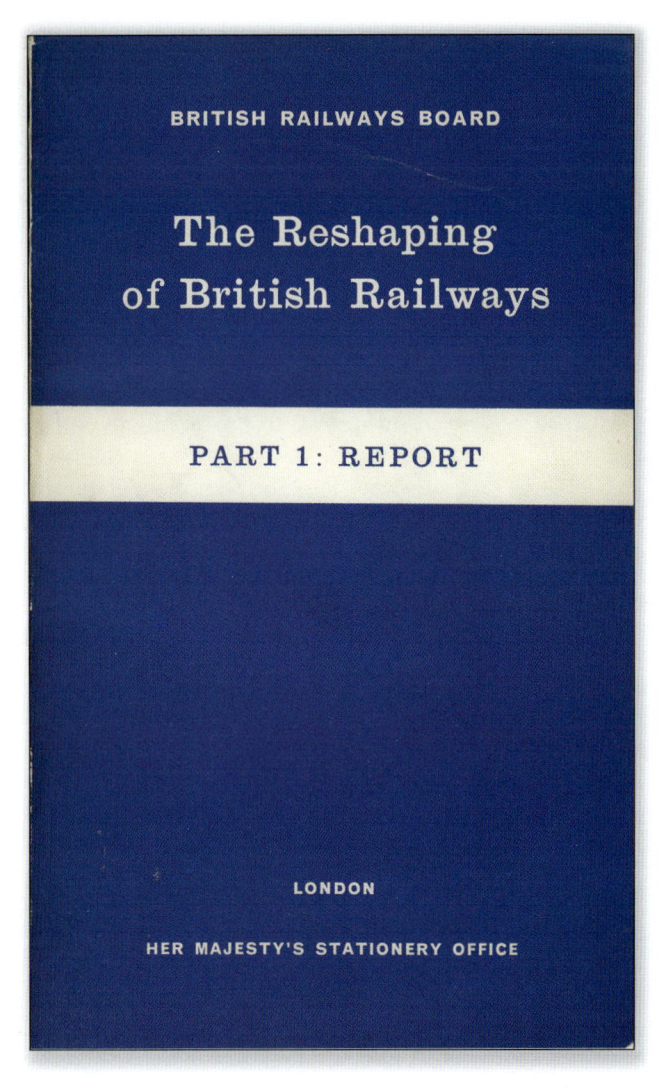

Beeching Report. This report from 1963 changed the way the railway was run and put it on a business footing for the first time since 1948. Remembered now for the maps of line and station closures, it also laid the foundations for Inter City travel and equipped rail freight to become part of the logistics chain. *Peter Waller Collection*

rail closures'.[155] This was effectively abandoned within weeks of the election when the Transport Minister, Tom Fraser,[156] told the House of Commons that he could not reverse the closure decisions taken by Ernest Marples,[157] his Conservative predecessor.[158]

The incoming Labour administration declined to renew Beeching's contract and he left the BR chairmanship in 1965.

He had made some irreversible changes at BR though, and from then on, the railway's management began to see itself more as a business and less as a deficit-funded public service. After the failure of the Transport Commission to manage the money, the Ministry involved themselves much more closely in every aspect of railway planning and finance, with its own economists, many of whom, like Stewart Joy, were single-minded in their focus on the financial effects, rather than the wider social and economic outputs the railway was expected to deliver.

Joy was a hawk in these matters, and for him, Beeching had failed, because his 'prognoses were hopelessly optimistic'.[159] The analysis of the report 'was lacking in arithmetic, logic and a sense of priorities'. 'The superficiality of the Beeching Report,' he wrote, 'was to cost BR and the country a lot in wasted resources in the following years.'

---

[155] 'Labour will draw up a national plan for transport covering the national networks of road, rail and canal communications, properly co-ordinated with air, coastal shipping and port services. The new regional authorities will be asked to draw up transport plans for their own areas. While these are being prepared, major rail closures will be halted. *1964 Labour Party Election Manifesto 'The New Britain'*.

[156] Tom Fraser (1911–88), Labour MP for Hamilton, 1943–67; junior minister at the Scottish Office, 1945–51, shadow Secretary of State for Scotland in opposition, then Minister of Transport, 1964–65. He left school at 14 when he began work as miner, working underground until his entry to Parliament. His two legacies as Transport Minister were the 70mph speed limit on motorways, and less happily, authorising the closure of 1,071 miles of railway lines. See *Holding the Line*, particularly Chapter IV. In May 1967 he resigned from Parliament to become chairman of the North of Scotland Hydro-Electric Board.

[157] Alfred Ernest Marples (1907–78), Conservative MP for Wallasey 1945–74, was one of the most colourful and controversial politicians of the twentieth century. Revelations of his private life and sexual proclivities, which did not see the light of day until January 2020, were even more sensational than any examination of his political career. Until then Marples was remembered chiefly as the Postmaster-General who introduced Premium Bonds and the Transport Minister who appointed Dr Beeching as chairman of the British Railways Board with the clear remit to carry out a massive series of line closures. As we recount in Chapter III of *Holding the Line*, allegations of conflicts of interest blighted, but did not destroy, his ministerial career, and the account of his overnight flit to France on the Night Ferry pursued by the Inland Revenue for tax fraud reads like an episode from one of Jeffrey Archer's more racy novels. All of this was put into the shade by the veteran investigative reporter Tom Mangold (described by *The Times* in August 2009 as 'the doyen of broadcasting reporters'), who published in the *Mail Online* on 30 January 2020 an account of the evidence given to Lord Denning in July 1963 by a woman who called herself variously 'Mrs Ann Bailey' and 'Mrs Smith' shortly before he concluded his report into the security risks posed by Christine Keeler's relationships with War Minister John Profumo and Yevgeny Ivanov, a Russian spy. Mrs Bailey was a voluntary witness who described in lurid detail the arrangement between Marples and her. She was paid to dress him in women's clothing and beat him. She said she was a full-time prostitute; Marples' sexual preferences were unusual 'with whipping the least extreme'. Mangold's source was Thomas Critchley, Denning's secretary, who kept a diary that had been read by Mangold. All of this was kept out of Denning's report on the Profumo scandal, and remains locked up in the Cabinet Office.

[158] *Hansard*, Col. 196, 4 November 1964.

[159] Joy, op. cit.

But Joy also blamed government for their acceptance of deficit grants for so long, which avoided the need for BR to confront the basic underlying macro-economic problem that, even if all the savings proposed in the Reshaping Report had been achieved, BR would still have been about £70 million short of breaking even. The other principal criticism of government was on closures, where he concluded that: 'With the unthinking agreement of BR, the Government had the best of both worlds. The 1962 Act left the onus on BR to prove that particular loss-making services were not in the public interest ... and the Government could then act as the protector of the public interest by refusing the application.'[160] At the end of the day, the deficit was a stick with which to beat BR.

These problems were the source of great tension between BR, the civil servants and ministers. The latter could not understand how, with all the investment, debt write-offs and deficit financing, BR could still not become profitable. Even though the traffic costing service had been established as long ago as 1951, and Beeching had brought in his own experts, there was no clarity on why or where the money was being lost. Indeed, fifteen years later, the problem remained, and the driving force behind Sir Robert Reid's establishment of the five business sectors prior to privatisation was the fact that the costs only came together on his desk on the basis of regional accounting. Nobody below the Chief Executive had the full picture or could compare costs and revenue.

Given that his effective time in office was only three years, Beeching made a number of radical changes very quickly, apart from the closure of branch and cross-country lines. The cultural change he brought ran deep through the industry and had a lasting effect, as did his focus on the growth businesses of intercity travel, bulk freight and a more effective pricing policy for both. But with 20 per cent of BR's costs being met by government, BR was still no nearer becoming the commercial enterprise that everyone assumed it should become, and consequently the relationship with civil servants was uncomfortably close, and BR was keen to restore its independence when the 1968 Transport Act put grant aid for passenger lines in place of deficit financing.

Beeching's departure in 1965 also illustrates the result of what happens when government is unclear on what it wants, and is focused on tomorrow's headlines than on the long-term policy they are pursuing. Tom Fraser, as minister, had been criticised by Labour MPs and unions for the continuing closures, which had become unpopular, and by his failure to address the question of a co-ordinated transport policy. Beeching was prepared to undertake a study that would look at comparative costs of road, rail and internal air services as a prelude to preparing an integrated policy. In fact, BR had undertaken some work on comparative road and rail costs as part of its work for the Trunk Routes study that did indeed show that road haulage was not meeting the costs it imposed on the road network. This brought in opposition from the road transport unions and particularly from Frank Cousins,[161] who claimed to have 'sacked' Beeching,[162] and the Cabinet agreed that Lord Hinton[163] should undertake the study in February 1965, while Beeching left BR after four years to return to ICI in June 1965. Lord Hinton's reports were never published and no further moves toward transport integration were taken until Barbara Castle's white paper, while the road haulage industry continued to use a rapidly improving road network subsidised by the taxpayer, without scrutiny.

Whilst Beeching recognised the external value of suburban railways outside London, realising that they could not be funded by BR, it was Castle who both found a way to recognise this value through grant aid payments for individual lines, as well as creating the 'magnificent seven' passenger transport executives that were able to invest in local rail services and provide integrated public transport in the areas they covered. Initiated by a Labour minister, it was the Conservative John Peyton who consolidated the line grants into the 'public service obligation' grant that ensured that government continued to support the benefits that the railway brought that could not be captured in the fare box. The pretence that the railway, with all its historic obligations and the costs of its own infrastructure, could be profitable in a skewed transport market finally ended in 1974.

The railway after Beeching and with the end of steam was a much simpler network to manage and many supervisory and management functions were combined, with area managers replacing stationmasters at individual stations and many of the district offices being combined in larger divisions. In 1971 a report was produced by BR with consultants McKinsey on a new and streamlined 'field' organisation designed to accelerate this process, simplify management and to save costs. Preparations were extensive and thorough, and new offices were built to house the new organisation, some of which still exist at railway centres like Woking. In the event, it was strongly opposed by the clerical union the TSSA and agreement

---

[160] Ditto.

[161] Frank Cousins (1904–86) General Secretary of the Transport & General Workers Union 1956–69, except for brief period between 1964 and 1966 when he served as Minister of Technology in Harold Wilson's first Labour government. A seat in the House of Commons was found for him in Nuneaton when the incumbent was given a peerage, but he found Parliament uncongenial and returned to his old job in the T&GWU in 1966, having resigned from the Commons.

[162] Quoted in Gourvish, *British Railways 1948–1973*.

[163] Christopher Hinton, Baron Hinton of Bankside OM KBE FRS FREng (1901–83) was a British nuclear engineer, and supervisor of the construction of Calder Hall, the world's first large-scale commercial nuclear power station. He had left school at 16 to become an engineering apprentice at the Great Western Railway in Swindon. He was appointed to the House of Lords in 1965. He was a special adviser to the Ministry of Transport on transport planning.

Stations became very run down in the post-Beeching period. Here at West Hampstead Midland (now West Hampstead Thameslink), the timber structure has long gone, and been replaced with a light, airy new building on the opposite side of the line with a staffed ticket office and gateline, with step free access to platforms, and good information about connections to London Overground, as well as the Jubilee Line at this major north London interchange. The undergrowth on the platform has gone too. *Christopher Austin*

King's Lynn with the arrival of a train from Hunstanton. Dark and gloomy by day, the station was little better at night as it was still lit by gas when this picture was taken in 1965. *Christopher Austin*

could not be reached. The decision was taken in 1975 not to proceed but to continue consolidation on a piecemeal basis. The exercise had been a costly one, a huge diversion for management of the industry and unsettling for staff, particularly management, supervisory and clerical staff. Its failure was another signal for ministers and officials in government that BR was not able to manage its costs and administration effectively, although even here, the minister, Fred Mulley, had intervened to call for stability, stirred to action by his Sheffield Park constituents, who were unhappy that the new administrative headquarters were to be at York rather than Sheffield.

Despite the positive developments of Beeching's approach to InterCity and freight, the railway of the mid and late 1960s was a dismal place, dark and unwelcoming, rather dirty, with low morale among the rapidly declining staff numbers. At every depot and works, lines of rusting steam locomotives awaited scrapping, while goods sidings were full of surplus wagons awaiting disposal. Staff were withdrawn from stations, leaving gaunt old buildings, boarded up and often vandalised. Station canopies made platforms dark and rather threatening as they either had no glazing, or it had been blackened by the locomotive smoke of years. Many were demolished, leaving the stations bleak and windswept with flimsy bus shelters giving little shelter from the elements. A big problem with unstaffed stations was lack of information on train running, although basic long-line public address systems, often giving information from a nearby signal box, made an appearance from an early stage.

The contrast with today's stations could not be more stark. Not only are they lighter and more welcoming, but most will have real-time information on train running, good lighting, CCTV coverage, tactile surfaces and other assistance for visually impaired passengers. They will probably have cycle storage, and will have local maps to help passengers find onward bus connections or guide them to their destination on foot. Much of this was started by BR, but it has to be acknowledged that more has been done in the last twenty years than was done before, particularly with local station adoption, flower beds, cleaning and supervision by volunteers showing clearly that someone cares about the station and the local community. Government has consistently supported community rail partnerships and station adoption but the work itself is down to volunteers and the support they get from train operating companies and the dedicated staff that work for them.

BR Chairmen

There were fourteen chairmen of British Railways during its half century of existence, and of these, Richard Marsh[164] had a unique insight, having been Minister of Transport in the Wilson government and then BR Chairman a decade later. His views are therefore particularly relevant in the context of the relationship between a minister and a nationalised industry. In Marsh's view the role was similar, in that neither were experts but had to rely on advice from those that were, and the chairman's most important task was to choose the right people.

The minister's powers, he said, were quite limited – the power to hire the chairman and board members (but not to fire the latter), and to approve or reject the board's capital investment programme and its research and development budget. In theory, therefore, the minister should have no involvement with the running of the railway, but political pressures and the responsibilities of the Permanent Secretary as Accounting Officer meant that, in practice that was not possible. In the case of BR, which was loss making throughout his period as chairman, 'a strange situation arises, therefore, involving a major source of conflict … What, under one set of statutes, seems to the board political interference is, from the Permanent Secretary's viewpoint, the legitimate discharge of his responsibilities to Parliament.'[165]

Marsh's conclusion was that 'no Government has ever been able to provide a long-term consistent policy which would enable Government and the nationalised industries to work together to achieve sensible long-term policies. Without consistent policies it is impossible for large industrial organisations to work efficiently.'

His relationship with his first (Conservative) Transport minister, John Peyton,[166] was good, as was evident twenty years later when, both in the House of Lords, they worked together on an amendment to the Railways Bill that would have allowed BR to bid for franchises. However, following the 1974 election and Labour's return to government, Fred Mulley[167] replaced Peyton, and relationships soured to the point at which Marsh was being sidelined by both ministers and civil servants. His term of office ended in dissatisfaction and disappointment, but his analysis of the problems is quite perceptive.

His successor, Peter Parker, adopted a very different approach as a newcomer, with vast business experience and the ability to enthuse and inspire everyone he came into contact with. He has perhaps left the clearest account[168] of relationships between nationalised industries and government. In his own inimitable way he identified the problem succinctly: 'Was the Minister the champion of the industry, jousting for it in the government, or was he its scourge, championing the taxpayer? Whose side was he on? And was the chairman of the board of the industry (say mines or railways) the agent of his political master, or was he in business, competing, taking risks in the market place in research and development?'

Parker identified this as the key weakness in the industrial policy of Britain: 'the unfruitful coupling of politics and industry'.

When Parker became BR Chairman in 1976, his first meeting with his Secretary of State, Tony Crosland,[169] highlighted this dichotomy. Crosland had produced an integrated transport green paper, but Parker could not accept it as it implied a reduced railway. It was, he said a 'depressing, sophisticated muddle, eventually published in orange covers and something of an embarrassment all round'.

---

[164] Richard Marsh (1928–2011) was Labour MP for Greenwich (1959–71), and succeeded Barbara Castle as Minister for Transport in 1968, serving until 1970. In 1971 he was appointed by the Conservative government as Chairman of British Rail, the job he held until 1976. He joined the House of Lords as Lord Marsh in 1981 and sat as an independent cross-bencher.

[165] *Off the Rails*, Richard Marsh, Weidenfeld & Nicolson, 1978.

[166] John Peyton, Lord Peyton of Yeovil (1919–2006), Minister of Transport (later renamed Minister of Transport Industries in the Department of the Environment) from 1970 to 1974. Conservative MP for Yeovil, 1951–83. As Transport Minister, he refused to approve the plans for swingeing cuts in the rail network proposed in his department's 'Blue Paper' in 1972 (leaked to the *Sunday Times* by a civil servant) and gave instructions that the network should remain at its 1974 level. When in the Lords in 1993, he opposed railway privatisation and successfully proposed an amendment to the Railways Bill that British Rail should be permitted to bid for franchises, which was subsequently overturned in the Commons.

[167] Fred Mulley (1918–95), Labour MP for Sheffield Park, 1950–83. He was twice Minister of Transport, 1969–70 and 1974–75, and held various other ministerial positions in the Labour governments in 1964–70 and 1974–79.

[168] *For Starters*, Sir Peter Parker, Jonathan Cape, 1989.

[169] Anthony Crosland (1918–77), Labour MP for South Gloucestershire, 1950–55; Grimsby 1959–77. Minister throughout the 1964–70 Labour government, and from 1974 until his sudden death in office when Foreign Secretary. He was Secretary of State for the Environment, March 1974–April 1976. See *Holding the Line* Chapter VIII for a description of the bitter clashes between Crosland and the rail unions and the environmental activists who campaigned successfully against further Beeching-style closures.

The other feature of ministers, as can be seen from Appendix 2, is that their tenure of office is short and when Crosland moved to become Foreign Secretary, his successor, William Rodgers,[170] had different ideas, more in tune with Parker's views.

Unlike his predecessor, Richard Marsh, Parker saw it as being 'up to us in BR to make the running on the railway. We should not look to Government for too many answers until we had put together our own business-like propositions. It was little use asking them what they wanted of us until we knew what we were capable of. Could we have a popular well-loaded railway? We had to take stock of our competitiveness and above all recapture the interest of the nation in their public service. Britain was baffled by BR, and more than a little bored.' Parker noted that many people who came to see him started discussion by talking about 'the problem with the railways ...' while Parker wanted to talk 'about the opportunities for railways'.

Perhaps most successful in terms of managing relationships between railway and government was Sir Robert Reid with Transport Secretary Nicholas Ridley.[171] Reid was an experienced operator and an excellent manager, who enjoyed the confidence of government and was, to a greater extent than his predecessors, allowed to get on with the job with less interference from ministers and civil servants. This was helped by his personal friendship with Ridley, with whom he spent time fishing on the River Spey. Reid demonstrated his control of industry costs and kept BR within the all-important public sector borrowing requirement. For his part, Ridley approved an investment programme including East Coast Main Line electrification, which is Reid's worthy memorial, and advised Margaret Thatcher not to attempt the privatisation of BR.

More than that, Reid reshaped the railway with his sector management proposals, which produced some high-profile benefits recognised by a sceptical public, in InterCity and Network South East, while new rolling stock also transformed the economics of 'Other Provincial Services', which, under Gordon Pettitt became sufficiently confident to rename itself Regional Railways. Both InterCity and Trainload Freight became profitable. Given the dire position in the 1960s and '70s and the subsequent trauma of privatisation it was, as Roger Ford commented, something of a 'golden age' for BR. As Terry Gourvish said, 'there was an authority and purpose in an integrated railway led by a strong manager'.[172]

Widely regarded by his managers as the best chairman BR ever had, he put in place an organisation that was similarly held in high regard and produced some excellent results before it was swept away by privatisation in a way that most managers and staff found difficult to understand. The cost of the privatised railway in its first year was 38 per cent higher than that achieved by Reid's business structure for BR.

But this change and BR's last chairmen are the subject of the next chapter.

The Beeching whirlwind of the 1960s saw a fundamental reappraisal of the role of the railway and a huge change in the way it was managed, quite apart from the line and station closures for which the period is best remembered. In particular, it saw the foundations being laid for the parts of the railway that were transformed and given new life by his report, particularly InterCity passenger trains and intermodal freight. The 1970s saw this continue, but with the added impetus of the 1973 oil crisis. The crisis led to petrol rationing and worries about dependency on oil from the Middle East, and BR took the opportunity through corporate advertising to highlight the potential for the electrified railway, which could draw from a variety of power sources. The campaign was pitched around efficient use of scarce energy and security of supply rather than around environmental concerns, which at that time were not part of mainstream thinking. The crisis did benefit BR in terms of journeys transferred to rail and in making the case for electrification, but did not have the lasting effect that might have been expected after the shock of fuel rationing. This was partly because the crisis led to the development of the North Sea oilfield and partly because government focus continued to be concentrated on concerns over the cost of the railway rather than on its potential to play a much greater role in meeting Britain's transport needs. Only four short years separated the crisis and the dismal 1977 Transport green paper.

---

[170] William Rodgers (born 1928) was Secretary of State for Transport 1976–79. He was MP for Stockton-on-Tees, 1962–83. He was one of the 'Gang of Four' who founded the SDP in 1981 but lost his seat in 1983. He was created a life peer in 1992, and was leader of the Liberal Democrats in the Lords, 1998–2001.

[171] Nicholas Ridley, Lord Ridley of Liddesdale, (1929–93), Conservative MP for Cirencester and Tewkesbury 1959–92, created a life peer in 1992. Prior to entering Parliament he was a civil engineering contractor in the north-east of England. He was one of Margaret Thatcher's most loyal supporters (whom she described as 'one of us') and served as a minister in successive departments almost throughout her period as Prime Minister, including Secretary of State for Transport, 1983–86; for the Environment, 1986–89; and for Trade and Industry, 1989–90. On 13 July 1990, he was forced to resign as Secretary of State for Trade and Industry after an interview was published by *The Spectator*. He had described the proposed Economic and Monetary Union as 'a German racket designed to take over the whole of Europe' and said that giving up sovereignty to the European Union was as bad as giving it up to Adolf Hitler. His spell as a Foreign Office minister (1979–81) was notable for his attempt in secret to reach an agreement with the Argentine government over transferring sovereignty for the Falkland Islands; had he succeeded the Falklands War would not have occurred. Ridley was the second son of the third Viscount Ridley and the daughter of Sir Edward Lutyens, the architect. He was a talented artist, whose art teacher at Eton said he was 'better than his grandfather'. A chain-smoker, he died of lung cancer not long after he joined the House of Lords.

[172] *British Rail 1974–97*, Oxford University Press, 2002.

Integration and Co-ordination

At the time of nationalisation, great emphasis was placed on the need for transport integration, encouraging each mode to do what it was best at. Buses and trucks could replace trains on small rural branch lines, and could feed into the trunk rail services at principal towns where freight concentration centres could be established. An example of this was at Taunton, where an old water tower just east of the station still bears the legend 'Taunton Freight Concentration Depot'. It opened in November 1963, replacing local goods depots in the area with a road delivery service. At the same time a new coal concentration depot replaced twenty-two small coal wharves at local stations, with coal drops to allow larger hopper wagons to be used and to cut handling costs.[173] But it was all too late and the goods depot with its modern handling facilities closed, along with the coal concentration depot in 1972, following the rapid change away from coal fires at home.

Terminal facilities. Taunton in 2021. The closed bus station is in the distance, and buses now call at stops around the town centre. There are no toilets, catering, real time information, waiting rooms or staff on hand, for long distance or local services. The town (pop 64,000) is also served by Great Western and Cross Country at the railway station, where a £7m refurbishment has just been completed, providing facilities worthy of the town.
Christopher Austin

In Northern Ireland, 'integration' was a euphemism for rail closures. The establishment of the Ulster Transport Authority in October 1948 by combining the Belfast & County Down Railway and the Northern Irish Road Transport Board led very quickly to the first B&CD closures in January 1950, and three months later the whole of the B&CD network, apart from the line to Bangor, had been replaced by buses.[174]

---

[173] *Engineering* magazine, January 1964.
[174] Newcastle–Castlewellan remained open, served by Great Northern trains via Banbridge until 1955.

This did not happen in the rest of Great Britain, where 'integration' meant to most people getting buses and trains to connect. This was to the regret of economists like Beeching and Joy, whose mistake was to see the two modes as interchangeable. We now know that they are not, but quite distinct with their own characteristics, producing different responses from their customers. Buses are affected by traffic congestion, which damages performance on some routes very badly; their terminal facilities are rudimentary or non-existent[175] and no real-time information was provided in the time of the rail closures, nor indeed later in the last century. Rail controls its own infrastructure, which allows faster journey times and greater reliability. Rail is a premium product that could be priced accordingly but, through government control of BR and regulation of half of fares latterly, most local train fares are cheaper than the parallel bus service.

The railway companies pioneered many rural bus services, starting with the GWR between Helston and the Lizard in 1903. These were all subsumed by local bus operators by the early 1930s and the railways were part owners of many of the companies between the wars. These services were used to extend the reach of the railway, and in some cases to test the market for a potential railway extension rather than to replace existing rail services with a cheaper alternative. The policy was commercially driven with no direct government involvement, although from 1930 onwards the traffic commissioners were involved in approving and policing performance on the routes operated. The result of this was that, right down to the late 1960s, railway companies and latterly BR were able to object to new bus routes that threatened the viability of existing railway lines, although in practice this had little effect.

Cost reduction, however, was the driving force of the bus substitution proposals of the 1970s and '80s, and governments took a keen interest in that. Some worthwhile experiments were carried out to see whether buses could be better integrated with trains with through ticketing, better information and, initially, some subsidy from BR, and these were introduced between Peterborough, Wisbech and King's Lynn, and between Kettering and Corby. Other links were delivered post-privatisation as part of a franchise commitment, including Virgin's Luton to Milton Keynes service and Wessex Trains' 'Helston branch line', which extended to designating the bus stop at Redruth railway station as 'platform three'. More recently, a 'virtual branch line' has been introduced between Totnes, Kingsbridge and Salcombe, a reminder of the GWR motor bus service between Kingsbridge station and Salcombe from 1909 until 1929.

In spite of these differences, the government – and BR – continued to pursue the idea of bus substitution, even though the savings it could yield were minimal. However, by the 1970s, the more important issue was the lack of co-ordination between transport and land use planning. Between the wars, out of town 'trading estates', such as the extensive site at Slough, had been established with good rail connections. However, the new generation of business parks established around the developing motorway network did not even consider such links, and were anyway often located away from the railway network. Some retail parks like Meadowhall, Bicester Village or Lakeside in Essex have benefited from the provision of better rail links, but many have not, rather than being integral to the developments, which have, in consequence generated huge quantities of car traffic, overwhelming the highway system. A classic example is at Cribbs Causeway in north Bristol, located near the junction of the M4 and M5 motorways, but so far from the railway network that it is almost entirely car dependent. The consequent congestion backs up from local roads and blocks the motorway itself, so that local traffic to a regional shopping centre blocks traffic on the strategic national road network – the very antithesis of good planning.

In London the new Covent Garden fruit, vegetable and flower market was built on former railway land at Nine Elms locomotive depot. It opened in 1974, and even though the site was linked to the railway and efforts were made in Parliament and elsewhere to ensure that rail access was maintained, this was refused by the Covent Garden Market Authority.

Similarly, business parks and distribution centres have been laid out for the lorry, and the motorway network using greenfield sites away from urban centres, and often remote from the railway, too. Even when next to the railway, these is no siding connection, with a handful of exceptions such as Daventry or Warrington.

The 'silo' approach of government means that this has never been tackled effectively, and so over a thirty-year period the logistics industry developed a network almost exclusively using lorries, with distribution depots away from the railway network, setting in stone a system that was wholly road dependent, in spite of the cost to the Highways Agency of high maintenance requirements as a result of increasing lorry weights, and the huge cost to the environment as well.

---

[175] British Coachways was the new group set up with Grey-Green and Wallace Arnold after the deregulation of long-distance coach services under the Transport Act, 1980. They set up in competition with National Express coach and InterCity rail services, and established a 'coach station' in the derelict site of the former Somers Town goods depot (where the British Library is today.) The booking office and witing room were in portacabins, and there were not even any toilets, for which passengers were directed to use those at the adjacent St Pancras station. British Coachways was disbanded just two years later in 1982.

Land use and transport planning have generally been poor in Britain, but here at Meadowhall, the huge shopping centre and the station opened on the same day. The Tram connection was added in 1994. A class 142 heads towards Rotherham in 1994 with the new Supertram station on the right and the M1 viaduct in the background.
Les Folkard/Online Transport Archive

The SRA under Richard Bowker[176] set out to tackle the issue properly for the first time when Jim Steer[177] established a planning team, recruiting from land use planners, to work up regional plans setting out the current position and future prospects for economic growth and establishing the future potential rail demand for each British region.

The previous record of planning in Britain was not good, the most striking cases being the development of new towns in the 1960s and '70s. Basildon and Milton Keynes were designed as being self-contained, with residential and employment areas linked by road and footpaths or cycleways. The need for a main-line station was therefore seen as unnecessary. In practice, the existence of cheap housing so close to London generated huge demand for commuting, which was not what the planners intended at all, and the stations had to follow – Basildon in 1974 and Milton Keynes in 1984. To add insult to injury, the designation of Milton Keynes as a new city with a population target of 250,000 in January 1967 coincided almost exactly with Barbara Castle's decision to approve the closure of virtually the whole of the Oxford to Cambridge line that passed through Bletchley – incorporated into Milton Keynes.

Similarly, in the West Midlands, Telford Central opened in 1986, but Skelmersdale in Lancashire, which lost its station in 1956, has never been reconnected, in spite of its substantial increase in population.

---

[176] Richard Bowker CBE (b 1966) is the former chairman and chief executive of the Strategic Rail Authority, and a former chief executive of National Express and Etihad Railway in the United Arab Emirates. In 1989 he joined the London Underground as a graduate finance trainee; he was appointed co-chairman of Virgin Rail Group in 1999 and commercial director of the Virgin Group in 2000. He also founded the transport consultancy Quasar Associates. In 2012 he was appointed as the second ever independent non-executive director of the English Football League.

[177] James Steer (b 1948) CEng, FICE, FCILT transport consultant; founder, 1978, and director, since 2005, Steer (formerly Steer Davies Gleave) managing director, 1978–2002; director and founder, Greengauge 21, since 2005.

New Towns. Many new towns were entirely dependent on road and a railway station was not included in the original plans. Whilst Milton Keynes was designated as a new town in 1967, its station was not opened until 1984. Incredibly, Bletchley (within Milton Keynes' designated area) lost its direct services to Oxford and Cambridge from 1 January 1968, even though the line had not been listed for closure in the Beeching report. Here a Class 310 slam door unit leaves the new Milton Keynes station for Euston in 1984. *Geoffrey Tribe/Online Transport Archive*

The respective roles of the railway and the Underground in London were the result of the decision to have separate Railway and London Transport executives under the British Transport Commission from 1948 onwards. The extension of the London area by the creation of the Greater London Council in 1965 meant that there were more BR stations within Greater London than Underground stations, and the new council took a much closer interest in what BR did, particularly after the proposed Fleet line extension was rejected on the grounds of cost in 1979. BR resisted the creation of a PTE for London, but co-ordination was formalised through a BR/LT Liaison Group, which did some good work on modest issues such as transferring the City Widened Line between King's Cross and Moorgate from LT to BR for the Midland electrification to Moorgate, and agreeing access for Bakerloo Line trains to Stonebridge Park depot in return for restoring a more frequent Bakerloo service as far north as Harrow & Wealdstone.

In 1981, the new Labour administration under Ken Livingstone,[178] the leader of the Greater London Council, introduced a 'Fares fair' policy, cutting Underground and bus fares and introducing zonal fares and travelcards. BR was prevented by government from participating and initially the disparity between fares lead to a big swing from rail to Underground, particularly in north London,

---

[178] Kenneth Robert ('Red Ken') Livingstone (b 1945) is a retired hard-left politician who became leader of the GLC in a coup that deposed Andrew (later Lord) McIntosh, the centrist incumbent, in 1981. The policies adopted under his leadership provoked Margaret Thatcher to abolish the GLC in 1985 but he got his revenge by becoming the first elected Mayor of London in 2000 (after Thatcher had left office) as an independent, having failed to win the Labour nomination. He was re-elected in 2004 as the Labour candidate, but lost to Boris Johnson in 2008. He was Labour MP for Brent East, 1987–2001. He was suspended from Labour Party membership in 2016, having been accused of anti-Semitism, and resigned in 2018 before the disciplinary case against him was concluded.

GN Electrification. Whilst a number of LNER suburban lines transferred to London Transport to become part of the Northern and Central Lines, one LT line (from Drayton Park to Moorgate) became part of the GN electrification scheme in 1976. Here, a class 313 unit for Welwyn Garden City is seen at the Moorgate terminus. *Geoffrey Tribe/Online Transport Archive*

where the Piccadilly line paralleled the Great Northern and the Central line took traffic from the Great Eastern. The London Borough of Bromley successfully challenged the policy in the courts, arguing that as no Underground services operated in the Borough, they should not have to pay, and it was ruled unlawful. Fares had to rise to a level above that before 'fares fair', and the traffic quickly switched back to rail (up to 40 per cent), with consequent overcrowding.

The clash between Ken Livingstone and Prime Minister Margaret Thatcher eventually became irreconcilable and led eventually to the abolition of the GLC in 1985, with LT becoming a new nationalised industry, London Regional Transport formed in 1984. With no co-ordinating authority for transport in London, the government stepped in directly and Transport Secretary Nicholas Ridley chaired a steering group to bring together BR and LT with his own civil servants. An initial task was to undertake a number of corridor studies where BR and LT and services overlapped, 'to reduce wasteful competition', a strange remit from a Conservative government that normally encouraged it. The Marylebone closure proposal[179] emerged from such a study, but thankfully was not implemented. The period did, however, allow the introduction of a travelcard to cover BR as well as LT services. Originally a premium product, Capitalcard, in 1985 it was merged with Travelcard in 1989.

BR's Parliamentary Relationships

The railway served the whole country and almost every constituency had a station or length of line, or constituents whose livelihood depended on it. By the early 1980s, MPs had gone beyond writing to the chairman and were using the railway's periodic private Bills as a way of highlighting their constituency concerns, culminating in the blocking of BR's regular private legislation with northern MPs opposing the development of a rail link to Stansted Airport[180] in favour of priority investment for a rail link to Manchester Airport.[181] The result of this was that BR appointed from 1982 a manager to work with Parliamentarians to overcome as many problems as possible and to work with ministerial special advisers to encourage the 'payroll vote'[182] to support the Bill at second reading stage.

---

[179] See *Holding the Line*, Chapter XIV.

[180] See the British Railways Bill second reading debate on 15 March 1983, *Hansard*, vol. 39, col. 183. The rail link to Stansted Airport was opened in 1991.

[181] Eventually provided in 1993.

[182] This was just over 100 MPs who were ministers or Parliamentary Private Secretaries who could be relied on to vote according to the party whip.

Airport links. BR provided or built new rail links to three major airports and upgraded or built new stations to serve five others. A class 317 unit upgraded for working Stansted Express from the eponymous airport to Liverpool Street is shown at the airport station in 2005. *Geoffrey Tribe/Online Transport Archive*

One of your authors, Chris Austin, was BR's Parliamentary Affairs Manager between 1987 and 1997, when the level of engagement with Parliament was extensive, and this continued until the end of 1996. In his report for that year, it was noted that there were 1,037 Parliamentary questions on railways and twenty-three debates in the Commons on railway issues, as well as four in the Lords. There were three rail-related All-Party Parliamentary Groups and the Transport Select Committee held several rail inquiries, including one on railway financing, one on the West Coast Main Line and one on safety following an accident at Watford Junction during the year. Parliament also dealt with the Railway Heritage Bill and the Channel Tunnel Rail Link Bill during the session, and rejected the Central Railway Group's proposal for a new railway from the Channel Tunnel to the West Midlands, using much of the formation of the former Great Central, but also threatening to wreck the extensive network then being developed by Adrian Shooter for the Chiltern line out of Marylebone. There had been 13,000 objections to this scheme. The BR team had produced a constituency guide to help the new parts of the privatised railway and, with Railtrack, organised seminars for the new companies on managing Parliamentary relationships and lobbying with speakers including MPs, MORI and Transport 2000.[183]

Channel Tunnel Rail Link

At the end of the BR era, the development of the Channel Tunnel Rail Link is perhaps the best illustration of the fraught relationships between BR and government and the mistrust and deliberate obfuscation by ministers in order to implement their inconsistent policies, which included some irreconcilable objectives.

During the passage of the Channel Tunnel Bill, and the negotiation of the inter-governmental agreement, the fiction had to be maintained, to satisfy the Prime Minister (Margaret Thatcher) and the Treasury, that this was a stand-alone project, with no requirement for public

---

[183] Now the Campaign for Better Transport, Transport 2000 was founded early in 1973 largely on the initiative of the then assistant general secretary of the NUR Sidney Weighell to bring together public transport users, environmentalists, amenity groups, academics, the railway supply industry, and the rail unions to campaign against rail closures and support sustainable transport.

Channel Tunnel Rail Link. HS1 was a political hot potato in the 1990s and clearly demonstrated the mismatch between the commercial requirements for a new railway and the string of inconsistent Government demands on its route and ownership. Despite Government insistence that it should be a private sector project, it was largely built with Government funding and guarantees provided by John Prescott who brought practical solutions to a complex situation. *Andrew Fox*

expenditure, which was, indeed, outlawed by section 42 of the Channel Tunnel Act, 1987.[184] To this end, the optimistic Eurotunnel forecasts for future demand had to be maintained in order to provide confidence for the banks from which Eurotunnel was raising finance.

BRB's predictions were more modest, that additional capacity would not be needed until the turn of the century, and so the planning for the introduction of through passenger and freight services via the Channel Tunnel was based on using Boat Train route No. 1 (via Tonbridge) with new connections to take it to an extended Waterloo station, with freight either travelling via the South London line or Tonbridge–Redhill and then the West London line to a terminal at Willesden. The depot for rolling stock servicing and maintenance was to be at North Pole, which intrigued both French and Belgian railway planners. The second stage of the development was in relation to services running beyond London, including sleeper services, and the third was to provide a new high-speed line between the Channel Tunnel and London.

Public pressure added impetus to the latter as the media stressed the comparison between France, where the *ligne à grande vitesse* (LGV Nord) from Paris ran right to the tunnel approach at Coquelles, with a new international station at Lille and a smaller one near Calais, and the British side where a slower, conventional railway, albeit with a top speed of 100mph, would take people on to London. A Jak cartoon in the *Evening Standard* showed the nose cone of a high-speed train emerging from the Tunnel with passengers walking forward to a connecting double-deck tram and gives the idea, even though it was false in every respect. President Mitterand[185] of France spoke of a high-speed dash across France and through the Tunnel, with the pleasure of a leisurely journey through the delightful Kent countryside, and British politicians ground their teeth.

---

[184] This was, however, repealed by the Transport Act, 2000.

[185] François Marie Adrien Maurice Mitterrand (1916–96) was the longest-serving President of France in history, serving from 1981 to 1995. He was the first left-wing politician to assume the presidency under the Fifth Republic. His father was a railwayman who worked as an engineer for the Paris Orléans railway. Mitterrand held ministerial office several times under the Fourth Republic. He opposed Charles de Gaulle's establishment of the Fifth Republic. Although at times a politically isolated figure, he outmanoeuvred rivals to become the left's standard bearer in the 1965 and 1974 Presidential elections, before being elected President in 1981. He was re-elected in 1988 and remained in office until 1995. His legacy of social reform included the abolition of the death penalty.

With no immediate need to press ahead with the high-speed line, BR started by identifying possible routes. The whole of the Channel Tunnel preparations including planning a high-speed link fell to a small team under Malcolm Southgate.[186] Southgate was an experienced operator, and had been Divisional Manager of the South Eastern, which covered the routes between London and the Channel Tunnel. In keeping with BR's normal policy of keeping costs down, the team was small and much of the route optioneering was carried out by Nick Alexander.

Four options made use of existing route corridors through Kent, with extensive tunnelling under south-east London, and there were four options for the London terminal (White City, St Pancras, King's Cross and Stratford). The options were published in July 1988, and after a peaceful August, sheets of flame erupted from Kent and south-east London in September. The openness of the consultation and the fact that the propositions were a work in progress resulted in uncertainty and property blight on a massive scale.

It was well beyond the ability of the small BR planning team to handle, particularly after Nick Alexander revealed that much of his work had been done at home on the kitchen table in order to meet deadlines.

Apart from the genuine concerns of those living on the line of one of these routes, other people had an eye on compensation and other discreditable lobbyists sought to gain from the uncertainty and confusion. One even hired a trailer with a huge bank of loudspeakers and broadcast at high volume the alleged sound of a high-speed train passing, making sure that the press photographs included children with hands over their ears to make the point. It was dishonest but depressingly effective in PR terms.

The following year, BR settled on a single route option and King's Cross as the terminal. To reduce tunnelling costs, the existing line from Fawkham Junction via the Catford Loop would be used, with a new tunnelled route leading from a junction at Warwick Gardens, between Peckham Rye and Denmark Hill stations, to approach a new low-level station at King's Cross from the south-east, with connections on to the routes to the north.

MPs along the route were hostile and an impressive opposition was mounted to the scheme. At the same time, the government were being pressed by consultants Ove Arup, to adopt an easterly approach across the Thames estuary to Stratford (which they would engineer). The French planners were bemused. They knew about Stratford from their studies of Shakespeare at school, but what had that to do with London?

The government were also determined that the line should be built by the private sector and without subsidy, to meet the requirements of s.42 of the Channel Tunnel Act, 1987.

The new line would be the first main line built in Britain since the opening of the Great Central Railway in 1899, and although the Japanese and the French had by the late 1980s an impressive network of high-speed lines, there was no such experience (and the confidence that goes with it) in Britain, with a requirement to thread it through the congested peri-urban environment of Kent, a very different proposition from striking through the open landscape of Picardy in the case of the LGV Nord.

Again, the government allowed too many conflicting objectives to intervene in the decision-making, instead of focusing on the primary objective of creating a fast route with capacity for passengers and freight customers as the best solution for their needs. Not only was this a major and complex engineering project in its own right, but government wanted:

- To assume forecasts of passenger demand consistent with those on which the Channel Tunnel Usage Agreement was based
- For it to be built and run by the private sector
- To use the Stratford station as an engine for regeneration of east London
- To provide services beyond London to the north, even though all the studies showed that these were not commercial
- To avoid the 'nimby' problems of their own supporters in Kent and south-east London
- To do this at no cost to the taxpayer
- To provide an intermediate station at Ashford, even though forecasts showed it not to be justified.

These objectives were irreconcilable, and the end result was a route that did require substantial taxpayer support (negotiated subsequently by John Prescott as Deputy Prime Minister). It is still run by the public sector, with the controlling interest with SNCF, and services beyond London never developed. The lobbyists' predictions were never fulfilled, and the question of noise has never been an issue since services started in 2007. Indeed, it is often hard to hear the trains through Kent above the noise of the adjacent M20. Ashford International station turned out to be something of a white elephant, particularly after construction of Ebbsfleet, and Stratford has never been served by international trains, although it did prove very useful in moving many thousands of people during the 2012 London Olympics.

However, the stunning conversion of St Pancras station, threatened with closure in the 1960s (which was prevented

---

[186] Malcolm Southgate (1933–2013) was a career railwayman who rose to the position of deputy managing director, Eurostar UK (formerly European Passenger Services Ltd), 1990–2000. In 1964, he became the youngest stationmaster at a London terminus when appointed to King's Cross at the age of 30. He served with British Railways as Divisional Manager, South Eastern Division, 1972; Chief Operating Manager, 1975; Deputy General Manager, 1977, Southern Region: Director of Operations, 1980; Director of Policy Unit, 1983. BRB: General Manager. LMR: 1983. Director: Channel Tunnel, BRB, 1986.

largely due to the sterling opposition of Sir John Betjeman, the poet laureate[187]) is perhaps the high point of this sorry saga. The station is magnificent and so much better than the other termini at Bruxelles Midi and the Gare du Nord in Paris. It is something of which Britain can be justly proud, as one of the finest railway stations anywhere in the world. The journey time to Paris of 2 hours 10 minutes and to Brussels of 2 hours brings those cities as close to London as Manchester or Leeds, and provides a much pleasanter journey than flying, as well as one that is carbon neutral, drawing supplies of French electricity generated by nuclear power.

But the way in which this was achieved was primarily as a result of muddled government thinking and the lack of any clear transport strategy. It also created huge and unnecessary problems for BR and its managers who, at the same time, were also having to cope with restructuring for privatisation and impossible financial targets. Government decisions were not taken with BR, but with private sector consultants, and decisions were shamefully withheld from BR. Even though the southerly route to King's Cross produced the best rate of return, the Secretary of State, Malcolm Rifkind, had decided on the easterly route to Stratford. This came to a head on 8 October 1991 when Sir Bob Reid had travelled to Blackpool for a meeting with Conservative MPs at their annual conference at Blackpool. But, for your authors, who had arranged this, the significance was not Reid's arrival, but that of the Board's Chief Press Officer, Syd Preston. Preston was a doyen among press officers and knew exactly what was going on, even though he rarely left his office in Euston House. When we met him off the train at Poulton-le-Fylde, we knew the forthcoming meeting planned with Rifkind would be game-changing, and so it proved. Rifkind met Reid in the Ruskin Hotel and told him that the government had rejected BR's proposals and would adopt the Ove Arup scheme with the line running to Stratford. This was included in his speech to the conference the following day. It was seen by the media as a complete defeat for BR and for Reid personally. The government still expected BR to pick up the pieces and work with Arup and Trafalgar House to develop and implement the project through the joint venture company Union Railways.

The final blow in this saga of shoddy treatment came three years later in April 1994, when the government took European Passenger Services away from BR and transferred it to a separate government-owned company, just one month prior to the opening of the Channel Tunnel by the Queen and President Mitterand on 6 May 1994.

Its treatment as an independent operator has had the long term effect of reducing its effectiveness as it is not well integrated with the national network. Indeed, during the Covid pandemic, its very future was in doubt as government-imposed restrictions prevented passengers travelling, and there was initially no support mechanism designed to keep the service on 'hot standby' compared with the rest of the national network where trains continued to run for essential workers and to be ready as and when travel restrictions were eased.

---

[187] Sir John Betjeman CBE (1906–84) was an English poet, writer, and broadcaster. He was Poet Laureate from 1972 until his death. He was a founding member of the Victorian Society and a passionate defender of Victorian architecture. He failed to save the Euston arch, but triumphed at St Pancras, where there is a statue of him. He began his career as a journalist and ended it as one of the most popular British Poets Laureate and a much-loved figure on British television. He wrote and broadcast extensively about railways, particularly *Metro-Land*, He had two railway locomotives named after him – one on the pier railway at Southend-on-Sea, and a British Rail class 86 AC electric locomotive, 86229, was named *Sir John Betjeman* by him at St Pancras station on 24 June 1983, not long before his death.

6

Fifty Years of British Railways

'Apart from the sanitation, the medicine, education, wine, public order, irrigation, roads, a fresh water system and public health, what have the Romans ever done for us?'
'Brought peace.'
'Oh, peace? Shut up!'
Monty Python's *Life of Brian*

Aunt Sally: Which was the Target?

Hindsight has allowed a view of the achievement of the 'Big Four' to be made in Chapter 4, and now it is over a quarter of a century on from privatisation it allows us to take a measured view of the achievements of the BR period.

This is not straightforward because much of the written commentary of the period is affected by the views or prejudices of the writers, either on the question of ownership, or on the effectiveness of the management or by their views on industrial relations or economic viability. It also against the background of press coverage that was always downbeat and frequently hostile.

How far was this the fault of BR, and how much of the railway as a national institution?

The humorous magazine *Punch* was first published in 1841, when railways were still new and developing. The magazine was merciless towards the failings of the railways, with the accidents, the open third-class carriages and the greed of directors being early targets. In an anthology published in 1907, the compiler recognised the huge improvements achieved and made a generous, but telling comment: 'Where Mr Punch in his wrath, as voicing the opinion of the public, was wont to ridicule and condemn the railways and all associated therewith, we are today as ready, and with equal reason, to raise our voice in praise. But ridicule is ever a stronger impulse to wit than is appreciation, and in these later days when we are all alive to the abounding merits of our railway system Mr Punch has had less to say about it.'[188]

We have already chronicled the PR problems of the Southern and the appointment of a public relations officer in the 1920s. So, we would argue that the criticism throughout the period of nationalisation was directed not only at BR as a hapless nationalised industry, but also to the railway as a national institution on which people relied, which in itself caused resentment.

One of British Rail's greatest failings was its inability to convince the public that it had been a successful guardian of one of the country's greatest assets. In other countries – like France, Germany, Switzerland, Japan, the Scandinavian states – the railways have been and remain a source of pride for their people. But in Britain they have constantly been the butt of cheap jokes endlessly repeated by comedians on TV and radio and in newspapers, and by MPs in Parliament.

The cleanliness of trains and stations, standards of catering (particularly the myth of curly sandwiches), delays, cancellations, overmanning and waste – these have all provided material for the railway's detractors – as well as the impression put about by hostile road lobby sources in the 1970s and '80s that the railways had had their day and were costing taxpayers vast sums in subsidies that would be better spent on other things (particularly roads).

---

[188] *Mr Punch's Railway Book*, The Educational Book Co.

Changing Perceptions: BR's Advertising

To its credit the British Rail board attempted to correct this negativity in the 1970s and '80s through creative, hard-hitting and often amusing advertising, using all the available media, particularly television and the press.

Previously they had used three main agencies, and to be fair to the firms concerned they had produced some excellent advertisements, some of which can be seen in the illustrations. BR was decades ahead of anyone else in warning of the consequences of climate change, over-reliance on oil supplies, the air pollution effects of heavy road traffic, and the stress of car driving (including one that daringly referred to 'the effect on family life', which could easily have been an advertisement for tackling erectile dysfunction).

Another advertisement headed 'As you can see, British Rail have to work a lot harder these days' claimed that the number of people working on the railway had been halved between 1962 and 1977, and the size of the wagon fleet reduced by 682,000 vehicles. 'Operating costs per train mile at constant prices have been reduced by twenty-five per cent.'

One advertisement, published in June 1978, tackled the issue of public subsidy and pointed out 'Every railway in Europe needs some support from the taxpayer. But ours needs less than most.' It cited Belgium, West Germany and France as countries that received up to five times more subsidy than Great Britain, and stated: 'Each year the Government requires British Rail to run passenger services which, although unprofitable, are socially vital ... Our contract with government is to run those services at a price which we agree each year in advance. In fact, we've met our contract for the second year running, and beaten it in 1977 by £27,000,000 ... Pound for pound British Rail are giving the nation good value for money. Especially when you take into account the social and environmental advantages that can't be measured in money alone.'

The most controversial advertisement in this series was the famous 'Highway Robbery' ad that appeared in June 1978 on the say-so of Frank Paterson, BR's chief freight manager, who was battling against the forces of the road haulage industry, the road-building lobby and the Transport and General Workers' Union. With the heading 'In 1978 Highway Robbery still exists on a huge scale', it showed a lorry driver dressed as a burglar taking money out of the wallet of a passing motorist.

Like the other BR advertisements that appeared at this time, it was aimed at political opinion-formers and decision-makers, and the medium of choice for them was *The House Magazine*, Parliament's own journal, which

Making the case for investment. A dramatic message in 1979, with the empty filling station and the electric APT powering past in the background. The alternative fuel message is just as relevant today as in 1979 when this advertisement appeared in the *New Statesman*. *History of Advertising Trust*

had been founded in 1977 by a then Labour MP Mike Thomas,[189] and Richard Faulkner, co-author of this book. 'Highway Robbery' was a two-page centre-spread and attracted huge attention.

This was exactly what Paterson wanted, and when he was summoned by Sir Peter Baldwin, Permanent Secretary at the Department for Transport, to be told off in the presence of the director-general of the British Roads Federation he was unfazed and unapologetic.[190]

That ad also attracted some exchanges in the House of Commons, as the following *Hansard* extract from 7 June 1978 makes clear:

David Madel (Con, South Bedfordshire): 'As Sir Peter Parker has described the road versus rail argument as "sterile", would not the Minister expect Sir Peter not to allow British Rail to go in for

---

[189] Mike Thomas (b 1944) was MP for Newcastle upon Tyne East, 1974–83 (Labour and Co-op until 1981, when he became a founder member of the SDP, losing his seat in 1983). Served on the BR Western Region board, 1985–92.

[190] See *Holding the Line*, Chapter XV, for a fuller description of this extraordinary incident and of the Didcot Distribution Centre scandal that led to it.

In 1978 Highway Robbery still exists on a huge scale.

To the tune of sixty million pounds. That's how much giant lorries are taking from Britain's taxpayers and ratepayers each year.

The sum represents the difference between what the State receives in fuel tax and vehicle duty from juggernaut operators and the true cost of the damage the juggernauts inflict on our roads.

A thirty-two ton lorry can do more damage than ten thousand cars. And the situation can only get worse; if EEC-size forty ton lorries are allowed into the country, the damage will be proportionately greater.

Action is needed to make juggernauts pay their way. They would then compete fairly with the railway, which has always had to pay the full costs of its own rail roads.

And British Rail is ready to compete on these terms. With a modern network of high speed, highly reliable services.

Carrying goods in bulk is a natural for rail. A single train can move the equivalent of fifty juggernauts.

Quickly, cleanly and at no extra cost to the community.

Railfreight

Highway Robbery. Speaking truth to power, the advert which upset the road haulage industry and the Department but made its mark with opinion formers. *Authors' Collection*

anti-heavy commercial vehicle advertising, which it is now doing, in view of the employment provided in that industry and the exports gained by it?'

William Rodgers (Secretary of State for Transport): 'There is a later Question on advertising. However, I have often said – and I repeat – that I do not think that there is any advantage in "knocking" copy in the transport industry or parts of the industry. Both the public sector and the private sector have a part to play, and I think that it is best for everyone to get on with it.'

David Crouch (Con, Canterbury) then attacked the whole corporate advertising campaign but got short shrift from the minister: 'Is the right hon. Gentleman aware that British Rail is now boasting of its great successes, at a cost of several hundred thousand pounds a year in advertising? What use is that to those who are compelled to travel by British Rail and suffer its growing inefficiency, as are commuters in the South-East?'

Mr Rodgers: 'I disagree with everything that the hon. Gentleman says. The efficiency of British Rail is improving. I believe that is widely recognised on both sides of the House. It is set out clearly in British Rail's most recent annual report. That being so, I see no reason for British Rail's not bringing to the attention of its passengers the facilities that it offers. I am glad to say, for example, that the advertising associated with the introduction of the HST on many new routes has been a great success. The high speed trains are now carrying up to 30 per cent more passengers than the trains that were previously running.'

Kenneth Lewis (Con, Rutland & Stamford) called for cheaper rail fares: 'Is it not a fact that the more we have special offers the more complicated they become and the greater the advertising and administrative costs involved? Would it not be better if British Rail reduced normal fares and kept the price to the ordinary passenger within limits? It would then still get the increased numbers, without having to spend so much on advertising.'

Mr Rodgers: 'The hon. Gentleman may feel that he can run British Rail better than the present chairman. I think that these are largely management decisions, which ought to be made by those who are professionally qualified to make them. It seems that reduced fares, which hon.

Members on both sides of the House generally want to see, must go with advertising so that people will know that they are available.'

Defence of BR's corporate advertising came from Ivor Clemitson (Lab, Luton East), who had clearly seen BR's international comparisons ad: 'Has my right hon. Friend seen the advertisement which seems to make a virtue out of the comparison between British Rail and other Western European countries with regard to the degree of subsidy received by British Rail? Does he agree with British Rail's assessment of the situation?'

Mr Rodgers: 'I am not familiar with the poster (sic). There can be a great deal of argument about exactly how subsidies here compare with those in other countries. The point of substance is that British Rail is providing an increasingly efficient service within rules and a subsidy agreed by the House. I think that it deserves the encouragement and good will of the House.'

The 'Agonising Beauty Parade'

The arrival of Peter Parker as BR chairman in 1976 had led to the Board deciding to change advertising agents, and mount an integrated advertising campaign managed by a single agency, with the messages BR had to communicate simplified. 'The agonising beauty parade', described by Parker in his autobiography[191] was won by the then not very well-known Allen Brady and Marsh (ABM) agency in 1977.

How ABM won is described on the website of the 22 Group creative consultancy:

> Peter Marsh of ABM, advertising extraordinaire and business pitch master, was known for his surprising presentation skills.
>
> Learn a thing or two from the greatest business pitches of all time …
>
> The pitch. That compelling moment in time. The pitch is the 100 metre sprint that stands between you and your business securing that deal. The art of the pitch is truly the art of persuasion and the number of ways we can go about this is infinite.
>
> The components of a really unforgettable pitch appear straightforward: be clear, be authentic, be memorable. But to execute a pitch so audacious that it goes down in business folklore takes something special …
>
> The year is 1977.
>
> The setting is Allen Brady & Marsh's (ABM) advertising agency.
>
> ABM are the mavericks of the advertising world, headed by the charismatic directors, Rod Allen and Peter Marsh. Marsh, or 'Mr Showbiz' as he was known, had the reputation of being a flamboyant performer who liked to surprise his clients mid-pitch, often with a musical number. With a background of performing on the stage, Marsh made sure his pitches would always stand out.
>
> The office of ABM is the stage to one of the most theatrical pitches in business history. The key players are ABM and Saatchi & Saatchi. At stake is a significant deal with British Rail. Saatchi & Saatchi are the heavyweight champions of advertising; ABM are the wildcards.
>
> When British Rail's team, headed by chairman Sir Peter Parker, enter the office of ABM their first impression is of disarray. The advertising agency is off-putting to say the least: overflowing ash trays, filthy coffee mugs, newspapers strewn on the floor. They are greeted by a surly receptionist who files her nails and refuses to look up and greet them before she has finished the page of her magazine.
>
> 'How long do we have to wait?'
>
> 'Dunno,' she replies.
>
> The British Rail team are kept waiting a full 20 minutes, all the time being wholly ignored by the receptionist and passing advertising staff. Just as they are about to leave in disgust, a door opens and the director of ABM, Peter Marsh, and his advertising team finally reveal themselves.
>
> 'You've just experienced how the public perceive British Rail,' Marsh says, to surprised faces. 'Now let's see what we can do to put that right.'
>
> Marsh and his team then launch into their pitch, outlining their plans to overhaul public opinion of British Rail.
>
> They are hired on the spot.

Parker described ABM as 'fresh and growing at the time, independent with an appetite for the pioneering work we needed'. They came up with an unexpected slogan 'This is the Age of the Train'. Although much parodied and mocked, particularly on bits of the railway with ancient rolling stock, it was one of those advertising slogans that stuck.

ABM proposed that the person to front the campaign should be Jimmy Savile.[192] Parker had reservations and asked that the market research be repeated. Parker wrote: 'Of the many television personalities tested on the questionnaires, Jimmy came up trumps because of people's perception that he would only do what he believed in, whatever the money … Jimmy would be genuine … Jimmy

---

[191] *For Starters* pp 293–298

[192] Sir James Wilson Vincent Savile OBE KCSG (1926–2011) was a television and radio personality who hosted BBC shows including *Top of the Pops* and *Jim'll Fix It*. As a teenager he worked in coal mines as a Bevin Boy in the Second World War. He raised an estimated £40 million for charities and, during his lifetime, was widely praised for his personal qualities and as a fund-raiser. After his death, hundreds of allegations of sexual abuse were made against him, leading the police to conclude that Savile had been a predatory sex offender —possibly one of Britain's most prolific. There had been allegations during his lifetime, but they were dismissed and accusers ignored or disbelieved; Savile took legal action against some of them.

served BR with the unique fervour which he radiated on behalf of all his good causes … His character is an astonishing and shrewd mix of innocence and experience, something of a Shakespearean fool, God's fool, the responsible clown who fixes all your dreams, who is generously mad and who owns a pale, heavenly blue Rolls-Royce and will give anybody a lift. And who loves trains. He fixed us cheerfully and firmly among the personal passions he devoted to hospitals and mental health.'

Later in the same chapter Parker revealed that he invited Savile to his office to meet executive members of the BR board, and 'we surprised him by giving him a gold pass for the year'. Savile asked if the award could be postponed for another year as he had just received an honour from the Pope.[193]

With the benefit of hindsight it is easy to condemn Parker for failing to see through Savile's superficiality and not ask questions about his disgusting sexual proclivities. In his defence Parker was not alone: scores of public figures, from the Pope, Prince Charles and Prime Minister Margaret Thatcher (who tried repeatedly to give him a knighthood, only succeeding at the fourth attempt) downwards had no knowledge of how depraved Savile was. It goes without saying that had the revelations about him emerged during his lifetime Parker's comments would have been very different.

One BR advertising campaign, launched in 1980, that did not feature Savile was a highly controversial but brilliantly effective corporate advertising campaign that aimed to convince 'opinion-formers' – defined as Conservative MPs, local authority leaders, heads of industry, senior civil servants, the media, and the travelling public, particularly commuters – about the realities of financing the modern railway.

Subjects covered included how much more cost-effective BR was compared with the eight largest European railways, the case for electrification (with the heading 'More of our financial resources could be used to save our natural ones', and saying that if 5,800 miles of BR's railway were electrified, that would save 120 million gallons of oil per year). Another described comparative costs of road and rail (making the point that the average cost per mile of building new sections of the M25 was £8.4 million, which was enough to buy four HSTs or electrify 28 miles of railway), while a third showed flags of countries around the world where Transmark, BR's transport consultancy subsidiary were selling British railway expertise – seventy-five projects in twenty-nine countries across six continents.

Each of the advertisements in the corporate campaign carried in small print an assertion that read: 'This is one of a series of advertisements designed to increase public awareness of the position of the railways in the national transport system and also in the life of the community as a whole. While the facts and figures contained in these advertisements are known and appreciated by those directly concerned in shaping the future, an industry as much in the limelight as ours has a duty to address itself to a wider audience, which needs to be well informed if it is to play its part in helping to form public opinion.'

How well the campaign succeeded in meeting these objectives was reflected in the improvement of the standing of railways as measured by the Opinion Research Centre. Parker wrote: 'There was a vast increase of questions on BR in the Commons – 32 in one day in January 1981, and half of them were to do with the lack of investment, our central message … The Secretary of State himself said, on Scottish television, 'In terms of cost-effectiveness, British Rail, I think, stands comparison with any other railway system in Western Europe.'

And the *Financial Times* said on 5 March 1981: 'In just eight months British Rail's corporate advertising campaign has created the desired effect in high places … The BR campaign is almost certainly the boldest, most vigorous use of corporate advertising by a nationalized concern seen in Britain to date.'

The health advantages of train travel comparing the heartbeats of train passengers and car drivers on a journey between Leeds and London. This one appeared in *Punch* in 1977. *History of Advertising Trust*

---

[193] *For Starters*, p.295.

Claire Perry MP, a junior transport minister opening Newcourt station on the Avocet line in Devon in 2015 with GWR regional planning manager Dan Okey. Photo opportunities like this mean that community rail is happily supported by ministers. *Christopher Austin*

Unsurprisingly, the ebullient Peter Marsh went out of his way to defend the right of nationalised industries to advertise and published his own advertisement in *Campaign* magazine on 22 April 1983 with the heading 'No bark. No bite.', showing a bulldog wearing a collar saying 'nationalised industries' and a gag over its mouth. The text read:

> Effective advertising is one of the most potent commercial tools available. To deprive an industry of its use is to ask it to compete in the market-place with its hands tied. There is no such thing as guaranteed customer sales. Nationalised industries must compete for new and repeat business and cannot be regarded as having a monopoly over customer decisions. In some cases this competition will be within the same market (The train versus the car, coach or plane).

New Lines and Stations

Within the tight financial constraints under which it operated and the general approach of planning a smaller and more efficient railway, BR did well to deliver local expansions to the passenger network, with fifty-eight new lines and 303 new stations between 1960 and 1996. Most of these were built in conjunction with a PTE or with the local authority. Inevitably, this dipped after privatisation, but Network Rail subsequently picked up the baton and the number of reopenings has continued to grow and indeed is being encouraged by the government's 'restoring your railway' programme. The figures are shown in the table overleaf:

The expansion of the network covered the whole country, with 186 new stations in England opened or reopened between 1960 and 1996, 77 in Scotland and 40 in Wales.

Penistone Line. As part of the process of abandoning the Woodhead route in 1980, trains from Huddersfield to Sheffield were diverted from Penistone to Barnsley to allow the direct route via Deepcar to be closed. A Pacer calls at Silkstone Common, one of two new stations on the route of the diversion. *John Meredith/Online Transport Archive*

Table 1. Lines and Stations Opened

Infrastructure owner	Lines	Stations
BR 1960–96	58	303
Annual average	2.1	8.4
Railtrack 1997–2001	8	26
Annual average	2.0	5.2
Network Rail 2002–17	35	77
Annual average	2.5	4.8

Source: Britain's Growing Railway, Railfuture, 2017

What did BR Ever Do for Us?

We can best answer this question by recording some of its more notable achievements, in addition to new stations. Here's a list of twenty-one of them, with the most impressive first:

1 The HST services on the Great Western and East Coast Main Lines were the fastest diesel trains in the world, rarely acknowledged by the media.

2 While other countries were building high-speed lines from scratch, BR was hugely successful in upgrading existing routes for 200kph running at considerably lower cost and so maintained the competitiveness of InterCity rail travel.

3 Independent research by Leeds University demonstrated that BR was highly efficient compared with other European railways and operated with a much lower level of subsidy than any other European network, apart from Sweden.

4 Efficiency improved dramatically during the BR period, with staff numbers coming down from 649,000 in 1948 to 121,000 in 1993–94, a drop of 81 per cent. Part of this was as a result of reducing the size of the network and technology changes, but it still resulted in a fourfold increase in productivity in terms of the number of passenger miles carried per employee.

5 It pioneered the hugely successful InterCity brand, which was widely copied throughout the world, notably in Germany. It remains a source of astonishment that this was allowed to wither and die on privatisation.

6 It was ahead of the game on introduction of market pricing, and led the field in airline-style marketing, while other European railways were stuck with an inflexible kilometric tariff. This resulted in very low-price 'super saver' fares and advance purchase (APEX) tickets, which allowed many more people to travel at affordable fares. The media, however, ignored this, and always quoted the first-class ordinary fare from London to Manchester as the comparator, misleading thousands of their readers into believing that rail travel was beyond their means.

7 BR maintained and improved a core network of 11,000 route miles, which was handed over to Railtrack in 1994 in substantially better condition than it was inherited on 1 January 1948.

8 It pioneered the tilt technology that allowed trains to operate faster on conventional track.

World's fastest diesel train. The high speed train transformed the market for Inter City travel and has had a very long and successful life. Originally introduced in squadron service on Western Region in 1976, it was also used on the East Coast and Midland Main Lines and on Cross Country services. Re-engineered and reconfigured it remains in service on Cross Country, Great Western and ScotRail at the time of writing. *Geoffrey Tribe/Online Transport Archive*

While not adopted by BR, this forms the basis of the Pendolino trains now used on the West Coast Main Line and in Italy.

9 It introduced and successfully operated the Freightliner network, one of the planks for future growth of rail freight today.

10 During the BR period, eight links to airports were provided at Birmingham, Gatwick, Heathrow, Manchester, Prestwick, Southampton, Stansted and Teesside.

11 Railcards offering discounts of a third on regular prices encouraged senior citizens, young people and less physically able passengers to travel and made the railway accessible to many more people.

12 BR pioneered the introduction of commercial hovercraft and fast ferry services on routes between Dover and Boulogne as well as to the Isle of Wight.

13 BR – and particularly Sir Peter Parker – kept alive hopes of building the Channel Tunnel following the decision of the Labour government to cancel the project on 20 January 1975, first by proposing a cut-price 'mousehole' with one single line on which trains would run in 'flights', then by supporting the tunnel that was eventually built with a double-track, 160kph railway opened in May–June 1994. BR successfully saw off ludicrous plans for a road tunnel or road bridge promoted by the motoring/road lobby.

14 BR pioneered the introduction of electronic signalling with the first Integrated Electronic Control Centre at Leamington Spa.

15 BR expertise was valued everywhere else in the world, apart from Britain, and was successfully sold through BR's consultancy arm, Transmark, in all six continents. In 1979, Transmark were running seventy-five projects in twenty-nine countries, including the USA and China, and had won the Queen's Award for Export Achievement,

16 The 'merry go round' concept was a highly efficient way of handling bulk freight including coal and aggregates.

17 The BR School of Transport in Derby and the management training centre at The Grove, near Watford, formed the basis of well-regarded training schemes for managers and for engineering and operating excellence. BR apprenticeships were highly regarded by employers across the engineering spectrum.

BR innovation. The Advanced Passenger Train used a sophisticated tilt mechanism to allow it to travel round curves faster than a conventional train. It also trialled the use of hydro-kinetic brakes. Here the gas turbine APT runs on trial near Cholsey on the Great Western main line in 1975.
Christopher Austin

18 BR Research at Derby were world leaders in railway research with ground-breaking work in many areas, including resin mouldings (HST nose cones and internal panels), seat design, battery technology development, rail/wheel interface, signalling and vehicle dynamics.

19 BR sold rail services and encouraged British tourism, with offices in Europe and America and agencies around the world. The Britrail pass was a hugely popular product for visitors to this country and BR pioneered its sale through airline booking systems.

20 Sir Robert Reid introduced a management structure based on business sectors, which gave managers full control of costs and freed them to focus on customer service and product development. For the first time, the business was based around the customer and not driven by the needs (and costs) of the engineer and the operator.

21 BR developed the MagLev (magnetic levitation) system of propulsion and applied it to an airport shuttle between Birmingham International station and the airport. The idea has now been taken up in China, with an 18-mile line linking Shanghai with its airport.

In his masterly business history of BR, Terry Gourvish aptly describes the approach of government: 'in Whitehall, an attitude to railways of at best neglect, at worst contempt.' British Rail, he said, 'provided comparatively safe, improving service, began to revolutionise marketing, and showed greater attention to customer care.

Birmingham International station was a BR initiative, opened in 1976, linked to the National Exhibition Centre by covered walkways and to the airport from 1984 to 1995 by the revolutionary magnetic levitation (Mag-lev) people mover, developed by BR Research at Derby. This picture shows its conventional replacement AirRail Link, next to a northbound Pendolino train in 2003. *Geoffrey Tribe/Online Transport Archive*

BR innovation. The first successful application of mag-lev was in the link between Birmingham International station and the adjacent airport, a product of BR Research. *Christopher Austin*

'The provision of safe and high-quality services, evident in the mid to late 1980s, was based on the establishment of firm hierarchical control and the setting of clear objectives.'

From the dysfunctional position of the railway under the BTC in 1948, and half a century of political interference and media antipathy, BR had produced a railway in 1991 of which the country could be proud, and in terms of efficiency and value for public money was better than most in Europe.

The authors recall a conversation in 1993 with one of the InterCity route directors, who indicated that the sector management organisation just put in place was the best he had experienced in his career, but that, even then, the dynamite sticks were being placed in the track to blow it all to pieces.

Gourvish reports the comments of John Welsby that: 'The fundamental problems of government having to choose how much it wishes to spend on supporting the passenger railway, and what are its priorities for the use of that support, have not been addressed by privatisation and will surely return.' Gourvish questions 'whether it was worth all the trouble and risk to dismantle what the two Bob Reids erected'.

Pacers. With no financial case to replace the first generation of diesel multiple units the prospects for provincial services looked bleak. John Welsby based the case for new rolling stock on a much cheaper design based on the Leyland National bus body and an innovative four-wheel chassis developed by BR Research at Derby. An early example is shown here at Doncaster on a stopping service to Leeds in 1984, prior to electrification of the ECML. *Harry Luff/Online Transport Archive*

7

The Great Privatisation Debate, 1992–97

'Absolutely dotty ...'
Lord Peyton of Yeovil, 1993

First Steps

Following the Conservative victory under Margaret Thatcher's leadership in 1979, the Board gave early consideration to the involvement of private capital and greater commercial freedom for their subsidiaries, but not to the core business of rail operations. Chairman Peter Parker was keen to do this as a way of securing investment for the subsidiary organisations managing ships, hotels, hovercraft and property. The new Secretary of State, Norman Fowler, was also enthusiastic about privatisation on this limited scale, and had secured a commitment in the Conservative manifesto to transferring the British Transport Docks Board and the National Freight Corporation to the private sector.[194]

A joint study was initiated under the Deputy Chairman, Michael Bosworth,[195] for BR and John Palmer, the Under-Secretary (Railways) at the Department for Transport.[196] The BR chairman was advised by Morgan Grenfell and ministers by Samuel Montagu. The study group reported in May 1980.[197] The objective of the study was to raise funding for BR's subsidiary companies, and allow public sector funding to be focused on the core railway.

The report identified the key structural problem that precluded the kind of public–private partnership envisaged by Parker and meant that the objective could only be realised through sale. That problem was the public sector borrowing requirement, which formed part of the overall public sector expenditure that the Chancellor, Sir Geoffrey Howe,[198] was determined to restrain. While the Board retained a majority holding in a subsidiary, funding would

---

[194] *British Rail 1974–1997*, Terry Gourvish, Oxford University Press, 2002.

[195] Michael Bosworth CBE (1921–2007) served in the Royal Artillery during the Second World War and qualified as a chartered accountant, working for Peat Marwick and Mitchell 1949–68, where he became a partner in 1960. He had a succession of board appointments at BR, including Chairman British Rail Engineering Ltd, 1969–71; British Rail Property Board, 1971–72; British Rail Shipping and International Services Ltd, later Sealink UK Ltd, 1976–84; BR Hovercraft Ltd, 1976–81; British Transport Hotels, 1978–83; British Rail Investments Ltd, 1981–84; British Rail Trustee Co., 1984–86; Director: Hoverspeed (UK) Ltd, 1981–89; British Ferries, 1984–90. He was Vice Chairman, British Railways Board, 1968–72, and Deputy Chairman, 1972–83.

[196] John Palmer CB (b 1928) was a career civil servant who served in the Ministry of Housing and Local Government, Cabinet Office, the Department of the Environment and then from 1976 in the Department of Transport, where he rose to be Deputy Secretary, 1982–89. He served on the British Railways Board and was chairman of European Passenger Services, 1990–94.

[197] *Introduction of Private Capital into the British Railways Board's subsidiaries.* Report of the joint BR/DTp team, 15 May 1980. TNA AN 179/73.

[198] Sir Geoffrey Howe, later Lord Howe of Aberavon, (1926–2015), was a major figure in the Conservative governments of the second half of the twentieth century. He was Conservative MP for Bebington, 1964–66, and then for the ultra-safe seats of Reigate, 1970–74, and Surrey East, 1974–92. Called to the Bar in 1952 and made a QC in 1965, Howe was Solicitor-General, 1970–72, and Minister for Trade and Consumer Affairs, 1972–74. In the Thatcher government he was Chancellor of the Exchequer, 1979–83; Foreign Secretary, 1983–89; Lord President of the Council, Leader of the House of Commons, and Deputy Prime Minister, 1989–90. He resigned in 1990, and made a speech in the Commons that the BBC reported as 'widely seen as a central factor in Lady Thatcher's downfall as prime minister'. They had disagreed over the EU and he broke ranks after the Prime Minister had declared at a

BR operated the largest shipping fleet in Europe. A year before sale to Sea Containers, mv *Ailsa Princess* is berthed at Weymouth in 1983 when on the Cherbourg route. *Geoffrey Tribe/Online Transport Archive*

count as public expenditure, as BR carried the ultimate financial risk. Only when the private sector owned the majority share in the company would it count as private expenditure. The external financing limit remained as a shackle on railway development throughout the existence of BR. This ended with the transfer of ownership and risk to private companies, but became an issue again when Railtrack was replaced by Network Rail, which was initially treated as being in the private sector. However, in 2014, the Office of National Statistics reclassified the company as a public sector one, its debt therefore scoring against the public sector borrowing requirement. It does, however, benefit from the cheaper cost of borrowing from government rather than from the market.

BR was a bit coy about this, perhaps because Peter Parker was still looking for some middle way, and the management brief to staff announcing the changes still portrayed it as securing private investment rather than 'selling the family silver'[199]: 'The reason that BR has agreed to the introduction of private capital into the main non-rail subsidiaries is that there isn't enough capital to go round at the moment, even to look after the railways properly. That is the problem. And 'do nothing' is not a solution to it.'[200]

The report recommended setting up a holding company for the subsidiaries to allow the private sector to buy into them, and this was established as British Rail Investments Limited (BRIL) under the Transport Act, 1981. This was a sensible arrangement, in that the study group revealed that British Transport Hotels and British Rail Hovercraft did not have the 'financial record' to allow them to be floated at an early date. Sealink, however, was capable of being floated in 1981–82, the report commented without any sense of irony.

Property was more complicated, as while there were some prime development opportunities in the major cities, there were also 1,500 miles of closed branch lines to look after, which at that stage were costing £650,000 a year to maintain.

BRIL pursued other opportunities too, but with less success.

European Council meeting that Britain would never join the euro. He described Thatcher's attitude to British negotiations in Europe as, 'rather like sending your opening batsmen to the crease, only to find … their bats have been broken before the game by the team captain'. The speech encouraged Michael Heseltine to challenge Thatcher for the leadership and within weeks she was gone. On leaving the Commons in 1992, he went to the Lords as Lord Howe of Aberavon, where he continued passionately to support Britain's membership of the European Union.

[199] Attributed to the Earl of Stockton (Harold Macmillan) in a speech to the Tory Reform Group in 1985.

[200] Quote from Sir Peter Parker in BR *Management Brief* of 15 July 1980. TNA AN 179/73.

The new business sectors came up with innovative solutions to improve the rail product, such as replacing EMUs with air conditioned loco hauled coaches on the Gatwick Express using Class 73 electro-diesel locomotives, developed by the London and South East Sector. This was so successful that InterCity took over the service in 1985. To deal with the growth in passengers travelling to and from Gatwick Airport, BR replaced EMU operation with Mark II loco hauled coaches from the LMR operated push/pull with a driving motor coach converted from an EPB. *Harry Luff/Online Transport Archive*

Gatwick Express. The prospect of private capital to invest in the Victoria–Gatwick service was pursued by Chris Lewin, the Project Co-ordinator, Private Capital, under the auspices of BRIL. At that stage, the service was fully integrated with Southern's Central Division services and the operation involved detaching a four-car unit from a Victoria–Horsham/Bognor service every 15 minutes at Gatwick Airport and attaching it to a following up train. Operationally and financially it would have been difficult to separate out such a service as a private operation. The cost base would have depended entirely on allocation of costs in what was an integrated network. It would also have involved substantial inefficiencies requiring its own management team. Philip Satchwell, the Board's Passenger Manager, London & South East, was scathing, pointing out that the operation only merited a manager at the lowly grade of MS1, not the panoply of a board of directors.

In the event, one of your authors, Chris Austin, who was one of Philip Satchwell's team, was responsible for the rolling stock commercial specification for a separate Gatwick Express operation with a locomotive hauled push-pull train running just between Victoria and Gatwick Airport non-stop. Although it used cascaded Mark 2 coaches, the new service increased rail's market share at Gatwick and was so successful financially that it was transferred to InterCity in 1985 and privatised as a separate franchise in 1996. Subsequently, and because for operational reasons it remained a part of the Brighton line service pattern, it was merged with the Southern franchise in 2008, although the trains retained their separate livery and branding.

Slough–Windsor

A mini privatisation of the Western Region's Slough–Windsor branch line was examined at this time as well, as a potential part of the BRIL portfolio. It was proposed by journalist and railway enthusiast Simon Neave, who with some financial backers had formed a company, Rail Limited, and approached BR in January 1983.

In earlier years, such a proposal would have been given short shrift by BR managers, but in these uncertain times a working party was set up by Board Member Jim O'Brien to look at all aspects of the proposal, including the WR Operations Manager, Ken Shingleton and the area manager at Slough.

The working party reported in July 1984 and from this, it is evident that it was the property rather than the railway that was the financial incentive for the proposal. The branch covered its costs with a small £20,000 pa surplus, but provided a huge £250,000 of contributory revenue for journeys beyond Slough, another indication of how hard it is to separate a service that is actually part of a much wider and integrated network. However, the railway land at Windsor was a big attraction, with the coach park (a former goods yard) bringing in income as well as opportunities around the station itself, although much of the station site had already at that stage been leased to Madame Tussauds for their long-running Railways and Royalty exhibition.

The railway would have been operated by two Leyland railbuses, with an occasional steam service, based at a new depot at Slough. Maintenance support would have come from the local bus garage. There was no resilience in such a service and no scope for growth, and the operation would have been run on a wing and a prayer.

The report also revealed that such a transfer of ownership would, under the law then applicable, have required prior closure consent from the minister.

The proposal never developed further and it was to be twelve years before the line was privatised as part of the Thames Trains franchise in October 1996.

Vale of Rheidol

This was a successful sale and was thus the first bit of operational railway (albeit a rather specialised one) to be privatised. This tourist narrow-gauge steam line was part of the Provincial sector and managed by the London Midland Region, whose General Manager, Cyril Bleasdale,[201] wrote to the trades unions in July 1987[202] to advise them that a review of the future of the line would be undertaken. The conclusion of the review was that the line should be sold separately, and Lazards were appointed as merchant banker advisers. Its estimated value was put at £250,000.

The sale is worth some consideration as it pointed up some of the complexity and cost of even a simple privatisation.

The sale required that the assets of the line should be vested in a new 'Vale of Rheidol' company through a Transfer Order approved by the Secretary of State. This in turn meant that the original Light Railway Order of 1902 had to be replaced with a new one in the name of the new company. The new company was then offered for sale by tender.

To avoid the risk of any challenge, it was decided that the closure process should be implemented in respect of the BR service, even though it was expected that the purchaser would continue to run trains in the summer in much the same way as BR had done.

The winning tender was from the Brecon Mountain Railway, and a press release confirming this was issued on 10 October 1988. One of the unsuccessful bidders, a consortium of railway staff, objected on a number of grounds, but the Board held firm in view of the gap between the BMR bid and that of the consortium. The Chief Executive, John Welsby,[203] did, however, agree to an *ex gratia* payment to the consortium to help cover the cost of their advisers.

Closure consent for BR was given by the Secretary of State on 28 March 1989 and the Transfer Order was made the following day. Brecon Mountain Railway started to run the line the following month.

The BMR bid was £306,500, against which has to be set the costs of redundancy for the BR staff of £150,000 and site separation costs of £15,000. BMR claimed compensation for the costs of repairs to bridge No. 2 over the River Rheidol and a settlement of £30,000 was offered.

Lazards' costs were agreed at £20,000 a month and a success fee of £60,000. The cost of their bill is thought to be some £240,000.

Thus the net loss on the sale of 'Y Lein Fach' (the little line) by the Board was £128,500, to which should be added the administrative costs of the Transfer Order and the Transport Users Consultative Committee's closure hearing. Added to the advisers' costs of the other four unsuccessful bidders, it meant that the net cost was very substantial.

It was an ominous foretaste of the costs to come after 1992.

Meanwhile, privatisation proceeded steadily with the sale of hotels, ships, hovercraft, and a number of other specialist businesses such as Meldon Quarry, while others such as Taunton Concrete Works were closed. Most significantly were the sale of railway workshops, such as Doncaster, York

---

[201] Cyril Bleasdale OBE (1934–2022) was a retired railway manager who was Managing Director of *Railnews* from 1996 until his death. His career included Managing Director, Freightliner Ltd, 1975–82; Director, InterCity British Rail, 1982–86; General. Manager, BR London Midland Region, 1986–90; Director, Scotrail, 1990–94.

[202] Papers in TNA, AN 18/1533.

[203] John Welsby CBE (1938–2021) was Chief Executive, 1990–98, and Chairman, 1995–99, British Railways Board at the time of privatisation. His previous career was in the Government Economic Service, 1966–81. He was BR's Director of Provincial Services, 1982–84; Managing Director, Procurement, 1985–87; and a Member of the Board, 1987–99. The Conservative government led by John Major owes a huge debt of gratitude to Welsby for seeing the controversial and sometimes chaotic privatisation process through and for keeping the trains running, and it is inexplicable that he is the only Chairman of BR not to have been awarded a knighthood.

The sale of the Vale of Rheidol line by BR marked an early and costly attempt to sell non-core businesses. The line has subsequently prospered and is a successful heritage railway and one of the 'Great Little Trains of Wales.' *Geoffrey Tribe/Online Transport Archive*

and Springburn, while others including Swindon, Ashford and Shildon were closed. These sales were supported by government and were seen as sensible steps that did not involve the core railway activities. This approach was also endorsed by the Prime Minister, Margaret Thatcher.

However, in 1990 she resigned as party leader and was succeeded by her chancellor, John Major, who went on to win a fourth successive Conservative victory in 1992. Thatcher was a hard act to follow, and, sensitive to charges that the party had 'run out of steam' after eleven years, Major was keen to demonstrate his party's innovative thinking, and chose to show this, *inter alia*, by railway privatisation. This duly appeared in the party's manifesto for the 1992 election so that when the Conservatives unexpectedly won, the policy proposal became a firm commitment.

Privatising the Railway: Theoretical Structures

During the summer of 1988, private discussions took place between British Rail and the Department under the heading of 'Long Term Options for the Railways' about privatisation of core railway activities. This was intended by the civil servants to allow them to work through the issues and to be in a position to brief ministers on the options, but had become a priority as a result of newspaper speculation at the time. The work was also intended to inform advice to be given to ministers in advance of the 1988 Conservative Party Conference and in advance of autumn conferences being organised by two right-wing think tanks, the Centre for Policy Studies and the Adam Smith Institute.

In a welcome change from earlier years, when network size was being considered, BR was involved in these discussions, which were chaired by John Palmer. As it happened, the initial meeting on 1 June 1988 also included Richard Allen, who had been seconded from the Department to BR's Policy Unit, although the papers reveal that he batted for BR throughout the discussions. The second meeting on 25 July involved Board Member Derek Fowler.[204]

---

[204] Derek Fowler CBE (1929–2006). After a number of financial appointments with local authorities, he worked for the British Railways Board as Internal Audit Manager, 1964–67, and Management Accountant, 1967–69, Senior Finance Officer Western Region, 1969–71; Corporate Budgets Manager, 1971–73; Controller of Corporate Finance, 1973–75; Finance Member of the Board, 1975–78; a Vice-Chairman, 1981–90; and finally Deputy Chairman, 1990.

The record of the discussions[205] reveal no preconceptions and a proper discussion of the options that might be available, should the government decide to go down the route of railway privatisation. Indeed, the initial discussions indicate a desire to take time for full consideration of the options and that a period would be required for any new structure to demonstrate a 'track record' on financial performance before privatisation could be undertaken.

From the outset, however, it was evident that while BR clearly preferred the 'unitary' option of privatising BR as a single entity, the Department could see that ministers would be looking for something more radical, involving competition.

In setting out its objectives for privatisation at this early stage, the Department made clear that 'Maximising Exchequer proceeds from any sale is not an objective.' This was to be overturned in a somewhat cavalier way subsequently by the Chancellor Kenneth Clarke,[206] as we shall see. In the meantime, the initial objectives set out by DfT were reasonable:

- Provide a better service to the customer
- Improve efficiency
- Free enterprise from public sector control and
- Widen share ownership.

In practice none of these, apart from the first, was destined to be achieved.[207]

To this list though should be added taking capital expenditure for rolling stock off the public sector borrowing requirement.

The working assumptions at this early stage were that the infrastructure would probably remain state owned, and that access charges would be low, allowing most train operators to run without subsidy. Light touch regulation was also assumed. Indeed, at the initial meeting in June, the possibility was considered that it might be possible to rely on existing competition and consumer protection law, rather than set up 'a regulatory apparatus'. 'The presumption was that any regulation of fares and quality could be limited to areas where the railway had a quasi-monopoly,' wrote Richard Allen in his note of the meeting. Both sides recognised that rail had only a small share of a market dominated by the car and the juggernaut.

There was also a recognition that any division of BR by region or business sector would be faced by the problems of allocation of costs and revenues. To their credit, the civil servants recognised at this early stage that the railway operated as a network and that any division would create somewhat arbitrary interfaces. This meant that the option of a split by sector was effectively ruled out at this early stage. To inform the discussion, the BR Policy Unit carried out an analysis of inter-regional passenger and freight flows. Whilst in terms of passenger numbers, the regions were fairly self-contained, in terms of revenue 50 per cent of Scottish Region income related to cross-border fares and the figures were 30 per cent for the London Midland and Western Regions. The dominance of Southern Region commuting flows to central London meant that their national figure for cross-border flows was rather lower, at 17 per cent. Regional boundaries were even less relevant to freight traffic, where 39 per cent of revenue was generated by inter-regional flows.[208]

The following year, in 1989, the discussions on structure and finances continued at the Department's behest, but with no clear idea from the Secretary of State (Paul Channon[209]) on the approach the government favoured. A paper to the Board in April 1989,[210] reviewed again the possibilities of break up by region, by sector, or a unitary privatising of BR or as a holding company with subsidiaries. The paper is interesting in identifying at an early stage the pitfalls in creating a track authority, which were prophetic and accurate: 'The Infrastructure Authority will be a monopoly supplier, one stage removed from the final customer,' it said. 'The Infrastructure Authority would essentially be a spending authority with weak incentives to reduce costs vigorously. Separation of track and train would make it far more difficult to reduce costs – or increase quality – by intelligent specification of track standards to meet train requirements.'

Board members reading this would have been well aware of the efforts made by their chairman Sir Robert Reid to get engineering costs under control in making them subservient to the needs of the five businesses or

---

[205] TNA AN 18/104.

[206] Kenneth Clarke, Lord Clarke of Nottingham (b 1940) was Conservative MP for Rushcliffe, 1970–2021. Fifth longest-serving minister in recent times, having been a member of the governments led by Margaret Thatcher, John Major and David Cameron for a total of twenty years. He had been Chancellor of the Exchequer, Home Secretary, Lord Chancellor and Justice Secretary, Education Secretary, Health Secretary and Minister without Portfolio; the two jobs denied him were Foreign Secretary and Prime Minister, principally because he remained a staunch pro-European while the Conservative Party drifted away to become Euro-sceptic. He contested the Conservative Party leadership three times – in 1997, 2001 and 2005. He was awarded the CH (Companion of Honour) when he finally resigned as a minister in 2014, and was ennobled in 2020.

[207] See Conclusions, Chapter 11.

[208] Paper from the Policy Unit to the BR Board dated April 1989. TNA AN 175/10.

[209] Henry Paul Guinness Channon, Lord Kelvedon (1935–2007) was Conservative MP for Southend West, 1959–97. A member of the Guinness family, he was selected as a candidate while still an undergraduate at Oxford. His father was Sir Henry 'Chips' Channon MP. He served as a minister in the governments of Edward Heath, 1970–74, and Margaret Thatcher, including as Secretary of State for Transport, 1987–89.

[210] Board paper on the structural options for privatisation, 26 April 1989. TNA AN 175/10.

sectors he had created. The move to a track authority put the engineers back in the driving seat, and the cost of infrastructure provision rose inexorably thereafter.

There would be other problems too: 'Customers would lose out as a result of the complex and bureaucratic inter-company process required to produce timetables, plan infrastructure maintenance, manage reliability, etc.'

'Heavy government involvement' would inevitably be required to regulate the monopolist track authority and the responsiveness of the industry would be significantly reduced by the complexity of the structure involved.

An Infrastructure Authority would account for some 35 per cent of BR expenditure, but such a proposal would have the effect of subsidising costs directly rather than relate them to provision of specified services, so weakening control.

Thus, at this early stage the structural flaws that led to the increased cost and complexity of the railway were correctly identified, but ignored by government in the policy they subsequently chose to adopt.

Watching this from outside the industry in 1989, Sir Peter Parker's wise words were prophetic. This would not free government from its responsibility for transport but, on the contrary would increase it: 'Privatisation will do little to lessen the role of any Government coping with congested airways and roadways as the lava of traffic pours over cities and countryside. It would be sad if the debate about the ownership of railways gravitated to political extremes again.'[211]

There was some jockeying for position by theorists who advocated different approaches to privatisation, with the Centre for Policy Studies[212] advocating a geographical split with a reversion to the 'Big Four' companies, the approach said to be favoured by the Prime Minister, John Major. The Adam Smith Institute,[213] on the other hand, wanted to go for a functional split with on-track competition. Most of the reports strongly advocated competition, as if rail was not already in competition with road and air, and some authors evidently had no idea of how railways actually operated, subordinating practical issues to economic theory.

There was also an assumption that privatisation would result in greater efficiency and a network that could be profitable, despite the flawed competitive structure for transport in Britain. But BR had been relatively efficient in the way it ran the railways, and in particular had been ruthless in stripping out costs under Sir Robert Reid, and many lines would continue to need government support. To ensure value for money for the taxpayer, competitive tendering would be required to demonstrate this, as well as to attach conditions to operators relating to other improvements during their franchise term. The reducing support requirement from many of the initial franchises came more from increasing revenue and passenger numbers, rather than from cost-saving efficiencies.

The 1992 Election

Parker's warnings – and the opposition of Conservatives like Nicholas Ridley – were not heeded by the new Conservative government formed under John Major's premiership, following the defenestration of Margaret Thatcher in 1990. There were two significant policies adopted that ran completely contrary to her thinking. One was the introduction of the National Lottery (which had always been opposed by Thatcher because of her strong non-conformist upbringing), and the other was privatisation of the railways.

While there was much that went wrong in practice in the years following the passage of the Railways Act, 1993, no one could argue that it was not clearly set out in the Conservative manifesto for the 1992 election. It is worth reproducing the passage from it in full:

The Railways

We believe that the railways can play a bigger part in responding to Britain's growing transport needs, and are investing accordingly. Next year alone, British Rail's external finance will top £2,000 million. The new Passenger's Charter will help to raise the quality of service. For the first time ever performance targets will be set, widely published and rigorously monitored; fare levels will reflect the standards set; and discounts will be paid to regular travellers where performance targets are not met.

We believe that the best way to produce profound and lasting improvements on the railways is to end BR's state monopoly We want to restore the pride and local commitment that died with nationalisation. We want to give the private sector the opportunity to operate existing rail services and introduce new ones, for both passengers and freight.

A significant number of companies have already said that they want to introduce new railway services as soon as the monopoly is ended. We will give them that chance.

Our plans for the railways are designed to bring better services for all passengers as rapidly as possible. We believe that franchising provides the best way of achieving that. Long term, as performance improves and services become more commercially attractive as a result of bringing in private sector disciplines, it will make sense to consider whether some services can be sold outright.

In the next Parliament:

- By franchising, we will give the private sector the fullest opportunity to operate existing passenger railway services.

---

[211] *For Starters, a life in management*, Jonathan Cape, 1989.
[212] *Reviving the Railways*, Andrew Gritten, Centre for Policy Studies, October 1988.
[213] *The Right Lines*, Kenneth Irvine, Adam Smith Institute, 1988.

- Required standards of punctuality, reliability and quality of service will be specified by franchises; subsidy will continue to be provided where necessary; arrangements to sustain the current national network of services will be maintained; and through-ticketing will be required.
- A new Rail Regulator – who will ensure that all companies have fair access to the track – will award the franchises and make sure that the franchisees honour the terms of the contract.
- BR's accounting systems and internal structures will be reorganised. One part of BR will continue to be responsible for all track and infrastructure. The operating side of BR will continue to provide passenger services until they are franchised out to the private sector.
- The franchise areas will be decided only after technical discussions with BR. But our aim will be to franchise out services in such a way as to reflect regional and local identity and make operating sense. We want to recover a sense of pride in our railways and to recapture the spirit of the old regional companies.
- We will sell BR's freight operations outright. We will also sell its parcels business.
- We will be prepared to sell stations – which we want to be centres of activity – either to franchisees or independent companies.
- The Railway Inspectorate will be given full powers to ensure the highest standards of safety.

The Railways Act, 1993

The Railways Bill was introduced in the House of Commons by the Secretary of State, John MacGregor, on 21 January 1993.

It received Royal Assent on 5 November 1993, and contained 154 clauses and fourteen schedules. It was a substantial piece of legislation.

To the casual observer, the Bill gives little clue as to what was proposed. It is not a strategic document, setting out the government's requirements of the railway, and gives little indication of how it was intended to operate. Railtrack, for example, is not mentioned, nor is the Association of Train Operating Companies (now Rail Delivery Group). It is essentially a framework document, setting out the licensing, access and regulatory process, the powers and constraints on the new offices of the Franchising Director and the Rail Regulator, along with the powers and duties of the Secretary of State. It covered duties of the Transport Users' Consultative Committees, powers of PTEs and, most importantly, the power of the British Railways Board to restructure the organisation and to transfer subsidiary companies to the private sector. Special provisions were made to provide for the continuation of railway services in the event of a company going into administration, although at the time this was assumed to be a train operator, not the infrastructure company Railtrack, which was put into administration in 2001.

Once the government had secured their majority in the second reading debate in the House of Commons, there was never really any chance that the Bill would not go through, or that it would be amended significantly. As mentioned above, there was a bold attempt in the House of Lords to amend the Bill to allow BR to bid for franchises, with the amendment introduced by Lords Peyton and Marsh (both former Transport Ministers) and indeed the Lords approved it. When the Bill was returned to the Commons to consider Lords' amendments though this clause was removed. So, it went back to the Lords, where it was reinstated, but was again removed by the Commons subsequently, with the government confident that it would not be reinstated a third time, by the Lords, in the light of the experience that led to the Parliament Act, 1911.[214]

An amusing incident accompanied this as, by tradition, the Commons form a 'reasons committee' to articulate the reasons for rejection of the Lords' proposals. Normally something of a formality, the opposition members decided to use it as a delaying tactic on this occasion. Writing in *The Independent* on 5 November 1993, under the headline 'Delaying tactics in a tiny, airless room: Donald Macintyre goes behind the Speaker's Chair to see how the Lords were kept waiting', Macintyre described what happened:

> Perhaps only Lewis Carroll could do it justice. It certainly strains credibility that there is such a thing as the 'Committee of Reasons', still less that it meets in a small, dark, airless, wood-panelled room behind the Speaker's Chair called the 'Reasons Room'.
>
> … it was in the stifling, if surreal, setting of the Reasons Room that it gradually dawned on John MacGregor, the Secretary of State for Transport, that he was losing his final chance of getting the BR privatisation Bill back to the Lords by the deadline of 11.30pm. The business on the floor was completed just after 11pm. But the Lords could still have debated the measure had it not subsequently been held up by the Reasons Committee.

Alex Carlile,[215] the QC and Liberal Democrat MP for Montgomery, had not even heard of the

---

[214] This was the Act that removed the powers of the Lords to block a money Bill after they had rejected the Liberal government's budget proposals, and provided powers for the elected House to override Lords' opposition to a Bill originally introduced in the Commons.

[215] Alex Carlile (b 1948) was Liberal Democrat for Montgomeryshire, 1983–97, member of the House of Lords as Lord Carlile of Berriew since 1999, sitting as an independent cross-bencher since 2017. He is a distinguished human rights lawyer who became a QC at the age of 36. In 2001 he was appointed as the independent reviewer of terrorism legislation, and was awarded CBE in 2012 for services to national security.

'Committee of Reasons' until he was appointed to it by the whips moments before it met. But he certainly knew what he was there for. The task agreed between the Liberal Democrats and Labour for Mr Carlile and Brian Wilson,[216] the Labour representative on the committee, was to maximise the Government's embarrassment by ensuring that the meeting went on long enough to send the Lords home without passing the Bill.

The Reasons Committee is an ad hoc select committee whose task it is to draft the official explanation of why the House of Commons has rejected amendments by the Lords. Until Wednesday it had always been a mere formality and rarely took more than 15 minutes. And when Mr MacGregor arrived with Roger Freeman,[217] his deputy at transport and Michael Brown,[218] the Tory transport whip, that is exactly what he expected.

The five committee members sat at the table which dominated the room, leaving the chair at the head empty. The clerk, Frank Cranmer, began by asking the senior MP to take the chair.

It was Mr MacGregor, but Mr Carlile quickly said that the motion to propose a chairman was 'debatable'. Mr MacGregor asked the clerk if this was true. 'Yes,' the clerk replied.

Mr Carlile then proposed Mr Wilson as chairman and embarked on a long speech detailing his attributes as a Parliamentarian and potential chairman, dwelling eloquently on the arguments of 'vested interest' which told against Mr MacGregor chairing a meeting to 'bludgeon' through his own Bill. As he spoke, Mr Wilson ostentatiously took off his jacket and loosened his tie. As Mr MacGregor began to realise that a filibuster was under way, he said: 'This is scandalous.' Wagging his finger at Mr Brown, he said: 'Take a note of this.' He told the opposition MPs he was ready to expose them on the Commons floor.

Mr Wilson, in an elaborate show of protocol, withdrew while the vote was taken, returning to 'congratulate' Mr MacGregor, elected by three to two.

Mr Carlile now proposed an amendment to the draft 'reasons'. As the argument, devoid of the usual Parliamentary niceties, raged on, Mr Carlile's pager went off. Under the table he showed Mr Wilson the message from the whips saying: 'The Lords have adjourned. You can go now.'

But should the opposition MPs delay the business still longer? In theory, they could have gone on until the weekend, provoking a fresh constitutional crisis. Mr Carlile now wrote a message on a slip of paper to Mr Wilson. 'You had better go and get instructions from your whips. I'll keep it going.' However, the Labour and Liberal Democrat whips had decided they had had done enough. Mr Wilson and Mr Carlile were called off.

By using his chairman's casting vote, Mr MacGregor got his Bill. And the Reasons Room became a footnote in history.

After the Bill received Royal Assent, there was no turning back, but problems arose as the first steps were implemented. The first invitation from the new Franchising Director to tender for the ScotRail franchise did not include the Fort William sleeper and the level of protest was out of all proportion to the actual number of passengers it carried. The press dubbed the train the Deerstalker Express, while one of your authors received an excoriating letter from the impresario Cameron Mackintosh,[219] who assumed the train was being withdrawn and that it was BR's fault. So much for the efficacy of government messaging.

Two successful bidders had to be changed as a result of loss of confidence in them following newspaper revelations. The approved bid for the London, Tilbury and Southend line (now C2C) was rescinded when it was revealed that some unauthorised adjustment of figures

---

[216] Brian David Henderson Wilson CBE (b 1948) was Labour MP for Cunninghame North from 1987 to 2005. He was minister of state for trade, Scotland, Africa, and industry and energy. A brilliant, prolific and award-winning journalist, he was founding editor and publisher of the *West Highland Free Press*, a community newspaper based on the Isle of Skye that campaigned for land reform and the rights of crofters in the Highlands and Islands. He writes regularly for *The Scotsman* and occasionally for *The Guardian*, for whom he had been the Scottish football correspondent in the 1980s. He was the author of the official history of Celtic FC and is a non-executive director of the club. Since leaving Parliament, Wilson was UK Business Ambassador, 2012–19, and chairman of both Harris Tweed Hebrides, since 2007, and the Centre for Energy Policy, University of Strathclyde, since 2020. He has been a Member, UK Board of Trade, since 2017.

[217] Roger, Lord Freeman (b 1942) was Conservative MP for Kettering, 1983–97, and Minister of State for Transport, 1990–94; Ministry of Defence, 1994–95; and Chancellor of the Duchy of Lancaster, 1995–97. Member of the House of Lords, 1997–2020. A chartered accountant by profession, he co-edited *All Change British Railway Privatisation* (McGraw Hill, 2000).

[218] Michael Brown (b 1951), newspaper political journalist, was Conservative MP for Brigg and Scunthorpe, 1979–83, Brigg and Cleethorpes, 1983–97. He served as an assistant government whip, 1993–94, resigning after the *News of the World* published pictures of him on holiday in Barbados with a 20-year-old gay man. During the 'Cash for Questions' Parliamentary scandal, Brown admitted to, and apologised for, accepting money to lobby on behalf of US Tobacco without declaring it. He was alleged to have received £6,000 from Ian Greer Associates to lobby on behalf of US Tobacco, and to have failed to declare it in the Register of Members' Interests or to ministers. He was a supporter of a variety of right-wing causes, including the National Party in South Africa during the time of apartheid, and the Monday Club. He joined the Brexit party in 2019.

[219] Sir Cameron Mackintosh (b 1946) is Britain's leading theatre impresario and producer of stage musicals. He owns nine London theatres.

relating to revenue sharing with London Transport on the shared route section between Upminster and London had taken place to boost LTS revenue.

Similarly – and even more embarrassingly – the bid for Great Western had to be given to the management buyout team after the media and opposition MPs destroyed the credibility of a new company euphemistically called 'Resurgence Railways', characterising it as being run by a 'double glazing salesman'. This was a £100 company set up in January 1995, whose 'managing director' was John Ansdell. He had been a director of Conservatories and Windows (UK) Ltd, which had been wound up at Southampton County Court in May 1995 with around thirty creditors with no prospect of any of them being paid what was owed to them. Not inaccurately Brian Wilson,[220] Labour's transport spokesman, described Ansdell as 'a failed double-glazing salesman'.[221]

The putative vice-chairman of Resurgence Railways was Mike Jones, a railway manager and Conservative party activist who was a former chairman of John Major's Huntingdon constituency association and privatisation enthusiast. The *Western Morning News* said that Jones's involvement 'caused anger and astonishment in the Westcountry. There was widespread criticism that the company has no experience of running a railway – unlike the inhouse management team'.[222]

Jones makes an appearance in John Nelson's[223] book *Losing Track*.[224] Nelson reports that Jones was berated by Major at a time 'when attracting bidders looked problematic, complaining "You bloody told me this would work". Mike replied "Relax John, it will."' This vignette is an indication of how much nervousness there was at the top of government.

The policy was hugely unpopular with the public and the media, and the DfT published a glossy booklet in March 1994 to explain the policy and make a number of claims about the possibilities offered. The criticism came from sober, analytical publications like the *Financial Times*, where a leading article on 24 May 1993 had declared that: 'The Government has scarcely a friend in the world when it comes to the privatisation of British Rail.' Even the government's cheerleaders like the *Daily Mail* opined: 'That even its friends think it is a policy without sense. A privatisation too far, a gamble which, if it fails, could cost the Government the next election.' Prophetically, the Institute of Economic Affairs in June 1993 foresaw that 'Privatisation will be blamed by opponents for every minor failure of the system.'

After the legislation, the policy was subject to considerable criticism by the Transport Select Committee and also by the Public Accounts Committee, which held inquiries into the sale of both Railtrack and the train leasing companies (ROSCOs). The rolling stock fleet was split into three to stimulate the creation of a train leasing market, but with little success at the outset, as so much rolling stock was specific to the routes on which it ran, and, there was at the time a national shortage of coaches resulting from years of government restrictions on new train investment. The PAC reported that at sale the companies were undervalued, and reported that: 'We note moreover that the participation of the MEBOs in the sale enabled a small number of British Rail managers to become millionaires, making windfall gains of between £15 million and £33 million, and that this risks discrediting privatisation as a whole.[225]

Three railway managers had profited when the companies were resold by £15 million, £15.7 million and £33.5 million respectively. The PAC were critical of the Department, which had obtained only £1.8 billion from the sales, while the new owners sold on quickly, earning a combined total of £2.7 billion. This also had a longer-term effect on the lease costs of the older trains, such as the Pacers, which reflected the costs the new companies had paid for them, even though, as a BR asset, they had been halfway through their book life.

In December 1995 the Secretary of State, Sir George Young,[226] wrote to reassure anxious Conservative backbenchers (see Appendix 6). This was needed as the

---

[221] In a press release issued on 24 November 1995.

[222] *Western Morning News*, 17 November 1995.

[223] John Nelson (b 1947). Career railwayman who joined BR Western Region as a management trainee in 1968, rising to become General Manager of BR Eastern Region and Managing Director Network SouthEast. After privatisation he formed First Class Partnerships 1997–2015, was a Director of First Class Insight Ltd, 1997–2003; Renaissance Trains Ltd, 1999–2017; Hull Trains, 1999–2014; Laing Rail, 2002–06; Wrexham, Shropshire & Marylebone Railway Ltd, 2006–09; Tracsis plc, 2007–18; YourRail Ltd, 2008–09; Passenger Transport Ltd, 2011–.

[224] *Losing Track*, New Generation Publishing, 2019, p.128.

[225] The committee reported that: 'Mr Jukes of Forward Trust Rail told us that he had invested £110,000 and his total return was £15.9 million'. Mr Anderson of Porterbrook told us that he had invested £120,000 and his total return was £33.5 million. Dr Prideaux of Angel told us that he had put no money into the business and that the maximum benefit he could receive was £15 million. (Select Committee on Public Accounts, 65th report, Privatisation of the rolling stock leasing companies, 27 July 1998).

[226] Sir George Young Bt (b 1941), Conservative MP for Ealing, Acton 1974–1997; North West Hampshire, 1997–2015; ennobled as Lord Young of Cookham, 2015. Popular and respected Parliamentarian in both Houses, his ministerial career after 2010 included Lord Privy Seal and Leader, House of Commons, 2010–12, and government chief whip, 2012–14. He had been Secretary of State for Transport and responsible for rail privatisation, 1995–97. A lifelong opponent of smoking and the tobacco industry, he was removed from his job as public health minister in 1981 reportedly on the insistence of Denis Thatcher, husband of the Prime Minister, who was

Leading the cycling lobby of BR was Sir George Young, Bt, who was MP for Ealing, Acton when this picture, showing him and his children, was taken at Rowlands Castle. This was used in a BR poster campaign to encourage cyclists to use the train at a time when brake vans provided accommodation for them, as on the 4-CEP unit in the background. Later, Sir George became Secretary of State for Transport during the latter stages of privatisation, and later still joined the House of Lords as Lord Young of Cookham.
Photograph supplied by Lord Young

issue had been divisive, even though the end result was not in doubt. The letter presented the case in optimistic terms, of course, but made a number of claims that were destined not to be fulfilled.

It referred to a 'new era for our railways which will see better services to passengers at less cost to taxpayers'. Better services were certainly delivered, with a 20 per cent increase in the number of trains run in the first four years, but overall support costs have risen threefold compared with that required for BR. Direct comparisons are difficult as following the demise of Railtrack, Network Rail was in receipt of some direct grants from government that resulted in some reduction in track access charges for train operators, which in turn allowed some reduction in their support levels.

The same letter referred to the future flotation of Railtrack 'enabling it to plan investment for the future at levels which would not be possible in the public sector'. This too was an assertion that proved to be undeliverable in the long term.

Another claim was that by reorganising BR into Train Operating Units, the government had 'freed the existing managers to make improvements even before privatisation'. Anyone who saw the iron grip John Welsby retained on his managers during this period would know that this was not quite what happened. He would allow nothing that was not justified financially or which gave his managers an unfair advantage in the competitions to come. The improvements that were achieved, such as on Chiltern Lines, were justified, good for passengers and strengthened the business that was to be sold.

The Politics of Privatisation

What drove the policy of privatisation that caused the government so many problems, diverted the industry from its task for a decade and proved so unpopular with the public?

A good place to start would be the views of the Prime Minister, John Major, but in his memoirs published in 1999,[227] rail privatisation is scarcely mentioned. It was one of the main policy planks, for which his troubled administration is still remembered today, yet the references are few and far between.

On page 248 he takes a swipe at the Labour Party, claiming: 'It was an error of historic proportions for the Labour Party – from Michael Foot to Tony Blair – to have resisted, as they did, every single privatisation. To give one example, hundreds of millions of pounds more could have been raised in the market for improving our railways if Tony Blair and Clare Short[228] had not raised the foolish, but in 1996 all too credible spectre of renationalisation. Mr Blair now blithely tells us he never intended to carry out that threat; in effect that it was just so much characteristic candyfloss to gull the Labour party faithful. It did not seem so at the time.'[229]

Max Hastings,[230] then the Editor of the *Daily Telegraph*, wrote a leading article forecasting that the scheme would

---

close to the tobacco lobby. Young is a passionate cyclist and was persuaded by your co-author Richard Faulkner when he was working as an adviser to the British Railways Board in the 1980s to appear on a poster with his son and daughters and their bicycles to promote cycling and train travel. Married to Aurelia Nemon-Stuart, Young's father-in-law was the distinguished artist Oscar Nemon. Young is the sixth holder of the baronetcy, which dates back to 1813. All holders have been christened George.

[227] *John Major – The Autobiography*, Harper Collins, 1999.

[228] Clare Short (b 1946) was MP for Birmingham Ladywood, 1983–2010 (Labour until 2006, when she resigned the whip, then Independent until her retirement from the Commons). She held a succession of shadow front-bench jobs from 1985, including transport 1995–96. In government, Short was Secretary of State for International Development, 1997–2003, when she resigned in protest over the decision to invade Iraq. Her first job after leaving university was as a civil servant in the Home Office.

[229] *Ibid.*, p.248.

[230] Sir Max Hastings (b 1945) is a journalist, broadcaster, military historian and author who was editor of the *Daily Telegraph*, 1986–95, and the *Evening Standard*, 1996–2002. Among numerous awards he won Journalist of the Year, British Press Awards, 1982; What The Papers Say, Granada TV, Reporter of the Year, 1982; Editor of the Year, 1988; the Duke of Westminster Medal

From 1996, Eurostar trains ran from Paris and Brussels using the conventional Boat Train Route no 1 to reach London, but running into Waterloo via a new spur at Stewarts Lane. In 2007, the channel tunnel rail link (HS1) was completed and the terminus changed to St Pancras. Here in 1998 a Eurostar train accelerates through Sandling, having just joined the South Eastern main line at Continental Junction, the pantograph having been lowered before Saltwood Tunnel. *Geoffrey Tribe/Online Transport Archive*

be 'politically suicidal'. In subsequent discussion he asked Major 'Why?' to which the reply was: 'Because we want an efficient rail service, that's why.' Hastings challenged this on the grounds that popular belief at the time was that services would decline steeply after privatisation. Major replied: 'That's nonsense. And it isn't as if the railways are working very well at the moment, are they?'[231] In fact, in the early 1990s, BR was performing very well indeed. 'Organising for Quality' had delivered an effective, business-led railway with the best ever performance levels recorded for BR in 1993–94, the start of Eurostar services in 1994 and with passenger services making an operating profit.[232] Major spent more time reading the newspapers than reports on the businesses for which his government was responsible, so his impression was at odds with reality.

Many Conservatives were unhappy with the government proposals, notably Robert Adley,[233] the MP for Christchurch, who was at the time chairman of the House of Commons Transport Select Committee.

However, privatisation was a manifesto commitment on which the government had been elected, so abandoning it was out of the question. Instead, backbenchers sought to amend it in a way that it would not turn out to be the disaster they feared. Adley referred to it as 'the Poll Tax on wheels'. Before the second reading debate he indicated to colleagues, tapping his breast pocket, that he had got enough votes lined up to ensure the changes he planned would be successful.

---

for military literature, RUSI, 2008.

[231] Max Hastings, *Editor*, 2002.

[232] British Railways Board Annual Report and Accounts, 1994–95.

[233] Robert Adley (1935–93), Conservative MP for Bristol North East, 1970–74; Christchurch and Lymington, 1974–83; Christchurch, 1983–93. The most passionate supporter of railways on the Conservative benches, Adley was virulently opposed to rail privatisation. He died suddenly of a heart attack at the age of 58, having recently become chair of the Transport Select Committee. He was the author of numerous books – ten in total – on steam railways, and was a collector of models and artefacts.

It was not to be sadly, as he died on 13 May 1993, shortly after his Committee's report was published, recommending several changes, including the merger of responsibilities of Railtrack and the Franchising Director, the retention of network benefits (through ticketing and impartial information provision), and that BR should be used as a yardstick and enabled to bid for franchises.

This latter recommendation was picked up in the House of Lords by Lord Peyton (former Transport Minister) and Lord Marsh (former Transport Minister and former BR Chairman) who introduced amendments to the Bill to protect railway pensions and to allow BR to bid for franchises.

In a letter to William Camp[234] on 2 November 1995, Lord Peyton wrote: 'What I do find surprising is the way in which the Government gives the impression of really believing that the course on which they are embarked is a sensible and profitable one.'

The argument for allowing BR to bid for franchises was that it would provide a valuable yardstick to measure the efficiency of private sector bidders and would retain a corps of expertise that could be deployed elsewhere if this went wrong. The arguments against were that BR would be in a position to conceal its true costs, particularly overheads, and so would be competing unfairly with the private sector.

Earlier – on 17 June 1993 – Camp had written to Peyton, saying: 'The government will, of course, resist giving BR the right to bid for franchises, if only because it wants BR to go out of business. This surely is the main thing wrong with the Bill ... I understand BR will cease to operate as such from 1 April next year. So who is going to take back any franchised routes that private operators make a mess of or decide not to persevere with? It looks as if there could be quite a vacuum – notwithstanding the large number of new quangoes [sic] created by the Bill. One of these, Railtrack, is the root of the problem. It should never exist ... Railtrack's functions should be embodied in BR, which will have a continuing role to play on the train side if your amendment is carried. Why should it not run the track as well, making routes available to private operators as and when justified (for a number of reasons, including the ability to raise capital where BR is strapped for funds). A pragmatic approach is surely more likely to succeed than a totally doctrinal one which asserts that BR (though curiously not the new Railtrack) is per se rotten and not to be tolerated. It is not too late to abolish Railtrack ...'

Will Camp's foresight back in 1993 is remarkable. He did not live long enough to see the collapse of Railtrack in 2002, or the increasing activities of Directly Operated Railways to take over failed franchises – let alone the establishment by another Conservative government of 'Great British Railways', which it appears may not be that different from the British Rail that Camp envisaged could work with private sector train operators.

As the government now says in the Williams/Shapps review, the railways are 'too fragmented, too complicated and too expensive to run'.

The Prospects for the Privatised Railway

The government did not really expect to see growth in the privatised railway. In their view, privatisation was about introducing competition, raising standards for passengers, improving efficiency and 'ending the BR monopoly'. 'Radical changes are needed,' said the white paper.[235] Within the industry and the political world there was a strong suspicion that privatisation would provide the cover for the large reduction in the size of the network that the railway's enemies had hankered after since the 1970s (see *Holding the Line*, *passim*).

Passenger traffic had been relatively static and freight traffic had been declining along with the manufacturing and extractive industries of Great Britain, accelerated by government financial targets for the freight sectors that forced the abandonment of all but the most profitable rail freight flows.

Consequently the received wisdom was that the industry was in long-term decline, and this is reflected in the language used in the discussions leading up to privatisation. It also explains the constant attempts during the previous thirty-five years to reduce costs by cutting production, and indeed cutting the network, which we dealt with in detail in our first book.[236]

The extent of this misconception is described in a working note submitted by Coopers & Lybrand (one of

---

[234] William Newton Alexander Camp (1926–2002) was public affairs adviser to the British Railways Board hired in 1977 by Peter Parker, a contemporary from Oxford, to advise on corporate communications strategy. In Camp's obituary (*The Guardian*, 29 January 2002) Ian Gilmour wrote: 'Under Camp's guidance, the railways adopted an aggressive, largely successful stance during the debates of the 1980s over the role and scale of their operations.' His earlier career included a highly successful spell at British Gas, where he was responsible for the 'High Speed Gas' campaign and a controversial one at the British Steel Corporation, where he resisted the efforts of the Heath government to denationalise the industry and was eventually fired by the chairman Lord Melchett on the instructions of ministers. Camp was an entertaining novelist, writing a number of his books on the train from his home station of Guildford to Waterloo. He was a Labour Party activist, a youthful Parliamentary candidate, and close friend of politicians on the left of the party such as Michael Foot and Peter Shore. As eventually reported in *The Times* on 5 July 2018, Camp has the distinction of being the only person on Marcia Falkender's 'lavender paper' controversial 1976 resignation honours list put forward for a peerage to have his name crossed out. Your co-author, Richard Faulkner, was recruited by Camp to work on *Steel News* in 1971, and remained as his consultancy business colleague until the late 1990s, including Camp's entire time advising the British Railways Board.

[235] *New Opportunities for the Railways*, July 1992, Cm 2012.

[236] *Holding the Line*, Richard Faulkner and Chris Austin, OPC, 2012.

BR's advisers on privatisation) to the BR Policy Unit dated 5 April 1989, entitled *Addendum to BR Business Forecasts*: '1,7 One factor in all the forecasts is the inclusion of the "negative time trend," an underlying fall in rail demand by around 2 per cent annually presumed to be due to factors such as higher car ownership.'

A sensitivity test allowed that the fall might be as low as 1.5 per cent, but none of the experts suggested that the opposite might happen, and that the railways were poised on the brink of phenomenal growth that would double their passenger volume over a fifteen-year period. Yet all the signs were already in place to hint that this might be so: traffic congestion, parking restrictions, fuel costs and emerging environmental concerns. Even the time efficiency of working on the train was then appreciated, although not to the extent made possible subsequently by the digital revolution and the availability of wi-fi on most trains.

The economic experts had again failed to see what was happening or appreciated the seismic changes in passenger demand that followed privatisation or the future collapse of coal as a primary fuel source, and a basic traffic on which the railways had been founded 170 years earlier.

The Rush to Sell Railtrack

Initially, it was intended that Railtrack would remain publicly owned as an independent provider of infrastructure on which competing operators would run. But the lure of both income for the Treasury and spreading share ownership more widely to make the sale irreversible, led to the government decision to sell Railtrack, in the same way as the popular sale of British Gas, through a share flotation. This took place in 1995 and the immediate rise in Railtrack shares was a clear indication that they had been underpriced to the detriment of the taxpayer and with windfall benefits to the new share owners. The then chancellor Kenneth Clarke talked of the benefits of doing this 'for the budget arithmetic' in a memo to John MacGregor, but there was no discussion of whether or not this would meet the future needs of the railway and its customers, or indeed, meet the needs of the nation.

The assumption by opinion formers at the time was that the efficiencies of privatisation coupled with the value of the land holdings of the company and the scope for raising money for investment through innovative financial models meant that it could not fail. Events were to prove them wrong.

From the outset, the company saw itself as a property company rather than a transport or even an engineering company and acted accordingly. It was excited by the commercial opportunities it assumed existed in many of Britain's larger railway stations, and pursued these with the zeal of a hyperactive estate agent, rather than as the guardian of priceless national assets that needed to looked after for the benefit of passengers and the wider community.

Weak on train operations, where much of the expertise remained with the train operators, they even had a period without a chief engineer. Their approach could be confrontational, and a combination of incompetence coupled with more than a little arrogance led to some disastrous decisions in relation to the West Coast Main Line upgrade project, and the financial consequences of the Hatfield accident in 2000 which brought them to their knees.

The company was put into administration by the Labour Secretary of State, Stephen Byers,[237] in October 2002, and a new company, Network Rail, was set up, with the help of the SRA, publicly owned, intended to be overseen by 100 stakeholders and still subject to oversight by the Rail Regulator (see Chapter 8).

The Cost of Privatisation

The 'railway problem' in the eyes of politicians and the press had been that of costs, since 1955 when British Railways ceased to trade profitably. Under the chairmanship of Sir Robert Reid, and his sector management structure, the finances of the railway were again under control, and support levels had reduced since the *annus horribilis* of 1982.

In his paper to the Board in April 1989,[238] Richard Allen highlighted this achievement:

> Public support for the Railways has fallen from £1182m in 1983 to an expected £492m in 1989/90 ... Government financial objectives for 1986/87 were met and those for 1989/90 are set to be exceeded for the supported Sectors, but not for the non-supported Sectors.

Rail finances, he said, were 'improving but fragile', but only InterCity, Freight and Parcels would be profitable, Network South East could be made to break even with real fares increases, but Provincial would continue to require subsidy. In other words, this would be different from the other privatisations of conventional profitable commercial operations such as gas, or British Airways.

The government white paper on the policy, *New Opportunities for the Railways*, said nothing on the cost of the privatised railway, but focused on the benefits to passengers and staff, and to efficiency. Labour, in their opposition to the subsequent legislation, were the first to articulate the probable increase in costs of the privatised railway.

---

[237] Stephen Byers (b 1953) was Labour MP for Wallsend between 1992 and 1997, and North Tyneside, 1997 to 2010. During his ministerial career, he was Chief Secretary to the Treasury, Secretary of State for Trade and Industry, and Secretary of State for Transport, Local Government and the Regions.

[238] Board paper on the structural options for privatisation, 26 April 1989. TNA AN 175/10.

Network SouthEast. Chris Green launched the network in 1986 based on a coherent approach to the railway in the South East. With its distinctive, bright livery and the characteristic red lamp-posts, No 50018 *Resolution* heads an Exeter train through Vauxhall in 1990. *Peter Waller*

Later on in the process, Parliamentary questions sought to reveal the cost of privatisation, and one around halfway through the process put it at £373 million for BR, Railtrack, the Department and OPRAF combined.[239] This would have covered fees, studies, restructuring costs and so on, but even so could only represent a fraction of the costs eventually incurred. The costs of BR redundancies, the continuing transaction costs of the privatised industry, the massive increases in the cost of engineering work as a result of compensation payments to train operators are all examples of fundamental cost changes that make comparisons with the previous unitary regime virtually impossible. Then there were other costs as well. What was the cost of the five-year gap with no rolling stock orders, of the eight-year gap in forward planning and the endless restructuring as government tried to make the system work and to exercise more control over it? BR, OPRAF, the Strategic Rail Authority and the Department's Rail Directorate all came and went in quick succession, and many studies, most recently the Williams/Shapps Review, indicated that further change was on the way.

Could Labour have Stopped it?

By 1995 it was evident that the Labour Party, which enjoyed opinion poll leads of 20 per cent or more, would be likely to win the next general election. This created some nervousness in the City of London, and the offers for sale documents of Railtrack had to include references to the potential political threats arising from a possible change of government.

There were lengthy debates within the Labour Party over what it should say to potential investors. Brian Wilson had written to John Ansdell of Resurgence Railways (see above) on 15 November 1995 setting out 'the approach which an incoming Labour government will adopt':

'We will abolish OPRAF as a separate organisation and the Franchising Director would then report to the British Railways Board, who will be responsible for the national rail network. Further franchising to the private sector will of course cease and, equally, you should understand that there would be no question of your franchise being renewed at the end of its contractual term. In this way, the entire passenger rail network will become publicly controlled and publicly accountable again; and in due course publicly owned also.

---

[239] Parliamentary Question, 23 October 1995, quoted in Privatisation Q&A, a guide for staff produced by the BRB in February 1996. NRM, K10/23.

'You will be expected by the Labour government to adhere strictly to the terms of the franchise agreement, particularly in relation to service performance and in terms of co-ordination with other operators. We will lay stress on the absolute priority of safety and of running a reliable service within the previously agreed levels of financial support, focusing on the needs of your passengers and the welfare of your staff. Any evidence of breaching the conditions of your franchise could result in its forfeiture and we would have no hesitation in asking the regulator to review the existing conditions of your licence if there is any evidence that they are not being fulfilled in every respect.

'You should also be aware that no undertakings can be given at this stage that there would not be further changes as a result of new primary legislation.

'If the company was to find itself unable or unwilling to continue operations under these conditions, it would of course be open to you to seek to negotiate an early release from your contractual obligations, and the franchise would be restored to British Rail. As you have had prior notification of Labour's intentions in this respect, you will understand that there could be no question of compensation, should you decide to give up the franchise prematurely.'[240]

Whether it was because of Wilson's letter, or the revelations in the media that Ansdell's double-glazing company had failed with creditors left inadequately reimbursed, Resurgence Railways withdrew its bid for the Great Western franchise on 5 December 1995 and the company was liquidated not long afterwards.

The approach adopted towards franchisees in Wilson's letter was consistent with the conclusions of a major piece of work undertaken by him and colleagues in 1993–94, when he published a document entitled *Putting the Railways Back Together Again*, following extensive consultation with numerous experts and interested parties.

The central dilemma for the Labour Party at that time was to decide what it should do about Railtrack. Wilson and other members of the Labour front bench were not short of advice. William Camp, for example, wrote privately to him on 6 December 1994, saying: 'To stop rail privatisation from getting off the ground, we really do need a firm commitment to renationalise Railtrack. The only way the Tories can launch it by doubling (they have already) and perhaps even trebling the subsidies paid to TOCs. This is a scandalous waste of taxpayers' money which Labour should not tolerate. This implies that anyone foolish enough to buy shares in Railtrack should not be compensated at his buying price.'

The Labour Party leadership would not, however, go along with a policy as radical as Camp proposed, primarily because they did not want 'New Labour' to be seen as anti-business and anti-City.

Gordon Brown told Brian Wilson that there was no need for Labour to commit itself to the nationalisation of Railtrack because the company would collapse anyway (which is of course what happened in 2002).

Instead the party's manifesto for the 1997 election said this:

Railways

The process of rail privatisation is now largely complete. It has made fortunes for a few, but has been a poor deal for the taxpayer. It has fragmented the network and now threatens services. Our task will be to improve the situation as we find it, not as we wish it to be. Our overriding goal must be to win more passengers and freight on to rail. The system must be run in the public interest with higher levels of investment and effective enforcement of train operators' service commitments. There must be convenient connections, through-ticketing and accurate travel information for the benefit of all passengers.

To achieve these aims, we will establish more effective and accountable regulation by the rail regulator; we will ensure that the public subsidy serves the public interest; and we will establish a new rail authority, combining functions currently carried out by the rail franchiser and the Department of Transport, to provide a clear, coherent and strategic programme for the development of the railways so that passenger expectations are met.

Notwithstanding the immense effort that he had put into creating a credible and coherent policy for tackling the railways' problems post-privatisation, and which were widely admired by railway managers, academics and fellow politicians on the centre and left, Brian Wilson was never made a minister in the Department for Transport by either Tony Blair or Gordon Brown. He served with distinction in other ministerial roles, but as far as the railways were concerned, he was the best minister they never had.

Some Conclusions

The Conservatives' policy was a leap in the dark, a radical experiment where neither the government nor the British Railways Board could predict the outcome. In this sense, it was certainly irresponsible, and was carried out in a timescale that allowed little time to work out the detailed policy or to implement the changes on the ground.

It was designed to be irreversible, but from the outset, constant changes were required, and the railway today bears little relationship to that of twenty-five years ago. Some of the fundamental flaws in the policy were fully recognised in the Williams/Shapps review in May 2021, which acknowledges: 'Breaking BR into dozens of pieces was meant to foster competition between them, and together with the involvement of the private sector, was supposed to bring greater efficiency and innovation. Little of this has happened. Instead the fragmentation of the network has made it more confusing for passengers, and more difficult and expensive to perform the essentially collaborative task of running trains on time.'

---

[240] Copy of letter supplied to the authors by Brian Wilson.

Lords on the line. Lord Rosser, formerly TSSA General Secretary, and Lord Faulkner of Worcester (co-author) on the east-west rail route near Claydon as part of a visit organised through one of the All-Party Parliamentary Groups which foster engagement between the railway and parliamentarians. *Christopher Austin*

Sir Bob Reid and John Welsby in 1993 as Chairman and Chief Executive of the British Railways Board. *BRB annual report and accounts 1993/94*

The overriding objective was to deliver it prior to the 1997 election regardless of any problems encountered or changes that should have been made at an earlier stage. A ruthless guillotining programme (the 'star Chamber') was set up by DfT to force decisions to meet this timescale. This was a tough target for ministers as they were dependent on the new Franchising Director, Roger Salmon[241] to let the contracts, which as we have seen above were closely watched by opponents of the policy. It was indeed a close-run thing and the last franchise, Scotrail, was let on 31 March 1997 just prior to the general election on 1 May. Most freight companies had also been sold by this date, although Railfreight Distribution was not finally sold until November of that year.

It was driven by political dogma with the arguments fashioned to justify the outcome. The policy could have been developed more effectively by using the work of the Department under John Palmer, and involving the Board instead of imposing decisions on it. The driving force came from a 'Westminster bubble' view of the world, formed from media coverage and 'think tank' reports rather than coherent briefing from DfT officials or BR based on facts.

Arguably, it set back planning on the railway by around ten years and created a huge gap in investment in rolling stock, resignalling and particularly in electrification.

Managers inevitably took their eyes off the ball during this extended and difficult process, and performance dropped. It could, however, all have been so much worse, but two things stand out during this turbulent period.

The first was the role of John Welsby as BR Chairman, who ensured that his people did what was required in a timely and efficient manner. Without his calm authority and firm grip on the process, we do not believe the programme would have been delivered within a single Parliament. Without him, the process would have been fairly chaotic, would have extended uncertainty and risked service quality collapsing as management focus inevitably shifted and as a result of job insecurity.

The second was the remarkable determination of most railway managers to carry on running the railway safely and reliably during this seismic upheaval. The new processes were not well thought through and many problems arose during implementation, but the relationships between managers whose experience and mutual respect had been built during their time with BR ensured that, by and large, passengers were unaware of the problems and the train service continued to run fairly seamlessly. Some managers actually welcomed privatisation, thinking that it would give them a freedom to manage that they could not have under BR. Some indeed, did initially make good use of their opportunities, and some, in the right place at the right time, made fortunes when their management buyouts were sold on and they were able to enjoy the profits of sale. For others, though, the initial freedoms they enjoyed were soon to be replaced by even more constraints as regulation tightened and every change required DfT consent under franchise agreements that were highly prescriptive, running to over 1,000 pages of detailed requirements.[242]

---

[241] Roger Salmon was a merchant banker with Rothschilds who had been involved in a number of privatisations including the gas and water industries.

[242] The West Coast Partnership Agreement of 2019, for example, ran to four volumes and a total of 1,370 pages.

What BR Could Have Done

At the end of this chapter it is appropriate to address the question of what BR could have done with the level of resource put into the privatised railway. It is, of course, a purely hypothetical proposition, as the political reality was that resources would not have been made available to BR, but a number of points can be made.

With the benefit of hindsight, it is now clear that had BR continued to operate, Britain would have had a cheaper railway than it does today. Passenger numbers would not have grown so significantly as BR would have controlled growth through pricing and a lot of money would have been saved in not expanding capacity as much as has been done. BR would have continued to live within its cash limits, although the requirements of higher safety standards, such as the Train Protection and Warning System (TPWS),[243] and replacement of Mark I rolling stock would have meant that there was precious little money for investment in enhancements.

The railway would have avoided a decade of disruption and reorganisation when staff and managers were pushed hard by government to reorganise within a tight timescale – a period when normal development work stopped. It continued long after privatisation was essentially complete in 1997, as further reorganisations took place to make the system work, particularly around the collapse of Railtrack and its replacement by Network Rail in 2002.

There was a five-year hiatus in investment, with no rolling stock orders placed for five years between that for the 'Networkers' in 1993 and the first of the new Chiltern class 168 units in 1998. Everything stopped while new structures were established, plans developed and funds raised. Strategic planning stopped for a rather longer period, because of the need for BR to prepare for the changes, starting in 1992 and lasting until the shadow Strategic Railway Authority got into its stride, around 2000, perhaps eight years.

Chiltern Railways were the first train operator to order new rolling stock after privatisation, with their class 168, one of which is shown here, at Quainton Road, during a VIP tour of lines north of Aylesbury, supporting the emerging plans for the East/West Rail project. *Christopher Austin*

---

[243] TPWS is designed to reduce the likelihood and consequences of a signal being passed at danger (SPAD), or a train exceeding permissible speed, either at a permanent speed restriction or on the approach to a set or points or buffer stops.

Had BR continued, rolling stock investment would have been relatively stable, at just over 200 vehicles a year, the number required to keep the average age steady.

Electrification would have been carried out more efficiently and with greater cost-effectiveness than proved to be the case with Network Rail, and that would have been a BR priority for both cost and environmental reasons.

Other investments, such as resignalling, would have taken place earlier than was the case under Railtrack, and the time and money wasted on trying to apply radical technical innovation such as moving block signalling would not have held up projects like the West Coast Main Line upgrade.

Most significantly, the creation of Railtrack and subsequently Network Rail had the effect of putting the strategic management of the railway back in the hands of the principal spending organisation, and its engineers, from which Sir Robert Reid had worked hard to remove it just a decade earlier. One clear effect of this on passengers was the nature and extent of engineering works and the trend to close a railway while work was undertaken, rather than using two tracks out of four, or putting in single-line working. The disruption caused to passengers' journeys over the eight years spent upgrading the West Coast Main Line was of epic proportions.

Some things would not have been so good, however: Stations were repainted regularly at the beginning of each franchise (to reflect the new corporate identity) and its end (under the contractual requirement to make good 'dilapidations'), and stations generally are in a much better condition than under BR's ownership, when expenditure was squeezed out by the need to put the bulk of the civil engineering budget into track maintenance and renewals.

Further major station development would have taken place and BR was experienced in making the most of partnerships with developers to achieve this, but it would have been on a more modest scale and, as John Welsby told a meeting of the Retired Railway Officers Society in 2018, BR would not have spent £800 million at Reading. The extravagant scale of the changes at Birmingham New Street would probably not have happened either.

Passenger growth would not have been so high, as government pressure (and BR's approach) would have been to manage demand through price, rather than plan to expand capacity for demand created by cut-price travel. Significant growth would have taken place but would have been more gradual. Similarly, we do not believe that train mileage would have increased so quickly as it did after privatisation. Frequencies generally would have been lower than exist today, but performance would have been better as a result.

Before the first privatised trains ran, the Secretary of State (Sir Brian Mawhinney[244]), announced a real reduction in regulated fares, replacing the cap imposed on BR of RPI +1 by RPI −1 for four years. While this was a sweetener to encourage acceptance of the policy, it did bring tangible benefits to passengers and helped to encourage the increase in ridership that was a feature of the post privatisation period.

Most significantly perhaps, government would have retained absolute control of the costs of the railway without taking the public criticism for shortcomings of the service, which it could have continued to attribute to BR. By taking control, ministers also were forced to take on responsibility and be directly accountable to passengers, which is not a tenable position for any government.

---

[244] Brian Stanley Mawhinney, Lord Mawhinney (1940–2019), was Conservative MP for Peterborough, 1979–97, and North West Cambridgeshire, 1997–2005. Appointed to House of Lords in 2005. Held a succession of ministerial offices, including Secretary of State for Transport, 1994–95, serving as Chairman of the Conservative Party and Minister without Portfolio, 1995–97. He was knighted in the 1997 Dissolution Honours.

8

Labour in Control, 1997–2010

'Railways are a growth industry. Their most sustained attempts to drive away their customers have not succeeded.'
Christopher Fildes, *The Spectator*, July 2001

Passenger Growth and Service Expansion

The Conservative government had developed a narrative of poor-quality services and management that they deployed to justify the policy of privatisation of BR, much in the way the Labour Chancellor of the Exchequer, Hugh Dalton, had in 1947 to justify nationalisation. Before losing his seat in the 1992 election, the minister Francis Maude was in charge of the campaign to keep the media supplied with examples of the shortcomings of BR, and particularly its chairman, the second Sir Bob Reid. The incoming Labour government could have turned this round and actively supported railway staff and managers (who were virtually all of BR origin) but instead chose to criticise performance and operation of the railway on the grounds that every failure was down to privatisation. This would have been a reasonable tactic to deploy if there had been a plan to change the organisation, its objectives and its funding, but there was initially no such plan and even the 1998 white paper did not propose to unpick the structure put in place by the Major government. The result was continuing tension between ministers and civil servants and some disenchantment in the companies being criticised and their staff.

In spite of this, passenger growth took off coincidentally with privatisation, partly as a result of service development (more trains), a higher public profile and growth of very cheap advanced purchase tickets. As new rolling stock orders eventually came through, they too improved the product and encouraged passenger growth, particularly as new trains with power points and wi-fi enabled passengers to make more productive use of their time on the train. The period also coincided with demographic changes, and in particular the metrocentric development of businesses with a return of activity to city centres like Leeds and Manchester, which encouraged an increase in rail commuting.

Mention should also be made of the rapidly improving information on services, which meant that potential passengers no longer had to leaf through voluminous timetables, but could find the information on times (and fares) relatively easily online. The effective work carried out by National Rail Enquiries eventually extended this to the growing phenomenon of social media and to information, payment and ticketing via mobile phones. This has made the railway highly accessible to young people in particular, who now use the system with confidence and at prices they can afford.

The new companies were quick to build links with the communities they served and the MPs representing them, to the extent that Great North Eastern Railway (GNER), for example, built a formidable level of support in Yorkshire and the North East, which they drew on heavily when it came to franchise renewal. On local services, the development of community rail partnerships and station adoption schemes led to close involvement of many communities with their railway, with improved perceptions and practical help in landscaping land around stations and deterring vandalism and trespass. Others, like Connex, failed to do this, so continued to be regarded with dissatisfaction and even anger by some of their customers, for whom rail commuting was a distressed purchase with little by way of competitive choice.

West London Line. BR started a basic service in 1994, and started to tap a large market travelling across the river via Clapham Junction, which has been successful given traffic congestion and its effect on bus services and the comparative speed of the train. Local stations along the line have opened up new markets and provided useful interchanges with the Underground at West Brompton and Shepherds Bush. A Connex class 319 calls at Kensington (Olympia) in 1998.
Geoffrey Tribe/Online Transport Archive

In contrast with the initial failings mentioned in the previous chapter, some companies got off to a good start. GNER[245] quickly established a reputation for excellence and Chiltern broke the logjam of rolling stock orders by procuring class 168 units. They also won a twenty-year franchise from the newly established SRA based on ambitious plans to double the line between Princes Risborough and Aynho Junction, provide additional rolling stock and construct the spur at Bicester to allow a new London–Oxford service to be run.

On the other sign of the coin, some did not shine and in 2002 the Connex South Eastern franchise was terminated by the SRA, not for its poor performance but for coming back for more money than agreed to deliver its franchise commitments. The GNER franchise ended when its parent company, Sea Containers, filed for bankruptcy in 2006. Its successor, National Express, found it could no longer meet the terms of its franchise and effectively handed the keys back to the department in 2009.

Most recently, South Eastern had its franchise terminated early when it was revealed that it had failed to return £25 million of government funding due under the agreement.

Welsh government has taken over the running of the Wales & Borders franchise and Scotland did the same for the Scotrail franchise in 2022. Other franchises were suspended as a result of the Covid pandemic, and have been replaced by passenger service contracts overseen by the department.

It is worth observing that, while BR was prevented from bidding for franchises under the Railways Act, 1993, of the eighteen franchises currently in place, no fewer than ten are owned or part-owned by overseas state railways, while a further three are run by DfT, one by Transport for Scotland and one by Transport for Wales, leaving just three wholly private sector operations.

The full list of agreements at the end of 2021 is set out in Appendix 8.

---

[245] Great North Eastern Railway (owned by Sea Containers Ltd).

Under Christopher Garnett's inspired leadership, Great North Eastern Railway (GNER) built a strong reputation for innovation and good customer service on the East Coast Main Line from 1996. The financial position of its holding company Sea Containers Ltd and demanding franchise terms meant that it lost the franchise in 2007. During its franchise the mainstay of the service was the Class 91 with Mark IV carriages. A southbound service is shown here at Edinburgh in 2000. *Geoffrey Tribe/Online Transport Archive*

Investing in growth. Chiltern Railways under their MD Adrian Shooter were active in investing in infrastructure for growth. Their first project was to provide a down platform and footbridge at Princes Risborough (which they still own) to overcome the bottleneck of a single through platform at this busy station. It also now provides access to platform 4, used by the Chinnor & Princes Risborough heritage railway trains. *Geoffrey Tribe/Online Transport Archive*

Transport for Wales took over the franchise for Wales and the Borders in 2021. Here a Class 175 at Shrewsbury displays the new livery. *Peter Waller*

Customer Service

In general, reasonable services to passengers continued to be provided under privatisation, as the same staff, managers and equipment were being used. South West Trains allowed the number of drivers to reduce in the pursuit of 'efficiency', but soon reversed this policy when cancellations started to rise and the penalties started to bite. Some operators fell short of the standards expected on cleanliness and, when challenged, fell back on the strict terms of the contract (franchise agreement) rather than seeking to provide the standards expected by passengers and the SRA.

But when the first franchise agreement was prematurely terminated with Connex in 2002, it was not because of poor standards, about which there were many complaints, but for financial inadequacy and seeking to vary the terms of their franchise agreement, the terms of which they could no longer meet.

On the freight side, the principal new owner, the English, Welsh and Scottish Railway, a subsidiary of the Wisconsin Central Railroad, invested heavily in new locomotives and, in a departure from BR practice, wagons. Indeed the demand was sufficient for manufacturer Thrall to establish production at the recently closed carriage works in York for four years from 1998 to 2002. The operator was more customer-focused than had been possible for BR with its unrealistic government-imposed financial targets, and some traffic was recovered to rail and new traffics gained.

Railtrack was not so good with its customers and stakeholders and proved a difficult partner for agencies such as local authorities to deal with, requiring payment for any work done to consider new rail projects to benefit local communities and contracts required even for attending planning meetings. It was the first sign that the private sector was not entirely made up of innovative entrepreneurs who would transform the railway, but included a collection of rather lacklustre bean counters who were unwilling to do anything new unless it were underwritten by the Franchising Director or the SRA beforehand. When third parties attempted to engage with Railtrack over new infrastructure investment (*eg* a station opening) it was commonplace for NR's quote to contain a 'contingency' of plus or minus 30 per cent.

EWS bought the lion's share of the rail freight business in 1995 and invested heavily in new locomotives and wagons. The standard design was the General Motors Class 66 loco built in Canada which have proved to be reliable and effective. *Geoffrey Tribe/Online Transport Archive*

Strategy: the 1998 White Paper

The greatest post-war opportunity for the railway perhaps came with John Prescott's white paper of 1998, *New Deal on Transport*, a ten-year plan charting a positive direction for the railway. It was an unusual, and perhaps unique overview of the issues relating to transport and its effect on peoples' lives and the economy. It was a huge and comprehensive document of 152 pages covering all modes, and had some important pointers for rail. The main structural change proposed was the formation of the Strategic Rail Authority, which would be charged with producing the strategic vision for the railway, with a strong encouragement for growth, integration, and accountability for the private sector providers. In particular, the white paper indicated the need to plan the railway as a network, rather than a collection of franchises, and to link it with local authorities and agencies' objectives and land use planning. There was a strong emphasis on expanding rail freight, providing capacity on routes where passenger services were being improved and managing rail freight grants to encourage transfer from road. It was clear from the document that expectations were high that the railway could also simplify fares, expand accessibility, and improve security, particularly for women travellers, and to let passengers have a louder voice in developing plans.

It was an exciting and challenging document, and was a bold move away from the silo approach of earlier rail white papers. Costs were still clearly a concern, but the emphasis was as much on value for money rather than the earlier approach of minimising support levels. It could be argued that there were some internal inconsistencies or that, at least, the programme was too demanding to tackle all these issues at the same time, but it was bold and progressive and sought to make the most of the railway in the state in which the Blair government found it after privatisation.

So, when this was followed a long eighteen months later by ministerial guidance, it was disappointing to see that this was essentially tactical and short term. It came in the form of a letter dated 15 February 1999 from the Transport Minister, Lord Macdonald,[246] to Sir Alastair Morton, who was at that point Chairman both of the British Railways Board and of the Shadow Strategic Rail Authority (SSRA). Apart from setting out how he should approach BRB's residual responsibilities, and the process of establishing the SRA, it gave no overall vision of what the railway should be doing, but still required the SSRA to produce an initial strategic plan within the first six months following an assessment of the network's capability. There was a general injunction to seek to improve performance, integration and value for money in negotiating new or extended franchises, but these would, in any case require the prior consent of the Secretary of State. There was a general requirement to bring forward from time to time proposals for increasing investment to increase capacity and for integration with other transport modes, but nothing relating to objectives, targets, or success criteria and precious little on freight.

Eight months later, the Hatfield accident set in train a series of events that meant the priority became restoring the network and safety-related expenditure, and it was clear by early in 2001 that this is where the money would go, and that most of the opportunities so tantalisingly offered in July 1998 had been taken away to pay for the shortcomings revealed by Hatfield.

The Strategic Rail Authority realised that, following these disasters, the case for rail had to be made again and made more strongly if it were to succeed in regaining public and political confidence and securing the future funding the industry would need. In 2003 the Authority produced both a strategic plan and 'Everyone's Railway', the wider case for rail, which did this, but again, sadly, within a year government plans to disband the SRA were being prepared and in 2005, another major restructuring of the railway meant that the continuity was lost, strategies were not followed through and there was again no leadership for the industry. The only remaining benefit for rail managers was the longer planning timescale than that which BR had endured. Instead of budgets being set annually (and then revised in the course of each financial year), planning was on the basis of the five-year Network Rail 'control periods' and the contractual commitments in franchises, which were typically of seven years' duration.

Safety Management

On 12 December 1988, a collision occurred at Clapham Junction as a result of a signal wiring error during the Waterloo Area Resignalling Project, and thirty-five passengers died with 500 being injured. The accident came at a time of public concern about the vulnerability of passengers in Mark I slam-door rolling stock, and of overcrowding. Unusually, the government asked Anthony Hidden QC[247] to hold a formal investigation into the causes of the accident and the circumstances surrounding it, rather than the railway inspectorate. While the immediate cause of the accident was not in doubt, Hidden's report into the context of it was thorough and his ninety-three recommendations covered a very wide range of issues affecting not only BR, but the Department and the emergency services.

In the context of this book, Hidden recognised the risks of major reorganisation, its effect on both morale and the management of projects and of the safety of the railway. The key recommendations in this context are:

> 34. BR shall require that any future reorganisation shall be properly planned, effectively resourced and implemented to an agreed timetable which takes account of all relevant problems.
> 50. BR shall ensure that the organisational framework exists to prevent commercial considerations of a business-led railway from compromising safety.[248]

These recommendations stemmed from the reorganisation of the Southern Region S&T department, but were about to be replicated on a much larger scale by BR with Organising for Quality, where the lessons of Clapham were still fresh in the minds of BR managers, and the even greater upheaval of privatisation starting three years later, where there was little reference to these prescient recommendations.

After the privatisation white paper had been published, the Health and Safety Commission, which was at that stage responsible for Her Majesty's Railway Inspectorate, published a report on the safety issues to be addressed as a result of privatisation. There were thirty-eight recommendations to keep the railways safe in a 158-page document that included nineteen appendices. Recommendations included the requirement for each company to produce a railway safety case, the reporting and review of incidents, and provision for continuing safety research. Most importantly (but not unexpectedly), the report asserted the continuing central role of HSC/HSE as the regulatory authority on railway safety.

In their authoritative history of Her Majesty's Railway Inspectorate, Ian Prosser and David Keay reflected the risks involved in the major changes at privatisation, saying: 'As well as contributing to the liberalisation agenda, there was

---

[246] Angus ('Gus') John Macdonald, Lord Macdonald of Tradeston (b 1940) Minister for Transport in the Department for the Environment Transport and the Regions under John Prescott, 1999–2001. Member of the House of Lords, 1998–2017, and Scottish Office and Cabinet Office minister. A former marine fitter who worked in the Glasgow shipyards, 1956–63, he became a journalist on *The Scotsman*, 1965–67; and a successful producer, presenter and executive on Granada Television, Channel 4, and Scottish Television.

[247] Sir Anthony Hidden QC (1936–2016), Judge of the High Court of Justice, Queen's Bench Division, 1989–2003.

[248] *Investigation into the Clapham Junction Railway Accident*, Cmnd 820, HMSO, November 1989.

still the "day job" of ensuring that the rail network was managed safely. It is well known and understood that change presents new safety risks, not least because individuals can become preoccupied and distracted as to the security of their own employment. This period undoubtedly put additional strain on the industry and it is testament to the dedication of all rail staff that safety standards did not deteriorate in the run-up to privatisation.'[249]

Following privatisation, a series of fatal accidents at Southall (September 1997), Ladbroke Grove (October 1999), Hatfield (October 2000), and Potters Bar (May 2002) took place, and were blamed by the media on privatisation. The root cause of the first two was signals passed at danger, while the latter two were caused by the condition of the track. Of the four, the one that had the biggest effect was that at Hatfield, where a rail shattered underneath a passing train. The condition of the rail was known and it had been earmarked for replacement, which had been delayed by the problems and cost of arranging a track possession and the effects of the incentive regime set up at privatisation, which discouraged taking emergency possessions. It led to the imposition of 20mph speed restrictions throughout the country, and the collapse of the national timetable. A month after the accident there was a total of 3,400 sites where gauge corner[250] cracking had been identified, and it was a further seven months before the bulk of these had been cleared and something approaching a normal service had been restored.

The full story is told elsewhere, particularly in the HMRI report and in Terry Gourvish's history,[251] but for the purposes of this book, the effects of this resulted in a collective nervous breakdown by the railways (as Sir Alastair Morton told an industry emergency conference in November 2000), and led to increased road congestion and a big boost for domestic airlines. The principal politicians, Tony Blair as Prime Minister and John Prescott as Secretary of State, were hugely frustrated at the inability of the industry to sort out its problems in reasonable time. Most importantly, it caused a collapse of public confidence in the railway, by its big customers like the Post Office as well as passengers. Worse still, the subsequent reviews that led to increases in Railtrack's budget to tackle the maintenance and renewals backlog came largely from the budget of the newly formed SRA, with a premature end to many of the improvement projects being planned in response to Prescott's upbeat 'New Deal' ten-year plan set out in his white paper of 1998. Within two years, mismanagement by Railtrack had squandered the opportunities offered by a supportive government and set in train a series of events that was to lead to its own demise.

The reviews of safety management that followed the Clapham Junction accident led to a renewed focus under the second Sir Bob Reid, led by Board member David Rayner and Safety Director David Maidment, and one of your authors worked with them to produce a safety plan in 1991. At the end of the BR period, in the financial years 1993–94 and 1994–95 no passenger was killed in a train accident. At the same time, the high level of track worker deaths was reduced from an annual average of over eight in the 1980s to zero in 1994.[252]

The febrile atmosphere of the early years of privatisation meant that it was blamed for every railway problem, and this was made worse by the HSE, which was quicker to criticise the industry and its managers than to identify the underlying issues on railway safety and help the industry put them right. This was replicated by the Secretary of State, John Prescott, and gave a clear field to the media to focus on the blame game, making it difficult to have an informed public discussion on what needed to be done. Ian Prosser and David Keay wrote: 'Bluntly, HSC and HSE routinely poured petrol on the flames of public concern and with no political air cover, the unprotected rail industry was left to largely fend for itself – a task for which it was both unprepared and ill-equipped. Reputational damage was immense.'

In 2006, Alastair Darling took the decision to move HMRI from HSE to the Office of Rail Regulation.

After the accidents referred to above in the early years of privatisation, significant efforts have been made by railway companies and regulators to manage safety consistently and as the overriding priority, reflected in the lower number of accidents recorded compared with earlier decades, but occasional accidents, such as that at Carmont in August 2020, remind us that constant striving is needed to continue to drive down numbers towards zero.

The Strategic Rail Authority

The SRA was the vision of John Prescott to fulfil Labour's election pledge in the 1997 election manifesto to 'provide a clear, coherent and strategic programme for the development of the railways so that passenger expectations are met,' as well as Tony Blair's ill-defined 1997 election manifesto promise to reconstitute British Rail as a publicly owned, publicly accountable company holding the public's interest in the rail network. It was designed to combine functions of the Franchising Director and the Department for Transport and, in a neat touch, the vehicle to set it up in shadow form was the British Railways Board, which still existed, although it no longer ran trains. To lead it, a strong man with a proven track record in raising investment from the private sector was

---

[249] *Her Majesty's Railway Inspectorate from 1840*, Ian Prosser CBE and Eur Ing David Keay, Steam World publishing, 2019.

[250] The 'gauge corner' was the upper corner of the rail, facing inwards towards the other rail that together supported the train.

[251] *British Railways 1997–2005. Labour's Strategic Experiment.* Terry Gourvish. Oxford University Press, 2008.

[252] *British Rail 1974 –97. From Integration to Privatisation*, Terry Gourvish, Oxford University Press, 2002.

Rt Hon John Prescott MP, Deputy Prime Minister 1997-2007. *Shutterstock*

chosen, Sir Alastair Morton. The full implementation of this project, however, had to await legislation in the form of the Transport Act, 2000, which did not receive Royal Assent until 30 November 2000, over three and a half years after the election of May 1997.

Morton was a giant of a man, intellectually and in terms of his drive, energy and his financial skills, used to command and someone who did not suffer fools gladly. He worked well with John Prescott, whose vision he shared and with whom he was comfortable working. Not so, with the civil servants, whom he saw as too often getting in the way of what needed to be done, and he had no patience with the restrictions imposed by government on the actions that the SRA was allowed to take, and the need for his decisions to be cleared with No. 10 first.

Sadly, John Prescott was by then at one remove, grappling with his responsibilities as Secretary of State for Environment, Transport and the Regions at Eland House at Victoria, as well as being Deputy Prime Minister. Three Transport Ministers passed through the revolving doors in Great Minster House (where the Transport Ministers and civil servants were based) in quick succession in 1999 and the legislation was piloted through by Lord Macdonald, with whom Morton did not have the same rapport.

The senior civil servants were ill prepared to meet the needs of the incoming government, but to be fair to them, this was as much to do with a lack of clear direction from ministers as a desire to obstruct. On one thing, however, they were clear, and that was their desire to control the costs of the railway and they did not want to cede this responsibility to another agency. They duly went along with the implementation of the 1998 white paper proposals to set up the SRA, although the work to do so was largely undertaken by Sir Alastair Morton, its first Chairman, and his team.

The industry was shaken by the Hatfield accident, as described above, and subsequently by Railtrack being put into administration by the Secretary of State, Stephen Byers, in 2002. Apart from the effect of Hatfield, the company had failed to deliver the planned upgrades to the West Coast Main Line and the project had to be rescued by the SRA.

After Morton resigned in 2001, he was replaced by Richard Bowker, who, initially was offered only a three-year contract, which gives an indication that the mandarins expected to change things sooner rather than later. Bowker, however, insisted on a five-year term, quite properly given the amount of work required by the Authority to deliver on the government's objectives and sort out the previous lack of leadership. Nevertheless, the civil servants persuaded the Secretary of State, Alastair Darling, that further radical change was required, and the SRA's role duly ended in 2005 when the responsibilities for franchising, major projects and strategic direction were taken on directly by the Department.

Whilst this change was badly handled by the Department, it did have two significant benefits that unexpectedly improved the relationships between the industry and government. It involved the creation of an expanded rail division, with a number of professional railway staff transferred to it who both infused expertise and saved a fortune in consultancy costs. Among the highly respected professionals moving across were Stuart Baker and Peter Wilkinson. It also breached the walls between the Department and the industry as many of those transferred from the SRA had good industry links, and this helped to break down the distrust and secrecy that had existed previously. Thereafter, it was easier to have a dialogue with the Department instead of waiting for the next diktat.

With the welter of criticism that surrounded the SRA, it is important to recall the important steps it did take during its brief existence. In particular, the project to upgrade the West Coast Main Line was out of control and the SRA put in place an achievable specification and brought costs down from over £11 billion to around £8 billion, while delivering most of the planned benefits in terms of journey time and capacity improvements.

The lack of any overarching strategy previously meant that huge new orders of third-rail electric trains had been placed to replace slam-door trains on train operating companies in the south-east, to meet a government commitment. These trains were more powerful than those they replaced, had air conditioning as well, and the existing traction supply system on the former Southern Region could not cope with their additional power requirements. The fragmentation of the industry, coupled with the lack of practical railway experience by many of the new players, meant that the need to support the more powerful new trains with enhanced traction current supplies had been overlooked. Again, it was the SRA that pulled together a credible plan to do this and provide the required depot facilities and a deployment programme that met the government's requirements as well as those of manufacturers, operators and Railtrack, and had to carry the £652 million cost on its budget.

All these additional costs due to Railtrack's shortcomings and additional government demands (on eliminating Mark I rolling stock) meant that little money was left for the enhancements in the ten-year plan, and Railtrack was not keen to undertake them anyway. Nevertheless, Bowker persuaded them to deal with three major impediments to expansion and performance on the Great Western main lines by doubling 7 miles of singled line between Probus and Burngullow in Cornwall, expanding the capacity of the bottleneck at Filton Abbey Wood and providing a new platform four on the down side at Swindon, to avoid down trains having to cross and recross down and up main lines to serve the station (a cost-cutting nonsense dating from the 1960s.)

Jim Steer, the internationally renowned transport planner, was recruited by Bowker to undertake the huge task of linking rail planning with local authority land use plans for the first time, to start to steer railway investment towards the needs of the railway's future customers. It was the SRA that started to address the needs of freight and upgrading the capacity of routes from the principal container ports to cater for the burgeoning demand for container trains.

The cost of local services, particularly on the Northern Rail franchise, became a source of serious concern to the Department (and the Treasury), which led to a Northern Rail Review of their services in 2006 with a view to cutting services to a level that was considered more likely to be affordable.[253] It was the SRA (under one of your authors) that worked up the Community Rail Development Strategy, which helped policy makers to understand the real value of local lines, and engage with community groups to improve stations and make the case for enhanced services, which meant that these lines delivered much better value for money than they had before.

At the same time, the SRA had to deal with the fallout (and the budgetary consequences) of the Hatfield accident, the collapse of Railtrack, and the growing demands for station and service improvements across the country. Not a bad record for an organisation that lasted only five short years until it was put down by government.

The Collapse of Railtrack

Railtrack never really recovered from the trauma of the Hatfield accident on 17 October 2000, and the disastrous investment decisions on the West Coast Main Line. Public perception, never good, was hardened by the decision of the company to pay a dividend to shareholders in 1999–2000 despite the company's losses that year of over £½ billion.[254]

Even before Hatfield, the conclusion had been emerging in government and the SRA as well as among train operators that Railtrack was not fit for purpose and discussions on alternatives had started. Initially, the SRA and the Regulator had been involved, but as the financial situation worsened, the urgency of doing something became more acute and during the summer of 2001 the serious discussions were between No. 10, the Treasury and the Department. When the decision to put Railtrack into administration was made on 8 October it was done by the Secretary of State, Stephen Byers, following a decision on the previous Friday that had been made without the involvement of the rail industry and particularly the Regulator, Tom Winsor,[255] and the SRA under Sir Alastair Morton.

The affairs of Railtrack plc (not Railtrack Group) were put in the hands of four administrators from Ernst & Young, an expensive process, both in terms of their fees, but also because there followed a huge increase in spending to restore the network wrecked by huge numbers of speed restrictions.

With the benefit of hindsight, the removal of Railtrack was inevitable in the light of their continued financial problems, poor management and the arrogant approach of the company to its customers and sponsors, as well as its poor operational performance. The secretive way in which it was done, however, marked a new low point in the relationship between government and industry and a breach of trust that took a long time to heal. It led directly to the end of the SRA, replacement of the Regulator by a regulatory board, and did huge damage to the reputation of the industry.

As in other cases where major changes to the industry were planned, government was working under financial and time pressures and was trying to secure a number of disparate outcomes, so it is no surprise that the results were sub-optimal.

In this case, the changes took place during the tenure of an inexperienced Secretary of State, and in the interregnum at the SRA between Sir Alastair Morton and Richard Bowker (Bowker formally took over as Chairman nine weeks after Railtrack had been put into railway administration, on 1 December 2001). The objectives were to:

---

[253] Described in *Holding the Line*, Chapter XVIII.

[254] Christian Wolmar *Fire & Steam*, Chapter 15. Atlantic Books, 2007.

[255] Sir Thomas Winsor (b 1957) was the second Rail Regulator and International Rail Regulator for Great Britain from 1999 to 2004. He was in post at the point at which Railtrack was put into railway administration. A lawyer by profession, he was appointed Her Majesty's Chief Inspector of Constabulary in 2012. In the 2015 New Year's Honours List, it was announced that Winsor was to be knighted. In 2017, he was additionally appointed as the first Her Majesty's Chief Inspector of Fire & Rescue Services, overseeing an expanded Her Majesty's Inspectorate of Constabulary and Fire & Rescue Services.

1. Keep the period of railway administration as short as possible as costs were going through the roof, and in the initial euphoria, the hope was to keep the period as short as three months. In the event, it was to be a year before the company was sold on 3 October 2002. The Administrators' fees exceeded £20 million and, together with the fees of advisers, cost government a total of £51 million.

2. Restore the network to some semblance of normality in the interests of passengers as quickly as possible, although this too took longer than planned, and the speed restrictions imposed for rail defects were not finally cleared until seven months after the Hatfield accident.

3. Find a solution that would not put Railtrack expenditure on the public sector borrowing requirement.

4. Run a competitive process for the purchase of Railtrack.

5. Produce a solution that would not put at risk other private finance initiative projects that the Chancellor of the Exchequer, Gordon Brown, was keen to promote.

6. Replace Railtrack with a company that was run more efficiently and could rely on a lower call on public funds, even if that involved limiting the powers of the Regulator.

7. The solution should not result in breaching Brown's 'golden rule' that public sector borrowing should be for renewals and enhancements only and not to subsidise operations and maintenance.

As well as these considerations, the question of compensating Railtrack's shareholders had to be considered, although government was not keen to countenance this initially.

The government had also to deal with the resentment understandably felt by the Regulator and the SRA in being excluded from the decision, and also with the reaction from train operators, which had contractual rights with Railtrack and were adamant that some form of economic regulation of the industry had to remain.

In wider political terms, these events played out against the aftermath of the 9/11 atrocities in America, and the first US bombing of Al-Qaeda bases in Afghanistan took place on the day Railtrack's administration was announced.

It was indeed that coincidence of timing that gave rise to one of the most difficult incidents affecting the Department for Transport, Local Government and the Regions, its civil servants and ministers during the life of the 1997–2010 Labour government. The Secretary of State's political adviser, Jo Moore,[256] who had a particular responsibility for media relations, sent an email round the office on that date, suggesting that the 11 September 2001 attacks made it 'a very good day to get out anything we want to bury. Councillors' expenses?'

Not surprisingly, there was media outrage but Byers and Moore managed to withstand that. Four months later, however, in February 2002, there was an even bigger row that this time involved the Department's head of news, Martin Sixsmith,[257] a former BBC news reporter. He had issued a warning – leaked to the media – to Jo Moore saying that she should not attempt to 'bury any more bad news' on the day of Princess Margaret's funeral, and implied that that was what she was attempting to do with unfavourable railway statistics.

Moore's position was seen as untenable, and her resignation was announced on 15 February, along with that of Sixsmith. Sixsmith denied that he had agreed to go, and it transpired subsequently that Byers had insisted on that.

Unfortunately for Byers, the Department's Permanent Secretary, Sir Richard Mottram,[258] was in the middle of negotiations with Sixsmith at the time of the Byers announcement about the resignations. According to Sixsmith, Mottram said to a colleague as Byers headed to the interview studios: 'We're all fucked. I'm fucked. You're fucked. The whole department is fucked. It's the biggest cock-up ever. We're all completely fucked.'

Sixsmith included this quote in an interview with the *Sunday Times* about his 'resignation'; it was picked up extensively in the media – which usually reported it as 'f***ed' – and by the House of Commons Public Administration Committee, which interviewed Mottram on 7 March 2002. Tony Wright,[259] the chairman of the committee, commented to him that, 'Our note-takers have trouble with asterisks.'

---

[256] Jo Moore (b 1963). Former press officer for local authorities in London and later the Labour Party's chief press officer. Moore then served as Chief Press and Broadcasting Officer during the Labour Party's 1997 general election campaign. In 1998 she left her job to work part-time as an account director at a lobbying company, and was then appointed by Stephen Byers, initially part-time, as a Special Adviser, from 17 February 1999. Following her resignation she retrained as a teacher.

[257] Martin Sixsmith (b 1954), author and broadcaster who was the BBC correspondent in Brussels, Warsaw, Moscow and Washington. He was twice Director of Communications for the Government Information Service (1997–99 and 2001–02).

[258] Sir Richard Mottram (b 1946) was a career civil servant, who worked in a succession of government departments and rose to be Permanent Secretary in the Office of Public Service and Science, 1992–95; Ministry of Defence, 1995–98; DETR, then DTLR, 1998–2002; Department for Work and Pensions, 2002–05; Intelligence, Security and Resilience, and Chairman, Joint Intelligence Committee, Cabinet Office, 2005–07.

[259] Dr Anthony Wayland Wright (b 1948) was Labour MP for Cannock and Burntwood 1992–97 and Cannock Chase, 1997–2010. He was a long-serving and distinguished chairman of the Public Administration Select Committee, 1999–2010. He resigned from the House of Commons to resume his academic career as Visiting Professor in Governance and Public Policy, University College London, and Professorial Fellow, Birkbeck, University of London.

Mottram responded: 'I find the subject of the remarks I am alleged to have made with the asterisks one of the most tedious subjects I have ever had to deal with … What is actually the case is that much to my regret, actually, these remarks appeared in the newspapers, they were uttered in private to one person, with one other person in the room and they were quite clearly over the top in a number of respects, not least in describing the nature of the crisis we were engulfed in.'

Mottram's career survived these traumatic events, and he moved to become Permanent Secretary at the Department for Work and Pensions in May 2002. Byers, however, resigned as Secretary of state at the same time and has not hold ministerial office since.

Byers's troubles did not end then as three years later – in October 2005 – he was forced to make a personal statement of apology to the House of Commons for 'inadvertently' misleading the Transport Select Committee about when he first became aware of Railtrack's financial difficulties. This information came out during a court action brought on behalf of 48,000 Railtrack shareholders, who alleged that Byers and the government had deliberately damaged their interests by engineering Railtrack's collapse into administration.

The Guardian on 17 October 2005, reporting on Byers' statement to the House of Commons, described the outcome of the trial as follows:

> The claimants had accused Mr Byers of 'misfeasance in public office'. They alleged that he had plotted to engineer a situation that would leave Railtrack no choice but to go into administration. The trigger was his refusal to give the company extra cash in October 2001, and his intention had been to harm shareholders' interests.
>
> The judge said, however, that no engineering was necessary on Mr Byers's part to push Railtrack into administration. The company's financial position was so weak that, without additional government money to which it was not entitled, it would be unlikely to be able to pay its debts.
>
> The government can be said to have failed to avert Railtrack's insolvency but that cannot be said to be a fault in the government unless one can postulate a duty on government to have funded Railtrack without limit and without condition, a hopeless proposition.
>
> Mr Justice Lindsay noted that not only were the company's finances seen as being a mess, but the evidence presented to him was that it had 'allowed the railways to become a complete shambles'.

The Regulator Sets out the Cost

The rising costs of Network Rail following its establishment caused alarm throughout government and the industry, and NR's first business plan, published in March 2003, revealed a funding requirement almost double that allowed for in the Regulator's previous review of access charges in 2000.

Consequently an interim review of access charges was undertaken by Winsor during 2003, which resulted in a settlement totalling £21.45 billion for the five years, funded by direct grant, access charges and borrowing, but well beyond the budget provision that the SRA had, leaving a huge problem for government, which had no option but to pay up. However, it was not to be repeated and from this point onwards, it led to considerations of the restructuring of the industry yet again, a review of the Northern Franchise including service cutbacks and line closures and a determination that henceforth they would be in control (see Chapter 10).

What drove this huge increase in costs and was it justified? Part of it related to the huge programme of work stemming from previous accidents, including the £½ billion Train Protection and Warning System programme designed to prevent signals being passed at danger, and part to improving knowledge by the infrastructure operator of the condition of its asset base. Part of it resulted from the changes that inevitably followed from privatisation. Much of the railway expertise had been removed by Railtrack and replaced by the extensive use of contractors who had no historic knowledge of any particular stretch of track but relied on maintaining it to 'group standards'. The judgement exercised by BR civil engineers could no longer be used to defer or bring forward track renewals or major maintenance projects and it was no longer possible to require that track should be maintained to a certain standard (linked to the operational performance of trains) without providing the funding to do so. Cutting the overall budget and expecting BR to manage the consequences was no longer an option, as performance was tied up in commercial contracts with train operators and contractors. Added to this, everyone erred on the side of caution, particularly after Hatfield when some, including the maverick MP George Galloway,[260] referred to corporate manslaughter or called for charges against Railtrack and its directors.

So, the approach was cautious in terms of setting group standards and in meeting them, with each party making sure that they and their staff were not at risk of failure. Coupled with a contractual matrix where each participant in the contracting process not only included their profit element but also their adviser costs

---

[260] George Galloway (b 1954) is a British politician, broadcaster, and writer who represented four British constituencies as an MP, first for Labour in Glasgow Hillhead from 1987 (when he defeated Roy Jenkins), and then for Glasgow Kelvin. He joined the Respect Party in 2004 following his expulsion from the Labour Party in 2003 for bringing the party into disrepute, including having called on British troops to disobey orders; he won Bethnal Green and Bow in 2005, did not contest the seat in 2010, and then represented Bradford West, for three years until 2015, having won it in a by-election in 2012.

After becoming the youngest ever chair of the Scottish Labour Party in 1981, he was general secretary of the London-based charity War on Want from 1983 until 1987. He is passionately pro-Palestinian and anti-Zionist.

Open Access operations. The complexity of regulation was predicated by the assumption of on-track competition between operators. In fact it has had minimal effect and is inconsistent with making best use of the infrastructure. Here a Grand Central Class 180 is seen at East Boldon. *citytransportinfo (CC0 1.0 Universal Public Domain Dedication)*

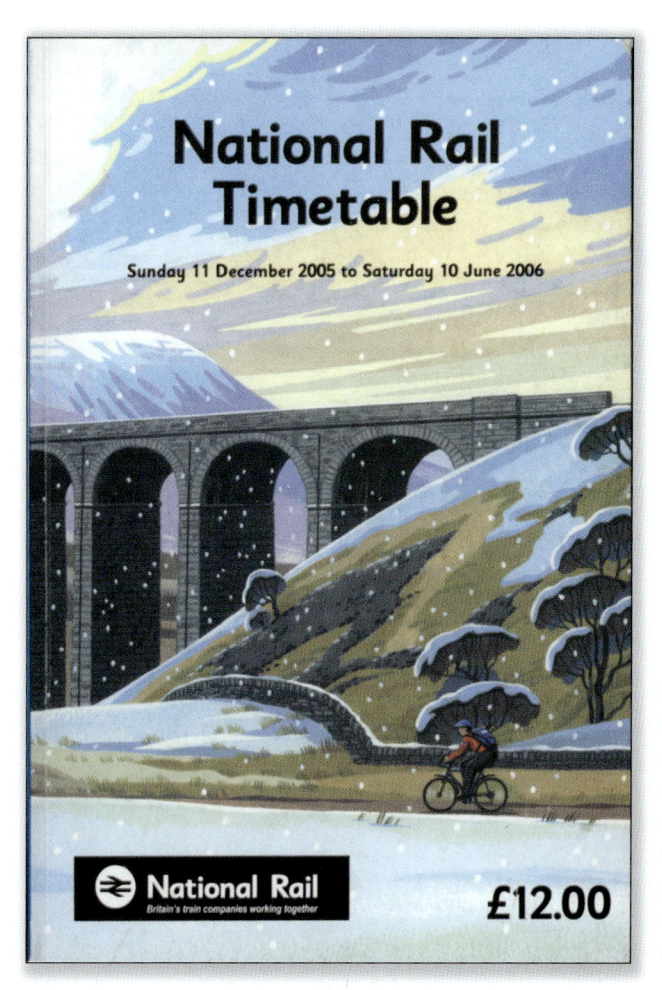

(particularly legal advice), it is perhaps not surprising that costs had risen sharply compared with those of the integrated public sector railway.

BR had worked wonders in running a cost-effective railway and part of that involved using track renewals as a financial regulator, so that in good years, more could be done and in lean years, less. Not only was that no longer possible, but it had left something of a backlog of deferred renewals that did not immediately affect the safety of the line or even its ability to support high line speeds, but would require rectifying at some stage.

So, while the escalating cost on infrastructure in 2003 came as something of a shock to government, it simply meant that the railway would require proper levels of investment in the future, with the downside that the government might deem that as unaffordable in terms of national spending priorities.

National Rail timetable 2005/6. With the demise of BR, Network Rail took over production of the national rail timetable until this final version in 2005. Other publishers continued to produce print versions until 2019. The covers were attractive railway scenes, as here, but no trains were shown to underline the impartiality of the publication between competitive operators. Timetable information is now available on line or through train operators' Apps. *Peter Waller Collection*

136

Open Access Operators

Competition between open access freight operators has been seen to be successful and the near monopoly exercised by the English, Welsh and Scottish Railway at the start has changed to a more balanced picture, as a result of new operators entering the market, and the collapse of the dominant EWS traffic in coal.

On passenger services, however, the picture is very different, and in general open access and franchise operations are essentially incompatible on a capacity-constrained route. It is acknowledged that the presence of more than one operator will tend to increase demand on a route, but brings with it a number of problems.

Passengers do not like the constraint of tickets limited to one operator, and this adds to the impression of fares complexity, which, together with misleading media reporting on fares levels, is a deterrent to rail travel.

Some passengers transfer from the franchise operator to the open access operators, reducing the former's income and reducing the value of the franchise. The consequence is that the principal franchise operator on the route will provide a lower premium, or require a higher subsidy to operate the service specified. Unsurprisingly, the Treasury is not keen on anything that diminishes the value of a premium-paying franchise. The same issue would still be of concern with the new rail passenger contracts.

On a capacity-constrained route, like the East Coast Main Line, optimising the use of the limited capacity requires the skills of an experienced timetable planner, rather than the regulatory process that has different objectives around ensuring impartial access.

The few open access operators that do exist have sought to fill gaps in the market and have accepted the regulatory constraints (in relation to stopping patterns, for example) and the system has brought some benefits to passengers in places like Hull, where the current level of service would not have been met by the franchise specification alone (and was not met previously by British Rail).

In practical terms, though, open access is of little relevance. There are around fifty trains run by open access passenger operators a day, out of a total of around 20,000. A new operator, Lumo, run by First Group, has added five trains each way between London and Edinburgh, compared with the twenty-three run by LNER and six by Avanti West Coast, although more are promised in the future.

9
The Freight Story

'A goods train! The shame of it!'
Gordon the big engine in *The Three Railway Engines*
Rev. W Awdrey, 1947

Freight Growth and Decline

Today the railway is scandalously underused for freight and some of the capability to play a greater part has been lost both in terms of route capacity and in staff and management capability. Some of this is due to changes in transport requirements, and to the de-industrialisation of Britain as production has migrated to Asian countries and the Far East, particularly to China. Some blame should be attached to the railway's poor management of the system they operated, and an unwillingness to adapt to changing transport requirements until the era of the Beeching Reports. Government inaction in the twentieth century, following surprisingly heavy-handed regulation put in place in the nineteenth, also played its part, as did political pressure from the road haulage industry and its allies and the undue influence they had on officials during the 1960s and '70s.

The main cause for the decline in rail freight is the downward trend of British industry, particularly extractive and manufacturing industries, with heavy industry like coal, shipbuilding and steelmaking bearing the brunt.

Coal

The first railways were built to carry coal, and for almost 150 years used steam locomotives fired by coal. It powered heavy industry, produced gas and electricity, and was used to heat homes. In the period 1909–13, the average annual tonnage of coal produced was 270 million tons (274 million metric tonnes), and in 1912, 225.6 million tons (229 million tonnes) was lifted by rail.[261] Some of this was long haul, such as the heavy Midland Railway coal trains from the Nottinghamshire and South Yorkshire coalfields to Cricklewood, or the later 'windcutter' trains on the former Great Central between Annesley and Woodford Halse from 1957 – block coal trains headed by the superb '9F' locomotives, a great example of efficient railway operation with steam.

Much of the coal traffic, though, was relatively short distance, notably that from colliery to power station, and one of the positive aspects of the Beeching Report was the creation of 'merry-go-round' trains, with higher-capacity 45-tonne coal hoppers behind a class 4 diesel locomotive, running continuously between loading point at the washery and the power station. Great loops at mines like Selby and power stations such as Radcliffe on Soar or Drax allowed these trains to move slowly under the loading hoppers at one end or over the discharge hoppers at the other, without stopping. This traffic was very profitable and helped support other freight flows. The Beeching Report of 1963 indicated that 'the Coal Board expected to increase their output to 200 million tons by 1966 and to sustain that level thereafter'.

However, radical change took place following the miners' strike of 1984 and the subsequent privatisation of the electricity supply industry under the Thatcher government. The cartel between BR, the National Coal Board and the Central Electricity Generating Board was broken and market forces led to a big switch to imported coal, particularly through ports like Hunterston on the Clyde, and Immingham on the Humber. While market

---

[261] Gourvish, *British Railways 1948–73*.

THE FREIGHT STORY

Coal was the reason for building much of the nineteenth century railway network and its core traffic for almost 200 years. Here a coal train from South Wales approaches Salisbury in 1961 behind an ex GWR 2-8-0. At that stage the Western route joined the Southern at Salisbury station rather than at Wilton Junction. The splendid collection of semaphore signals were pneumatically operated from Salisbury West signal box and the low pressure cylinder can be seen on the lattice post just below the diamond sign.
Christopher Austin

The huge number of smaller collieries with limited facilities meant coal wagons had to be handled individually, rather than in block trains and loading facilities meant the standard coal wagon was only 16 tons without continuous brakes. A WD 2-8-0 locomotive plods slowly along the Dearne Valley line in South Yorkshire.
John Meredith/Online Transport Archive

Before the days of North Sea gas. A train of coke hoppers is hauled past the former Finchley Road (Midland) station by a WD 2-8-0 heading north. The sidings are now occupied by Homebase and Sainsbury superstores and car parks. *Harry Luff/Online Transport Archive*

forces applied a downward pressure on rates in a shrinking market, the longer haul meant that rail revenue remained high. Costs inevitably increased with the greater length of haul, and capacity increases were needed with a huge upgrade programme on the Settle and Carlisle line, for example (only saved from complete closure in 1989), and the redoubling of the line between Gretna Junction and Annan in 2008, the flows being too great to accommodate on the West Coast Main Line.

At the same time, growing environmental awareness led to a flue gas desulphurisation plant being installed at Drax, which required large quantities of limestone, which was brought in by rail, principally from Horton in Ribblesdale on the Settle and Carlisle line.

Rapid reductions in coal traffic followed the decision to move away from coal-fired power stations in 2015.

Table 2. Reduction in Coal Traffic by Rail

Year	Freight moved (bn net tonne/km)	Freight lifted (m tonnes)
2014/15	6.50	44.0
2015/16	2.32	19.8
2016/17	1.43	12.0
2017/18	1.24	9.8
2018/19	1.17	10.5
2019/20	0.37	6.2

Source: ORR

Other Goods Traffic

Government attention has always been on passenger services rather than freight as 'freight does not vote'. However, people do, and during the nineteenth and early twentieth century the political pressure from industrialists, traders and farmers was a powerful inducement to governments to legislate to regulate or control the rates charged and the quality of service provided.

After the First World War, the railway lost its quasi-monopoly position, but the regulations remained in place while traffic leeched away to the unregulated, embryonic road haulage sector. Even after some modest controls on lorries were introduced in 1930, road haulage succeeded because it could price just under the published railway tariff to take the traffic. The haulage industry was mainly made up of owner drivers, with low overheads and capable of offering a very flexible service (and price) to their customers, while the railway was cumbersome and slow to adapt, and stories of delay, damage or pilferage of consignments by rail circulated widely with huge reputational damage, which the railway was slow to deal with.

Hauliers also benefited from the road-building programme at no additional cost, and for years paid less in licence fees than the damage they caused, as lorry weights increased steadily from the 1950s onwards. The railway tried to respond by grouping local freight terminals together, by building strategic marshalling yards to speed up the transfer of wagons from one service to another, but they failed to tackle the poor productivity of the great city centre goods depots. Dick Hardy,[262] in his portrait of Dr Beeching referred to them as 'those bastions of restrictive practices where enormous economies could have been made.'[263]

Patterns of distribution were changing too, and increasingly traders preferred to control the distribution of their products through their own fleet of lorries rather than consigning them to a third party. It also reflected the need for transport to be integrated with production as part of a seamless process that avoided costly stockholdings by delivering to destination 'just in time'. The way the railway was managed was not conducive to that and the traders were to some extent expected to fit in with the times the railway was prepared to ship and deliver their products.

By the late 1950s the system was in poor shape. Wagons were too small as the 10-ton open truck had its origins in the pre-history of railways and was more of an eighteenth-century concept than something fit for the middle of the twentieth century. Transits were too slow, and information for customers was often not available, so wagons could be 'missing' for days. Worst of all was the unreliability. Retrenchment was inevitable and as depots were closed in the mid-1960s following the Beeching Report, the railway ceased to be a network for wagon load traffic and the focus was then on trainload business. Coal for power stations underpinned the network, and paid much of the cost.

Dr Beeching's analysis in his 1963 report, *The Reshaping of British Railways*, was well researched and summarised the position accurately: 'The slow and semi-random movement of wagons, and their dispersal over many small terminals where they cannot be collected or delivered very frequently, has necessitated the provision of an enormous fleet of wagons.[264] Also, because of their random motion, all these wagons have to be capable of coupling and running with one another and of going almost anywhere on the system. This compatibility requirement, coupled with the size and cost of the fleet, has been a great obstacle to technical progress, since the new always has to mate with the old. In consequence, evolution of improved rolling stock has been very slow.'

His conclusion was that new wagons should provide new services running directly between principal centres of production and consumption rather than being staged through marshalling yards. His prophetic conclusion from the analysis of different classes of freight traffic was 'that the only traffic which the railways can carry in much larger volumes in the future is general merchandise'. He was right, although he could not foresee that much of this general merchandise would be coming from overseas in containers via UK ports, rather than from British manufacturers.

The second Beeching Report, *The Development of Railway Trunk Routes*, published in 1965, was bullish about the prospects for rail freight, forecasting a doubling of freight tonne miles over twenty years, compared with a 5 per cent reduction in passenger miles between 1964 and 1984.

In 1946, there were no fewer than 1,252,000 wagons in use on the railways,[265] so keeping track of them using the manual spreadsheets of the daily wagon return was complex, costly and ineffective as the return recorded total numbers of each wagon type, rather than the fleet numbers of individual wagons. There were 5,175 goods depots in 1962, served through 602 marshalling yards,

---

[262] Richard Hardy (1924–2018) was, in the words of the *Railway Hub* (21 August 2020) 'one of the last remaining professional links with the "Big Four" and a railwayman who commanded as much respect in the preservation era as he did during his illustrious career with the LNER and British Railways. Known affectionately in his autumn years as "the Grand Old Man of Steam", and widely regarded as the elder statesman of the heritage movement, he made a meteoric rise through the rail industry's hierarchy, becoming a shedmaster at the astonishingly young age of 22, running another five major depots before he was 35, and then overseeing the massive changeover from steam to modern traction on the busy Stratford district of the Eastern Region. Unlike many of his fellow managers, Dick was a rail enthusiast at heart and never lost his passion for locomotives and their crews.'

[263] *Beeching, Champion of the Railway?* RHN Hardy, Ian Allan, 1989.

[264] 848,591 wagons in 1963, down from 1,209,380 on nationalisation.

[265] Beeching Report, 1963.

and the volume of data required called out for record keeping involving more than pen, paper and telephone. The Total Operations Processing System (TOPS) computer system, introduced in 1975, was the very effective answer to this problem, providing real-time information on the location and status of every wagon on the system, but was too late to save the network of individual wagon load traffic that had been reduced following Beeching's report by 85 per cent by 1973. The rolling stock was at last renewed too, with a fleet of air-braked vans and open wagons capable of higher speeds and of carrying greater loads. 'Speedlink' was launched in 1977 and lasted until 1991, when recession coupled with a high cost base led to closure of the network. Even with its demise, 70 per cent of the traffic was retained through running more block trains through the much-reduced, but effective, 'enterprise' network. However, the railway's reputation and its limited network still meant it was at a disadvantage compared with the more flexible lorry and the burgeoning road network, where the government was a willing partner in upgrading it at public expense to carry first 38-tonne lorries, then 40-tonne, latterly 44-tonners, and now 48-tonne vehicles for intermodal trips.

Government Role

Government and Parliamentary interest in rail freight has generally been low, and it is noticeable in looking through the long list of government and Parliamentary inquiries into the railways (set out in Appendices 4 and 5), that one report out of 110 is devoted to freight on rail. Generally, the government approach from the 1978 white paper onwards was that rail freight was part of the 'commercial' railway and should produce a return sufficient to cover its asset replacement costs. At the same time, no attempt was made to control the unchecked growth in the number and weight of juggernauts on a highway network that was provided at public expense.

The exception to this government indifference was the provision from 1974 onwards of rail freight grants to help with the cost of provision of terminals or rolling stock where there was a saving of 'sensitive lorry miles', which meant heavy lorry miles on single-carriageway roads. After privatisation, the grants remained, but became freight facility grants, although the scheme had to be suspended by the SRA in 2003–04 when cuts in their budget meant abandoning virtually all non-committed expenditure.

International Freight. Two class 09 diesel shunters unload continental ferry wagons from the train ferry at Dover Western Docks. The ships carried more rail freight to France than travels through the Channel Tunnel today. *Geoffrey Tribe/Online Transport Archive*

International

The low level of rail freight through the Channel Tunnel has been particularly disappointing, given the longer-distance journeys involved, and the potential reliability available from the fixed link compared with a sea transit. Indeed, at the time of writing, the freight tonnage travelling through the Channel Tunnel is only about half that carried through by rail via the train ferries until the Dover–Dunkirk train ferry ceased operations in 1995. During the planning phase of Eurotunnel, the forecasts were as high as 22.5 million tonnes, compared with the 1 million tonnes that used this route in 2016. So what went wrong?

There is the basic structural problem in that the smaller loading gauge used in Great Britain requires use of specialist wagons or the transhipment of intermodal traffic at Barking, where a link to HS1 marks the northern limit for Continental-gauge freight rolling stock. A second problem is the imbalance of trade between Britain and Europe, with a consequent lack of outbound manufactured goods to balance the inflow of imported products. The inconvenient truth is that Britain no longer manufactures products in sufficient quantity to form regular complete trainloads to any single European destination.

Surprisingly, this has been accompanied by a marked unwillingness of the private sector to group traffic into trainloads and an unwillingness of the only two Channel Tunnel freight operators (DB Cargo and GB Railfreight) to undertake that function themselves. Some traffics like mineral water, car components and steel have been very successfully carried by rail since the tunnel opened, but it is particularly disappointing that intermodal traffic has failed to develop.

A further problem has been SNCF, over whose network all Channel Tunnel traffic has to pass in order to reach countries beyond, in terms of their performance and willingness to engage on traffic that originates in Britain. A particular problem here is the impact of the relatively frequent strike action by French railway staff, which makes transits unreliable. Another is Eurotunnel's charging regime, governed by the Inter-Governmental agreement, which means it is cheaper to send a container through the Channel Tunnel on a lorry on the Eurotunnel shuttle than on a through freight train.

In December 2020, the scenes of 5,500 juggernauts parked on the runway of the former Manston airport and

Market failure. Britain's logistics are too dependent on the highway network and when this fails as here, with Operation Stack in place on the M20 in Kent, the chain quickly seizes up and life is heavily disrupted. Brexit documentation, P&O redundancies and holiday traffic have all contributed to triggering this recently. *Shutterstock*

along the M20 was a clear indication of the shortcomings of a just-in-time delivery system almost completely dependent on trucks. When things go wrong, it is a system vulnerable to delay and is in any case unsustainable, as we are a long way from decarbonising the trucking industry. Rail, however, could be the electrically hauled, sustainable trunk haul system for the future, helping to decarbonise the whole logistics chain. But this needs financial incentives and leadership from government, and probably a higher cost of transport to deliver the environmental benefits required.

In the case of Channel Tunnel, successive governments have been pretty supine, accepting the market failure, which has meant that proper use has not been made of the unique national asset of the Tunnel, and too much traffic remains on road with the environmental and physical damage caused by the juggernauts that carry the goods instead. Indeed, there has been pressure from the European Commission to increase large goods vehicle weights to 60 tonnes, so far resisted in the UK. Investment in the highway infrastructure to take these greater weights is, of course, carried out at public expense by local authorities or the Highways Agency and does not fall as a direct cost on the road haulier. Enforcement is not good either, and when checks are set up, they usually reveal large numbers of overweight lorries. To be fair, the regulations are byzantine in their complexity, and the DfT acknowledges that they 'have been amended many times, which makes it very onerous to piece together the latest form of the regulations', and recommends a commercial publication to see the full picture as the full regulations on the internet are not understandable.

Apart from passing on the upgrading costs to hauliers, simplifying the regulations so that they can be understood and then enforcing them, government also needs to encourage actively the transfer to rail freight for environmental reasons as part of decarbonising freight haulage, and to invest in better transfer arrangements to ease the transfer between UIC gauge and British gauge at Ashford or Barking.

[266] Source: Rail Freight Group.

Potential for Freight Growth

The principal potential for rail is, as Beeching recognised, intermodal traffic – cargos packed in containers, which may be white goods, electronic devices, or supermarket supplies, for example. With much of the former sourced from the Far East, demand through the ports has been strong for many years now and constrained only by the limitations of capacity on the rail network. Selective investment here, particularly on the Felixstowe branch, and the West Coast Main Line as well as on the cross-country route from Ipswich to the East and West Coast Main Lines, has been successful. Already one in four sea containers arriving at a UK port is carried inland by rail, and each freight train takes sixty HGVs off the road.[266] Increasingly, rail is being used for inland intermodal as well, linking distribution centres like Daventry and Hams Hall and the main container terminals for delivery to the supermarkets' own distribution depots. Part of this is driven by the economics of the operation where long trunk hauls are involved, and part by the increasing average age and shortage of truck drivers and the difficulties in recruiting younger people as drivers. Mostly though it is driven by the environmental imperative to decarbonise transport, increasingly insisted on by retail customers. When it comes to heavy haul over long distances, rail is years ahead of road haulage in terms of providing low-carbon solutions, with scope to improve further as electrification is extended over more of the network. Together with this is a need for more terminals, notably in the South-West, where very little freight at all is carried. This is an area where government support will be needed either directly or through the sub-regional transport bodies and Local Enterprise Partnerships (LEPs), both financially and in the planning system as, despite the environmental advantage of shipping by rail there are always local protests about the location of new freight terminals.

Nineteenth-century governments were keen to intervene on freight rates and conditions to protect users while rail had a virtual monopoly of goods traffic, in spite of the strong competition between companies that then existed. This appetite diminished as road haulage developed after the First World War and became the dominant mode in the 1950s, although they were slow to free the railways of the shackles of the earlier legislation and their 'common carrier' liabilities, and this tardiness undoubtedly limited the ability of the railways to respond to this competitive threat. However, it was the changing nature of logistics and the railway's adherence to the huge network of small terminals until the mid-1960s, coupled with poor performance and restrictive practices, which ended the traditional method of handling goods traffic on the railway.

The future of freight. Intermodal trains, like this one from Felixstowe in 2012 demonstrate the scope for rail freight growth. The picture also shows the constraints of working over the single track Felixstowe branch.
Geof Shephard/CC BY-SA 3.0

With the one exception of freight facility grants and their successors, government's intervention on freight has not really helped the railway or the environment. From 1978 onwards, the only policy has been to avoid any subsidy for freight, which was seen as a 'commercial' activity for the railway. The government's 'hands off' view is well described in the 1976 'orange' consultation paper on Transport Policy:[267]

> 3.12 But what of the belief that a dramatic environmental gain would accrue if only we shifted a large amount of long-distance freight traffic from road to rail? Alas, it is a pipe-dream. To begin with, no large-scale shift of such traffic is practicable. British Rail already hold the major share of bulk long-distance traffic which is particularly suited to rail haulage ... And even if all freight movements of more than 100 miles were transferred to rail, total road traffic would be reduced by only 2–4 per cent. Again, in the unlikely event of a 50 per cent increase in rail freight, this would reduce total road traffic by less than 2 per cent and goods traffic by under 8 per cent.

The paper goes on to argue that the transfer to road for delivery would lead to increased lorry movements in sensitive urban areas. Grants, it said would be hard to justify on social and economic grounds and be ineffective as decisions on transport were often not decided on the basis of charging. Quantity licensing of road transport would increase costs and bureaucracy and cause serious confusion in industry. It goes on to argue that some roads may bring environmental gain (sic):

> 5.10 Rail Freight is also failing to meet its costs even though only avoidable track costs are charged to it. In 1975 the subsidy to British Railways attributable to freight traffic amounted to about £70m. There are no social grounds for such a subsidy. Neither ... is there a justifiable case for a general subsidy to rail freight.

The tone of the argument and the selective use of figures reflect both Tony Crosland's view and those of a government unprepared to make the most of the existing rail network to deliver environmental and wider social and economic benefits. This flawed thinking continued to be the basis of government policy on rail freight for the remainder of the time it was run by British Rail.

Rates of Return

Rail freight was badly damaged by government action in the run-up to privatisation, partly as a result of its policies in relation to the core businesses of iron and steel and electricity generation, which were the bedrock of the rail freight sector, and party because of the impossible financial targets they set BR in relation to freight. The result of these two factors together was a steep decline in rail freight tonnage to under 100 million tonnes lifted in 1994 for the first time. It had halved over the twenty-year period since the 'commercial' target had first been set.

The steel industry had been privatised (for the second time) in 1988 and the electricity supply industry in 1991. The aftermath of the 1984 miners' strike had led to massive contraction and colliery closures, and the coal industry itself was privatised in 1994 (the same year as Railtrack). The new owners were looking to reduce their costs and this included reducing the profits that BR made from coal haulage as well as purchasing cheaper overseas coal, which changed patterns of distribution in a way that required some ingenuity from BR, with its fixed infrastructure based on British collieries, rather than ports.

In 1989, the government had set trainload freight the target of a 6 per cent rate of return on its assets, with a rise to 8 per cent by 1994–95. This was an eye-wateringly high figure in a sector that was highly competitive and where margins were notoriously small, even for road haulage where the government provided the infrastructure. In order to meet this target, BR was forced to abandon some flows that covered their costs, but did not meet the required rate of return. Cement, in particular, was a victim of this unrealistic target and in total 3 million tonnes of rail freight were lost as a result.

This did produce some bad publicity, and the Rail Freight Group accused BR of 'poisoning the well' for the new freight companies. But the finger should really have been pointed at government and the undeliverable objectives. This all occurred at the same time as rail freight was being reorganised and prepared for privatisation, again an example of trying to make too many major changes at the same time, while expecting delivery of the service to continue as normal. Unsurprisingly, the targets were not met, although the cost base was considerably reduced. It seemed to be driven by the Department's obsession with cost transparency and exposing and eliminating any cross-subsidy between profitable and marginal traffics. This was itself something of an academic exercise, given the fairly arbitrary assumptions that have to be made on an integrated network in the way costs are allocated. However, the major customers supported this approach as it gave them the opportunity to negotiate even more competitive contracts to their own benefit. The losers in this battle were the environment and those whose lives were blighted by the increase in the number of juggernauts carrying traffic forced off the railway.

Privatisation

Government lack of understanding of the way that rail freight worked was evident too in their approach at privatisation. Competition was a political imperative, and so the (by then) small residual rail freight operation was divided into five companies, designed to encourage competition, despite the fact that the real competition was

---

[267] Transport Policy. A Consultation Document. Department of the Environment, HMSO, 1976.

from road haulage. But the market decided otherwise and four of the five were bought by a single purchaser, Wisconsin Central Railroad, with Freightliner being sold separately with a £75 million dowry. Wisconsin subsequently sold out to Canadian National and the principal freight company is now owned by Deutsche Bahn. Freightliner has expanded into heavy haul and also operation of engineering trains for Network Rail. The specialised business of transporting nuclear fuel in flasks for reprocessing at Sellafield was bought by Direct Rail Services, a subsidiary of British Nuclear Fuels Ltd, and so a public sector company. GB Railfreight, a spin-off from Anglia Railways, has expanded to become a significant freight operator for both heavy haul, container and Network Rail traffic. Other niche freight operators have also started up, although some have subsequently given up.

Overall, the freight sector has survived and prospered since privatisation, although this is belied by the overall decline in carryings resulting from the rapid reduction in the use of coal for electricity generation. It has had a particularly important role to play since the Covid pandemic shut down so much of the economy, making sure that supermarket shelves could be restocked and delivering other commodities such as building materials where work has continued. Freight lifted grew from privatisation until 2014–15, but has declined since by 39 per cent, largely as a result of the sharp decline in coal carryings. A better indication is provided by statistics for freight moved, which follows a similar pattern, reaching a peak in 2013–14, followed a fall of 27 per cent in tonne miles subsequently.

In their consultation paper of March 2020, the Department recognised that: 'Rail is one of the most carbon efficient ways of moving goods over long distances,' and that rail freight is becoming more efficient. Again: 'The Government recognises the economic and environmental benefits of rail freight: the sector plays an essential part of the UK economy' [sic]. Yet, there is no suggestion in that paper of any significant attempt to encourage, let alone enforce, mode switch to limit the environmental damage from road haulage. Yet, the implications of the facts set out are clear, particularly as there is currently no practical way of decarbonising heavy goods vehicles. The most sustainable system would be one based on a rail trunk haul, with local deliveries by electric vehicle from the distribution depot. Government intervention may also be required to deal with the market failure in the electricity supply industry, which had pushed costs up to levels that in 2021 meant that Freightliner had to change from electric to diesel locomotives in order to remain competitive, even before the war in Ukraine.

Rail freight is better understood by government now, and this is supported in the Williams/Shapps review. 'Freight trains reduce road congestion, connect markets over long distances and are much less carbon intensive than road freight. They have played a crucial role in keeping food and medical supplies moving during the pandemic and the freight sector will be key to building back better as we look to support economic recovery across the country.' This is a welcome change from the rhetoric of the 1976 'orange' paper and a recognition that rail freight should not be judged on its financial rate of return alone. It is also seen as a successful outcome of privatisation, and the white paper sets out to support 'the dynamic rail freight operators who have transformed that market as coal and steel traffic declined'.

10
Back in Public Control, 2005

'Privatise in haste – repent at leisure'
Frank Paterson MBE, 2002

Abolition of the SRA

After the turbulent years culminating in the collapse of Railtrack, Alastair Darling,[268] was put in charge at Transport with a remit to calm things down and keep the railway out of the headlines. He was seen as a 'safe pair of hands' to achieve this, but he had three problems. Like many of his predecessors, he had no vision for the railway nor any ambition to do anything other than keep the lid on costs. His second problem was his Treasury training, and there is no doubt that he was shocked by the burgeoning cost of the railway and his inability to control it. The third was that he was in thrall to his civil servants, who wanted to regain control.

Relationships between Darling and Bowker started in a promising way, and a strong bond was formed between them that infuriated the civil servants further. While Bowker had a plan and was steadfastly pursuing it to deliver on the major projects in hand, to hold train operators to their franchise obligations, and to control the runaway expenditure of the newly formed Network Rail, none of this earned him any friends within the industry. The reality was that the other strong players, Network Rail, the Regulator and the civil servants, were all jockeying for control and the only one that Darling could tackle directly was the SRA. In a futile attempt to cut costs and to simplify the top-heavy management of the industry, which was a consequence of the flawed privatisation of the preceding government, he decided to abolish the SRA and take back control himself.

By the beginning of 2005, the bulk of the industry was back under public ownership or control. Network Rail was a public sector company, overseen by the public sector ORR, and the SRA was a non-departmental public body and specified both services and major investment. Management of infrastructure maintenance had been brought back in house by Network Rail. The train and freight operators were in the private sector, but the former were entirely dependent on the SRA for funding as they specified the service levels and the enhancements. The ROSCOs were private sector companies, but entirely dependent on leases related to SRA specification of services and approval of contracts (to reduce residual risks). As so much of the rolling stock was route specific, this was not, in any case a normal market.

The SRA had been a creation of John Prescott when he was Secretary of State and had no support from the civil servants, who wanted to wrest control back again and who had always seen the authority as a temporary measure. The relationship between the two had been irreparably damaged by the approach of the SRA's first chairman, Sir Alastair Morton, who worked well with Prescott, but was contemptuous of the officials when they did not agree with him and took pleasure in

---

[268] Alistair Maclean Darling, Lord Darling of Roulanish (b 1952), Labour MP for Edinburgh Central, 1987–2005; Edinburgh South West, 2005–15. Secretary of State for Transport, 2002–06. Also served as Chief Secretary to HM Treasury, 1997–98; Secretary of State: for Social Security, 1998–2001; for Work and Pensions, 2001–02; for Scotland, 2003–06; for Trade and Industry, 2006–07; Chancellor of the Exchequer, 2007–10. He campaigned for a 'No' vote as chairman of Better Together, 2012–14. Member of the House of Lords, 2015–20.

showing it. Unsurprisingly, the civil servants resented this, and were critical of the way the SRA was managed, but above all, the financial performance of the organisation that, as we saw in Chapter 5, had been emasculated by the need to find additional funding for Network Rail and unfunded government commitments. The SRA also had to deal with the financial inadequacy of some of the TOCs and it became the default organisation to pick up the tab for any expenditure that did not belong elsewhere, such as station accessibility and power supply enhancements on the former Southern Region lines when slam-door rolling stock was replaced. This was one of the more expensive unforeseen results of the track/train split that had resulted from privatisation.

Generally too, there was an underlying resentment that salaries at the SRA were higher than those of the civil servants, and they criticised the extensive use of consultants as well as the delay by Morton in producing a strategic plan (Morton called his initial document a strategic 'agenda' as so much remained uncertain post-Hatfield). Subsequent plans were deemed by the Department to be lacking in financial detail and they did not like *Everyone's Railway – the Case for Rail*.

Removal of the SRA without replacement resulted in no single body being in overall control of the railways. Government wanted to take strategic control and Network Rail thought it was taking over the strategic direction of the industry.

But nature abhors a vacuum, and the default position was that DfT were in charge. This was highlighted in 2014 by a National Audit Office report, the Head of which, Amyas Morse,[269] said: 'At the moment there is a gap between the Department's stated desire to play only a strategic role in the rail industry and how it is acting. It needs to ensure that the industry understands its policy on the procurement of trains and produce a detailed integrated plan bringing together infrastructure, rolling stock and franchising strategy.'[270]

The lack of clear strategic objectives leads to uncertainty and confusion for the industry and means continued disappointment of politicians and commentators, who have failed to make clear their expectations.

Indeed, during the passage of the Railways Bill in 2005, an amendment was introduced in the House of Lords by Lord Bradshaw,[271] whose long railway experience included time as BR's Director of Policy and as an SRA Board Member. Together with Viscount Astor,[272] his amendment would have introduced a requirement for the government to produce a long-term strategy for the railway but was defeated by a small majority. As the intention was to transfer this responsibility to the Department for Transport following the abolition of the SRA, this was something of a missed opportunity.

Ironically these issues have been addressed in the latest white paper on the creation of Great British Railways, which after just sixteen years recreates a much-needed organisation to provide leadership for the railway and to take responsibility for the delivery of services to passengers and capacity for freight operators. The Secretary of State has retained extensive powers to direct the industry and to approve all significant expenditure, and it will require a proper working relationship between the two to provide the results forecast by the white paper.

Costs and Complexity

On privatisation, BR was split into over 100 companies (dubbed by Sir Peter Parker as 'The Origami Railway'[273]), and the principal consequence was that inevitably transaction costs increased as relationships were set down in contracts, prepared by expensive lawyers and requiring compliance teams to check that their terms were being met. The Williams/Shapps white paper describes the issue well: 'Co-ordination is governed by a costly, inflexible spider's web of often adversarial relationships penalties and disconnected incentives.'

In the nineteenth and first half of the twentieth century, railways were independent private companies providing essential public services, and regulated in the interests of public and staff by government.

Since 2005, we have had a railway specified by government, presumably in the public interest, but also heavily regulated by a nominally independent body – ORR – but with the inherent costs of a complex structure of suppliers and the high transaction costs that go with that.

---

[269] Amyas Charles Edward Morse, Lord Morse KCB (born 1949), was the Comptroller and Auditor General of the National Audit Office, 2009–19. He led the Coopers and Lybrand practice in Scotland before moving to London to manage the London City Office, subsequently becoming executive partner of Coopers and Lybrand UK. Recommended for appointment to the House of Lords as a cross-bench peer by the House's Appointment Commission in 2021.

[270] NAO report, *Procuring New Trains*, 9 July 2014, HC 531.

[271] William, Lord Bradshaw (b 1936). Career railwayman who joined Western Region of British Railways as a management trainee in 1959, rising through a succession of appointments to Chief Operations Manager at BR HQ, 1978; Director of the Policy Unit, 1980; and finally General Manager of Western Region, 1983–85. Special Adviser to Transport Select Committee, House of Commons 1992–97; served on the Strategic Rail Authority 1999–2001, and the Commission for Integrated Transport, 1999–2001. An active Liberal Democrat, he was a member of Oxfordshire County Council, 1993–2008, and from 2001 to 2015 was Lib Dem spokesman on transport, House of Lords, to which he had been appointed in 1999.

[272] William Waldorf Astor, 4th Viscount Astor (b 1951), was a government whip, and junior minister in the House of Lords, 1990–95. He joined the House in 1973, succeeding his father, the 3rd Viscount. He was successful in the election for hereditary peers in 1999 following the passage of the House of Lords Act.

[273] In a speech to the Railway Study Association in March 1993.

The 1.30pm train from Bristol Temple Meads to Portishead calls at Ham Green Halt on Saturday 17 February 1962. The train called on Wednesdays and Saturdays to serve the nearby hospital. This station would not be restored when the line reopens to passengers, but would stop at nearby Pill.
Christopher Austin Collection

Not only is this expensive, but it is highly inefficient and partly explains why the industry costs so much more than it did under BR and why projects take so long and are so costly.

The reopening of the railway from Bristol to Portishead involves a 3½-mile (5.6km) extension from the existing freight route at Portbury on a former rail route where the track remains (although requiring replacement). This modest little scheme has been in development since 2008, but subsequently became unaffordable when the original cost of £58 million rose to an unbelievable £145 million. To be fair, the costs included upgrading the line through the Avon Gorge for higher speeds as well as reopening the short link to Portishead. This should really have been picked up and corrected as part of the GRIP[274] process, with a sensible trade-off between journey time and cost leading to a workable solution, but this did not happen and the project was delayed while a more modest and affordable scheme was developed. Under the recent white paper, *Great British Railways*, the approach of Network Rail's project SPEED approach ('better, greener, faster, cheaper') should avoid this sort of problem in future, and the trade-offs can be properly made by a single authority with an interest in both trains and track.

Government requirements are now for a Development Consent Order as well as the various planning consents required for a new line and stations. To achieve this, the applications have required 287 documents with an incredible total of 20,735 pages, which total 6.1km if laid end to end,[275] longer than the line being reopened.

All credit to the local authorities and railway managers, who have stuck with the project despite all these setbacks, and we hope they will be successful. As we recorded in our book *Disconnected!*, the line closed to passengers in 1964 despite warnings from the Ministry of Housing and Local Government that house building proposals would put strains on the road network, and as early as 1966, the local council was lobbying to have the line reopened. Their time has surely now come. But as this example shows, the bureaucracy is out of control, and the costs (currently £116 million) are now at a level that will prevent many useful railway schemes being implemented in the future. In October 2021, the timescale for the ministerial decision on the line was extended by six months to allow fuller consideration of the environmental issues. The Development Consent order was finally approved in November 2022. The present framework does put extraordinary obstacles in the way of expanding (or in this case, reopening) parts of the rail network.

Electrification

The story of railway electrification reflects the problems the rail industry has experienced over many years in securing the sort of investment in the network that is commonplace throughout Europe, and brings a wide range of industry and societal benefits that have not yet been recognised or acknowledged by successive governments.

The first electric railway in Britain was as early as 1883 – the Volks Electric Railway on the Brighton seafront, which is still with us – and this was followed by the City & South London Railway in 1890, the Liverpool Overhead Railway in 1893 and the Waterloo & City line in 1898. In terms of suburban electrification, this was pioneered by the Mersey Railway in 1903, the Lancashire & Yorkshire in 1904 and the North Eastern on Tyneside also in 1904. In London, after earlier experiments, the Metropolitan and District Railways started regular electric services in 1905

---

[274] Governance for Railway Investment Projects – a Network Rail Process designed to flag up unaffordable schemes at an early stage.

[275] Philip Haigh writing in Rail magazine 927, March 2021.

The pioneering Volks Electric Railway in Brighton was the first electrified line in Britain and opened as early as 1883, with a gauge of 2'8½". It is the oldest electric railway in the world. *Barry Cross Collection/Online Transport Archive*

and the London Brighton and South Coast Railway (LB&SCR) launched its 'elevated electric' service on the South London line on the overhead system in 1909. The Southern continued enthusiastically electrifying its suburban network during the 1920s, converting the overhead line supply on the central section to third rail in 1925.

Main-line electrification began in 1915 when the North Eastern Railway electrified the Shildon–Newport line at 1500v DC with overhead wires, and prior to the Grouping in 1923 had developed plans to electrify the East Coast Main Line between Newcastle and York, producing an express passenger locomotive that was trialled on the Shildon line. The Southern started to electrify its longer-distance routes to the south coast, starting with the Brighton line, inaugurated in 1932.

Initially, the investment was made with capital raised by the railways themselves, although the Brighton line was facilitated by the ending of Passenger Duty (on first- and second-class tickets) in 1929, on the understanding that the railways used the capitalised value of the duty for improvements for passengers. The Southern used their £2 million for electrification.

The admirable Weir Committee report of 1931[276] (which included LNER Chief General Manager Sir Ralph Wedgwood[277]) on Main Line Electrification highlighted the advantages and drawbacks of main-line electrification that had become possible, following establishment of the National Grid, and recommended that priorities for investment should be based on traffic density.

The LNER had prepared plans for electrification between Manchester, Sheffield and Wath (MSW) in the 1930s, as well as for Liverpool Street to Shenfield, but the war intervened and post-war government controls on resources[278] restricted the bullish forecasts of the post-war investment plans made by the Big Four in the early 1940s.

---

[276] Report of the Committee on Main Line Electrification, Ministry of Transport, HMSO, 1931.

[277] Sir Ralph Lewis Wedgwood (1874–1956), 1st Baronet, the great-great-grandson of Josiah Wedgwood, founder of the famous pottery firm that bears his name, joined the North Eastern Railway at the age of 22 straight from Cambridge University. In the First World War he was Director of Docks, GHQ, France (and made an honorary brigadier general), 1916–19; Deputy General Manager, North-Eastern Railway, 1919–21; General Manager, North-Eastern Railway, 1922; Chief General Manager, London and North-Eastern Railway, 1923–39; Chairman, Railway Executive Committee, 1939–41; Chairman, Indian Railway Inquiry Committee, 1936–37. The LNER named class A4 No. 4469 *Sir Ralph Wedgwood* (renumbered 60006 by British Railways) in his honour.

[278] Particularly the decisions of the Sir Edwin Plowden's Investment Programmes Committee in 1947, which aimed to prioritise resources across industry.

Right: Electrification. Early North Eastern Railway electric train at New Bridge Street in Newcastle in 1904.
John Meredith Collection/Online Transport Archive

Below: The Shenfield electrification was planned by the LNER but completed by BR in 1949. Here two class 306 units head back to Liverpool Street in 1956, in the days before yellow warning panels on the trailer ends. *Marcus Eavis/Online Transport Archive*

Nevertheless, the Shenfield scheme was completed under British Rail in 1949, although MSW was dependent on building the new Woodhead tunnel and was not finished until 1954.

The 1955 modernisation plan included Kent Coast electrification, as well as Great Northern suburban and the Euston–Birmingham, Manchester and Liverpool lines. Scrutiny by the Select Committee on Nationalised Industries and the Stedeford Committee in 1959 and 1960 resulted in delay and the cancellation of the Great Northern scheme, where inner suburban services were not electrified until 1976. The Kent Coast scheme continued, but the case for the West Coast scheme was not effectively made by the BTC, and Dr Beeching, as a member of the Stedeford Committee, questioned the figures closely, on the basis that 2,500hp diesel locomotives would be more cost-effective. The BTC approval had been based on traffic density rather than

The LNER planned the Manchester-Sheffield-Wath electrification, but, with the war intervening and the need to build a new Woodhead tunnel, it was not completed until 1954. Here the 1500v DC locomotive *Minerva* is seen at Manchester (London Road) – now Piccadilly – with a train from Sheffield in 1960.
J. Joyce/Online Transport Archive

detailed financial analysis, and when that was done, it showed the diesel option to be better financially. By that stage, though, some £11 million had been spent on the scheme and after further analysis and argument, it was allowed to proceed. Regardless of the figures, the railwaymen saw electrification as the future, but, as happened subsequently, failed to convince the economists in the absence of supporting figures, as indicated in a letter from Sir Brian Robertson[279] writing on behalf of the Commission to Sir Ivan Stedeford: 'While the estimates show that in the short term … the comparative economics of the two systems are not wildly different, they have more confidence in the ability of an electrified service (where the density of traffic justifies its introduction) to stand up to the growing competition of air and road transport.'

Government reports on railway electrification were produced in 1920, 1928, 1931, 1960 (Stedeford Committee) and 1981, the latter being undertaken jointly by BR (Michael Posner[280]) and the Department (John Palmer). This indicated a strong case for a widespread electrification programme that would produce an 11 per cent return on capital. It was designed to produce a strategic framework that would allow BR to submit individual proposals and to encourage the supply industry to prepare for a regular programme of work. Sadly, the government was not in practice committed to a long-term programme and each project remained to be authorised separately on its merits in isolation. The disastrous strikes of the following year meant that all bets on investment were off, and it was a great personal triumph for Sir Robert Reid that he secured approval to electrify the East Coast Main Line to Leeds and Edinburgh, completed in 1991.

BR managers showed great ingenuity in securing incremental investment to extend the electrified network, notably Gordon Pettitt[281] with Tonbridge–Hastings (1986) and South Croydon to East Grinstead (1987), and Chris Green[282] on electrification to Norwich and Harwich (1985)

---

[279] General Sir Brian Robertson, Lord Robertson of Oakridge (1896–1974), was a distinguished soldier who served in both the First and Second World Wars, and afterwards as Military Governor and UK High Commissioner, Allied High Commission, in Germany. He was invited by Churchill to become chairman of the British Transport Commission in 1953, and served until succeeded by Beeching in 1961. He was given an hereditary peerage in 1961. BR Western Region named the first of their Warship class diesel-hydraulic locomotives, No. 800, *Sir Brian Robertson* in 1958.

[280] Michael Posner (1931–2006) was a member of the British Railways Board, 1976–84. He was a Cambridge don and Whitehall adviser to successive Labour governments in the 1970s and played a pivotal role safeguarding social science research in the UK.

[281] Gordon Pettitt (b 1934), distinguished career railwayman who joined British Railways at the age of 16 in 1950, and then served through to 1992 in a number of high-profile management positions, including Freight Sales Manager, Eastern Region, 1976; Chief Passenger Manager, Western Region, 1978; Divisional Manager, Liverpool Street, 1979; Deputy General Manager, Southern Region, 1983; General Manager, Southern Region, 1985; Director, Provincial, 1990–91, Managing Director, Regional Railways, 1991–92. President: Bluebell Railway Preservation Society since 2014.

[282] Chris Green (b 1943) began his career in 1965 as a trainee manager with British Rail in the West Midlands, becoming area manager at Hull in 1973. Showing dynamic leadership, he became manager of ScotRail in 1984, BR Sector Director, London & South East in 1986 and launched Network SouthEast to unify London suburban rail services, with a bold and bright corporate colour scheme. In 1992 he was appointed managing director of the InterCity sector, with a remit to create a new integrated and profitable business (from that April), which he achieved with a particular emphasis on customer service. In 1999, after privatisation, Green was invited back into active rail industry management as Chief Executive of Virgin Rail Group on a five-year contract with a twofold mission – to deliver a markedly improved service on the existing network and ensure the £1.8 billion worth of new class 390 *Pendolino*, class 220 *Voyager* and class 221 *Super Voyager* trains would be delivered on time. From 2005 to 2010 he was a non-executive director of Network Rail.

BR electrified the Great Eastern main line to Norwich in 1985 using Class 86 locomotives and cascaded Mark IIE/F coaches. A train in Anglia Railways livery is seen at Norwich station in 2003. *Geoffrey Tribe/Online Transport Archive*

Electrification of Birmingham's cross city line took place in 1992 and the southern end of it is the town of Redditch. The station was relocated in 1972 following closure of the line south to Evesham where passenger services ceased ten years earlier. The line is single as far as Barnt Green where it joins the line from Gloucester, with a crossing loop provided at Alvechurch in 2014. *Geoffrey Tribe/Online Transport Archive*

and, more surprisingly, Cambridge–King's Lynn (1992) and the Southminster, Romford–Upminster and St Albans Abbey branches (all in 1986). Branksome–Weymouth followed in 1988 and Portsmouth–Eastleigh and Southampton in 1990. In most cases, these schemes were justified on the basis of being able to use existing rolling stock on the newly electrified line, by more intensive use of the existing fleet, while saving the costs of the diesel units (and in a number of cases the diesel depots) they replaced.

The investment hiatus that came with privatisation brought a halt to electrification for nine years. In 2007, Director of Rail Strategy in the Department, Mark Lambirth, asserted that further electrification would be questionable as, within fifteen years, a new technology, like hydrogen, would provide an alternative to diesel trains. This was reflected in yet another white paper of that year, launched by Secretary of State Ruth Kelly.[283] 'The case for network-wide electrification will be kept under review; it is not made yet. The right long-term solution for rail will be the one that minimises its carbon footprint and energy bill. That depends on the relative rates at which the carbon footprint of electricity generation declines and the rate at which options become available for low-carbon, self-powered trains, neither of which can be forecast at present.' Additionally, the government noted that it would generally be more cost-effective to implement electrification after the migration to cab-based signalling, rather than before.[284] (The latter comment was based on the desirability of avoiding the cost of immunising conventional signalling from traction current interference.)

Industry lobbying by Adrian Shooter[285] for ATOC and Iain Coucher[286] for Network Rail led to approval to electrify the Great Western and Midland Main Lines in 2009 and work started on the Great Western in 2010. Network Rail had very limited experience of main-line electrification and had to rely heavily on consultants to plan and contractors to implement the work. It was grossly mismanaged, with costs rising from £874 million in 2013 to £2.8 billion five years later, and the original completion date of 2016–17 had slipped. Delays and cost overruns led to electrification being 'paused' in June 2015 by Secretary of State Patrick McLoughlin[287] to allow Network Rail to focus on Great Western, and for the incoming Chairman, Sir Peter Hendy,[288] to analyse the problem. He reported on the whole of Network Rail's enhancement programme in November 2015, and in November 2016, Transport Minister Paul Maynard[289] announced that the electrification between Thingley Junction and Bristol Temple Meads would be deferred indefinitely, along with Filton Bank, Didcot Parkway to Oxford and the Henley and Windsor branches. In July 2017, the Transport Secretary announced that electrification between Cardiff and Swansea would not go ahead, as most of the benefits

---

[283] Ruth Kelly (b 1968) was Labour MP for Bolton West, 1997–2010. A former economics writer on *The Guardian*, she served as a minister in a number of roles including Secretary of State for Transport, 2007–08. She left Parliament to pursue a new career in academic life.

[284] Delivering a Sustainable Railway, DfT Cmd 7176, July 2007.

[285] Adrian Shooter CBE (1948-2022) joined British Rail in the 1970s as a management trainee. Area Manager, St Pancras, 1984–87; Managing Director, Red Star Parcels, 1987–89; Director, Parcels Business, 1989–93; Managing Director, 1993–2001, Chairman, 2002–11, Chiltern Railways. He has been chairman of Vivarail, a company overhauling London Underground D78 Stock and upcycling them into new British Rail class 230 DEMUs. He owned the Darjeeling Himalayan Railway class 'B' steam locomotive No. 778 (originally No. 19), which he operated on the Beeches Light Railway in the grounds of his residence in Oxfordshire. Carriages to accompany the locomotive were commissioned from Boston Lodge works.

[286] Iain Coucher (b 1961), Chief Executive of Network Rail, 2007–10, formerly Deputy Chief Executive from 2002. In 1999 he had formed a transport consultancy, Coucher Pender Ltd, in partnership with a colleague, Victoria Pender. Through the consultancy, they provided freelance management services to Tube Lines, one of the infrastructure maintenance companies under the London Underground public–private partnership in which the company was responsible for modernising three tube lines, with Coucher serving as Tube Lines' Chief Executive from 1999 to 2001.

[287] Patrick, Lord McLoughlin (b 1957), was Conservative MP for West Derbyshire, 1986–2010; Derbyshire Dales, 2010–19. A former mineworker at Littleton Colliery, 1979–85; and then marketing official, NCB, 1985–86, he was a junior minister in various positions from 1989 to 1997, starting at the Department of Transport. When the Conservative-led coalition government was formed he was made chief whip, 2010–12, and was then a successful Secretary of State for Transport, 2012–16. He was Chancellor of the Duchy of Lancaster, 2016–18, and chairman of the Conservative Party, 2016–18. He was created a life peer in 2020.

[288] Sir Peter Hendy (b 1953) has been chairman of Network Rail since 2015. From 2006 he was Commissioner of Transport for London, and before that – from 2001 – managing director of Surface Transport for Transport for London. He started his career in the public transport industry in 1975 as a London Transport graduate trainee. He moved up the career ladder, eventually taking on the role of managing director of CentreWest London Buses Ltd, managing it under London Transport ownership. Hendy was appointed CBE in the 2006 New Year Honours for his work in keeping public transport in London running in the aftermath of the 7 July 2005 London bombings. Following the successful operation of transport during the 2012 Olympic and Paralympic Games, he was knighted for services to transport and the community in the 2013 New Year Honours. Since 2019 he has been a trustee of the Science Museum Group, and serves on the Railway Heritage Designation Advisory Board. He also chairs the National Railway Museum advisory board. His brother is Labour peer John, Lord Hendy KC. Created a life peer (Lord Hendy of Richmond Hill) in 2022.

[289] Paul Maynard (b 1975) has been Conservative MP for Blackpool North and Cleveleys since 2010. He served as Parliamentary Under-Secretary of State for the Department for Transport from 2016 to 2018 and again from 2019 to 2020. He self-identifies as disabled, and has cerebral palsy.

St Albans Abbey. An opportunistic electrification scheme by Chris Green, justified by saving a DMU and the empty mileage to and from the nearest depot at Bletchley. A Community Rail Partnership has helped revive the line's fortunes. *Christopher Austin*

could be achieved by using bi-mode trains. Midland Main Line electrification was cut back to the route between Bedford, Kettering and Corby.

The government's strategic vision for rail of 2017, *Connecting People*, makes no mention of electrification, apart from a passing reference to South Manchester, but has some finger-wagging strictures for the industry: 'Other transport modes have made significant progress in improving their environmental performance, and rail cannot afford to be complacent.'[290]

More recently, the political emphasis has been on hydrogen trains, even though this is a new technology for rail that has yet to be tested in squadron service. More than that, the production of hydrogen is itself both costly and carbon intensive, even though it produces no harmful emissions at the point of use. This might in the future be dealt with by producing hydrogen by electrolysis, but that too uses huge quantities of energy. A great deal of energy is lost in the production, distribution and conversion back into electricity.[291] Its volatility as a fuel is also relevant in a rail application. It may be possible to overcome these disadvantages over time, and hydrogen trains may have a role, but the concept is not suitable for high-speed lines or those with significant freight flows where hydrogen is unable to generate sufficient power. It would be suitable for deeply rural lines where electrification could never be justified financially, perhaps 10 per cent of the network. Other routes may benefit from battery electric or other forms of hybrid trains, but it is important that a start is made on electrifying the rest of the network, where it will provide huge environmental benefits.

The position is set out very clearly in Network Rail's Traction decarbonisation strategy, which identifies routes where high-speed operation, freight flows or volume of traffic requires electrification, and identifies a network of 11,000 single-track kilometres to be electrified, 76 per cent of the existing non-electrified network. Time is short and an early start needs to be made to meet the 2050 target, and specification and funding of such projects is these days with government.

Today, the arguments for electrification may be simply stated:

1. An electric train is simpler than a diesel one and its weight is lower as it requires only traction motors and associated electrical equipment, but does not carry the weight of diesel engines, generators for traction current and fuel.
2. This relative simplicity means that it is also cheaper to maintain, and its availability is higher.
3. It does not need to return to a depot to refuel.
4. Its ability to grab power from the overhead line means that it has a high rate of acceleration compared with the alternatives.
5. In environmental terms, it produces no emissions at the point of use, including in inner-city areas where principal stations are located.
6. The electricity used can be produced from any source, including renewables and nuclear where carbon emissions are very low. In particular the train itself can produce about a fifth of the power required by use of regenerative braking, where the traction motors become generators as the train slows, returning power to the overhead line for other trains in the electrical section to use.

The two principal drawbacks are capital cost and lack of flexibility. The first is usually justified by the reduction in maintenance costs, but the payback period will depend on the relative costs of electricity and fuel oil. In environmental terms, it is a no-brainer.

The second drawback is that electric-only trains can only use electrified routes, and diversions using non-electrified lines are not possible, unless the trains are diesel-hauled over these sections. This drawback can be overcome by use of bi-mode trains, which provide a lot of flexibility but at the penalty of additional weight and complexity, driving higher maintenance costs.

This drawback is, of course, diminished as more of the network is electrified, providing wired alternatives when required.

There is considerable scope for infill electrification – wiring connecting routes between existing electrified networks. The classic example is the 2-mile connection

---

[290] *Connecting People; a Strategic Vision for Rail*, DfT, Cmd 1519, November 2017.

[291] Roger Ford, *Modern Railways*, March 2021. In the same issue, Ian Walmsley puts it even more succinctly: 'Hydrogen wastes 30 per cent of the energy needed to produce it.'

between Willesden and Acton, which would enable connection between the Great Western Main Line and the West and East Coast Main Lines and East Anglia for electrically hauled freight, linking the ports in the east, and the Channel Tunnel, to South Wales. The environmental and political benefits of electric freight are huge and the only way to decarbonise the logistics industry effectively.

Advances in battery technology also mean that in some cases (typically branch lines with modest speeds) it would be possible for power to be provided by batteries, which can be recharged during the layover time under the wires at the junction station.

Electrification proposals usually go along with renewal of signalling, and in earlier years in conjunction with track renewals, or take place when a diesel fleet needs replacement.

Until well into the twenty-first century, the case for electrification was made solely on financial grounds, but now it is possible to place value on decarbonising the railway, and the best way to do that is through electrification.

The government has set the target to replace all conventional diesel trains by 2040, but has no electrification programme planned to achieve this. Instead, they appear to be placing their faith in the trials of hydrogen trains.

As a consequence of this, the amazing decision was taken to rebuild the initial phases of the East-West Railway (Oxford–Bedford) as a non-electrified route despite the huge network benefits that would accrue by linking three north–south routes together[292] and the value of the route for diversion of electric services during engineering work. Clearly, this was done to ensure the route reinstatement itself fitted the investment criteria with the appropriate benefit–cost ratio. But the BCR analysis is not these days fit for purpose, given the requirement for the railway to fulfil dozens of objectives above and beyond the normal transport criteria. If you need it to meet the low-carbon objective, the levelling up agenda, accessibility criteria or 'building back better' after the Covid pandemic, the railway can deliver it, but there will be a cost. It is simply unrealistic to think that these additional benefits can be delivered at the support level required simply to deliver the contracted train service.

Over 100 years governments have been reporting on electrification, its advisability, technical standards and its method of delivery. There has been something of a reluctance throughout this period to embrace the concept for the greater part of the network, even though it is commonplace elsewhere in Europe. There have been too many studies and too many attempts to put off the inevitable requirement to electrify in common with every other European railway. It well illustrates the timescale problem, in that ministers need projects to produce results within the five-year Parliamentary term, or preferably within their own term of office that, as is shown in Appendix 2, is only eighteen months since privatisation. Great Western electrification, even in its truncated form, took nine and a half years to complete, and the mismatch is clear.

Governments are beguiled by new technology and the claims of the promoters of innovation. Funding trials and embracing something new is relatively cheap and appeals to politicians, even where a practical solution already exists, but requires funding over time for a substantial programme of work, the benefits of which will be enjoyed by their successors. The technology of electric traction is well proven and the timescale for implementation pressing, but governments remain obsessed with innovation, as expressed by Transport Secretary Grant Shapps: 'Investing in innovation is crucial in decarbonising transport.'[293] But we need to recall that George Stephenson himself is credited with saying: 'But I tell you, young man, that the day will come when electricity will be the great motive power of the world.'[294]

The UK is only twenty-first in the European league table of lines electrified. Thirty-nine per cent of Britain's route network is electrified, for example, compared with 58 per cent in France, 86 per cent in Belgium and 65 per cent in the Netherlands and Italy. It is a classic example of the effects of a short-term funding regime based on political timescales and priorities, rather than a long-term strategy with cross-party support and consistent funding. The dilettante approach to alternative and untested low-carbon technologies has proved to be little more than a distraction from the principal task of getting the wires up.

Perhaps this is now better recognised, and the recent white paper affirms that 'electrification of the network will be expanded …' and that 'electrification is likely to be the main way of decarbonising the network'. Better than that, it also foresees an Environment Plan in 2022 that will establish rail as the backbone of a cleaner future transport system. This is welcome after the relentless negativity of the 2007 white paper detailed above.

High Speed Two: Andrew Adonis's Vision

The one Transport Minister in recent times who succeeded in breaking the pattern of disappointed expectation and lack of delivery was Andrew Adonis, a Labour life peer who volunteered to become Secretary of State for Transport in June 2009 because he saw the opportunity to make a real difference to the fortunes of the railway, having previously been a minister of state in the same department. His

---

[292] Great Western Route from Didcot to Oxford and Birmingham, Chiltern Line from Marylebone, West Coast Main Line and Midland Main Line, the latter two being already electrified and the first as an electrification priority.

[293] DfT press release, 10 March 2021.

[294] Dow's *Dictionary of Railway Quotations*.

enthusiasm for taking on the transport job in Cabinet singled him out from many other politicians, who were either given it as a consolation prize in a demotion that usually led to the end of their ministerial career or who saw it as a stepping stone on to a grander job in government. Not Adonis: for him creating a new railway infrastructure was the most important legacy imaginable.

Among the decisions planned, taken and announced by Adonis was the electrification of the Great Western Main Line from London Paddington to Bristol, Cardiff and Swansea, and the electrification of lines in north-west England from Manchester to Liverpool and Manchester to Preston.

Adonis was also responsible for the partial redoubling of the North Cotswold Line from Oxford to Worcester – a route with which he had a particular affinity as a member of the Cotswold Line Promotion Group, having been a pupil at Kingham Hill School, which he had attended as a boarder with the help of a local authority grant.

These investment decisions, however, paled into insignificance compared with High Speed Two – the most important railway project of the last 120 years – which owes its existence almost entirely to the foresight and steadfastness of Andrew Adonis.

He explained the decision to proceed with HS2 in a lengthy statement to Parliament on 11 March 2010. This is an extract of what he had to say:

Prime Minister David Cameron and Lord Adonis pictured at the ceremony to mark partial redoubling of the Cotswold line on 20 March 2009, just prior to their private discussion on HS2 as described in chapter ten. On the right is President of the Cotswold Line Promotion Group, and co-author of this book, Lord Faulkner of Worcester as well as Mark Hopwood CBE, Managing Director of Great Western Railway. *Richard Faulkner Collection*

> I am today publishing HS2 Ltd's report, together with the Government's proposed high-speed rail strategy, which is based on HS2 Ltd's analysis. In summary, this strategy is for the development of an initial core high-speed network which would link London to Birmingham, Manchester, the East Midlands, Sheffield and Leeds, with high-speed trains running from the outset through to Liverpool, Newcastle, Glasgow and Edinburgh. This Y-shaped network of about 335 miles in total, with branches north of Birmingham running either side of the Pennines, would be capable of carrying trains at up to 250mph and could be extended to other cities and to Scotland.
>
> There are six principal reasons why the government are proposing this strategy. The first is transport capacity. The extra capacity provided by a high-speed line would more than treble existing rail capacity on the West Coast Main Line corridor. This is not only because of the new track, but also because of the far greater length of train that high-speed lines and stations make possible, and the segregation of high-speed trains from other passenger and freight services.
>
> By contrast, the most ambitious conceivable upgrade of existing rail lines to Birmingham would yield less than half this extra capacity, at greater cost in terms of both money and disruption than a high-speed line, and without most of the journey time savings. This analysis is critical to the argument as to whether investment in high-speed rail unjustifiably diverts investment from the existing railway. The most likely alternative over time is to spend more achieving less. This accords with the experience of the recent £9 billion upgrade of the West Coast Main Line, whose benefits, though considerable, were essentially incremental and came after years of chronic disruption to passengers and businesses. Furthermore, by transferring long-distance services to the high-speed line, large amounts of capacity would also be released on the existing West Coast Main Line for commuter and freight services, including services to key areas of housing growth around Milton Keynes and Northampton.
>
> Secondly, the journey time savings from such a line would be significant. The journey time from London to the West Midlands would be reduced to between 30 and 50 minutes, depending on stations used, with Manchester, Leeds and Sheffield all brought to within 75 minutes of London – down from almost 2 hours 10 minutes now – and through services from Glasgow and Edinburgh to London down to just 3½ hours.
>
> Thirdly, however, the connectivity gains of high-speed rail come not only from the faster trains but also from the new route alignments which comprise the proposed 'Y' network of lines from London to Birmingham, and then north to Manchester, and north-east to the east Midlands, Sheffield and Leeds. This new network would provide a once in a lifetime opportunity to

overcome the acute connectivity limitations of the Victorian rail network, with its three separate and poorly integrated main lines from London to the north, each with its own separate London terminus.

By contrast, the high-speed line, routed via the West Midlands, would not only slash the journey time to London from Manchester, Leeds and Sheffield; it also nearly halves journey times from these cities to Birmingham. So the East Midlands, the North-West and the North-East gain dramatically improved connections within the Midlands and the north, as well as to London. These connections would be further enhanced by the northern hub proposals to upgrade the trans-Pennine route from Manchester to Leeds.

Fourthly, this high-speed network would enable key local, national and international networks to be better integrated. In particular, by including on the approach of the high-speed line to central London an interchange station with the new Crossrail line just west of Paddington, the benefits of both Crossrail and the high-speed line are greatly enhanced. Such a Crossrail interchange station would deliver a fast and frequent service to London's West End, the City and Docklands, giving a total journey time, for example, from central Birmingham to Canary Wharf of just 70 minutes, and from Leeds to Canary Wharf of just 1 hour 40 minutes. This Crossrail interchange station would also provide a fast, one-stop Heathrow express service to Heathrow in place of the long and tortuous journey to the airport currently experienced by passengers arriving at Euston, King's Cross and St Pancras. Similarly, an interchange station close to Birmingham Airport would provide an efficient link to the M6 and the M42, the West Coast Main Line, the wider West Midlands and the airport itself.

Fifthly, high-speed rail would be a sustainable way forward. High-speed trains emit far less carbon than cars or planes per passenger mile, and the local impact of high-speed lines is far less than that of entirely new motorway alignments in terms of land take and air quality. For these reasons the government take the view that high-speed rail is preferable both to new intercity motorways and to major expansion of domestic aviation, even if these were able to deliver equivalent intercity capacity and connectivity benefits.

Finally, HS2 Ltd assesses that all these benefits far outweigh the estimated costs. With the project yielding more than £2 of benefit for every £1 of cost, HS2 Ltd estimates the capital cost of the first 120 miles of the line from London to the West Midlands at between £15.8 billion and £17.4 billion. This is broadly similar to the cost of Crossrail, which is being built over the next seven years.

The cost per mile beyond Birmingham is then estimated to halve, taking the overall cost of the 335-mile Y-shaped network to about £30 billion. This cost would be phased over more than a decade after the start of construction, which would not begin until after the completion of Crossrail in 2017. Indeed, the high-speed line would be the transport infrastructure successor project to Crossrail, deploying its skills base and project management expertise, and with a similar annual rate of spend.

The arguments adduced by Adonis in this statement have stood the test of time, and remarkably the HS2 project has largely survived, despite one change of government and five different Prime Ministers. He had persuaded Conservative leader David Cameron of the merits of HS2 in a private meeting without officials present in Cameron's house in the Cotswolds, to which the two of them went together on 20 March 2009 following an event at Charlbury station (which was in Cameron's constituency) to celebrate the start of the work to redouble 20 miles of the Cotswold Line.

Some of the figures quoted by Adonis in his March 2010 statement have proved to be under-estimates – objectors in Buckinghamshire succeeded in adding to the costs by getting sections of the line put into tunnels, for example – and his assertion that Crossrail would open in 2017 was too optimistic: it opened in 2022.

One major disappointment was the decision by the Conservative government in 2021 to abandon – at least for the foreseeable future – the eastern leg of HS2 from the East Midlands to Sheffield and Leeds, and not to proceed with a new high-speed line from Manchester to Leeds via Bradford. As Lord Adonis said in the Lords on 14 October 2021 (before the decision was announced):[295]

> To understand the significance of the potential cancellation of the eastern leg of HS2, you just need to consider what will be the journey times between the major cities of the Midlands and the north and London after HS2, if it is not built. Birmingham to London would be half an hour, Manchester to London would be an hour, Leeds and Sheffield to London would be 2 hours, and Newcastle to London would be 3 hours. Where is all the investment and the new social activity in the country going to happen if, for the next few centuries – because we build railway lines to last centuries – that is the pattern of communications between the Midlands and the north of this country and the economic powerhouse of London, which will always continue to be so because it is our dominant city? It is absolutely essential that the eastern leg of HS2 proceeds.

---

[295] *Hansard Vol 814*, Col. 1985-87. 14 October 2021.

Bradford too would have liked to see its two stations linked across the city centre and the Midland Railway secured Parliamentary powers in 1896 and again with a different scheme in 1911, but the First World War meant that this was never completed. In the 1960s the city was more interested in link roads and offices than a rail connection, and the original station sites were subsequently redeveloped for retail and law courts. PTE proposals came to nothing and more recently, changed Government plans ruled out a link between the two lines. The picture shows the new terminus opened to replace the original Midland station in 1990 in order to release land for redevelopment.
Geoffrey Tribe/Online Transport Archive

Bradford Exchange was originally used by both Lancashire and Yorkshire and Great Northern trains, but with the closure of a number of local lines the station was rebuilt in 1973 on a more modest scale and the original site released for redevelopment. In 1977 a bus station was added alongside and the station renamed Bradford Interchange in 1983. The picture shows the station in 1975 with the remains of the old Exchange station behind.
John Meredith/Online Transport Archive

Because we are a democratic community, with very powerful political spokespeople from the eastern side of the country, it is stark staring obvious that, if, by an act of great negligence, Her Majesty's Government do not proceed with the eastern leg of HS2 now, when the leg to Manchester opens and there is a massive political controversy about the delayed journey times, much poorer communications, much lower capacity and lack of connectivity with Crossrail – because the Old Oak Common interchange will of course be available only to people coming from Birmingham and Manchester – the political campaign to build the eastern leg will be unrelenting. In a classic failure of planning, we will build the eastern leg of HS2 and it will go through to Sheffield, Leeds and Newcastle, but it will be done 30 or 40 years later than it should have been. In that interval, an enormous amount of damage will be done to the society and the economy in the east Midlands, Yorkshire and the north-east of the country and to the connectivity between Edinburgh – because the HS2 trains would go there – and London.

One argument in favour of HS2 that has grown significantly over the past decade has been climate change. High Speed 2 is essential to achieving net zero emissions and tackling climate change. Today, a high-speed rail journey would typically yield a 90 per cent reduction in CO_2 emissions compared with flying the same route. When electrical power generation is fully decarbonised, this will be a 100 per cent saving. Rail freight reduces carbon emissions by 76 per cent compared to road, and passengers travelling on High Speed 2, will emit almost seven times less carbon emissions per passenger kilometre than the equivalent intercity car journey. Phase 1 of High Speed 2 will make a significant strategic contribution towards a carbon-neutral economy, with the whole-life carbon footprint of its construction and operation being less than one month's road transport greenhouse gas emissions.

High-speed railways have the desirable effect of attracting passengers from shorter-distance air services and longer-distance car travel. As Ian Walmsley pointed out in *Modern Railways*:[296]

> HS2 stands or falls on modal transfer from road and air, but that's no problem because high-speed rail achieves exactly that. The problem starts when you look at the Department's figures for modal transfer, which are unbelievably low. The calculations bring in many factors, but primarily the good old Passenger Demand Forecasting Handbook (PDFH) from British Rail days. This is the one that predicts the revenue bonus for introducing new trains, based on the pre-privatisation idea that new trains were always better. This works but only to a certain extent, as it predicts incremental change. By contrast, a big change produces a tipping point bringing about a much bigger modal transfer than the PDFH predicts.
>
> The DfT sticks to these traditional incremental change calculations rather than stated preference surveys, which are common around the world and tend to predict a much bigger modal transfer. All over the world road and air traffic has moved to high-speed rail when it becomes available, yet predictions for HS2 show just 1 per cent of its business coming from air and 4 per cent from cars.

Most major economies in Europe and the Far East have built a new network of high-speed railways. The one aspect that is common to all these countries is that none has regretted it, and virtually all have expanded this network, having built and operated their first lines. Not only do they solve the problem of how to meet growing passenger demand for rail travel, they also achieve huge environmental benefits.

An example of how HS2 is enhancing the environment is their commitment to create a green corridor along its tracks, with 7 million new trees and shrubs already being planted along the Phase One route, and the establishment of a woodland fund to restore existing ancient woodland and create new ones. There will be 650 hectares of new woodland. That contrasts with the 29 hectares of woodland that will be lost over the 140 miles of HS2 – that's out of 3.19 million hectares of woodland in the UK, of which around 1 million is described as 'ancient woodland'. Ian Walmsley quotes *The Independent* as saying that when contractors widened just 2.5 miles of the A21 in Kent they took out 9 hectares – almost a third of the HS2 total. No wonder he describes the ancient woodland argument as 'green tripe'.

Walmsley also deals with what he calls 'the biggest fantasy' – that if HS2 were cancelled the money would be spent reopening closed railways. The principal proponent of this is the so-called the Taxpayers' Alliance, a shadowy organisation that refuses to disclose the source of its funds, although a number of individuals and companies with links to the road and construction lobbies are known to be involved.

No one is a stronger supporter of reopening lines that should never have been closed than your authors – much of our second book[297] on the politics of the railways after Beeching is devoted to this subject – but it is risible to suggest, as the Taxpayers' Alliance does, that it makes sense to switch funds from a major infrastructure project that will bring huge benefits to the whole of the country and earn a positive rate of return, benefiting at least 20 million people, to branch line reopenings such as Beverley to York and Keswick to Penrith, which would always need public subsidy and benefit 20,000 people at best.

---

[296] 'HS2: Stand Up And Be Counted', *Modern Railways*, August 2020.
[297] *Disconnected! Broken Links in Britain's Rail Policy* by Chris Austin and Richard Faulkner, Oxford Publishing Company, 2015.

Devolution or Balkanisation

The main-line railways down to 1939 were run through a hierarchy of district offices in places such as Cambridge, Cardiff and Carlisle, with managers in close touch not only with local staff, but also with local authorities, local communities and local businesses. The stationmaster was not only responsible for the safe working of his station and section of line, and for supervision of the commercial responsibilities of the ticket office and the goods office, but was also a sales representative for the railway, both passenger and goods. The military-style structure of the railways meant that districts were subordinate to the head office structure, and so a balance was held between local needs and those of the strategic network managed by the companies themselves. It was not perfect, but it worked well and continued under BR, with the need to balance priorities across the country brilliantly depicted in the 1952 British Transport Film *Train Time*.

Capacity on a mixed-traffic railway is limited by the nature of the line and its signalling, and priorities were crudely but simply handled through the priorities set out in the *Signalmen's General Instructions*, and in the signal box bell codes, with express passenger trains taking priority and an unfitted local goods train being at the bottom of the list.

With the continuous rationalisation of track layouts and capacity throughout the 1960s and '70s and the merging of districts into fewer but larger divisions, pressure on capacity increased while decision-making became more remote. Local contact through the stationmaster was eroded as they were replaced by area managers and subsequently lost and the railway became more remote and faceless in dealing with the local communities it served.

Dr Beeching's *Reshaping Report* in 1963 made clear that, outside London, suburban networks could not be justified without financial support. Cities like Bristol and Edinburgh lost almost all their suburban networks as a result, and a political solution was identified by Barbara Castle as Transport Minister with the creation of the 'magnificent seven' Passenger Transport Executives under the Transport Act, 1968.

The power of the PTEs increased steadily and all have revived local rail networks that were declining rapidly under the national control exercised by BR and the malign influence of the Treasury and the Department. Manchester and Newcastle have replaced heavy rail with light rail routes, while others like Strathclyde, Liverpool and Birmingham based development on big capital investment projects for new cross-city lines and rolling stock. South and West Yorkshire have reopened stations and lines, and all have encouraged the modal shift from road to rail in the process, and have supported the economic growth of the regions they serve.

Tyne and Wear Metro decided at the start to develop a metro system based on BR lines, but separate from them with their own lightweight rolling stock, and first services ran in 1980. This shot from 1983 shows the original rolling stock and livery on a train for St James at Tynemouth. *Geoffrey Tribe/Online Transport Archive*

Manchester chose both to develop its suburban rail network and create a light rail system Metrolink, using both converted heavy rail routes, new construction and street running. Metrolink planning followed lack of Government approval for the rail tunnel project between Piccadilly and Victoria stations. Starting with the Bury line in 1992, Manchester now has the most extensive light rail network in the country. Here, a tram for Altrincham is shown in 1997.
Geoffrey Tribe/Online Transport Archive

Along the way, there have been many conflicts between BR and PTEs on the allocation of capacity between longer-distance trains, freight and local passenger services. Some, like Manchester's Castlefield corridor, remain to be resolved, others have been sorted out through the separation of infrastructure (Tyne & Wear Metro) or of PTE and other services (Merseyside).

As well as the PTEs, considerable autonomy has been transferred to Scottish government, to the London Mayor and to Welsh government and, more recently to Transport for the North for a range of PTE and regional services. Not only was the railway split into over 100 companies by privatisation, but the strategic responsibility for service specification and investment has been split between a dozen agencies. Given that the railway runs as a network with many shared facilities between the different companies, this is a concern and will want careful management in the future. Artificial divisions that break up journeys or force a change of train are not generally in the interests of passengers. Services that end at a political boundary, rather than one determined by where the majority of passengers want to go, represent a poor way to run a railway. One nonsensical example is provided by the services to Kirkby on Merseyside, where the single platform has two sets of buffer stops, one marking the terminus of the frequent Merseyrail electric service from Liverpool, and the other the end of the diesel-operated branch line from Wigan.

Nevertheless, the authors acknowledge that these devolved lines have prospered in a way that would not have been possible under BR. Is it plausible that the Edinburgh–Glasgow route via Bathgate would have been rebuilt, and indeed electrified, without Scottish government specification and funding? Or that the North London Line would have seen such a busy and frequent service along its core route with all stations rebuilt or refreshed and fully staffed? And where would the Ebbw Vale line have been if it had not been for the decision of Welsh government that it was required for regeneration of the valley following closure of the steel works?

Balkanisation. With the creation of the Merseyside PTE, electrification plans were drawn up for services around Liverpool, but on the line to Wigan and Bolton only extended to Kirby in the PTE area. From 1977, through services ceased and passengers were obliged to change trains using this rather exposed, but level interchange. Passenger journeys do not always sit well with political boundaries. *Geoffrey Tribe/Online Transport Archive*

Most of this is about money and objectives, and in theory BR could have done the same if it had been given the remit and the funds to accomplish it. In fact, BR did particularly well in reopening lines in South Wales to Aberdare and Maesteg, as well as the Robin Hood line in Nottinghamshire and Derbyshire, for example. However, more was not possible under the political structures and financial imperatives of the time, and it has to be acknowledged that devolution has brought benefits to railways in general and local services in particular.

BR did well in working with local authorities on line and station reopenings, as described in Chapter 6, and their total of 303 stations opened or reopened between 1960 and 1996 reconnected a lot of local communities to the network (although it would have been far better had many not been closed as a result of the Beeching Report).

In recognising this, and in considering ownership and management structures for the future, however, it is essential to hang on to the benefits of the national network, and the ease of travelling between the parts of it that BR provided. It is also important to continue to work within a pragmatic framework to avoid the situation where a largely empty, off-peak, two-car local train takes the path that is needed by a Freightliner train keeping sixty HGVs off the road. HS2 will help to solve the conflict between stopping and fast passenger trains on the Coventry–Birmingham corridor, for example, but there will be plenty more points of conflict as environmental imperatives encourage more and more people and products to switch to rail.

Lord Steel of Aikwood, the former Liberal Democrat leader, leaves the first up train on the Borders Railway at Edinburgh Waverley, almost fifty years after he had joined protesters at Newcastleton on the day the Waverley route had closed. *Christopher Austin*

The Williams Review

The review was launched in September 2018 by Chris Grayling following the disastrous timetable changes on Northern Rail and Great Northern/Thameslink/Southern, which had proved to be unworkable and resulted in extensive delays, inconvenience to passengers and a lot of bad publicity for railway and government. The study was commissioned to look at the future of the rail industry and how rail services are delivered. The review was carried out by Keith Williams, a former chairman of British Airways, chairman of John Lewis and Chairman and Chief Executive of Royal Mail. Following the pattern of earlier government inquiries, nobody from the rail industry had been asked to serve on the group advising him, but a late decision saw Dick Fearn[298] able to contribute and bring his extensive industry knowledge to the inquiry.

Essentially complete by the beginning of 2020, just prior to the first lockdown, the report had to wait fifteen months before publication after extensive revision and the Secretary of State, Grant Shapps, deciding that it should bear his name as well as that of Williams. The Williams/Shapps report is a remarkable document that shows signs of the extensive involvement of No. 10 in the way it was presented in its published form. It is not couched in the measured language of the Civil Service but is, in contrast to previous similar reports, relentlessly upbeat and hugely aspirational in its promises, which is exciting in terms of the vision it outlines, but raises public and political expectations to a level that will be difficult to meet.

It is remarkable too, in that it gives a forthright assessment of the failings of the Conservative privatisation policy that led to so many of the problems it identifies, yet still manages to suggest that a large element of blame rests with the industry itself.

It puts the Secretary of State in pole position in terms of making all key decisions relating to the railway, giving 'strong statutory and administrative controls for Ministers'. This is supported by the ten key outcomes it sets out together with no fewer than sixty-two commitments.

For the first time it gives a much clearer idea of the external benefits the industry is expected to deliver, in addition to the core task of providing rail passenger and freight services. The list is long, and some are quite demanding, and they are set out in outline here:

Biodiversity. 'A sustainable, long-term approach to land management on the network will support biodiversity, while also improving reliability and reducing the risk of landslips and flooding.' There will be 'a new duty to conserve and enhance biodiversity set out in the Government's Environment Bill'.

Connectivity. 'Partnership with other key infrastructure providers, such as broadband innovators, will help boost the country's drive towards a revolution in connectivity.'

Costs. Cost savings of £1.5 billion a year are expected from GBR.

Diversity. 'The new body will recruit more broadly than before.' Great British Railways are 'to employ more people with retail experience'. The paper puts a premium on non-railway experience, a surprising comment, given that the opening words of the report are: 'We want our trains to run on time.'

Economy. Local engagement is expected from Great British Railways at regional level, to support

---

[298] Anthony Richard Fearn, former BR managing director of South Eastern, divisional director of Thames & Chiltern, Railtrack zonal director and subsequently Chief Operating Officer and then Chief Executive of Iarnrod Eireann from 2003 to 2013. He was also chairman of the Bluebell Railway from 2013 to 2019.

small and medium-sized enterprises and start-up companies.

Environment. 'The 30-year strategy will be a key mechanism that Ministers will use to ensure that the railways respond to public priorities such as levelling up, the environment, housing and regeneration.' 'the rail estate could support carbon offsetting and sequestration for the wider economy, including through extensive tree planting'. 'Renewable power generation on the rail estate will be increased.' An Environment Plan 'will establish rail as the backbone of a cleaner future transport system'.

Levelling up. 'The railways are a public service, paid for by taxpayers and passengers to connect places and foster economic growth through levelling up across our towns, cities and regions.'

Local economic development. 'Opportunities to better unlock housing, local economic growth and social value will be explored.'

Research. 'Great British Railways will become the primary focus of RD&I[299] initiatives across the sector, delivering priorities set by ministers.'

Training. 'A cross-sector advisory body will advise on skills, training, leadership and technology.'

Even in a document of 112 pages, packed with detail, inevitably some questions remain unanswered. If Great British Railways is to be the 'guiding mind' of the industry, how does that sit with the responsibilities of the devolved authorities in Scotland, Wales and London, which have authority over services within their own areas?

People planning and training is advocated with a requirement to attract and retain a diverse workforce. If this results in a return to national conditions of service and national collective bargaining, this would inevitably impact on costs as pay rates are 'levelled up' and unions assert the power to call national strikes.

Finally, we should not let go unnoticed one of the greatest compliments that the Conservative government appears ready to pay to the legacy of British Rail, so often consistently and unfairly derided by their ministers and spokespersons at the time of privatisation and subsequently. We refer to their decision to retain the classic BR double-arrow logo as GBR's symbol, which was first launched in January 1965, though with one important and controversial change.

The original design was of a white arrow on a bright red background, and was the work of Gerry Barney, then a 24-year-old lettering artist, who drew it literally on the back of an envelope in 1964 during his daily commute from Ealing Broadway to the Design Research Unit in Bond Street. 'The only thought I had was railway lines coming and going,' he told *The Guardian*, whose reporter Matthew Weaver had tracked him down.[300]

Rather than keeping the logo red and white, which is used across Great Britain to direct people to railway stations and appears on press and TV advertisements including those for the Rail Delivery Group (RDG), the Secretary of State, Grant Shapps has reimagined it in four shades of green – 'a single familiar brand with a bold new vision for passengers – of punctual services, simpler tickets and a modern and green railway that meets the needs of the nation,' he said.[301]

The RDG approached Barney for his view on the colour change, the above supportive quote at the ready. 'No way,' he said when the quote was read to him, and in the same *Guardian* article he describes it as 'a load of old bollocks'. He said he was pleased that the RDG was using his original design properly in their TV ads, but why would they want to change it?' I don't know if it can be updated, it's so simple. They should just leave it well alone – if it ain't broke, don't fix it.'

---

[299] Research, development and innovation.
[300] *The Guardian*, p.3, 22 September 2021.
[301] *Op. cit.*

11

Analysis and Conclusions

*'And noble statesmen do not itch
To interfere in matters which
They do not understand …'*
W S Gilbert, *Iolanthe*, 1882

Over almost 200 years politicians have sought to intervene and control railways without being quite clear on what they want to achieve. Initially, the objectives were clear and related to protecting the public interest on safety, fares and freight rates, based on the concessions they had created through enacting the legislation that permitted the creation of the railway in the first place. Later, the interventions were for more broadly based objectives, including protection of employees, restricting industrial action and meeting the needs of the nation in a variety of ways, from the needs of the war effort, to improved efficiency or as part of a wider social policy such as common ownership, or private sector involvement.

Ministers' Perspectives

The time in office for ministers is short – on average only eighteen months over the last twenty-five years. Unlike the great offices of state – Chancellor, Foreign Secretary, Home Secretary, Transport is a relatively lowly portfolio in the Whitehall hierarchy, and ministers who are offered the post are either on the way up to the more celebrated ministries, or on the way down, and possibly out. Very few have actually wanted the Transport portfolio, and their time in office and their names are soon forgotten.

Who can now name six Transport Ministers who have really made a difference or left their mark on the industry? Many might be able to recall Ernest Marples, for all the wrong reasons, and perhaps Barbara Castle, recalled as the minister who did not drive a car, but better remembered for setting up the passenger transport executives and saving the great suburban networks in the city regions around which the PTEs were created. She is also remembered, however, for approving the closure of over 300 services that were in the Beeching Report, and some, like Oxford to Cambridge, which were not.

Some might recall Richard Marsh as the only man to become both Transport Minister and to chair the British Railways Board, and Lord Adonis deserves to be remembered as the first minister to understand the potential of rail infrastructure investment and for his support for HS2 and the start of a network of high-speed lines that other European countries started building over fifty years ago.

Who remembers the others, though, or that that the mighty Sir John Reith[302] was, for a short time, Minister of Transport? His successor as Minister of War Transport, John Moore-Brabazon,[303] might be remembered for the aircraft that bore his name, but not for his work in relation to railways.

---

[302] John Charles Walsham Reith, 1st Lord Reith (1889–1971), was Minister of Transport in 1940, having been ennobled in that year. He had previously been Chairman, Imperial Airways, 1938–39, and first Chairman of British Overseas Airways Corporation, 1939–40. He is principally remembered as the first General Manager of the BBC, 1922; its Managing Director, 1923; and Director-General, 1927–38. He was also Minister of Information in 1940.

[303] John Moore-Brabazon, 1st Lord Brabazon of Tara (1884–1964), was Unionist MP for Chatham, 1918–29; Wallasey, 1931–42. Junior Transport Minister, 1923–24 and 1924–27; Minister of Transport, 1940–41; Minister of Aircraft Production, 1941–42. Pioneer motorist and aviator.

Lord Brabazon of Tara (left) at the handover of the silver model of the first Bulleid pacific *Channel Packet* to Andrew McLean of the National Railway Museum. The loco was presented by the Southern Railway in 1941 to his grandfather John Moore-Brabazon who was at the time Minister of Transport. Looking on is the then chair of the All-Party Parliamentary Group on Heritage Rail Nicky Morgan MP, now Baroness Morgan of Cotes. Lord Brabazon was himself a transport minister in the Lords between 1986 and 1989 and 1990-92. *Christopher Austin*

As we have seen, railway projects are long term, so legacy projects are difficult, as if a minister starts them, it will be a successor that reaps the benefits. In the simplistic world of tabloid newspapers and social media, the unfortunate minister is seen as accountable for everything, including punctuality. Surprisingly, ministers have embraced this responsibility at the despatch box, even though privatisation gave them the opportunity to make clear the dividing line between responsibility for policy and that for day-to-day operations.

Privatisation provided the opportunity to adopt a more strategic approach, but ministers failed to do this and always felt obliged to intervene, either to criticise the train operators or Railtrack, or to pledge tougher standards to improve performance.

Too many ministers have been quick to intervene to comment on accidents, instead of leaving it to the industry and its safety regulator to sort out what has to be done, as they have been doing systematically and effectively for 180 years.

Since 2005, ministers have taken back control of the railway more directly, and the opportunity to delegate responsibility for almost every aspect of the railway has been lost. A new opportunity, however, is offered by the formation of Great British Railways to delineate clear boundaries between policy and delivery.

Regulation, Control and Ownership

Looking at the evidence of government legislation and inquiries, it is perhaps surprising to see the extent of government intervention in the nineteenth century

The period between the wars is, by contrast, relatively untroubled with legislation, apart from the creation of the Big Four in 1921 and major changes in and around London with the formation of London Transport in 1933.

The railways were a source of public comment and ridicule, particularly the unfortunate Southern Railway in the early 1920s when the first steps towards managing public expectations and replacing media myths with a few facts were taken by the newly appointed Public Relations Assistant John Elliot. Yet, ministers did not feel the need to intervene, and left it to the railways to get themselves out of the headlines.

The move into bus ownership, the formation of Railway Air Services and even international services via the Dover–Dunkirk train ferry were left to the railways to manage. Government involvement, where it occurred, tended to be beneficial, such as the payment of interest charges for a fifteen-year period on borrowing for railway capital projects under the Development (Loans Guarantees and Grants) Act, 1929.

During the wartime years the railways were under government direction.

It might have been thought that, with nationalisation, the railways would be, as in wartime, under direct government control with the policy being set by ministers and implemented by British Railways, but it was not to be like that.

Nationalisation in 1948 was not just a consolidation of the railways under a single management, but a grouping of all British transport – railways, buses, road haulage, canals, docks, ferries and hotels. It had a hopelessly big portfolio and, with two thirds of a million staff employed by the railways alone, and spread throughout Great Britain, quite unmanageable. The objectives were as rambling and incoherent as the range of activities involved. There was the Labour commitment to public ownership, the desire to see co-ordination of transport (with some blurred vision on the role of competition in transport), and a naïve desire for the railways to be both a public service and to be profitable even though the transport market was hopelessly skewed by public ownership of the highway network that was free for motorists and HGV drivers to use, once their vehicles had been taxed.

Folkestone Harbour. The packet port of Folkestone remained in railway ownership after 1948, while larger railway ports like Southampton and Immingham became part of the Docks Executive. The steep connection to the main line at Folkestone East meant that boat trains required three of these R1 class tank engines to lift the train, a problem that was solved when the line was electrified in 1962. The station and branch were last used in 2009 and formally closed in 2014. *J. Joyce/Online Transport Archive*

This lack of clarity was destined to be repeated forty-five years later with privatisation. Again, the objectives were complex and conflicting. The policy was driven by the desire to see the industry in the private sector, but was hopelessly complicated by the parallel objectives of encouraging on-track competition, reducing the cost to the public purse, and the desire of the Treasury to benefit financially from the sales process. At the same time, there was an expectation that it would free the private operators to innovate and to make big cost savings. However, that proved to be unachievable as BR was one of the most efficient railways in Europe with one of the lowest subsidy rates, and the biggest savings had already been made by BR. In the event, the financial success of the first round of franchises was based on growing the market, not on efficiency savings.

The privatisation of the infrastructure turned out to be a disaster and Railtrack was placed in administration in 2002, being replaced by the government-owned body Network Rail.

Plans for privatisation made the mistake of treating rail as if it were in a silo, not part of the wider transport market, and had already been shaped by competition from airlines and from roads, where the latter remained publicly owned with no proper charging mechanism for their use. At the same time, the government lacked the faith in the private sector to deliver what was required by passengers, and so an intrusive control mechanism was included in the plans on passenger service levels and fares, later extended to station facilities and other minutiae.

The requirement to provide a universal common carrier service for goods traffic was abandoned in 1962, as was the concept of the railway as a nationwide public service provided for every part of Great Britain. The government had traditionally been opposed to supporting railway services financially (apart from the worthy attempts through the Light Railways Act, 1896, to provide lines in rural areas that, even at that time of quasi monopoly, could not be justified commercially).

An opportunity was lost when the Inter City brand was allowed to die on privatisation. The legend lived on, however, and its 50th anniversary was marked by Virgin by naming a class 91 power car at Kings Cross in 2016. Three inter City directors, (L to R) Chris Green, Cyril Bleasdale and John Prideaux stand in front of the locomotive. *Christopher Austin*

Government financial support was required from 1955 onwards when BR as a whole first ceased to trade profitably. The pursuit of the profitable core of the railway network effectively stopped with the Railways Act, 1974, requiring BR to provide a service 'broadly comparable to that in existence at 31 December 1973'. It was finally put to bed with the ministerial refusal of closure of the Settle and Carlisle Line in 1989. Financial support was always grudgingly given, and was never quite enough to provide the level or quality of service being sought. The assumption by the department was always that BR could close the gap with unspecified 'efficiencies'.

A handful of lines have been retained with a token service to protect them against the potential of future use, and while this has been criticised, it is a positive device to avoid more closures. The classic example of this is Stockport to Stalybridge, where neither BR nor the PTE (nor more recently DfT and Transport for Greater Manchester) have required services along the route, which has to be retained for freight. A weekly service maintains the option for future use when required. Such nominal services have been dubbed 'Parliamentary trains', although the term derived from Gladstone's act, which was about the maximum fares to be charged on at least one service a day.

In short, Britain is seeking a system with French TGV speeds, Swiss-style performance, at Japanese levels of subsidy, with Italian fare levels. The government has in past decades sought to reorganise rather than fund the railway properly (in 1923, 1948 and 1992). Privatisation has provided a salutary lesson for government in terms of the actual cost of providing a safe, sustainable, affordable, accessible and attractive rail system, first with Tom Winsor's Railtrack settlement of 2003, secondly on the cost of replacing failed franchises, and more recently on the huge cost of maintaining a fully functional railway without many passengers during the Covid lockdowns. It is perhaps a good sign, though, that government wished to keep the network open in this way for its essential role in moving freight and carrying essential workers.

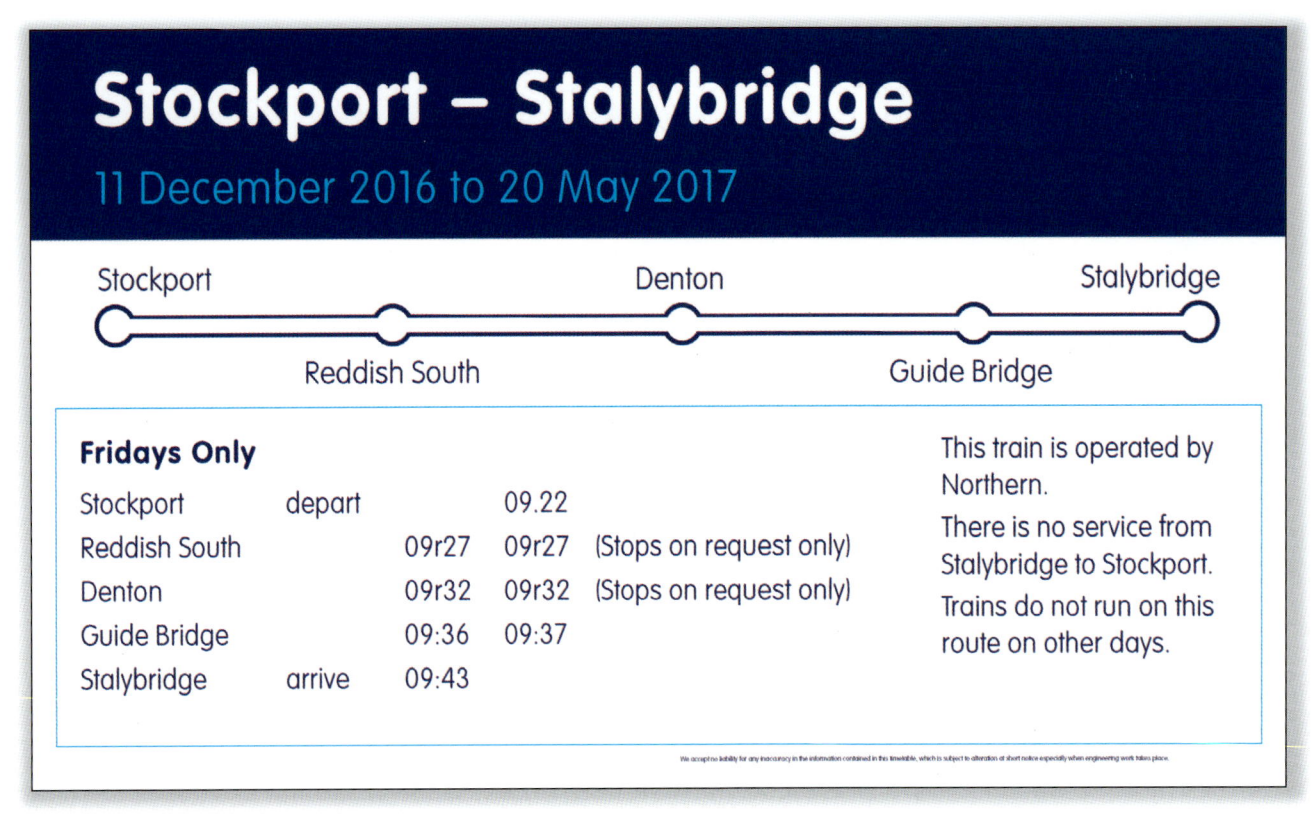

Stockport – Stalybridge
11 December 2016 to 20 May 2017

Stockport — Reddish South — Denton — Guide Bridge — Stalybridge

Fridays Only

Stockport	depart		09.22	
Reddish South		09r27	09r27	(Stops on request only)
Denton		09r32	09r32	(Stops on request only)
Guide Bridge		09:36	09:37	
Stalybridge	arrive	09:43		

This train is operated by Northern.
There is no service from Stalybridge to Stockport.
Trains do not run on this route on other days.

The Stalybridge 'Pullman.' The timetable for the weekly train between Stockport and Stalybridge for 2017, loosely called a 'Parliamentary' train. *Authors' Collection*

The clearest example that rail's effectiveness depends on wider transport policy and decent leadership exists in the approach to freight on rail, which has reduced steadily with the decline in British manufacturing and the extractive industries. The growth of imports from the Far East, and particularly China, has led to huge rises in demand for transport through the principal container ports – Felixstowe, the Thames ports, Southampton and Liverpool, where rail's share has been constrained by lack of capacity rather than lack of demand. Railways are also important in handling building materials, oil, cement and cars, but many areas are scarcely touched by rail, as described in Chapter 9. Opportunities exist for distribution of products to supermarket warehouses and distribution centres for the online retailers, but there are few incentives for customers to consider rail against the lightly regulated road haulage industry, where no infrastructure charges are made and government is perennially willing to adapt the highway network for ever larger and heavier juggernauts.

As early as 11 October 2018, Chris Grayling's statement to the House of Commons turned the privatisation policy on its head and, with no sense of irony, he listed the problems his predecessors had created by the hasty and ill-conceived policy of 1993:

> Network Rail, which represents a third (38 per cent) of the industry (based on spend), is nationalised. It is also responsible for over half (54 per cent) of the daily disruption.
>
> But no matter whether it is a failure of the track, a fault with a train, or a customer incident, it is because there is little resilience or margin for error in the system that, when things go wrong, the knock-on effect can last for hours.

Engineering work is costly and disruptive, but a lot safer than it used to be. Here track is being relaid at Topsham on the Exmouth branch in Devon. *Christopher Austin*

This problem is compounded because the railway is run by multiple players without clear lines of accountability.[304]

These failings were expounded in greater detail by the Williams/Shapps white paper, as described in Chapter 10.

Now the railway is supported to the extent of £7.1 billion a year (including £2.6 billion for HS2) and the value of it is better understood by government. The endless engineering work closures and diversions are at least an indication that the backlog of infrastructure renewals and new projects are being addressed.

The relationship between government and industry is more open, the benefits brought by the railway are better understood and there is greater clarity about what is being bought through the franchise agreements or service contracts and the interventions being funded through Network Rail. However, the relationship continues to exclude the industry on too many occasions, such as during the preparation of the Integrated Rail Plan for the North and Midlands, which, again, was handed down from Mount Olympus, rather than being worked up with the industry, let alone stakeholders.

Renationalisation

Since the start of the privatisation process there had been calls for Labour to renationalise the railways, and it formed part of their manifesto for the 2017 election.

In this section we review the lessons of the past 100 years of government influence and control and assess the factors underlying questions on future ownership.

Over this period we have seen:

- Private vertically integrated companies lightly regulated by government.
- Government control in wartime, exercised with the industry through a Railway Executive Committee.
- Merged private sector companies (a government construct) lightly regulated by government.
- A nationalised industry responsible to the British Transport Commission.
- A nationalised industry responsible to the Secretary of State.
- A fragmented privatised industry part specified and more closely regulated by government through quangos.
- A publicly specified and largely publicly owned industry with the private sector acting as suppliers but tightly controlled by government as shadow managers.

The only variant we have not seen since 1844 is an unregulated private sector operation.

In fact, through all these changes, the trains have continued to run (although they almost came to a stand in 2001 post-Hatfield) and the conclusion has to be that there is no 'right' answer to the question of ownership.

Our conclusion therefore is that ownership is not the primary issue in order to run a successful railway. The key issues are the strategic direction of the industry, the specification of the requirements of the network, how services are funded and some consistency and stability in the way the railway is organised.

The railway is not a normal commercial business. It is expected to provide a safe and seamless national service of high quality at low cost and to support many areas of government policy beyond simply that of transporting people and goods. It is expected to be universally accessible, to provide for growing and changing demand on a capacity-constrained network and both to meet local demand and to support regeneration where this is required. It is expected to provide generous compensation when things go wrong, even when this is beyond the control of the operator, like flooding or misuse of level crossings by car or truck drivers. At various times the railway has been criticised for lack of capacity for special events or sudden surges in demand, even though this was eliminated by the Beeching Report with government and Parliamentary approval. It is expected to keep ticket offices open while eliminating their need by facilitating online booking, and to provide high levels of staffing while becoming highly efficient. It must also prioritise and promote diversity, inclusion and meet a host of other government policies as part of its daily activities. These may be good objectives, but none of this had (before Williams/Shapps) been clearly enunciated in any government policy document, and there has, amazingly, never been a national strategy setting out the nation's requirements from its railway, let alone consistent and adequate funding to pay for it.

Experience teaches us that when future changes come, it will again be the political imperatives that dominate. While it will be claimed that the changes are needed for reasons of accountability and to ensure that passenger interests are put before profit, the reality will be that it is about extending government control, driven by dogma or theories about organisational structures, or by political imperatives regardless of the effect on passengers (and freight customers) and staff. It will be to meet the political priorities of the day, rather than the long-term needs of people and freight customers.

In spite of this, and in view of previous experience, it would be worth asking a few simple questions as a test to see whether any radical change of organisation or ownership is needed and if so, how far it should go:

1. Will the changes be safe? Will they increase or diminish risks and how will any risks be managed? The Hidden Report (into the 1988 Clapham Junction accident) highlighted the risks inherent in any organisational change.

2. Will the change benefit passengers, and if so, how?

---

[304] *Hansard*, cols 318–321, 11 October 2018.

3 Will the change benefit freight customers?

4 What effect will the changes have on staff?

5 Who will be continuing to plan investment while the changes are taking place? Previous experience shows that there is a hiatus in planning for around a decade when major changes are undertaken, which does not serve passengers well.

6 How will the changes actually improve services or decision-making, or offer better value for money?

7 How much more will the changes cost to implement? (They always cost more – never less).

And perhaps the key question for any government thinking of tinkering with the ownership or structure:

8 What do you want the railway to deliver through this change that it is not delivering now?

The argument about ownership continues, so we need to review how far that affects the performance of the railway and how it works for passengers and freight customers. In practical terms, in 2023 most of the railway is publicly owned or publicly controlled, even before the implementation of the Williams/Shapps white paper.

1 Passenger services are publicly specified and procured. The service level specification is the responsibility of the Department for Transport, which also has to approve any change to it, including enhancements and many other very detailed aspects of the operation of trains and stations such as the opening hours of ticket offices and the provision of station toilets.

2 The railway network is owned and the major stations are managed by Network Rail, a public sector organisation.

3 The Department also sponsors the major infrastructure enhancements and pays part of the cost of the network through direct grant.

4 The network and access to it is regulated by another public sector body, the Office of Rail and Road.

5 The train operators are private companies, but now work to emergency measures agreements or rail service contract agreements where revenue risk is with the Department.

6 The train leasing companies are privately owned, but most rolling stock leasing contracts are underwritten by the Department to protect the residual value of the contract at the end of the contract term.

7 The freight companies are in the private sector.

A number of franchises have, however, failed and are being run by an operator of last resort (OLR), which is a public sector company reporting to the Department for Transport. The history of OLR intervention is as follows:

- *South Eastern Trains* operated the South Eastern franchise from 2003 until 2006, after the Connex South Eastern franchise was terminated by the Strategic Rail Authority. London & South Eastern Railway ran the franchise from 2006 to October 2021, when it was stripped of it for not declaring £25 million of revenue. South Eastern Trains (an OLR company) has operated it since then, and is continuing to use the South Eastern name.

- *East Coast* operated the InterCity East Coast franchise from 2009 until 2015, after National Express East Coast defaulted. That franchise passed to Virgin Trains East Coast, but in 2018 that company also defaulted, and the InterCity East Coast service has been operated by OLR London North Eastern Railway.

- *Northern Trains* has operated the Northern franchise since 1 March 2020, after the Arriva Rail North franchise was terminated by the Department for Transport.

- *Transport for Wales Rail* has been the Welsh Government's operator since 7 February 2021, after the Wales & Borders franchise operated by Keolis/Amey Wales became unviable as a result of the Covid-19 pandemic.

- *ScotRail Trains* controlled by Transport Scotland took over the ScotRail franchise from Abellio ScotRail from April 2022.

The Williams/Shapps white paper is based on continued involvement of the private sector as train operators, rolling stock leasing companies and contractors and suppliers, and the nature of the paper is driven by the political reality that wholesale change to a fully public sector railway would not at this stage be acceptable.

Reorganisations

Organisational change on the scale of privatisation (or nationalisation) is hugely disruptive. The industry has to refocus on changing the organisation, developing new objectives, recruiting new staff and redeploying or making redundant those not transferring. There are training and relocation costs, redundancy payments, offices to rent, new computer systems to set up and a host of other activities that detract from the core task of running a safe, reliable and punctual railway. Management attention shifts from these key requirements and customer service slips, manifest sometimes in poor punctuality, and always in confusion about who is responsible for what.

The managers of the Big Four experienced this in the 1930s, noting that the changes they wanted at the outset took a decade to achieve. The risks of constant reorganisation is summed up by an experienced railway manager, Gerry Fiennes, who wrote in 1968: 'For many months the few top people who keep the momentum up are distracted from their proper job. Punctuality goes to hell.

Safety starts to slip. Don't reorganise. Don't. Don't. Don't.'[305] Thirty years later, another senior railway manager, Peter Rayner, made the same point about the last BR reorganisation, 'Organising for Quality': 'the Government asked for the structure of BR to be changed yet again. Terrible hypocrisy, really, for one of the Hidden recommendations and much of the text of his report was concerned with the dangers of reorganisation.'[306]

Changes in ownership are driven by political dogma rather than logic, so that in 1947, the practical arguments were subservient to the need to nationalise rail along with other forms of transport and other utilities as part of the move to give effect to clause 4 of the Labour Party's constitution, and the creation of a socialist society in a country hungry for change after six years of war. Similarly, the privatisation of the railway between 1992 and 1997 was as much about showing that the Major administration had not 'run out of steam' and could implement radical ideas in the way that his predecessor did. It is surprising that such a significant (if misguided) achievement as railway privatisation does not merit an explanation in Sir John Major's memoirs. All that upheaval and effort scarcely merits a footnote in his history.

Oversight and Scrutiny

Both government and Parliament have undertaken endless inquiries into the performance of the railway, particularly in the BR period, and many other organisations have weighed in with their thoughts and advice from the Centre for Policy Studies to groups of 'critical friends' like Railfuture or the Campaign for Better Transport.

In 1976 Peter Parker had found it all a bit overwhelming: 'It was hard to think of any industry more reported on: it was a wonder to me that BR management had not died of overexposure.' Pragmatically, he took the view that each inquiry offered an opportunity to spread the virtues of the railway and to increase its awareness, and treated each one in an amazingly positive spirit.

Appendix 4 lists the reports of Parliamentary select committees relating to railways, while Appendix 5 list government inquiries.

Expectations

Today, the position is, if anything, even more complex. The expectation is for a railway that runs safely, punctually and reliably, of course, for one that is the basis of a co-ordinated public transport system that fulfils social as well as financial objectives, although these have not previously been specified. It must be fully accessible and contribute to the government's environmental targets, even though there is no electrification plan in place and that even if electrification were limited to the rest of the main-line network, it would be a thirty-year project. Meanwhile, the requirements for a properly co-ordinated system, including reregulation of the bus network, road pricing, traffic restraint measures and controls over internal airlines are not even on the current policy agenda. The SRA's brave attempt to link land use and transport planning has been abandoned.

There is the perennial problem of a mismatch of timescales. Railway projects take a long time – new lines typically between ten and twenty years, electrification, five to ten years and rolling stock replacement, three to five years. Even changing the timetable is a two-year job. Politicians think in no more than five-year cycles, and preferably would like to see results within two or three years. Reports can be commissioned and delivered in two or three years and whilst costly, are still cheaper than major investment schemes. So, it is perhaps inevitable that many Transport Ministers have sought to make their mark through a 'review' rather than through the legacy of projects like new lines, electrification or major increases in capacity. Typical of this was Dr Brian Mawhinney, who launched a 'Great Transport Debate' in 1995 as an alternative to even developing a policy, let alone implementing it. In some ways, this was understandable at the time. The policy for railways was privatisation, while Professor Phil Goodwin's study[307] had demonstrated to the Treasury that you could not build your way out of the congestion problems on the roads, so it was not a propitious time to be suggesting radical new departures in either mode. Mawhinney's job was just to kick the can down the road for a few more months until the 'benefits' of privatisation came through.

Funding

The other common factor relating to the major changes to the structure of Britain's railways relates to money, and particularly to investment. The Grouping in 1923 came after the First World War, which had stretched the railways to the limit, financially and physically and had left a backlog of maintenance and renewals matched only by their customers' wishes to see improvements to services. Not only had the railways not been recompensed for the service they provided to the nation, and the government had played 'hard ball' on the compensation due to them, as we saw in the case of the North British Railway, there was no intention of providing public funding to pay for deferred maintenance and renewals. By merging the companies into larger groups they were able to raise the funds, and invest in electrification, new locomotives and dramatic speed improvements, including running the world's fastest train,[308] but this was in spite of, rather than because of, the government's approach.

---

[305] *I Tried to Run a Railway*, G F Fiennes, Ian Allan, 1968.

[306] *On and Off the Rails*, Peter Rayner, Novelangle, 1997.

[307] *Trunk Roads and the Generation of Traffic*, SACTRA, 1994.

[308] The GWR's *Cheltenham Flyer* running between Swindon and Paddington at an average speed of 71.4mph.

Similarly, the system suffered the same problems after the Second World War and, again, no structured programme for renewals and new works projects was possible because of impending nationalisation and lack of money. It started to be put right from 1949 onwards, with the ambitious Modernisation Plan following in 1955, but the hiatus was damaging to both customer service and to staff morale. Passengers returned in huge numbers to the railway after the war eager to take advantage of the ending of travel restrictions and desperate to have a holiday after six years. The year 1946 was a record one for passenger carryings. What they saw was a run-down and unkempt system but with the continuation of petrol rationing and while motoring remained expensive, rail saw continued growth for summer holiday traffic to the peak year of 1957. The strains on the system of handling such huge numbers are graphically described in *Summer Saturdays in the West*[309] and many people stuck in heavily delayed, overcrowded, dirty and old trains determined at that point to go and buy a car.

Covid 19 led to a national lockdown from March 23 2020. A couple of weeks later, this mid-morning shot of London Bridge station shows the dramatic effect of the restrictions. *Christopher Austin*

[309] *Summer Saturdays in the West*, David St John Thomas and Simon Rockborough Smith, David & Charles, 1973.

In the case of privatisation, there was no such backlog in maintenance to contend with, and renewals in modern form had delivered some substantial improvements in rolling stock and line speeds, but there was an evident need to do more. Channel Tunnel connections came out of the DfT budget and there was a strong case for further electrification as well as for new and improved stations. BR had one of the lowest levels of government financial support of any railway in Europe and was the subject of increasing expectations on environmental grounds. It was getting better at articulating its case in public as well, notably through the understated but highly effective publication of *Future Rail* in 1991. In theory, privatisation should have been able to give the railways freedom to raise capital to invest, and that might have worked if a more practical method of privatisation had been chosen. In the event, the complex contractual matrix increased risk for investors. In particular, train operating companies were designed to be 'asset light' and the infrastructure and rolling stock were owned by others. The private sector was risk averse under these circumstances and major investments had to be sponsored and guaranteed or funded by government.

Since 2005, most aspects of the railway have been under direct government control, but this too is not satisfactory. Even though a new rail division was created, there have been major problems with the sponsorship of major projects and the franchising process. Above all, the Department has not been able to provide the leadership required to make the industry function effectively, while ministers have, quite inappropriately, been left answering in Parliament for operational shortcomings, which are the responsibility of Network Rail or the train operating companies.

The Covid crisis has seen the end of the franchising system and even closer control of the production side of the railway by ministers. That has resulted in enough funding to keep a high level of service running, but in the long term is bound to lead to attempts to reduce the huge cost of this by cutting back. The government injunction not to use public transport during the pandemic has been hugely damaging and it took many months for public confidence to recover, once the crisis started to recede. Commuting levels and business travel will never recover to their 2019 levels, although the prospects for leisure travel are better. However, these changed circumstances will release capacity and create an opportunity for the railway to play a much greater part in meeting the travel needs of the nation for good environmental reasons, but the present political and industry structure does not encourage such an approach, although the Williams/Shapps white paper seems to point in the right direction.

Government has always kept a close eye on the railways and has not hesitated to intervene when public or political pressure has demanded it. Since 2005, however, government has been running the industry as well, and the pressures and uncertainty have grown. Appendix 5 lists the government reports and inquiries that have been held since 1830, and the list is long, with many more reports during the nineteenth century than might have been expected in that *laissez-faire* era. But add to this the number of Parliamentary inquiries from departmental select committees and the National Audit Office (see Appendix 4), and the level of scrutiny and intrusion can be seen fully.

Sixty-five inquiries over the last twenty-five years, mostly followed by a government response, show the level of commitment required from both DfT and the industry to service and to respond to these elaborate studies that now weigh down the shelves of the House of Commons library, with little to show in the way of implementation. Arguably, this is no way to run a business, even one so dependent on government support as the railway. There must be a better way of holding the industry to account than this scattergun approach, where the agenda depends on the committees themselves, with no attempt to co-ordinate them or space them out so that industry resources to service them can be more sensibly deployed.

12
Postscript

'The utter centrality of the railway system to the maintenance of decent daily life in a crowded, complicated island. It is up there with the NHS and the police, an essential shared source.'
Libby Purves, *The Times*, 21 November 2000

Like all good stories, this one has not ended, but continues to move forward, sometimes in surprising directions. Like most other major political changes, understanding their consequences only comes with hindsight and usually after a period of years rather than months.

We started to plan this book in early 2019, and at that stage it would have been impossible to predict that normal life would come to an end in 2020 with the first lockdown. Who could have predicted that the government's generous settlement would result in keeping a high level of rail services running throughout this unprecedented period? Who then could have predicted a rise in electricity prices so extreme that Freightliner could not afford to use its electric locomotives?

Other startling events were perhaps more predictable. The shortage of HGV drivers had been apparent for some time, and is replicated in Europe and the USA. This has led to some reputable hauliers starting to transfer some long-haul traffic to rail. Yet, as a nation, we have forgotten our history, and in all the comment on this shortage and the empty supermarket shelves that follow from it by experts and the media, the one obvious way of mitigating the crisis – moving more flows to rail – was not mentioned, although some freight forwarders and major ports like Felixstowe are attempting to increase rail's share.

Initially seen as a short-term interruption to normal life, it is already clear that some of the changes the Covid pandemic triggered will have a more profound effect. Conference calls have been around since the 1970s, but have never had much effect on the desire of business people to meet together and this need has been the source of much of InterCity's profitable business traffic. However, Covid stimulated the rapid development of Zoom calls and, while there will be many cases where physical meetings will be preferred for the networking opportunities they offer, and for serious negotiations, Zoom is here to stay, and will inevitably affect the long-distance business travel market.

By the same token, working from home has affected (but not destroyed) the commuting market and the huge and surging demand of the first part of the twenty-first century is not going to drive investment in the same way that it has in the past. More importantly, in political terms, rail was essential to the effective functioning of Britain's major cities and this was a key factor in convincing politicians of the essential nature of the railway. Crossrail has, at last, given London a regional express service through the capital that is the equal of any other in the World, and will be key to keeping London's competitiveness post Brexit. However, the ending of inexorable commuter growth is bound to affect the way politicians look at the case for yet more huge rail (and road) infrastructure projects, such as Crossrail Two.

Continuing strong growth is expected in the leisure market and the railway is now well equipped to deal with that, supported by a community rail network for many rural lines, attractive new trains such as the Stadler units on branch lines in East Anglia and the environmental pressures to use sustainable transport rather than cars to access the countryside.

The role of rail freight in terms of distribution was important throughout the pandemic and will continue to be so. In environmental terms, rail can be relatively easily decarbonised, whereas there is no solution yet in sight to do the same for the heavy goods vehicle. If we are serious about reducing our carbon footprint, government will have to encourage a shift to rail and this will be working with the grain of many companies that want to improve their green credentials.

Birmingham Curzon Street as it looked when the London & Birmingham Railway opened in 1838. The elegant building, a remarkable survival, will form part of the terminus for the first stage of High Speed Two. *Public Domain*

Environmental considerations continue to provide the strongest case for further rail development but, as in the past, the state of the economy and government resources will determine what is actually possible. Here, the high cost of the railway is a major drawback, as is the politicians' perception of the cost and the value for money offered compared with other expenditure on the key priorities of the NHS, or education, or tax cuts.

So the future is, as it was in 1923, 1948 and 1997, uncertain, but the prospects are reasonable. Huge effort will continue to be required to articulate the case for rail, to highlight its achievements, and to deal with unfair or inaccurate media criticism (particularly given the conspiracy theories that are a feature of social media), which plays to the natural scepticism of people in Britain.

Some things, however, we can forecast with certainty, including the inevitability of further structural change as politicians strive to leave their mark in a normally short period of office. Railways are a form of mass transit that seek to provide safe comfortable and enjoyable journeys for millions of very different individual passengers each year. Inevitably, some of these journeys will not meet the expectation or needs of some passengers, who will not hesitate to raise this with their elected representatives, so there will be more inquiries by government and Parliament into the state of the railways.

The third and more positive conclusion is that railways are special and attract both strong views and some exceptional people to work for them, people who are more motivated by the public service or environmental aspects of the job, rather than just the financial rewards. Such people are resilient and innovative and have in the past proved that they can deliver services to customers under a variety of ownership and regulatory structures.

The Williams/Shapps review proposes some sensible steps in the right direction, including closer co-ordination in the way the industry is run and an attempt to reduce the number of contractual interfaces. Success, however, will depend, *inter alia*, on a number of other factors, in particular:

1 Solving the inherent conflict between the Permanent Secretary of the DfT as Accounting Officer and the head of Great British Railways. Which is in charge, given the actions taken by the latter will have financial implications that will impact on the departmental budget for which the former is responsible?

2 Associated with this is the wider question of relative roles. Given the high cost of the railway, it will always be a matter of public scrutiny, but ministers must stand back from interfering and leave it to the industry to run. The minister's job is done when he has set out clearly the objectives for the next five to ten years and agreed with GBR the budget that will deliver that. Similarly, the industry has to deliver on a wide range of objectives beyond that of transporting passengers and freight, and has to do so in the most efficient and cost-effective way it can, and be able to demonstrate that.

3 The new organisation will be judged on agreeing a fares structure that meets the perceived requirement of simplification, while retaining very low fares (such as Super Off Peak) and still yielding the level of revenue required to meet government objectives on the proportion of costs that should be met by passengers. The role the railway plays in delivering social policies for the government has to be considered here as well as comparative costs with other modes if the objective is (as it should be) to continue to encourage passengers and freight to use the more sustainable mode.

4 The railway has a huge capacity to deliver benefits to its users, and also to those who do not use it but benefit indirectly from its services. Railway passenger services bring a reduction in road congestion, while many products are carried by rail freight as part of the supply chain. The transport market is skewed by the different methods of charging for road and rail, and the differential treatment of issues such as safety and sustainability. It no longer makes any sort of sense to pretend that rail can achieve a conventional 'profitability'. GBR will have a major task to manage costs justified by the benefits the railway brings, not least because so many of these remain unquantified.

5 Treasury pressure will always bear down on costs and look to minimise the requirement for public support. While not entirely happy with the thrust of the Williams/Shapps white paper, they did secure a commitment to reduce costs by £1.5 billion a year and could not think of any better alternative. At some stage they will want to return to the issue and compel further changes.

6 In particular, the new organisation will need to be seen as competent and well managed, a task that is made so much more difficult where a majority of commentators and officials believe they could manage it better themselves.

7 A cadre of competent and motivated railway staff, well managed, and a degree of organisational stability to allow them to focus on the core objective of delivering the safe, reliable and affordable railway specified in strategic terms by government.

As we identified in *Holding the Line*, we could so easily have ended up with a much smaller network after the closures of the 1960s and '70s and the mistakes of the modernisation plan. Good stewardship by BR during the 1990s and the growth that followed privatisation, together with significant investment, particularly in rolling stock, have enabled the railways to transform themselves, and offer services that people want and welcome, as shown by the doubling of passenger numbers pre-pandemic. The arguments now are no longer about what has to be cut out to meet inadequate financial support levels, but about how more can be found to meet the needs of rail passengers and freight customers. Environmental considerations strengthen rail's claim for investment to allow it to become the backbone of the nation's sustainable transport system, and it will continue to be an exciting time to be part of the rail industry.

The 11.10 Waterloo to Portsmouth Harbour accelerates through Vauxhall at the start of its journey, with the Palace of Westminster in the background.
Christopher Austin

Stop the Presses

The story continues, and even during the editing process of this book over a five-month period, we have seen three Prime Ministers and three Transport Secretaries with different policy approaches.

A financial crisis was triggered by Russia's invasion of Ukraine, the costs of the Covid pandemic and a Government fiscal policy that spooked the markets and led to the replacement of the Chancellor of the Exchequer. Inevitably, as part of the process of restoring confidence, a new period of austerity has been triggered, with government departments expected to make significant 'efficiency savings'. So, the medium term prospects for rail are difficult and at least will require the sort of changes planned in establishing Great British Railways, as described in chapter 10 above. The reduction in the number of industry interfaces this implies, and a collaborative approach to running trains and projects both reflect that the railway is a team game, not a solo sport. The close coordination that cut 25% from the costs of the Okehampton reopening project and delivered it ahead of schedule in just nine months, with ridership three times that forecast shows what can be achieved. Yet, the former Secretary of State (Anne-Marie Trevelyan – holder of the unenviable record for the shortest period of time for a transport secretary in office ever) accepted the deferment of the legislation required for the new organisation to operate effectively because of 'a lack of parliamentary time'[310].

The Government did however argue that much could be achieved without legislation, including 'workplace reform, delivering local partnerships, bringing forward a more long-term strategy for rail and reforming how we use ticketing'[311].

This procrastination has a parallel with the period from 1998 to 2001 when the Strategic Rail Authority was being set up, but had to operate in shadow form as time could not be found for the required legislation. The result will inevitably be a measure of drift and uncertainty while stability returns and legislation allows changes to be made.

Government support for the railway during the pandemic was claimed by the Government to be £16bn and this will be a stick with which to beat the industry for some years to come. Clearly these were wholly exceptional circumstances and reflected the level of service the Government specified. However, the continuing post pandemic support level is accepted as unsustainable by both government and railway managers and has to be reduced, in spite of the increasing labour costs and revenue losses that will result from current strike action. That would seem to imply reductions in staff numbers as well as outputs. The concern will be to ensure that, in the desperate search for short-term economies, long-term damage is not caused to the network through service or network reductions which, as we saw in *Holding the Line*, never produce the economies sought.

The difference is that while most people see rail as an economic good, the Treasury sees it as a financial asset. This makes it very difficult for the Department to plan and deliver a longer-term strategy for rail which incorporates the wide range of benefits they would want the industry to deliver.

Railways remain the key component of a decarbonised transport system and their importance in this context is perhaps greater than at any time in the last century. There is no doubt that their existence has both been sustained by Government support since 1955, but also held back by excessive Government interventions in their organisation and management and in the lack of overall strategic direction that ministers should be providing. The railways' capabilities are manifest when the management of the railways is restored to those competent to operate them, with a clear strategy and funding agreed to deliver the outputs of that strategy.

28 October 2022

---

[310] Evidence to Select Committee on Transport, 19 October 2022, HC 163

[311] Rail minister Kevin Foster (also in post for an extraordinarily short period of time) House of Commons Hansard 24 October 2022 col 26.

Appendix 1
Statutory Returns Required from the Railway Companies, 1901

At the end of the Victorian era, at the height of unfettered capitalism, it might be surprising to read of the detailed information that the government required the private railway companies to send it on a regular basis. These eighteen regular returns had to be sent to the Board of Trade, except where otherwise shown.

Accidents. Timely reporting of any movement accident to a train or to railway staff.

Accounts and Balance Sheets. Every half year a statement of accounts and balance sheet, signed by the Chairman, Deputy Chairman and Accountant, to be provided.

General Meetings. These should be held in February and August (unless otherwise specified by Act of Parliament) and should be advertised in prescribed newspapers with fourteen days' notice of date, time and place of the meeting.

Share Transfer Ledgers. These could be closed fourteen days before an Ordinary meeting but seven days' written notice was required in newspapers, as above.

Shareholder addresses. Companies were required to publish annually a list of shareholder addresses up to 1 December each year.

Annual Returns. Annually companies had to provide returns of their capital, traffic and working expenses for the preceding financial year using a form provided by the Board of Trade within fourteen days of their half-yearly meetings.

Return to Factory Inspector. Where they had a factory or workshop, the company should provide by 1 March each year a return of the number of employees during the previous calendar year, with details of age and sex.

Local Information. The annual accounts had to be sent to the Overseers of the Parishes and to the Clerks of the Peace for the counties through which the railway ran.

Continuous Brakes. Half-yearly forms required listing numbers of vehicles fitted with continuous brakes.

Loan Capital. Half-yearly return to the Registrar of Joint Stock Companies of loan capital authorised and actually raised.

Composition in Lieu of Transfer Duties. Half-yearly return to the Commissioners of Inland Revenue of the company's stock and funded debt.

Carriage of Cotton. Monthly return required showing quantity of cotton received or forwarded through the ports.

Passenger Receipts. A monthly return of passenger receipts to be sent to the Commissioners of Inland Revenue and Passenger Duty to be paid.

New Railways. Companies to give one month's notice of the opening of a new railway and a second notice ten days before opening.

Property Conveyances. Companies to produce to the Commissioners of Inland Revenue, conveyances of all property acquired, on which duty is payable, within three months of purchase.

Income Tax. Requirement on companies to pay income tax in four quarterly instalments.

Increase of Capital. Returns to Commissioners of Inland Revenue required within one month of any increase in capital.

Working Agreements. Notice to be given to shareholders of intention to enter into working agreements with other railways, and the consent of the Railway Commissioners obtained.

In addition to the regular reports, other government requirements included:

Fares on Tickets. Fares to be shown on every ticket, with a 40 shilling fine for each case where this was not done.

Statutory Notices. Notices had to be exhibited at all stations in relation to:

    Insurance of valuable parcels

    Dangerous goods

    General notices of the railway

    General bye-laws of the railway

    Explosives bye-laws

    Toll notices

    Shoddy, rags and mungo (in Yorkshire goods stations only)[312]

---

[312] Shoddy was cheap cloth, rags are fragments of cloth and mungo was an inferior cloth made of felted rags. West Yorkshire was a major provider of cloth of all sorts in the nineteenth century and many fine mill buildings remain, although now repurposed.

Appendix 2
Transport Ministers and Secretaries of State, 1919–2022

Date	Name	Party	Des
1919–21	Eric Geddes	Conservative(Coalition)	MT
1921–22	Viscount Peel	Conservative	MT
1922	Earl of Crawford	Conservative	MT
1922–24	Sir John Baird Bt	Conservative	MT
1924	Harry Gosling	Labour	MT
1924–29	Wilfrid Ashley	Conservative	MT
1929–31	Herbert Morrison	Labour	MT
1931–33	John Pybus	Liberal (National Government)	MT
1933–34	Hon Oliver Stanley	Conservative	MT
1934–37	Leslie Hore-Belisha	National Liberal	MT
1937–39	Leslie Burgin	National Liberal	MT
1939–40	Euan Wallace	Conservative	MT
1940	John Reith	National Independent (Coalition)	MT
1940–41	John Moore-Brabazon	Conservative(Coalition)	MT
1941–45	Lord Leathers	Conservative	MT
1945–51	Alfred Barnes	Labour	MT
1951–52	John Scott Maclay	Conservative	MT
1952–54	Alan Lennox-Boyd	Conservative	MT/MTCA
1954–55	John Boyd-Carpenter	Conservative	MTCA
1955–59	Harold Watkinson	Conservative	MTCA
1959–64	Ernest Maples	Conservative	MT
1964–65	Tom Fraser	Labour	MT
1965–68	Barbara Castle	Labour	MT
1968–69	Richard Marsh	Labour	MT
1969–70	Fred Mulley	Labour	MT
1970–74	John Peyton	Conservative	MT/MTI
1974–75	Fred Mulley	Labour	MT
1975–76	John Gilbert	Labour	MT
1976–79	William Rodgers	Labour	SST
1979–81	Norman Fowler	Conservative	MT/SST
1981–83	David Howell	Conservative	SST
1983	Tom King	Conservative	SST
1983–86	Nicholas Ridley	Conservative	SST
1986–87	John Moore	Conservative	SST
1987–89	Paul Channon	Conservative	SST
1989–90	Cecil Parkinson	Conservative	SST
1990–92	Malcolm Rifkind	Conservative	SST
1992–94	John MacGregor	Conservative	SST
1994–95	Brian Mawhinney	Conservative	SST
1995–97	Sir George Young	Conservative	SST
1997–98	Gavin Strang	Labour	MST
1998–99	John Reid	Labour	MST
1999	Helen Liddell	Labour	MST
1999–01	Lord Macdonald of Tradeston	Labour	MST
2001–02	John Spellar	Labour	MST
2002–06	Alistair Darling	Labour	SST
2006–07	Douglas Alexander	Labour	SST
2007–08	Ruth Kelly	Labour	SST
2008–09	Geoff Hoon	Labour	SST
2009–10	Lord Adonis	Labour	SST
2010–11	Philip Hammond	Conservative	SST
2011–12	Justine Greening	Conservative	SST
2012–16	Patrick McLoughlin	Conservative	SST
2016–19	Chris Grayling	Conservative	SST
2019–22	Grant Shapps	Conservative	SST
2022	Anne Marie Trevelyan	Conservative	SST
2022–	Mark Harper	Conservative	SST

Analysis

Total: 54

Average tenure of office: 21.7 months

Average tenure of office since privatisation in 1997: 17 months

Longest in office: Alfred Barnes, six years five months

Shortest term in office: Anne-Marie Trevelyan, seven weeks

Notes

This table shows the ministers with direct responsibility for railways. In general, Ministers of Transport up to 1969 and Secretaries of State for Transport had a seat in the Cabinet and reported directly to the Prime Minister. From 1970 to 1976, transport was represented by a junior minister reporting to the Secretary of State for the Environment. From 1997 to 2001, Transport Ministers reported to Rt Hon John Prescott MP as Secretary of State for Environment, Transport and the Regions (he was also deputy Prime Minister). However, Gavin Strang also had a seat in the Cabinet. From 2001–02, John Spellar reported to Stephen Byers as Secretary of State for Transport, Local Government and the Regions, and also attended Cabinet meetings.

Designation codes

MT	Minister of Transport
MST	Minister of State for Transport
MTCA	Minister of Transport and Civil Aviation
MTI	Minister for Transport Industries
SST	Secretary of State for Transport

Appendix 3

Principal Acts of Parliament Affecting the Nature and Structure of Railways in the United Kingdom, 1838–2022

Definition: This appendix lists the Public General Acts affecting the management of railways. It does not include railway private Bills or hybrid Bills. It does not include other Acts of general application that might also affect railways, nor ministerial orders made under delegated powers. Legislation having the greatest effect on the management of the railways or their competitive position shown in bold type.

1838, Railways (Conveyance of mails) Act, 1838.

1839, Highway (Railway Crossings) Act – railways to maintain gates at level crossings.

1840, Regulation of Railways Act – Board of Trade inspection of new railways.

1842, Regulation of Railways Act – Board of Trade could prevent opening of new railways if thought to be unsafe.

1842, Railway Passenger Duty Act – 5 per cent duty on passenger fares; requirement to keep records and report.

1844, Railway Regulation Act – Fares and safety regulation. Parliamentary trains.

1845, Railway Clauses Consolidation Act – Regulations relating to railway construction, provision of mileposts.

1845, Railway Clauses Consolidation (Scotland) Act.

1846, Gauge of Railways Act – only standard-gauge lines to be built in future.

1850, Railway Clearing Act – legal existence for Railway Clearing House.

1854, Railway & Canal Traffic Act – regulation of carriage of goods by rail and compensation provisions.

1863, Railway Clauses Act – Consolidated provisions on railway construction and safety. Level crossing safety.

1866, Railway Companies Securities Act – Half-yearly capital accounts to be made available to the Office of the Registrar of Joint Stock companies; available to shareholders.

1867, Railways Companies Act – Rolling stock and plant of operational railway not to be seized in payment of legal debt.

1867, Railway Companies (Scotland) Act.

1868, Regulation of Railways Act – Requirements for communication cords; uniformity of accounts.

1871, Regulation of Railways Act – Requirement for accident inquiries by Board of Trade and compulsory accident returns.

1872, Railway Rolling Stock Protection Act – Preventing creditors seizing operational rolling stock on hire.

1873, Regulation of Railways Act – Appointment of Railway Commissioners to hear complaints under the Railway & Canal Traffic Act, 1854; railways to keep their canals in navigable condition.

1873, Regulation of Railways (Returns) Act – returns to Board of Trade on signalling arrangements.

1878, Railway Returns (Continuous brakes) Act – details of rolling stock so fitted.

1879, Regulation of Railways Continuance Act.

1883, Cheap Trains Act – abolition of duty on urban fares, encouraging workman's fares.

1888, Railway & Canal Traffic Act – rates and charges – classification of goods for charging purposes.

1889, Regulation of Railways Act – continuous automatic brakes on passenger trains, block signalling.

1889, Light Railways (Ireland) Act – order making procedures for light railways in Ireland with Government backed loans or grants for their construction.

1893, Railway Regulation Act – Railway operating staff allowed to make representation to Board of Trade about excessive hours.

1893, Railway Servants (Hours of Labour) Act – provision for complaints of excessive hours worked by railway staff.

1894, Railway & Canal Traffic Act – regulation of railway rates.

1896, Light Railways Act – simplified process for building rural lines.

1900, Railway Employment (Prevention of Accidents) Act – Powers of Board of Trade to make safety rules, including brake handles on both sides of wagons.

1903, Railways (Electrical Power) Act – Powers for railways to use electric power and provide distributions systems.

1904, Railway (Private Sidings) Act – railways to make reasonable provisions to collect trader's traffic.

1905, Railway Fires Act – compensation for farmers whose crops had been damaged by fire caused by sparks from steam locomotives.

1911, Railway Companies (Accounts and Returns) Act – Form of annual accounts and returns of assets to be provided to the Board of Trade.

1912, Light Railways Act – Amends 1896 Act to increase financial support for Light Railway Order and allows Board of Trade to submit Parliamentary Bills to confirm an order if required.

1913, Railway & Canal Traffic Act – increasing rates and charges.

1914–1922, railways under Government Control under the Regulation of the Forces Act, 1871.

1919, Transport Act – Formation of Ministry of Transport

1921, Railways Act – Grouping of the 'Big Four'.

1923, Railway Fires Act (1905) Amendment Act – Doubling of liability limit and requirement for claims to be sent within seven days.

1929, Development (Loan Guarantees and Grants) Act – Government support for fifteen years on interest payments for capital expenditure. Abolition of Railway Passenger Duty.

1930, Railways (Valuation for Rating) Act – Railway Assessment Authority set up to determine rates for railway properties.

1933, London Passenger Transport Act – creation of London Transport, fares control in LPTB area.

1933, Road and Rail Traffic Act – Goods vehicle licensing; ministerial consent required to opening of new lines, stations and electrification schemes.

1936, Railway Freight Rebates Act – Railway rates to local authorities paid to a fund from which rebates could be given to freight customers.

1939–45 – Railways under government control under the Emergency Powers Defence Act, 1939.

1943, Railway Freight Rebates Act – Suspension of rebates on coal traffic.

1947, Transport Act – formation of British Railways.

1949, Railway and Canal Commission (Abolition) Act – transfer of Commission's responsibilities to High Court.

1953, Transport Act – denationalisation of road transport.

1954, Transport Charges &c (Miscellaneous Provisions) Act – Tidying up legislation relating to rates and charges following nationalisation.

1955, British Transport Commission (Borrowing Powers) Act – raising BTC borrowing powers to fund the modernisation plan costs.

1957, Transport (Railway Finances) Act – temporary borrowing powers for BTC to meet interest payments and future deficits.

1962, Transport Act – formation of British Railways Board.

1963, Offices, Shops and Railway Premises Act – health, safety and welfare of staff working in railway offices.

1968, Transport Act – PTEs established, National Carriers and Freightliner formed. BR finances restructured.

1969, Transport (London) Act – Duty of BR to work with GLC to co-ordinate transport in London; removal of Transport Tribunal powers over London fares; power of GLC over London closures.

1972, Transport (Grants) Act – grants to BR to compensate for pricing controls.

1972, Transport Holding Company Act – disposal of assets in Transport Holding Company.

1974, Railways Act – Objectives for a stable network and start of PSO grant.

1977, Transport (Financial Provisions) Act – Power to make grants to cover BR deficits.

1978, Transport Act – Freightliners Ltd transferred back to BR.

1980, Transport Act – Deregulation of coach services; abolition of Freight Integration Council and Rail and Coastal Shipping Committee.

1981, Transport Act – Paving legislation for privatisation of railway docks and formation of Associated British Ports.

1981, Transport Act, 1962 (Amendment) Act – The Speller Act; experimental reopening of passenger lines and stations.

1982, Transport (Finance) Act – Increased borrowing powers for BR.

1983, Transport Act – Financial arrangements and plans for Passenger Transport Executives.

1984, London Regional Transport Act – formation of LRT prior to abolition of GLC.

1985, Transport Act – Bus substitution and Disabled Persons Transport Advisory Committee

1987, Channel Tunnel Act – Construction and use of the Channel Tunnel, and associated railway works to Waterloo.

1991, British Railways Board (Finance) Act – Increased borrowing powers for BR.

1992, Transport and Works Act – Ministerial orders replace primary legislation for authorising new railways; drugs and alcohol controls.

1993, Railways Act – Privatisation.

1994, Transport Police (Jurisdiction) Act – restoring jurisdiction powers lost under the Railways Act, 1993.

1996, Railway Heritage Act – Designation of artefacts and records for preservation.

2000, Transport Act – Creation of SRA by merger of BRB and OPRAF.

2003, Railways and Transport Safety – Safety responsibilities transferred to ORR; RAIB set up; establishment of British Transport Police Authority.

2005, Railways Act – Abolition of SRA

Analysis

Nineteenth-century railway acts – 30 (or one every 2 years)
Twentieth-century acts until 1948 – 18 (one every 2.7 years)
Twentieth-century acts from 1948 – 27 (one every 1.9 years)
Twenty-first-century acts – 3 (one every 7 years)

Appendix 4
Parliamentary Inquiries and Reports on Railway, 1995–2022

July 1996. *DfT – Freight Facility Grants in England*. NAO. HC 632.

March 1998. *The Proposed Strategic Rail Authority and Railway Regulation*. ETR. HC 286.

December 1998. Railway safety. ETR. HC 30.

January 1999. *Regional Eurostar Services*. ETR. HC 89.

April 2000. *Ensuring that Railtrack Maintain and Renew the Rail Network*. NAO. HC 397.

August 2000. *Action to Improve Passenger Rail Services*. NAO. HC 842.

December 2000. *Recent Events on the Railway*. ETR. HC 17.

March 2001. *Department of the Environment, Transport and the Regions: the Channel Tunnel Rail Link*. NAO. HC 302.

March 2002. *Report on Passenger Rail Franchising*. TSC. HC 239.

February 2004. *Strategic Rail Authority: 2002–03 Accounts*. NAO. HC 1009.

February 2004. *Improving Passenger Rail Services Through New Trains*. NAO. HC 283.

March 2004. *The Provision of Rail Services in Wales*. WAC. HC 458.

April 2004. *The Future of the Railway*. TSC. HC 145.

May 2004. *Network Rail – Making a Fresh Start*. NAO. HC 532.

July 2005. *Maintaining and Improving Britain's Railway Stations*. NAO. HC 132.

July 2005. *Progress on the Channel Tunnel Rail Link*. NAO. HC 77.

December 2005. *South Eastern Passenger Rail Franchise*. NAO. HC 457.

November 2006. *Modernisation of the West Coast Main Line*. NAO. HC 22.

March 2008. *Reducing Passenger Rail Delays by Better Management of Incidents*. NAO. HC 308.

July 2008. *Delivering a Sustainable Railway*. TSC. HC 219.

February 2009. *Priorities for Investment in the Railways*. TSC. HC 38.

July 2009. *Rail Fares and Franchises*. TSC. HC 233.

June 2010. *Increasing Passenger Rail Capacity*. NAO. HC 33.

March 2011. *The Inter City East Coast Passenger Rail Franchise*. NAO. HC 824.

April 2011. *Regulating Network Rail's Efficiency*. NAO. HC 828.

December 2011. *Thameslink Rolling Stock Procurement*. TSC. HC 1453.

January 2012. *Cable Thefts on the Railway*. TSC. HC 1609.

March 2012. *The Completion and Sale of High Speed 1*. NAO. HC 1834.

April 2013. *EC 4th Railway Package*. TSC HC 1001.

May 2013. *High Speed 2. A Review of Early Programme Preparation*. NAO. HC 124.

June 2013. *Progress in Delivering the Thameslink Franchise*. NAO. HC 227.

December 2013. *High Speed Rail: on Track?* TSC. HC 851.

January 2014. *Crossrail*. NAO. HC 965.

February 2014. *Safety at Level Crossings*. TSC. HC 680.

February 2014. *Cancellation of the InterCity West Coast Franchise Competition*. TSC. HC 1086.

July 2014. *Procuring New Trains*. NAO. HC 531.

September 2014. *Security on the Railway*. TSC. HC 428.

October 2014. *Lessons from Major Rail Infrastructure Programmes*. NAO. HC 267.

January 2015. *Investing in the Railway*. TSC. HC 257.

November 2015. *Reform of the Rail Franchising Programme*. NAO. HC 604.

June 2016. *Progress with Preparations for High Speed 2*. NAO. HC 235.

October 2016. *The Future of Rail: Improving the Passenger Experience*. TSC. HC 64

October 2016. *Rail Technology: Signalling and Traffic Management*. TSC. HC 67

November 2016. *Modernising the Great Western Railway*. NAO. HC 781.

January 2017. *Rail Franchising*. TSC. HC 66.

January 2017. *Wales and Borders Rail Franchise*. WAC. HC 589.

April 2017. *Investigation into the South East Flexible Ticketing Programme*. NAO. HC 1130.

July 2017. *The Sheffield–Rotherham Tram-Train Project; Investigation into Modernisation of the National Rail Network*. NAO. HC 238.

July 2017. *Report of the Comptroller and Auditor General on the 2016–17 Accounts of High Speed Two (HS2) Limited*. NAO. HC 247.

November 2017. *Update on the Thameslink Programme*. NAO. HC 413.

January 2018. *The Thameslink, Southern and Great Northern Franchise*. NAO. HC 528.

March 2018. *An Investigation into the Department for Transport's Decision to Cancel Three Rail Electrification Projects*. NAO. HC 835.

May 2018. *The Cancellation of Rail Electrification in South Wales*. WAC. HC 403.

June 2018. *Rail Infrastructure Investment*. TSC. HC 582

September 2018. *East Coast Main Line Franchise*. TSC. HC 891

September 2018. *Investigation into Land and Property Acquisition for the Phase One (London – West Midlands) of the High Speed 2 Programme*. PAC. HC 1531.

December 2018. *Rail Timetable Changes – May 2018*. TSC. HC 1163

February 2019. *A Memorandum on the Crossrail Programme*. PAC. HC 1924.

May 2019. *Network Rail's Sale of Railway Arches*. PAC. HC 2137.

May 2019. *Completing Crossrail*. PAC. HC 2106.

January 2020. *High Speed Two: A Progress Update*. PAC. HC 40.

September 2021. Major Transport Infrastructure Projects. TSC. HC 24

July 2022. Integrated Rail Plan for the North and Midlands. TSC. HC 292

March 2021. *Trains Fit for the Future?* TSC. HC 876

July 2021. *Railway Infrastructure in Wales*. WAC. HC 438

Current Inquiries (at December 2022)

Started July 2020. *Reforming Public Transport after the Pandemic*. TSC.

Started December 2021. *Fuelling the Future: Motive Power and Connectivity.* TSC

Total – 67 (Average of 2.7 reports a year)

Notes

ETR – House of Commons Select Committee on Environment, Transport and the Regions

PAC – Public Accounts Committee

NAO – National Audit Office

TSC – House of Commons Select Committee on Transport

WAC – House of Commons Select Committee on Welsh Affairs.

This listing is by publication date

It excludes one-day evidence sessions.

It only includes rail-based enquiries and does not include wider transport inquiries in which rail may have featured.

In almost every case a formal government response was published to each substantive report, usually a few weeks after the committee's report was published.

Appendix 5

Government Reviews of Rail Policy, Including White Papers, 1839–2022

The reports listed are those relating solely to railways. Other reports, such as the Select Committee on Employers Liability of 1877, but which are of more general application, are not included.

1845 Advisory Board, chaired by Lord Dalhousie – reporting on new railway proposals. Ceased after a few months.

1846 Gauge Commission, Royal Commission – Decision on broad or standard gauge. (No railwaymen on the commission.)

1867 Royal Commission on Railways.

1877 Royal Commission on Railway Accidents.

1893/94 Royal Commission on Labour – Group B, Transport and Agriculture.

1899/1900 Royal Commission on Causes of Accidents, Fatal and Non-Fatal, to Servants of Railway Companies and of Truck Owners.

1911 Royal Commission report on the Railway Conciliation and Arbitration Scheme of 1907

1920 Future Organisation of Transport. WP. Cmd 787.

1928 Report of the Railway Electrification Committee (1927). Ministry of Transport. Electrification systems.

1930 Report of the Automatic Train Control Committee (1927). Ministry of Transport – Automatic Train Control systems and improving visibility of signals.

1930 Royal Commission on Transport, Roads and PSV licensing, co-ordination and development of transport.

1931 Report of the Committee on Main Line Electrification. Ministry of Transport – The Weir Committee on electrification of main lines.

1946 Railway (London Plan) Committee report. Ministry of War Transport

1953 Transport Policy, Ministry of Transport, WP – change of policy from integration to competition, Abolition of Railway Executive. BTC takes over.

1956 Proposals for the Railways, MoT, WP – Railway finances and review of 1955 Modernisation Plan.

1960 Guillebaud Report (government review by independent expert) – Railway Pay.

1960 Stedeford Inquiry, DfT – Structure of BTC, rationalisation.

1966 Transport Policy, WP – modernisation, support for socially necessary passenger services and co-ordination of modes.

1972 Railway Policy, WP – one of four policy WPs following on from 1966 WP.1976.

1977 Transport Policy, WP – pricing and support levels, objectives for BR.

1978 The Nationalised Industries – financial targets, performance indicators and labour relations.

1980 Monopolies & Mergers Commission report on London & South East Services.

1981 Review of Railway Electrification, DfT/BR.

1982 Serpell Report, Review of Railway Finances, BRB and DfT – network sizes.

1987 Monopolies & Mergers Commission Report on Network South East Services.

1993 New Opportunities for the Railways. WP – Privatisation.

1998 New Deal for Transport; Better for Everyone. WP – Prescott ten-year transport plan.

2003 John Birt's 'blue skies' thinking for Tony Blair – unpublished.

2004 The Future of Rail, WP – abolition of SRA; cost reduction.

2004 The Future of Transport – look ahead to 2030.

2006. *West Coast Main Line Progress Report*. DfT.

2007 Transport Study, Rod Eddington, WP – transport integration; expanding infrastructure.

2007 Delivering a Sustainable Railway, WP. Cm 7176 – Rail expansion.

2008, Competition Commission – Market Investigation into Rolling Stock Leasing.

2009 Britain's Transport Infrastructure; High Speed Two. DfT.

2010 Review of the InterCity Express Programme for DfT. Sir Andrew Foster.

2011 McNulty Review, Realising the Potential of GB Rail – value for money study.

2012 Reforming our Railways; Putting the Customer First, DfT, Cm 8313 – Fares and Ticketing, capacity, devolution, industry reform. Separate papers on a review of Ticketing and devolution published on same day.

2012 Laidlaw Inquiry – Lessons learned for DfT on West Coast Franchising. HC 809.

2013 Brown Review – Rail Franchising Programme. DfT. Cm 8526.

2015 Bowe Review – Planning of Network Rail's Enhancement Programme, 2014–2019. DfT. Cmnd. 9147.

2016 Shaw Report – The Future Shape and Financing of Network Rail.

2021 Williams/Shapps WP. Structure and organisation of the railway. CP 423.

2022 Integrated Rail Plan for the North and Midlands. DfT.

2022 Rail Environmental Policy Statement. DfT

Appendix 6

Letter from Sir George Young to Conservative Backbenchers on Privatisation

Rt Hon Sir George Young Bt, MP
House of Commons, London SW1A 0AA
Tel: 0171-219 6665 Fax: 0171-219 2566
E-mail: cyclebart@arcade.demon.co.uk

Hugh Dykes Esq MP
House of Commons
London SW1A 0AA

December 1995

Hugh

As we enter the Christmas recess, I thought it would be helpful to bring you up-to-date on progress with the Government's programme for the railways.

Our policy is aimed at driving up the quality of service on railways, and is being achieved firstly by restructuring British Rail, and placing it in the private sector; and secondly, by inviting bids for franchises to run the 25 passenger service companies.

We have made steady progress with sales of various parts of what was British Rail, such as the Rolling Stock Companies which were sold last month for £1.8 billion, and the sale of British Rail Telecommunications for £132 million. This means that about 50 per cent of the old British Rail stock.

In addition, we will be floating Railtrack on the Stock Market next spring, enabling it to plan investment for the future at levels which would not be possible in the public sector. I enclose a copy of Railtrack's press notice, which explains that Railtrack will be investing £1 billion a year over the next decade to deliver the railway network passengers deserve.

By reorganising the old British Rail passenger services into 25 separate companies, we have freed the existing managers to make improvements even before privatisation. On lines in your area, these include: double the frequency of trains between Birmingham Snow Hill and Marylebone; a new hourly service between Aylesbury and Marylebone; 600 extra seats on busy early morning commuter services to London; and major improvements to Marylebone station.

We now enter the most important stage of the programme, with the franchising of passenger services. The Franchising Director, Roger Salmon, has been impressed by the high quality of bids submitted to him, which are proof of the keen appetite in the private sector to run rail services, often in conjunction with a management and employee buy-out team. Some bidders have offered to replace or refurbish the rolling stock. As you may know, the Chiltern Line is to be franchised next year and the Franchising Director is making good progress with his plans for

---

this event. I enclose a letter published in The Times recently from a member of the public, looking forward to the benefits of rail privatisation.

For the first time ever, passengers have been given guarantees on services and fares that did not exist under British Rail. Each franchise has specified Passenger Service Requirements which they must meet, such as the frequency of trains, measures to reduce overcrowding, and the timing of first and last services. Key fares will be frozen to the Retail Price Index for the first 3 years, and will then fall below that for the following 4 years. In other words, passengers will have certainty about their fares right through into the next century.

In stark contrast is the position of our opponents. Since the entire Labour Transport team was replaced, we have heard from Clare Short and Brian Wilson that they would allow the franchises for passenger services to continue throughout their expected term of contract, namely 7 years. This means that Labour has admitted for the first time that, even if Labour were to win the next General Election, there would be private rail companies operating throughout the whole of the next Parliament. This is an astonishing U-turn in just two months, and demonstrates that Labour have realised that our vision for the railways is the right one.

We need take no lessons from Labour on the railways. After all, in their last two administrations, Labour closed 655 stations. In contrast, we have opened or re-opened 244. Labour have given no commitments to passengers on services, fares, or investment. We have given guarantees on all three.

I hope you will agree that this marks the beginning of a new era for our railways, which will see better services to passengers at less cost to tax-payers. I am determined to deliver this programme and I look forward to your support in the forthcoming year.

SIR GEORGE YOUNG Bt

Encs

Appendix 7
Minor Railways Excluded from the Railways Act, 1947

Standard Gauge

Corringham Light Railway
Derwent Valley Light Railway
Easingwold Railway
Liverpool Overhead Railway
Mersey Docks & Harbour Board
North Sunderland Railway
South Shields, Marsden and Whitburn Colliery Railway#
Swansea and Mumbles Railway

Narrow gauge

Ashover Light Railway
Ffestiniog Railway*
Isle of Man Railway
Manx Electric Railway
Snailbeach District Railway*
Talyllyn Railway
Ravenglass and Eskdale Railway
Romney, Hythe and Dymchurch Light Railway
Rye and Camber Tramway*
Snaefell Mountain Tramway
Snowdon Mountain Railway
Volks Electric Railway

* Operations ceased by 1947
# Nationalised on 1 Jan 1947 as part of the National Coal Board

Appendix 8
List of Passenger Service Agreements in Place in October 2022

Franchise	Type of contract	Owner	Public Sector?
Caledonian Sleeper	Temporary Measures Agreement	Serco	No
Cross Country	Direct award	Arriva	Yes – DB
East Anglia	Direct award	Abellio	Yes – NS
East Midlands	Direct award	Abellio	Yes – NS
Elizabeth Line	TfL concession agreement	MTR	Yes
Essex Thameside	Direct award	Trenitalia	Yes – FS
Great Western	Direct award	First Group	No
InterCity East Coast	Direct award	LNER	Yes – DOR
London Overground	TfL concession agreement	Arriva	Yes – DB
Northern	Direct award	Northern Rail	Yes – DOR
Scotrail	Direct award	Tnspt for Scotland	Yes – Sc Govt
South Eastern	Direct award	L&SER	Yes – DOR
South Western	Direct award	First/MTR	Yes – MTR
Thameslink, Southern & Great Northern	Direct award	GoVia/Keolis	Yes – SNCF
Transpennine Express	Direct award	First	No
Wales & Borders	Direct award	T'sport for Wales	Yes – Welsh Govt
West Coast Partnership	Direct award	First/Trenitalia	Yes – FS
West Midlands	Direct award	W Mid Trains	Yes – NS

(19 contracts, of which 16 are owned or partially owned by public sector companies, some UK organisations, and some based abroad.)

Open Access and other passenger operators

Eurostar (40 per cent owned by private investors)		SNCF, SNCB	Yes
Heathrow Express		Ferrovial	No
Hull Trains		First Group	No
Lumo		First Group	No
West Coast Railways Ltd		David Smith	No

Freight companies

DB Cargo (Owned DB)

DRS (publicly owned subsidiary of British Nuclear Fuels Ltd)

Freightliner (privately owned, a subsidiary of the Genessee & Wyoming Railroad)

GB Railfreight (privately owned)

Colas Rail (privately owned by French engineering company Bouygues)

Notes:

DB	Deutsche Bahn (German railways)
DOR	Directly Operated Railways (non-departmental public body sponsored by Department for Transport)
DRS	Direct Rail Services (subsidiary of the Nuclear Decommissioning Authority)
FS	Ferrovie dello Stato (Italian railways)
MTR	Corporation (Mass Transit Railway) in Hong Kong
NS	Nederlandse Spoorwegen (Dutch railways)
SNCB	Societe Nationale des Chemins de Fer Belges Belgische Spoorwegen (Belgian railways)
SNCF	Societe Nationale des Chemins de Fer Français (French railways)

Bibliography

The Birth of British Rail, Michael R Bonavia, 'Steam Past', George Allen & Unwin, 1979.

British Railway History, C Hamilton Ellis, George Allen and Unwin, 1954.

British Railways 1948–73. A business history. T R Gourvish. Cambridge University Press, 1986.

British Rail 1974–97. From Integration to Privatisation. Terry Gourvish. Oxford University Press. 2002.

British Railways 1997–2005. Labour's Strategic Experiment. Terry Gourvish. Oxford University Press, 2008.

British Transport since 1914, and Economic History. Derek H Aldcroft. David & Charles, 1975.

The Buildings of England, London 6; Westminster, Simon Bradley and Nikolaus Pevsner, Yale University Press, 2003.

Disconnected! Chris Austin and Richard Faulkner, Ian Allan (OPC) 2015.

Dow's Dictionary of Railway Quotations, Andrew Dow, Johns Hopkins University Press, 2006.

Editor, Max Hastings, 2002, Macmillan.

Fire and Steam, Christian Wolmar, Atlantic Books, 2007.

For Starters, a life in management. Sir Peter Parker, Jonathan Cape, 1989.

The Four Great Railways, Michael R Bonavia, David and Charles, 1980.

George and Robert Stephenson – the railway revolution. LTC Rolt, Amberley, 2009.

Gilbert Szlumper and Leo Amery of the Southern Railway. Edited by John King, Pen & Sword Transport, 2018.

Her Majesty's Railway Inspectorate from 1840. Ian Prosser CBE and Eur Ing David Keay. Steam World publishing. 2019.

Holding the Line, Richard Faulkner and Chris Austin, Ian Allan (OPC), 2012.

Irish Railway Record Society website, www.irishrailarchives.ie

I Tried to Run a Railway, GF Fiennes, Ian Allan, 1968.

John Major – The Autobiography. Harper Collins, 1999.

The Ministry of Transport Act, 1919, W A Robertson, Stevens & Sons Ltd, 1919.

The Network Southeast Story 1982–2014, Chris Green and Mike Vincent, Ian Allan (OPC), 2014.

Off the Rails, an autobiography; Richard Marsh, Weidenfeld & Nicolson, 1978.

Off the Rails, Andrew Murray, Verso, 2001.

Parliamentary website, www.parliament.uk

The Railway Interest. Geoffrey Alderman. Leicester University Press. 1973.

The Railwaymen, The history of the NUR, Vol. 2, Philip S Bagwell, George Allen & Unwin, 1982.

The Railways Archive website. www.railwaysarchive.co.uk

The Railways of Uxbridge, C T Goode, 1983

The Railway Year Book for 1901. Railway Publishing Company. 1901.

The Reshaping of British Railways (Beeching Report), BRB, HMSO, 1963.

Review of Main Line Electrification final report, DfT/BRB; HMSO 1981.

Sir Daniel Gooch memoirs and diary, Ed Roger Burdett Wilson, David & Charles, 1972.

Southern Electric 1909–1968, 4th edn; G T Moody, Ian Allan, 1968.

Summer Saturdays in the West, David St John Thomas and Simon Rocksborough Smith, David and Charles, 1973.

The Subterannean Railway, Atlantic Books, 2004

The Train that Ran Away, Stewart Joy, Ian Allan, 1973.

Who's Who, Bloomsbury Press

Acknowledgements

The History of Advertising Trust and Eve Reed
Peter Trewin
Brian Wilson CBE
Ivor Warburton
John Yellowlees
Lord Young of Cookham
Lord Adonis
David Faulkner CB

Index

Note: Images are shown in **bold type** and references to footnotes only are in *italics*.

Accidents:
   Armagh *7,19*
   Carmont *131*
   Clapham Junction *130, 131, 171*
   Hatfield *7, 10, 119, 130-135*
   Ladbroke Grove *131*
   Potters Bar *131*
   Southall *131*
   Watford Junction *92*

Accounting Officer role 85, 177
Adam Smith Institute 110,112
Adley, Robert, MP 117
Advanced Passenger Train (APT) **97, 104**
Advertising .63, 86, 97-101
Ailwyn, Lord 36
Airport policy 65, **66, 67**
Airport rail links **92**, 103, **104, 105**, 108,
Alderson, Sir Edward Hall 13
Alexander, Nick 94
Allen, Brady and Marsh (consultants) 99-101
Allen, Richard 110-101, 109
Amalgamated Society of Railway Servants
   (ASRS) 22, 26-27, 38
Anderson, Donald, MP (Lord Anderson of Swansea) . .49
Anderson, Frank, MP 42,44
Armaments manufacture and transport 55, 70, 73
Armoured train **68**, 71
Ashfield, Lord 60-62
Ashford 94, 110, 144
Asquith, Herbert Henry, MP 27-30, *58*
Associated Society of Locomotive Engineers
   and Firemen (ASLEF) 30-33, 40, 45, 50, 51
Association of Minor Railway Companies 75

Bagier, Gordon, MP 47
Baker, Stuart 132
Baldwin, Sir Peter 97
Balfour, Alfred, MP 43
Banbury, Sir Frederick, MP
   (Lord Banbury of Southam) 28, 32, 58

Barnes, Rt Hon Alfred, MP 74, 181
Barnes, George, MP 29
Barrington Light Railway 75
Barrymore, Lord 37
Barstow, Percy, MP 43
Barton, Clarence, MP .44
Basildon 89
Beaumont, Huntingdon 11
Beckett, Hon Rupert 36
Beeching, Dr Richard 79-86, 151
Beeching Report . . .17, 82-83, 138, 141, 161, 163, 171
Belcher, John, MP .44-45
Belfast and County Down Railway *80*, 87
Bell, Richard, MP 39
Bellamy, Albert, MP .41,42
Benson, Henry (Lord Benson) 79, *80*
Betjeman, Sir John 62, 95,
Beveridge report 72
Bevin, Ernest, MP 33
Big Four, The 37, 54-59, 63-65, 71-73, 78, 172
   Achievements 63-65
Birmingham Curzon Street **177**
Birmingham International 104, 105
Birmingham New Street 124
Bleasdale, Cyril **169**
Blenkinsop, William **12**
Block signalling 19, 124, 182
Board of Trade *8*, 15, 17-19, 22, 26-31, 36, 56,
   57, 61, 180
Bomb damage *36*, **70**, *77*, 78
Bonar Law, Andrew, MP 29, 31, 33, 55, 56
Bonavia, Michael Robert 72-74
Bosworth, Michael 106
Bowker, Richard 89, 132, 133, 147
BR achievements 96, 102-105
BR School of Transport 103
Brabazon, Lord, of Tara *166*, **167**
Bradley, Tom, MP 46-48
Bradshaw 67, 68. 71
Bradshaw, Lord 148
Brakes 19, **104**, **139**, 180, 182
BR Chairmen 85, 86
Brecon Mountain Railway 109

191

Brill 62
British Coachways *88*
British Rail Investments Ltd 107
British Railways and the Future *73*, *74*
British Railways Board . . .10, 17, 35, 80, 81, 113, 120, 131
British Transport Commission 10, 74, 78-80, 90
British Transport Hotels 107
British Transport Police 59, 183
Bromley, John, MP 33, 40-42
Broseley wagonway 11
Brown, Rt Hon Gordon, MP *52*, 121, 134
Brunel, Isambard Kingdom *15*, 18
Bryce, James, MP (Viscount Bryce) 26
Buchanan, Elizabeth 52
Buchanan, Richard, MP 47
Buffer Depots 71
Burden, Thomas William, MP (Lord Burden) 43, 44
Burgess, Frederick George, MP 42
Bus services 88
Bus substitution 88, 183
Butler-Henderson, Hon Eric Brand
 (2nd Baron Faringdon) 36, **37**
Buxton, Sydney, MP (Earl Buxton) 27

Cameron, Rt Hon David, MP **157**, 158
Campaign for Better Transport *92*, 173
Campbell-Bannerman, Rt Hon Sir Henry, MP . . .26,27,29
Carlton Club 30, 32
Carson, Sir Edward, MP 58
Castle, Rt Hon Barbara, MP
 (Baroness Castle of Blackburn) . . . *32*, 83, 89, 161, 166
Cecil, Rt Hon Sir Evelyn, MP (Lord Rockley) 37
Centre for Policy Studies 110, 112, 173
Champion, Arthur Joseph, MP (Lord Champion) . . .43, 46
Channel Tunnel Act, 1987 . . . . .92, 93, 183
Channel Tunnel Rail Link Bill 25, 92, 93
Channon, Rt Hon Paul, MP (Lord Kelvedon) 52, 111
Charleton, Henry, MP 40, 42
Chat Moss **14**
Cheltenham Flyer, The 63, *173*
Cheltenham (Lansdown Junction) **69**
Chiltern Railways **123**, **127**
Churchill, Sir Winston 27, *29*, 56, *61*, *77*, *152*
Churchill, Viscount 37
Clarke, Rt Hon Kenneth, MP
 (Lord Clarke of Nottingham) 111, 119
Clifford, James 11
Clinton, Lord 37
Closures, railway . .48, 81-83, 86-88, *92*, 135, 169, 178
Clynes, John Robert, MP .33
Cohen, Stan, MP 47, 48
Cold Meece **69**
Collick, Percy, MP 45, 46
Common user wagons 57, 74

Community Rail Network 10, 85, **101**, 125,
 133, 155, 176
Conciliation Act, 1896 26
Connex 125, 126, 128, 172
Cook, Rt Hon Robin, MP .49
Coronation Scot train **64**
Corporate identity *60*, **81**, 124
Corry, Dan 52
Coucher, Iain 154
'Coupon' Election, The 29, 30, 40
Cousins, Frank, MP (Lord Cousins) 50, 83
Covent Garden 88
Covid 10, 95, 126, 146, 156, 169, 172,
 174, 175, 176
Cowans, Harry, MP 48
Crane, Arthur Beresford 22
Cribbs Causeway 88
Crosland, Rt Hon Anthony, MP 85, 86, 145
Crossrail 18, 158, 160, 176, 185
Crow, Bob 51
Croydon airport **66**

Dalhousie, Lord 17, 186
Dalton, Rt Hon Edward Hugh John Neale , MP
 (Lord Dalton) .59, 77, 125
Dalyell, Tam, MP 49
Daventry 88, 144
Davies, Albert E, MP 44
Davies, Lt-Col David, MP .37
D-Day 8, 68, 73
Deerstalker Express, The 114
Denning, Lord *82*
Derwent Valley Light Railway 8, 75-6, 188
Development (Loans, Guarantees and Grants)
 Act, 1929 . . . . .167, 182
Dewar, Rt Hon Donald, MP 50
Didcot, Newbury and Southampton line 8
Direct Rail Services 146, 189
Dobbie, William, MP 42
Dobson, Rt Hon Frank, MP 49
Dowty retarders **79**
Dunkirk evacuation 68, 71, 73
Dunwoody, Hon Gwyneth, MP 49
Dyson, William 32

Easingwold Railway .75, 188
East London Line 61
East/West rail **122**, *123*, 156
Eccles 15, 43, 46
Economist, The 34
Edge Hill Light Railway 75
Eight Hour Day **34**, 39, 41
Electrification 149-156
 Branch lines 156
 Early projects 149-150, **151**

INDEX

East Coast Main Line *80*, 86, 150, 152,
   East Grinstead 152
   Great Northern 151
   Great Western 154, 156, 157
   Kent Coast 151
   Kings Lynn 154
   Manchester-Liverpool/Preston 157
   Manchester–Sheffield–Wath 74, **152**
   Midland Main Line 154-155
   NER 149-150, **151**
   Norwich/Harwich 152, **153**
   Ongar 62, 73-74
   Oxted line 74, 152
   Portsmouth-Southampton 154
   Shenfield 74, 150-151
   Southern *56*, 150,
   Tonbridge-Hastings 152
   West Coast Main Line 151, 152
   Volk's Railway 149 **150**, 188
   Weymouth 154
Elizabeth Line (see Crossrail)
Elliot, Sir John 63, **167**
Epping **73**
European Passenger Services *94*, 95, *106*
Eurotunnel *51*, 93, 143
Euston **14**, 95
Evening Standard 93, *116*
Express, Daily 32-33
External Financing Limit *80*, 107, 123

Fares 7-9, 11, 18-19, 54-55, 61, 88, 102, 111, 119,
           124, 129, 168, 169, 180, 182-183
Fares Fair policy 90-91
Faringdon, Lord Alexander *42*
Fatigue 19, 1182
Fawley 57
Fearn, Anthony 'Dick' 164
Ffestiniog Railway 75, 188
Field, Horace 20
Fielden, Edward Brocklehurst, MP 25
Field organisation 83
Financial Times, The 74, 100, 115
Finchley Road (Midland) **140**
Finsbury Park 62-63
Ford, Roger 86, *155*
Fowler, Rt Hon Sir Norman, MP
   (Lord Fowler) *24*, *25*, 106
Franchising 9, 112, 120, 132, 175, 184, 186
Fraser, Rt Hon Tom, MP 82-83
Freight 63, 81, 86, 87, 103, 111, 113, 118, 128,
      129, 133, 138-146, 160, 169-170,
                176, 183, 189
   Coal 11, 71, 87, 103, 119, 138, **139**, 140-141,
                145-146, 183
   Grants 142, 149, 184
   Intermodal .86, 143-144
   International **142**, 143-144
   Privatisation 122, 145-146
Freight charges 12, 19, 55, 182
Freightliner 103, 146, 163, 176, 183, 189
Fryatt, Captain Charles 55

Garnett, Christopher *127*
Gatwick Express 108
GB Railfreight .143, 146, 189
Geddes, Sir Auckland, MP (Lord Geddes) 30-31, 34
Geddes, Sir Eric, MP (Lord Geddes) . . .15, 31, 33, 55-56
Gibb, Sir George 60
Gladstone, William Ewart, MP **16**, 17, 19, 169
Gleneagles Hotel 65
Glenties (Co Donegal) 17
GNER 125-126, **127**
Gooch, Sir Daniel 15, 35
Gore-Brown, Colonel Sir Eric 72
Gourvish, Terry 86, 104-105
Government of Scotland Bill, 1913 59
Granet, William Guy 22
Great British Railways 7, 10, 118, 148
                        164-165, 167, 177
Great Central Railway 17, 28, 61, 62,
Great Northern Railway 12
Great Western Railway: 12, 63
   Broad gauge 15, 17, 61
   Bus services 88
   Cut-off lines **16**, 17
   New hotels planned .74
Greater London Council .90
Green, Chris **120**, 152, **155**, **169**
Grey, Viscount, of Falloden 36
GRIP process 149
Guest, Sir Freddie, MP 29-30
Gunter, Ray, MP 44, 46-48

Haig, Field Marshall Sir Douglas *28*, 58
Haigh, Philip *149*
Halls, Walter, MP 40
Halwill Junction – Torrington 57
Ham Green Halt **149**
Hammersmith 61
Hardie, Keir, MP 39
Hargreaves, Alex, MP .45-46
Harrison, James, MP 44
Haworth, James, MP 45
Heathrow airport 67, 103, 158
Heggie, Ian 52-53
Alexander Henderson MP (see Faringdon, Baron)
Henderson, Arthur, MP 33
Henderson, Joseph, MP (Lord Henderson) 42-43
Hendy, Sir Peter (Lord Hendy of Richmond Hill) 154
Herald, The Daily *31*, 32
Her Majesty's Railway Inspectorate . . .18, 113, 130, *131*

193

HS2	18, 157-158, 160, 163, 171, 184
HST	102, **103**, 104
Highways Agency	88, 144
Highway Robbery (advertisement)	97, **98**
Hill, Keith, MP	51
Hills, Adam, MP	42
Hinton, Lord, of Bankside	83
Holiday traffic	**143**, 174
Holland-Hibbert, Hon AL (Lord Knutsford)	36
Home Robertson, John, MP	50
Hood, John,	19
Horne, Sir Robert, MP (Viscount Horne)	31
Hotels	65, 74, 77, 106-107, 109
Hours of Labour Act, 1893	19, 34, 182
House Magazine, The	97
Houses of Parliament	27
Hovercraft	103, 106-107, 109
Howell, Charles, MP	46
Huckfield, Les, MP	50
Hudson, George, MP	35
Hudson, Walter, MP	39
Hurcombe, Sir Cyril (Lord Hurcombe)	67, 68, 72
Huskisson, William, MP	15
Hybrid bills	18, 60
Hynd, Harry, MP	45-47
Hynd, John, MP	43, 46-48
Inchcape, Lord	37
Incitement to Mutiny Act, 1797	32
Industrial relations	19, 27, 34
Integrated transport	8, 83, 85, 87-88 186
Institute of Economic Affairs	115
InterCity	8, 81, 86, 102, 119
Inverness	10
Irvin, Joe	52
Jackson, Glenda, MP	50
Johnson, Walter, MP	47-48
Joicey, Lord	36
Joint Lines	61, 74
Jones, David Thomas, MP	44, 46
Joy, Dr Stewart	80, 82-83, 88
Kensington Olympia	61, **126**
King's Cross	22, 29, 32, 45, 94-95, **169**
King's Lynn	**84**, 88, 154
Kirby	**163**
Labour Research Department	32
Laing, Dame Eleanor, MP	52
Lakeside	88
Lansbury, George, MP	32
Lardner, Professor Dionysius	12
Lathan, George, MP	41-42
Law, Arthur, MP	42

Lawrence, Hon Charles Napier, (Lord Kingsgate)	36
Leeds University	102
Lewis, Ronald, MP	47
Light Railways Act, 1896	7, 17, 18, 168, 182
Lindgren, George Samuel, MP (Lord Lindgren)	45-46
Liverpool and Manchester Railway	12, 13, 18
Liverpool Overhead Railway	**75**, 149, 188
Livingstone, Ken, MP	90-91
Lizard, The	88
Lloyd George, David, MP (Earl of Dwyfor)	8, 25-34
LNER track authority proposal	74
Local Enterprise Partnerships	144
Local Government Board	57
Locomotives:	
Butler-Henderson	**37**
Channel Packet	**167**
County of East Sussex	**108**
Intercity 50	**169**
Lloyd George	28-29
Lord Hurcombe	67
Owain Glendŵr	**110**
Resolution	**120**
Rocket	*13*, 15
Salamanca	**12**
Silver Link	**64**
Sir Felix Pole	*54*
Sir Frederick Banbury	37, **38**
Viscount Horne	*31*
London and Birmingham Railway	**13**, **14**, **177**
London Bridge	**174**
London General Omnibus Company	61
London Passenger Transport Board (see London Transport)	
London School of Economics	*31*, 43, 80
London Transport	
Area	
Bakerloo Line	90
BR/LT Liaison Group	90
City Widened Lines	90
Competition with main line railways	61-62, 90-91
Design	60
New Works Programme, 1935	62
Lowth, Thomas, MP	40, 42
Lullingstone airport and station	65-67
MacGregor, John, MP (Lord MacGregor of Pulham Market)	*52*, 113-114, 119
Maclay, John, MP	8
Mag-Lev	104, **105**
Maidment, David	131
Major, Rt Hon John, MP	10, 110, 112, 115, 116, 173
Mallaig extension	17
Manchester Ship Canal Railway	75
Manuel, Archibald Clark, MP	46-47
Mapp, Charles, MP	46-47

Index

March (Cambs) 10
Marek, Dr John, MP 50
Marples, Rt Hon Alfred Ernest MP
  (Lord Marples of Wallasey) 82, 166
Marsh, Rt Hon Richard, MP (Lord Marsh) 85-86,
  113, 118, 166
Marshalling Yards 79, 141
Mathers, George, MP (Lord Mathers) 41-42, 44
Matthews, Sir Ronald 74
Maurice, Major-General 29
McAdam, William, MP 43
McCartney, Sir Ian, MP 51
McClean, Andrew **167**
McKinsey (consultants) 83
McMillan, Tom, MP 47
Meadowhall 88, **89**
Meale, Sir Alan, MP 51
Meldon Quarry 109
Mellor, William 32
Merry-go-round trains 138
Metroland (Metropolitan Country Estates Ltd) 62
Metropolitan Police Act, 1829 59
Metropolitan Railway 61-62
Middleton Railway 11, 12
Mildmay, Hon Francis Bingham, MP
  (Lord Mildmay of Flete) .37
Milton Keynes .88-89, **90**, 157
Ministry of Transport 8, 24, 34, 56, 57-58, 182
Minor railways . . . . .75, 76, Appendix 7
Missenden, Sir Eustace 78
Mitterand, President Francois 93, 95
Modernisation plan, 1955 . . . . .8, 79, 80, 151, 174,
  178, 183, 186
Monslow, Walter, MP (Lord Monslow) 45-46
Moorgate 61-62. 90, **91**
Morgan, Baroness, of Cotes **167**
Morison, Kenneth 22
Morris, Percy, MP 44
Morrison, Herbert (Lord Morrison of Lambeth) . . .59-62
Morton, Sir Alastair *51*, 130-133, 147-148
Mottram, Sir Richard 134-135
Mulley, Rt Hon Fred, MP 84, **85**
Murray, Hon Arthur Cecil, MP (Viscount Elibank) 37

National Audit Office (NAO) 148, 175, 184-185
Nationalisation 8,10, 21, 56-59, 63, 72-74,
  77-79, 87, 96, 112, 121, 125,
  141, 167, 172, 174, 183
National Freight Corporation 106
National Rail Enquiries 125
National Union of Railwaymen (NUR) 26, 30-34,
  39-43, 46-51
(See also ASRS and RMT)
Network SouthEast 86, 119. **120**, *152*, 186
Newcourt **101**

New lines and stations 16-17, 57, 60, 101-102,
  173, 183
News, Daily 33
New Scientist 52
New towns 89, **90**
Nicholls, Henry R, MP 43
Night Ferry, The *82*
North British Railway 56, 58, 173
Northern Rail Review 133
North Pole depot 93
North Sunderland Light Railway 75, 188

Oakley, Sir Henry 22
O'Brien, Jim 109
O'Halloran, Michael, MP 49
Oil crisis 86, 97, 100
Ongar 62, **73**, 74
Open Access operation 9, 12, **136**, 137, 189
Operation *Stack* **143**
OPRAF (Office of Passenger Rail Franchising) . . .120, 183
ORR (Office of Rail and Road) 9, 59, 131, 147,
  148, 172, 183
Osborne judgement 39
Ownership (railway) 9, 56, 60, 72, 74, 77, **93**, 96,
  107, 112, 147, 163, 166-168,
  171-173, 177

Pacers **89**, **105,** 115
Page Arnot, Robert ('Robin') .32
Palmer, John 106, 110, 122, 152
Parker, Sir Peter *75*, 85-86, 99-100, 106-107,
  112, 148, 173,
Parliamentary Affairs Manager (BR) 91-92
Parliamentary powers 11
Parliamentary privilege 19
Parliamentary trains 11, 19, 169, 182
Passenger Demand Forecasting Handbook 160
Passenger Service Agreements 189
Paterson. Frank 97, 147
Peel, Sir Robert, MP 20
Penistone line **102**
Penzance 10
Perry, Claire, MP **101**
Peyton, Rt Hon John, MP (Lord Peyton) 83, 85, 106,
  113, 118
Pick, Frank *60*, 61-62
Pirrie, Lord 37
Plunkett, David, MP (Lord Rathmore) 29
Pole, Sir Felix 54
Poole, Cecil Charles, MP 42
Popplewell, Ernest, MP (Lord Popplewell) 44, 46-47
Ports (railway owned) 63, 78, **168**, 183
Prescott, Rt Hon John, MP (Lord Prescott) 20, 50-51,
  93, 94, 131, **132**, 147
Preston, Sydney 95
Prideaux, Dr John *115*, **169**

195

Princes Risborough 62, 126, **127**
Privatisation 9,10, 72-73, 86, 102, 105, 106-124,
125, 145-146, 148, 154, 162, 164,
167-168, 173, 175, 183, 187
   Cost 119-120, 135
   Politics 116-118
   Safety management .130-131
   Theoretical structures 110-112
Proctor, William Thomas, MP 43, 46
Public Accounts Committee 115, 184-185
Public Bill Office 18
Public Sector Borrowing Requirement 86, 106-107,
111, 134
Public Service Obligation Grants 83, 183
Punch magazine **26**, **34**, 96, **100**

Quainton Road 62, **123**

Rail, Maritime and Transport Union (RMT) 50, 51
(See also ASRS and NUR)
Rail Standards and Safety Board 10
Railtrack 102, 113, 115, 118-124, 128,
131-135, 168-169, 184
Railway Air Services Ltd 65, **66**, 167
Railway and Canal Traffic Acts 19, 22, 182
Railway and Canal Commission 19, 56, 183
Railway Clearing House 21, 22, 79, 182
Railway Clerks Association
   (RCA – see also TSSA) 21, 40-41
Railway Control Officers 66, 68
Railway Executive Committee 7, 25, 56, 67, 73, 171
Railway Liaison Officers 68
Railway Magazine, The 37, 58
Railway Mania, 1845 17
Railway offices in Westminster: 20-25
   LNWR 20, **21**
   MR 20, **23**
   NER **20-21**

   Railway Companies Association 22, 24
   Railway Executive Committee,
     Fielden House **24**, 25, 67
   BR 25
Railway strikes: 165-166
   1907 . . . .**26**
   1911 27-29
   1919 29-34
   Aristocratic volunteers during 1919 strike 32
   1982 152
Railways Act:
   1921 . . . . .24, *57*, 182
   1974 . . . . .169. 183
   1993 . . . . .112, 113-114, 126, 183
   2005 148
Rayner, David 131
Reading 17, 124

Regulation of railways 7, 11, **16**, *17*, 18-19, 22, 57,
111, 121-122, 131, 134, **136**,
138, 167, 182, 184
Reid, Sir Bob 95, 105, **122**, 125, 131
Reid, Sir Robert 79, 80, 83, 86, 104 105, 111, 112,
119, 124, 152
Regional Railways 86, **105**
Regulation of Railways Acts:
   1840 18
   1844 (Railway Regulation Act, 1844) *18*, *19*
   1868 22
   1889 . . . . .19, 22
Regulation of the Forces Act, 1871 . . . . .24, 56, 182
Renationalisation .116, 121, 171
Reorganisation 10, 56, 71, *80*, 123, 130, 172-173
Research 10, 51, 85, 102, 104, **105**, 130, 165
Revenue allocation (see page 79) 79, 80, 83,
109, 111, 115
Ridley, George, MP 42
Ridley, Rt Hon Nicholas, MP
   (Lord Ridley of Liddesdale) 86, 91, 112
Rifkind, Rt Hon Sir Malcolm, MP 95
Road safety 9
Roads Board 57
Robertson, General Sir Brian
   (Lord Robertson of Oakridge) 152
Robinson, John G 28
Rodgers, Rt Hon William, MP (Lord Rodgers) . . .86, 98-99
Rogers, George, MP 45-47
Rolling stock orders 73, 120, 123, 125, 126
Romeril, Herbert, MP 40-41
Romney, Hythe and Dymchurch Light Railway . . .57, 188
Rosser, Lord 48, **122**
Rosyth 56
Rowlands Castle **116**
Runciman, Walter, MP (Viscount Runciman) 30

St Pancras station *88*, 94, *95*, **117**
Safety regulation and management 18, 130-131, 182
Salcombe 88
Salisbury **139**
Sandling **117**
Savile, Jimmy 99-100
Sassoon, Sir Philip, MP 65
Scapa Flow 56
Scottish Government 59, 162
Sealink 106, 107, 109, 142
Select Committee on Nationalised Industries 79, 151
Serpell, Sir David 80, 186
Shapps, Rt Hon Grant, MP 7, 156, 164, 165
Shelmerdine, Sir Francis 66
Sherwood, George, MP 40, 42
Shipping services **65**
Ships 54, 55, 77, 106, 109
   Ailsa Princess **107**
   Belgrano 49

SS Brussels 55
SY Gondola 63
Shingleton, Ken 109
Shooter, Adrian 92, **127**, 154
Signalling 19, **70**, 74, **75**, 79, 103, 104, 124,
154, 156, 161, 182, 184
Signalling interlocking 19
Silkstone Common **102**
Silver Jubilee train **64**
Simon, Viscount John, MP 30
Simpson, Fred, MP 42
Skelmersdale 89
Slough-Windsor branch line 108-109
Smith, Sir Frederick *15*
Smith, Robert Haldane (Lord Smith of Kelvin) *119*
Snape, Peter, MP
(Lord Snape of Wednesbury) 47-48, 51
Southgate, Malcolm 94
Southwold Railway 8
Sparkes, Joseph, MP 43
Special advisers 52-53, 91
Speedlink 142
Spriggs, Leslie, MP 46-47
'Square Deal' campaign 24, 58, 63, 72
Stalybridge 'Pullman' 19, 169, **170**
Stamp, Sir Josiah 36
Stansted Airport 91, **92**, 103
*State and the railways, The; Alternatives to
Nationalisation* 74
Statutory returns 180, 182
Station adoption 85, 125
Stations 9, 63, 77, 79, **84**, 90, 95, 101-102, 113,
119, 124, 125, 133, 149, 155, 157, 161,
162, 163, 172, 183, 184
Stedeford, Sir Ivan 79, 152,
Stedeford Committee *79*, 80, 81, 151, 152, 186
Steel, Lord **164**
Steele, Tom, MP 43, 46-47
Steer, Jim 89, 133
Stephenson, George, MP **12**, *13*, 15, 18, 35, 156
Stephenson, Robert, MP **13**
Stockton, Sir Edwin Forsyth, MP 36
Stockton and Darlington Railway *13*, 59
Strategic Rail Authority (SRA) 120, 126, 129, 130
131-133, 147, 172, 173, 184
Abolition *10, 130, 132*, 147-148, 183, 186
Achievements 89, 119, 132-133
Creation 51, 130-133, 179, 183
Subsidy 8, 74, 94, 97, 99, 102, 113, 119,
121, 137, 145, 160, 168, 169
Surrey Iron Railway 12
Szlumper, Gilbert *66, 67, 68, 73*

Taff Vale case, 1901 38
Taunton: 17
Bus station **87**
Concrete Works 109
Freight Concentration Depot 87
Station **87**
Telford 89
Temple Franks, William *22*
Thatcher, Rt Hon Margaret, MP (Baroness Thatcher
of Kesteven) 86, 91, 92, 100, 110, 112,
Thomas, Ivor Owen, MP 44
Thomas, James Henry (Jimmy),
MP 30, 33, 34, **39**, 40, 42
Thomas, Mike, MP 97
Times, The *17, 31, 32, 33*, 82, *118, 176*
Timetables **68**, 69, **71**, **80**, **81**, 112, 125, 131, **136**,
137, 164, **170**, 173, 185
Tinsley yard **79**
TOPS 142
Topsham **170**
Townend, Arnold, MP 41
Trades Disputes Act, 1906 38
Trades unions 31, *32*, 33, 38, 44, *45*, 49,
51, 56, 78, 109
Train ferries **109**
Training 10, 103, 165, 172
Tramways Act, 1870 ....**8**, 17
Transmark 100, 103
Transport 2000 (see Campaign for Better Transport)
Transport and General Workers Union 50, 97
Transport & Salaried Staffs Association (TSSA) ...40, 44,
46, 47, *48*, 50, 51, 83,
(See also RCA)
Transport Acts:
1919 ....57, 190
1947 ....24, 57, 76, 78
1953 78
1962 19
1968 161
1981 107
Transport and Works Act, 1992 ....17-18, 183
Transport for Greater Manchester 19, 169
Transport for London 60, 189
Transport for Scotland 126, 172
Transport for Wales 126, **128**, 172
Transport Select Committee 49, 92, 115, 117,
135, 184-185
Tribune *32*

Ulster Transport Authority 80, 87
Underground Electric Railways of London 60-62
United Pointsmen and Signalmen's Society 40
United Railways Companies' Committee 20-21

Vale of Rheidol line 109, **110**
Vauxhall **120, 178**
Verney Junction 62
Vignoles, Charles **13**, *15*

197

Walkden, Alexander, MP (Lord Walkden) 41-42, *48*
Walker, Sir Herbert Ashcombe 56, 63
Walmsley, Ian *155*, 160
Wantage Tramway 8, **9**
Wardle, George, MP 39-40
War effort by the railways 24-25, 55, 166
    Armoured trains **68**, 71
    Bomb damage **70**, 78
    Buffer depots 71
    Evacuation trains 68
    D-day 8, 68, 73
    Dunkirk 68, 71, 73
    Workshops 55, 68
War memorials 55
Wartime management of railways 54, 57, 67-71,
                                                           77, 171
Warrington 88
Waterloo and City line 61, 63, 149
Watkin, Sir Edward William, MP 35, **36**, 62
Watkins, Frederick Charles, MP 42
Webb, Beatrice 31
Wedgewood, Sir Ralph 150
Welsby, John 105, 109, 116, 122, 124
Welsh Government 126, 162, 172
Welsh Highland Railway 51
West Coast Main Line upgrade 92, 103, 119, 124,
                                  132-133, 140, 144,
                                      157-158, 184, 186

Western Morning News 115
West Hampstead Midland **84**
Westminster offices
    (see Railway Offices in Westminster)
Weymouth **107**, 154
Whitehead, Phillip, MP 49
Whitelaw, Sir William, MP 36, 56
Wilkinson, Peter 132
Williams, Rt Hon Alan, MP .50
Williams, Keith *7*, 164
Williams/Shapps Review 7, 118, 120-121, 146, 148,
                                  164-165, 171-172, 175,
                                           177-178, 186
Willoughby, Sir Percival 11
Wilson, James W, MP .40, 42
Wilson, MJ, MP 36
Wilson, Mr S S 74, 76
Winsor, Sir Tom *133*, 135, 169
Winterton, Dame Rosalie, MP 52
Wisconsin Central Railroad 128, 146
Withered Arm, The **81**
Wollaton Wagonway 11
Wood, Sir William Valentine 72
Worker representation 56
Workshops, Railway 54, 55, 57, 68, 109

Yerkes, Charles 60
York (Layerthorpe) **76**

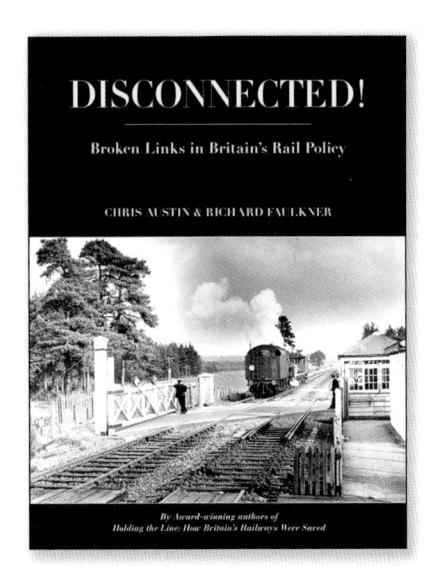

Disconnected!

Broken Links in Britain's Rail Policy

Chris Austin & Richard Faulkner

The Beeching closures and those of the 1970s and 1980s left a lot of gaps in Britain's railway network and a legacy of inadequate capacity. Which lines should Beeching and his successor have kept, and what lessons can we learn from the closures today?

Award winning authors Chris Austin and Richard Faulkner reveal the real stories behind some of the most controversial closures and draw some important conclusions for today's transport planners and politicians. They also pay tribute to some of the whistleblowers of earlier years, without whose intervention, the railway would be much smaller than it is today.

As well as the closure of key routes that would add value to the network today, the authors look at the loss of many city centre stations that have stretched capacity at the remaining stations and inhibited the growth of services.

Meticulously researched, this book also draws on the professional experience of the authors and includes much material never published before.

ISBN: 9780860936640

Hardcover, 160 pages **£25.00**

Holding the Line

How Britain's Railways Were Saved

Chris Austin & Richard Faulkner

At its zenith, there were 21,000 route miles of railway in Britain. Today the country's railways deliver more passenger miles than they did at their greatest extent despite a drastic reduction in the size of the network. Those cuts were the result of a campaign by a number of individuals who believed, erroneously as the passing of time has shown, that railways were a thing of the past and an impediment to progress.

Although the process of railway closures started early, it gained momentum in the 1950s and in the harrowing years following the publication of the Beeching report. However, as the original research by the authors of this book reveals, it could have been much worse and there were plans to reduce the size of the network even more drastically, to the point where only a few lines would have survived.

An understanding of what happened in the past is vital to understanding how today's railways struggle to meet the demands imposed on them. Trimming at the margins remains an attractive option for some policy makers who do not comprehend what happened in the past and the risk remains that previous errors may be revisited. Now available in paperback for the first time, this book shows how close Britain's railways came to being eviscerated and how the dangers of closure by stealth still exist, even today.

ISBN: 9780860936763

Paperback, 344 pages **£9.95**